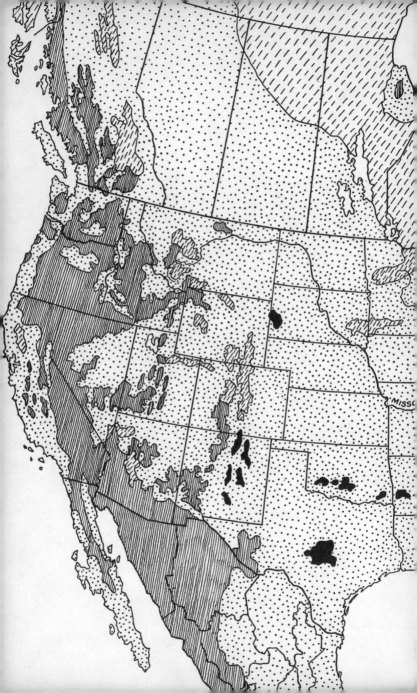

Generalized Map of
MAJOR FORMATIONS
OF NORTH AMERICA

 Sedimentary rocks

Igneous rocks

Metamorphic rocks
(with intrusive Plutonics)

 Plutonic rocks

MISSISSIPPI R.

OHIO R.

A Field Guide
to Rocks
and Minerals

THE PETERSON FIELD GUIDE SERIES
Edited by Roger Tory Peterson

THE PETERSON FIELD GUIDE SERIES

A FIELD GUIDE to ROCKS and MINERALS

by FREDERICK H. POUGH

*Illustrated with
photographs and drawings*

Fourth Edition

HOUGHTON MIFFLIN COMPANY BOSTON

Library of Congress Cataloging in Publication Data

Pough, Frederick H
 A field guide to rocks and minerals.

 (The Peterson field guide series)
 Bibliography: p.
 Includes index.
 1. Mineralogy, Determinative. 2. Rocks. I. Title.
QE367.2.P68 1976   549'.1   75-22364
ISBN 0-395-08106-8   ISBN 0-395-24049-2 pbk.

Printed in the United States of America

v 10 9 8 7 6 5 4

Editor's Note

THIS FIELD GUIDE differs from the others in the Field Guide Series in two important respects: its subject is inanimate and it can be used anywhere in the world.

One might argue that the recognition of minerals is considerably more difficult than that of birds or other living creatures. Whereas a bird may be hard to glimpse, it is relatively easy to identify. A mineral is easy to glimpse but often hard to identify. Its proper identification should be made on the basis of some knowledge of mineral "natural history" and "ecology," that is, the conditions under which it was formed and the environment in which it is usually found.

Frederick Pough maintains that the primary identification of most common minerals can be made on this visual appearance and a knowledge of the general conditions that surround them. However, the system used in the other *Field Guides*—that of "field marks" which can be pointed to by little arrows — is of little use here, because the minerals we find rarely show completely all of their distinctive features. One must resort to chemical tests and blowpipe tests for further information. Many new and relatively simple tests are described by Dr. Pough in this book.

Where other mineral guides have included identification tables, this book attempts to give the user the basic grasp of the subject that makes such tables unnecessary. Tables at best are cumbersome and can only organize superficial effects, leaving more fundamental relationships unnoted.

In this latest (fourth) edition of *A Field Guide to Rocks and Minerals* the text has been completely reset; several new minerals have been added and the localities of occurrence have been updated and expanded. The special uranium section that was added as a separate feature to an earlier edition is now incorporated into the mineral descriptions in the main body of the book where it properly belongs. The chemical tests continue to be an important feature of this guide. Many new color photographs have been added as well as a plate of photomicrographs of minerals.

Do not leave this book at home on your library shelf, but take it with you on your trips. Put it in the glove compartment of your car or in your knapsack. It is, essentially, a *Field Guide*.

ROGER TORY PETERSON

Preface to the
Fourth Edition

IN THE TWENTY YEARS that have elapsed since the First Edition of this *Field Guide,* there have been some changes of emphasis in mineral collecting and an unforeseen growth in the number of collectors. Mineral specimens have won popular recognition as objects of beauty and merit and many are now regarded as suitable accessories for elegant houses; they are approved by interior designers and their price has skyrocketed. At the same time, more and more sources have been ravished and seemingly inexhaustible deposits have given out, particularly those promising Mexican sources. An increasing recognition of investment values in fine specimens, supplementing the popular demand for colorful accents (worthless examples to the true mineral connoisseur, fortunately), has driven prices to levels that older collectors find shocking.

Seven minerals that were not included in the earlier editions have been added in this Fourth Edition. All are relatively rare, but popularity, especially at shows frequented by competitive-minded collectors, has shown them to be of enough general interest and sufficient availability in attractive specimens from dealers to justify their inclusion here. Scolecite, brazilianite, and euclase are among these.

The rise in interest and price of minerals has also had the fringe benefit of enormously improving the quality of specimens. Many are obtained by professional collectors who have researched old localities known for their attractive specimens and who then—often at some risk—have succeeded in obtaining outstanding examples that they have carefully preserved in order to reach a dealer's shelf in an unblemished state. Would that the old-time miners, with far greater chances of obtaining good specimens, had had the ability and skills of the present generation, who must search through their leavings. What wonders we would now have.

Sadly we must concede that the attitude of the general public toward mineral collecting has changed much more than has the attitude of those responsible for most mineral production. The majority of the mines still officially discourage any collecting. We have heard tales of the deliberate smashing of crystals in magnificient pockets by mine foremen; such vandalism is not only stupid, it is well nigh criminal, and should be stopped by any sort of pressure that collectors and aware individuals can apply. The wonders formed by nature are unique, and ore veins represent the seepings of cubic miles of magma. The mere occupation of the apex of a vein, although it does give a company the right to mine, should not be taken as justification of thoughtless destruction of objects of beauty and singularity for a few cents' worth of metal. Mines that encounter specimens of great artistic and scientific merit should be required to make some arrangement to preserve them for the world to view. Those who appreciate fine minerals should form themselves into groups to apply pressure in any legal way possible, through the press or as stockholders, to force the mine operators to arrange for specimen preservation in one way or another. It matters not how the mine companies arrange this. Ideally, the mine could collect and sell specimens and thereby make more profits for the stockholders. If the mine owners consider this too trivial, they can close their eyes to the miners' thefts, as many do, and in this way avoid getting a bad name. Or they could allow qualified collectors to do the collecting under reimbursed supervision when the mine is not working. Surely with goodwill and understanding something could be worked out, any required insurance coverage arranged, and any extra costs repaid.

The important thing is to save the specimens, and that must be done now, while the mine is working and while it is still in the shallower levels where pockets abound and secondary minerals have formed. It *cannot be postponed* for a more convenient time. The regrettably common production man's can't-be-bothered attitude must be replaced by intelligence and an enlightened recognition of the operators' public obligation to this and future generations as they plunder the earth. The mining engineers of the next decades could easily be the men who have been inspired in their youth by the very specimens so thoughtfully saved. The author pleads for coordinated action in this respect on the part of collectors organized into groups. Such are the Friends of Mineralogy, who have made a good start. In view of all that must be done, their efforts are only a beginning. Surely there must be some lawyers and insurance men among the world's lithophiles who could develop some sort of insurance coverage for the protection of the mine and quarry operators.

The writer wishes to express his appreciation to many who have helped in the preparation of the book. First and foremost, to the authorities of The American Museum of Natural History who gave the writer the experience and the use of collections so essential to the original work and to many of the illustrations. Guenever Pendray Knapp and Walter Holmquist were responsible for the major part of the work on the crystal drawings. Eunice Robinson Miles assisted with the tedious photographic chore of the black and white photographs, and the author did most of the color work. Jane Kessler Hearn aided by checking the blowpipe and chemical tests and the revision of the manuscript. Helen Phillips, of Houghton Mifflin Company, put in many extra hours on the difficult copy-editing job. Local collectors have helped through the loan of specimens and by giving locality information. They have also helped indirectly to determine the minerals included, because their constant stream of specimens for identification has shown where emphasis should be placed.

Since this is a practical work, intended to be of the greatest possible value to the amateur, the author would appreciate additional observations on tests and mineral occurrences that can be included in later editions of this *Field Guide*.

Contents

PART II

Mineral Descriptions

Illustrations

Additional crystal drawings throughout the text

About This Book

THE COMPILATION of a pocket *Field Guide* to mineral identification that is both comprehensive enough for the serious collector and basic enough for the beginner in mineralogy is a difficult task, and no selection can please everyone. All the common minerals are included here, as well as a few of the rare and intriguing ones that the collector may not encounter; but if he does they will thrill him far more than the usual find.

In the preparation of this guide an attempt has been made to simplify the identification of minerals for the collector and give as much information as possible to help the beginner form the habit of observing and testing. A certain minimum of application and equipment is requisite, as for other nature-study hobbies. A hammer and testing equipment are as essential to the serious study of minerals as a pair of field glasses is to the bird lover.

On the other hand, the book is not intended as a textbook of mineralogy. A *Field Guide* aimed primarily at identification is not the place for a complete course in crystallography and all the details of analytical chemistry. This is a practical book, with as much firsthand observational information as the writer could include in a limited space.

Tests: There are some departures here from descriptions of tests, procedures, and physical properties used in other books. The tests given here have actually been performed, and a great many interesting observations are included which are either original or have been forgotten in the three quarters of a century since blowpipe and chemical testing were in good repute. This aspect has been emphasized and the microscopic and X-ray methods of testing omitted because the latter are wholly unsuited to the training and the facilities of the average amateur, and their inclusion can only have a discouraging effect on the beginner.

Emphasis has been placed on the use of the ultraviolet light, a relatively new piece of equipment for the study of mineralogy and an extremely rapid means of distinguishing between some otherwise similar minerals. Used in this way, ultraviolet light becomes an essential addition to the collector's equipment. The use of cobalt nitrate is also emphasized in this *Field Guide,* for when we have to distinguish between only two minerals by some special type of behavior, as we do in this book, slight differences in reaction are immediately apparent.

It is perhaps the failure of the professional to think in terms of blowpiping, together with a lack of initiative among the amateurs, that has reduced the chemical testing and identification of minerals to its present secondary status. Some suggestions of new tests will be found in the testing section of the mineral descriptions; they are particularly appropriate to a book in which no attempt is made to distinguish by blowpipe tests one mineral from 2000 others. Here, on the contrary, the problem has been reduced—through the elimination of all dissimilar compounds—to the determination of which one of two or three like minerals is in question.

Illustrations: For this edition the plates are grouped at the center of the book. The black and white photographs are largely taken from specimens at the American Museum of Natural History, and most of the color photographs are of specimens in the author's collection. An attempt has been made in the main to select specimens typical of those that might be found by the amateur, and to illustrate to the best possible advantage the characteristic appearance, size, and associations of each mineral. They were photographed on widewale corduroy, about $5\frac{1}{2}$ stripes of which equal 1 in. (2.5 cm) in the picture (21 stripes equal 10 cm), so that an exact measure of the size of the specimens can be had if desired. However, with minerals it is more a matter of approximate size that is important, and this can be judged at a glance.

The crystal drawings on the legend pages opposite the plates usually show two different crystal habits: the left-hand one, or top drawing when they are vertically arranged, is the more common one; the right-hand (or lower) one a less frequent but important habit. Occasionally there is a sketch to emphasize a manner of growth.

Measurements: For this edition, metric equivalents have been added to supplement the traditional U.S. terms. However, minerals are not limited to exact dimensions, statistics that are important in the identification of most living things. *All measurements are approximations:* translating 1 in. into 2.54 cm, the exact equivalent, would imply a precision that is unintended and undesirable. So the policy in this book is to say 1-2 in. (2.5-5 cm) for average conditions; or, when the tendency in the crystals is on the large size, to convert it to 3-6 cm; or, if on the smaller size as an average, to 2-5 cm. The purpose of all dimensions mentioned is to give an order of magnitude. Some minerals normally form only minute crystals; others have crystals in the 1-6 in. (2-15 cm) range; and some crystals may be enormous and measurable in yards (meters). As a rule, the rarer minerals (rare because all the conditions for their formation are seldom present, with a resultant paucity of occurrence) tend to be in smaller crystals. Common minerals (common because they can form under a wide range of conditions in many localities) are more likely to be large. Often collectors are interested in obtaining the largest crystals possible; and frequently there is one exceptional locality to excite them. For *Field Guide* purposes it has been advisable to indicate the *normal dimensions*. Reference to the average sizes given will also help the show-specimen collector to realize just how notable a particular specimen is—at least in respect to the size of the crystals.

Along the fore edge of the back cover of the book is a longer conversion rule than the one given below:

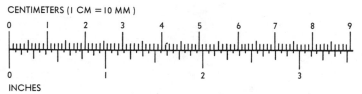

Comparison of centimeter and inch scales.

PART I

*An Introduction
to the Study of
Rocks and Minerals*

1

Your Mineral Collection

ROCKS AND MINERALS are fine introductions to the study of natural history and to a greater appreciation of nature, because they are tangible and often beautiful objects that can be preserved in collections. They do not fade and lose their beauty, like flowers; making a collection of them harms no living thing. Unlike many other objects of nature that may be arranged in collections, their preservation actually conserves them for future generations. Often, particularly in recent years, such accumulations from old collections have served useful purposes for scientific and economic studies of inaccessible and abandoned mines. Someday many old mines may come to life again, reopened because studies of specimens that were saved when the mines were running have indicated that other minerals occurring there are now of value, though they were thought worthless at the earlier time.

A general collection is best for the beginner, so that he will become familiar with the overall principles of mineralogy. Later he might better specialize in some narrower field. If mineral specimens are sufficiently large, pure, and typical, their definitive characteristics are more easily observed than in small, impure samples. They should be large enough in size and freshly broken or exposed in order to show a characteristic surface.

Read, observe, and learn all there is to know about each mineral, so that you will recognize each the next time you encounter it, even though it may appear in a different guise. Cultivate the acquaintance of other collectors in your vicinity and see their collections. You will thereby learn faster what good specimens look like. When you collect, keep a careful record of the place from which each example came.

Before visiting private property ask permission if you can, and hold back on the collecting in ore piles you may find at a mine or quarry. Even a few pounds of some minerals (like beryl) are valuable, and the quarry owner is not likely to be pleased to find his hoard stripped on a Monday morning after leaving it unguarded over a weekend. When you have the owner's permission, do not abuse the collecting privileges granted to you; one bad experience will put the whole mineral-collecting fraternity in a bad light. Do not clean out a locality or batter up crystals you cannot take out yourself — there will be other collectors after you. Encourage others to join you in the hobby. From today's collectors come tomorrow's professional mineralogists. Join local mineral societies and work to improve their meetings. *Study some*

3

phase of mineralogy and make yourself a master of it; you will get as much out of you hobby as you put into it. Visit museums and see what they have from your localities. Take pride in the museums and give to them, because they cannot exist without your support. The principal funds for the purchase of specimens may be your financial contributions.

There is in the basic sciences no more educational hobby than mineralogy. It combines chemistry, physics, and mathematics. A lifetime of study would not make you the master of every phase.

Care of the Collection

Collect specimens that are the right size for the space you have available. Crystallized specimens, when obtainable, should be the goal of the collector. Wrap them carefully and label the wrapper at once if you plan to visit several localities on a single trip.

When you arrive home wash them carefully to remove dirt and stains. Persistent iron stains can be removed by a soaking in oxalic acid to dissolve the limonite, but try the solution on an inferior specimen first to make sure that the acid does not attack the mineral itself. (A saturated solution of oxalic acid that has been diluted slightly is best: first dissolve all the dry acid crystals that will go into a water-filled glass or plastic vessel, then dilute the solution a little.)

When you are out collecting look particularly for calcite-filled veins, since calcite can be dissolved to expose insoluble silicate or oxide minerals. This is done by soaking the specimens in dilute acetic or hydrochloric acid in a plastic jar or an all-glass aquarium. Here, too, try out a small specimen first, to see whether the mineral you want to save is also attacked by the acid. Acetic acid is far safer than hydrochloric; dioptase, for example, can be ruined by hydrochloric acid, but has a fine luster after a brief, weak acetic-acid soaking to remove calcite.

Plan some sort of catalog and numbering system. A personally modified Dana number system is good.* Give the Dana number and then your own. Your first pyrite specimen would be 2911 — 1, your sixth pyrite would receive the number 2911 — 6. Paint a neat white rectangle on an inconspicuous place on the back of the specimen and when the paint is dry write on the number in India ink. The added protection of a thin coat of varnish will keep it from rubbing off when the specimen is handled or washed.

Arrange the collection in shallow drawers or on shelves in a nice

---

*The Dana numbers will be found in the classic mineralogy text used by all professional mineralogists: *Dana's System of Mineralogy,* 7th edition, rewritten and enlarged by Palache, Berman, and Frondel, to be completed in four volumes, three of which have been published.

and not too crowded display, and plan on some definite arrangement: locality, Dana order, groups of all ores of one metal, crystal
systems, etc.

Discard poorer specimens as you find better ones. Do not let
your collection become dirty and overcrowded, and avoid broken
and bruised crystals.

Finally, since your space and resources are both limited, consider
specializing in some field: one mineral, one group, one locality,
a crystal system, or the like. You cannot rival the overawing
accumulations of the museums, but you can easily excel them in
one or another specialized category.

Collecting Equipment

The equipment needed for the collecting of minerals is easily
obtained and is inexpensive. With more experience at specific
collecting localities, you will add tools as their need is shown.
Improvisation and originality are the mark of the experienced
collector, who may scorn the commonplace but more expensive
tools.

The first fundamental is a *hammer.* Any hammer will do, though
in most hard rocks the prospector's
pick will be found the most
acceptable (Fig. 1). This has a
fairly small tapered head and the
back is drawn out to a point. He
who tempers his own hammer
should be careful not to temper it
too hard, for steel splinters are
likely to fly off a very hard head.

Fig. 1 Prospector's pick

The best plan is to make the center the hardest point and the
edges fairly soft; this can be done by heating the head and carefully dropping single water drops on the center of the striking
surface, thus cooling the outer edges more slowly. The pick end,
in contrast, must be very hard or it will soon become dull; due
caution should be observed in its use.

Lighter hammers and sledgehammers may be needed for special
tasks; a light sledge is a useful thing to carry about in the car
if one usually drives when collecting. Cold chisels are also useful
for carefully working crystals out of solid rock, where they are
apt to be shattered by heavy blows. Very light hammers and the
picks your dentist has discarded are excellently adapted for finish-
ing the trimming of the specimen or for opening crystal pockets
after a mass has been brought home.

Next in utility to the collector is some sort of *magnifying glass;*
and for field work the inexpensive ones are ordinarily as useful

as the highly corrected lenses. In using them we generally look at selected small crystals and so do not really require the larger field of sharp focus of the more expensive lenses. Do not get too high a power, 8× to 10× is usually sufficient; a trained observer can see more with a 10-power lense than the beginner with a magnification twice as high. A 20× lens has a small field and too little of it is sharp at one view for it to have any use in ordinary field work.

A *collecting sack* or container of some sort stuffed at the start with enough wrapping paper to protect completely all the specimens collected is desirable when any prolonged trip is planned. Usually it is wiser not to start wrapping the day's haul until toward the end of the day — after a careful elimination of the first specimens that looked far better at the time they were picked up than they do after a couple of hours of collecting.

If one is collecting residual heavy minerals in loose gravels on slopes or in streambeds, a *shovel,* a *sieve,* and a *rake* will be found useful. Many collectors like to carry a *gold pan* and wash for gold "colors." Long deep pockets in solid rock cannot be brought home, but a short *stove poker* is ideal for freeing crystals from the walls. An *auto jack* will turn over boulders too heavy to turn by hand. All sorts of adaptations to overcome special difficulties are part of the fun of collecting. A portable *ultraviolet light,* which permits the collecting of fluorescent minerals at night, and a portable *Geiger counter,* for prospecting among radioactive minerals, are two more specialized tools that can give good results.

Once in the laboratory, specimens should be trimmed, washed, and, if necessary, cleaned up before they are cataloged and arranged.

Testing Equipment

The laboratory of the mineral collector will harbor many of the simpler reagents and equipment of the chemist. Though the testing methods of the professional mineralogist require much expensive equipment, the traditional blowpipe and chemical tests of the amateur (and the professional of the last generation) are still perfectly satisfactory. They could profitably be amplified by experimentation in using new equipment, new reagents, and new techniques.

The *Bunsen burner* is the fundamental piece of equipment when a source of gas is available. Bottled gas can be obtained in many places where piped gas is out of the question. Small disposable cans of bottled gas are available. Failing that, for field testing, an alcohol flame, a cigarette lighter, or a paraffin candle can be used, though none is as satisfactory as the gas flame. The air inlet of the Bunsen burner (named for a 19th-century German chemistry professor at Heidelberg) should be adjusted so that the flame is blue-violet, with a bright inner cone of blue unburned gas. The pressure should be kept down so that the flame burns quietly, without a roaring sound (Fig. 2). There are two parts to this flame. The hottest place is just above the center, where there is often a slight yellow touch. The lower part of the flame, just at the tip of the blue cone, has gas in excess and takes oxygen from anything placed within it. For this reason it is called the *reducing flame,* and oxidized compounds placed here will lose any removable oxygen, or will be "reduced."

oxidizing flame—
(faint yellow)

reducing flame—

blue (gas)—

Fig. 2 Bunsen burner

At the far tip of the flame, where the last of the gas is being burned, oxygen is now in excess, so objects heated in this part of the flame will be, like the gas, free to take oxygen from the air, to oxidize if they can; this part of the flame is known as the *oxidizing flame.* For certain tests (the bead tests discussed later) these two parts of the flame are important, and the beginner should practice with easily oxidized and reduced compounds in the borax beads (iron, for instance) to see where he gets the best results. He will learn how long it takes to change completely the color from that of the oxidized bead to that of the reduced bead and back again to the oxidized bead. The blue inner cone is relatively cool, so the bead should be held near its top, high enough in the flame to keep it red-hot, for if it becomes too cool it cannot react.

In conjunction with the Bunsen burner we use our lungs on a *blowpipe,* an equally fundamental piece of equipment (Fig. 3).

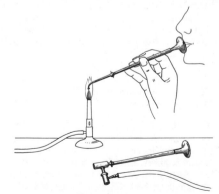

Fig. 3 Blowpipes

Blowpipes are of two types. One is a simple curved tube whose tip is held near the edge of the Bunsen burner flame, pointing slightly downward so that a needlelike blast of air goes across the top of the burner to direct a jet of flame horizontally or slightly downward onto a block of charcoal held on the other side of the flame. In this way bits of the unknown mineral can be heated in a pit on the charcoal for noting their behavior. This reaction is the one that mineral texts denominate as "B.B.," or "before

Fig. 4 Charcoal test

blowpipe" (Fig. 4). By varying the strength of the blast and the position of the flame, an oxidizing or a reducing flame may be applied to the test piece. A continuous air blast can be obtained by breathing steadily with the cheeks puffed out; the cheeks then apply the air pressure as the lungs are taking their next breath. A little practice in this technique is all that is needed to become an expert in blowpiping, capable of maintaining a uniform unbroken blast for several minutes at a time. For difficultly fused minerals and for reductions of compounds to metal, this intense heating may be necessary. Thin fragments held in forceps give best results when any trouble is encountered in the fusion.

A far better blowpipe, but one that is not widely used or generally available, has a gas connection leading directly to it (Fig. 3). When not in use it gives a yellow flame and can safely be set directly on the table. When it is in use, the charcoal block can be left on the table top — which should be of some acid- and heat-resistant type — and the danger of scorched fingers will be eliminated.

A pair of *tweezers,* preferably with stainless steel tips and double-ended (one end designed to hold itself closed) is essential for testing the fusibility of splinters of minerals that melt only with some difficulty in the Bunsen flame. Forceps that must be held together may become too hot near the tip, where they have to be held to keep them tight.

Charcoal blocks about $\frac{3}{4}$ x 1 x 4 in. (2 x 3 x 10 cm) are the most important bases for the support of test minerals. If charcoal cannot be obtained, a wood splinter can be charred deeply by working the blowpipe flame over the area in which the test mineral is to be placed. This will do for an occasional test, but if any considerable work is planned, obtain charcoal blocks from a chemical supply house. A small pit, $\frac{1}{4}$ in. (6 mm) across and about as deep, should be made at one end before the test is started. The mineral grain is then placed in this pit for blowphping, and will be less likely to blow away. A *mortar,* preferably of solid iron with a close-fitting ring and pestle, will be found useful for the crushing of mineral grains. A *magnet* of any common type is essential for the recognition of many iron minerals. *Test tubes* are glass tubes 6 or 8 in. (15 or 20 cm) long, and about $\frac{3}{4}$ in. (2 cm) in diameter. They are made of ordinary glass or Pyrex glass. Pyrex tubes cost a little more but are less likely to break and are preferable. They are used for all the acid-solution tests and for all liquid reactions.

The use of *glass tubes,* about $\frac{1}{4}$ in. (6 mm) in diameter, is occasionally of value in the testing of minerals. These are the *open-* and *closed-tube tests.* Ordinary glass tubes of this diameter, bought by the foot or yard, are broken into shorter lengths. A sharp-edged triangular file is used to groove the place where the glass is to be broken; then a quick snap with the fingers breaks the tube off in a clean sharp line without trouble. When a closed tube is desired, the glass should be cut to twice the final length, about 9 in. (23 cm), and the flame used to melt it at the middle, concentrating the flame at a single point as the tube is turned to heat it uniformly all around. Quickly draw the tube apart and melt back the short drawn-out ends by a rapid dip in the flame to form a rounded closure. Before using either open or closed glass tubes (in cases where you wish to determine the presence of moisture), heat them a bit before inserting the mineral grain to drive out the moisture of the air in the tube. The tube should be long enough so that the fingers can hold it in the Bunsen flame without its becoming too hot. If the tube should finally get too hot, a fold of paper wrapped around it and held together at the ends, like a cup handle, will insulate the fingers. This trick is also useful for holding test tubes if a metal holder is not available.

Since the amount of air in the closed tube has a negligible effect, merely noting the response of the sample to heat is sufficient. The open tubes, which should be held on a slant, permit a constant stream of air to pass over the hot sample. The deposits from this oxidizing treatment may be very different from those resulting from simple heat decomposition.

A *platinum wire,* shaped around the tip of a sharp lead pencil into a small loop, is also essential in testing. With this platinum wire the collector may observe the color given to the flame by chemical solutions of the unknown mineral. It usually takes the form of a quick flash as the liquid volatilizes. Also, the wire becomes the frame for beads of melted borax, salt of phosphorus, and sodium or lithium fluoride.

Reagents

The dry powder reagents that will be needed include a few ounces of sodium carbonate (Na_2CO_3), lithium fluoride (LiF), borax ($Na_2B_4O_7 \cdot 10H_2O$), sodium fluoride (NaF), and salt of phosphorus

[HNa(NH$_4$)(PO$_4$) · 4H$_2$O]. In addition there are the common liquid chemicals. Most important is hydrochloric acid (HCl), in two strengths, diluted: first, 2 parts of acid to 3 of water, and second, 1 part of acid to 5 of water. (In most localities it is desirable but not necessary to use distilled water for this simple testing). For calcite testing the lesser concentration is strong enough. Nitric acid (HNO$_3$) may be diluted 1 to 2 (often more). Sulfuric acid (H$_2$SO$_4$), diluted 1 to 6, is not often used and can be omitted. It is more hazardous than the others and will boil up violently when it is diluted unless one remembers to **ADD THE ACID TO THE WATER; NEVER, NEVER ADD WATER TO SULFURIC ACID!** Ammonia, chemically called ammonium hydroxide (NH$_4$OH), diluted 1 to 2 parts of water, is the opposite of acids and neutralizes them.

When the chemicals are obtained from a regular chemical supply house, a few substances not normally obtainable from the druggist should be purchased. These include the dry compounds cobalt nitrate [Co(NO$_3$)$_2$ · 6H$_2$O], silver nitrate (AgNO$_3$), potassium iodide (KI), dimethylglyoxime (dissolved in ethyl or grain alcohol, about all that will dissolve, added a little at a time), tin (Sn) metal in granules (this was formerly obtainable from toothpaste tubes but is not today, and tin-coated cans are too thin to use), and zinc (Zn) metal (this can be obtained easily, since it is the outer metal in ordinary flashlight batteries).

Testing Supplies Required for Laboratory Mineral Identification

Equipment:

Blowpipe

Charcoal blocks about 4 x 1 x ¾ in. (about 10 x 3 x 2 cm)

Glass tube ¼ in. and ⅜ in. (6 mm and 8 mm) in diameter

Small triangular file

Bunsen burner (alcohol lamp, compressed gas torch, or paraffin candle)

Balance or scale arranged for specific gravity determinations

Platinum wire (27-gauge)

Forceps

Magnet

Unglazed white tile

Set of hardness points or minerals of the Mohs scale

Ultraviolet light — best of all, two; one for longwave and one for shortwave ultraviolet. They give spectacular effects and are used only for this reason by most collectors till now, so you will want one anyway, even if you don't use them for some of the determinations in this guide.

Mortar (diamond mortar of iron, or agate)

Test tubes (12), holders, and rack

Reagents:

Wet

Hydrochloric acid (HCl) — usually sold concentrated, by the pound (kg), although a liquid. Buy the minimum quantity you can; dilute for use 2 to 3 and 1 to 5 of water

Nitric acid (HNO_3) — same as for hydrochloric acid

Sulfuric acid (H_2SO_4) — of minor usefulness; dilute 1 to 6 of water, **ALWAYS ADDING ACID TO THE WATER;** never add water to this acid

Ammonium hydroxide (ammonia) — dilute 1 to 2 of water

Ethyl alcohol — to dissolve dilute dimethylglyoxime

Calcium chloride solution — calcite dissolved in hydrochloric acid

Dry (buy smallest quantities obtainable, usually an ounce or so (30 g) except for borax)

Borax

Sodium carbonate

Salt of phosphorus

Lithium fluoride

Sodium fluoride

Cobalt nitrate

Ammonium molybdate

Dimethylglyoxime

Oxalic acid — dissolve in water to make solution for cleaning iron stain from specimens; buy 5 lb. (about 2 kg) at a time

Potassium iodide

Silver nitrate

Zinc (from battery casings)

Tin

2

Rocks and Minerals
and Where to Find Them

MINERALS are the building stones of the earth's crust. They are stony mixtures of one or more of the 92 relatively stable elements that man has found in the earth's surface and its rocks. They have pretty definite formulas and the things that go into them are the same no matter where the mineral is found. The quartz sand of Coney Island has one part of silicon and two parts of oxygen (called SiO_2 in chemical shorthand), just like the quartz sand of the Sahara Desert.

In scientists' attempt to cover all possible alternatives, the definition of a mineral has become so complex that it sounds almost meaningless to the beginner. In general, a *mineral* can be considered as a naturally occurring inorganic compound with fairly definite physical properties and chemical composition. Within their formulas, iron and magnesium may replace each other, as do sodium and calcium, but unless the replacement is very extensive the compound is regarded as the same mineral. Albite may contain no lime and 11.8% soda, or it may contain 4.0% lime and 9.5% soda. Minerals, then, can be recognized by their appearance and by various physical properties that are characteristic for each chemical combination.

Rocks, on the other hand, can be defined as extensive mineral bodies, composed of one or more minerals in varying proportions, which constitute an important part of the earth's crust. They cannot be positively identified by a series of simple tests, the product of which is a definite identification. The field classification must be given on the basis of the appearance, and for the average collector this is sufficient. The professional petrographer (the technical name for a man who studies the composition of rocks) will find it necessary to grind thin slices, which he then examines under the microscope. By a detailed study of one or more slices from a single rock exposure, known as an *outcrop*, he will then determine the exact name and classification of the rock in question. However, petrographers working in this way have made a list of names of rocks that could rival the mineralogist's list of minerals, and petrography has become very complicated. The rarer and newer names are so little used that even a geologist may find it necessary to look up their meaning each time. It is far better to use mineralogically descriptive terms in most cases. The common names listed below are old, universally accepted and understood, but it should be remembered that one cannot expect to make more than a field determination of igneous and plutonic rock samples without detailed laboratory work.

Geographical Distribution

For the collector the first indication about the nature of his rock specimen comes from the region where it was collected. The different sections of the United States can be broadly divided on the basis of the rocks that occur in them. (See front endpaper.) Volcanoes and their rock products, the lava flows and near-surface intrusions, abound in the West. Here and there mountainous masses of deeper-seated rocks that solidified more slowly and grew coarser in grain project above the surface. These are now separated in classifications from the lava rocks and are called plutonic rocks. They too solidified from a liquid, or were so changed by heat, pressure, and gases at considerable depth that they have the crystalline granular texture and uniformity of grain and grain size which could only have formed in this manner. In places, as in the Sierra Nevada of California and in the Rocky Mountains, great bodies of these rocks are exposed at the surface. To the east the underlying plutonic rocks are buried beneath deposits of rubbish from the bounding mountain masses, carried down and spread out over low plains or sunk in seabeds as the mountains decayed and were worn away. Only here and there in the Central States, as in the Black Hills, in the Ozarks, in Arkansas and Minnesota, do crystalline rocks rise above this great mantle of sediments so that the collector in the Midwest can see them and get samples. Occasionally we find indications that the millions of years have not been wholly uneventful as these sediments were laid down and then raised again. In various places later igneous activity has melted some lava (called *magma* when it is well below the surface of the earth) and let it eat its way up. Here and there in sedimentary beds we find streaks of a fine-grained dark rock which cut through the strata, giving isolated occurrences of igneous rocks in a great sedimentary terrain.

As we work farther east, past Ohio to Pennsylvania, we come to the place (all along the Appalachian mountain chain) where we again have an indication that the sedimentary rocks have been squeezed into great arches and basins, called *anticlines* and *synclines,* until we reach the area where the pressure has been great enough to change the sediments to a new type of rocks, the metamorphic rocks. In some places the burial, with the pressure, has been enough to restore completely the original igneous minerals, and in a few places even to melt the sediments into a new magma, which then squeezed upward to form another plutonic rock. This would have an unusual composition, because it was formed from sorted-out sediments instead of the complex original mixture of elements which went to make up the earliest igneous rocks. Here and there along the East Coast we have intrusions of magma to bring granite near the present surface with its associate, the very coarse variety known as pegmatite (see Pl. 6, entry 2).

The rock collector's variety will be as limited as that of the mineral collector if he is unable to visit a region other than that in which he lives. (See rear endpaper.) Areas in which all types of rocks meet are relatively few. Except for glacial boulders, the Midwestern collector is likely to be limited to his sedimentary rocks and the minerals that occur in them. The Californian or New Englander is lucky, for he can collect plutonic, some igneous, and many metamorphic rocks, with their host of related minerals and veins. Even a few sediments may be picked up, like the Maine limestones and the red sandstones of the Connecticut Valley with their dinosaur tracks and ripple marks, or the lightly consolidated, sometimes fossiliferous Recent West Coast sediments.

Rock Classifications

The Igneous Rocks

The rock types are classified into three great groups — igneous, sedimentary, and metamorphic — and subdivided into several divisions. Those which have formed from a molten state are either igneous or plutonic, though those words are often used interchangeably. The *igneous* rocks are those formed from *extrusive* lava which spilled out onto the surface, or from *intrusive* lavas (known as magmas) which have solidified quickly. The *plutonic* rocks have cooled and solidified at some depth and much more slowly. What this has meant to grain formation we shall see later. The igneous rocks, then, are rocks that have certainly hardened from a molten mass. They are characterized by a uniformity of texture — except for the *porphyries,* where larger crystals are embedded in a fine-grained groundmass. When they have flowed out onto the surface they are considered extrusives.

Extrusive Igneous Rocks

Obsidian (Pl. 3): Obsidian is a comparatively rare glassy rock that has not crystallized at all, because it has cooled too quickly for any atoms or ions to group into the regular arrangements of the minerals. Obsidian is locally abundant in the western United States but does not occur in the East. It will only be found where volcanic activity has taken place in relatively recent times, for with time obsidian tends slowly to crystallize into a fine-grained rock or to decompose by taking on moisture. No obsidians can be very old in the geologic sense.

Most often obsidian is gray to black, sometimes it is streaked with brownish red and black. Obsidian masses may have an interesting texture of flowage and reflect light from certain internal planes, which are sometimes delicately iridescent in greenish or violet, even silvery. This has been called rainbow obsidian.

Old obsidian flows sometimes take up water and change their glassy luster to a duller gleam. The moisture trapped in this altered rock makes it swell up when it is heated, and it turns into a glass froth, a sort of artificial *pumice*. This man-made substance, sold as artificial "perlite," is in fact not unlike natural pumice formed when a gas-filled mass of lava is hurled from a volcano. The gas bubbles within the lava expand before it freezes, to make the light glassy froth. Dull, partially altered obsidian is known as *pitchstone*. Sometimes a network of cracks develops in the obsidian, along which alteration extends, leaving a series of rounded, fresh glassy cores in a natural *perlite*. When such lava is mechanically eroded before the process of alteration is complete, rounded glassy pebbles are freed. The pebbles are often translucent and a light smoky color. They are locally collected by amateurs for cutting and are called "Apache tears." The western United States volcanic belt with its obsidian formations extends down into Mexico. Obsidian was a valued stone to the American Indians, the Aztecs, and Mayans for tools and decorative objects.

In composition, obsidian is high in silica and is the uncrystallized equivalent of rhyolite and granite.

Felsite: "Felsite" is a useful general name to apply to all light-colored fine-grained igneous rocks, which may be light gray, yellow, pale and deep red. The textures are so fine that it is not possible to see the individual grains, nor can they be recognized with a lens. Darker gray and greenish-gray fine-grained igneous rocks have long been specifically called felsite for want of a better term. The texture is known as felsitic. There are other names for the various compositions of rocks with these textures; for example, the granite mineral assemblage is called *rhyolite* (Pl. 3). However, unless one has a real reason for naming a specimen rhyolite it is safer to use the more general term. It is obvious that no better identification can be made without examining thin slices under the microscope. Some of the compact, very fine-grained sandy sediments can also be confused with felsites, and unless one knows the source of a specimen, and the type of rock expected in the region, it is impossible to make a positive identification on the basis of the hand specimen alone. An average hardness equal to or less than that of quartz can be determined by scratching a quartz crystal face — showing whether quartz is present (and it must be to be a rhyolite).

Basalt (Pl. 3): Most of the recent volcanoes (and many of the older ones did) now erupt a lava that solidifies to a fine-grained black rock composed largely of microscopic grains of a calcium-sodium (*plagioclase*) feldspar, pyroxene, and olivine, but with no quartz. This rock is known as basalt. Slightly coarser old sheets of basalt, now partially altered but still dark in color, are extensively quarried, crushed, and sold as "traprock."

The temperature at which basalt melts and freezes is much lower than that of rhyolite, and its lava is more fluid. Basalt flows will be longer and thinner than flows of rhyolite. The higher the proportion of silica, the more viscous is the flowing lava.

Intrusive Igneous Rocks

Molten rock does not always attain the surface and pour out as a lava flow. It may cool too rapidly and be trapped below the surface, frozen in thin dark seams that cut the other rocks. We call the thin seams *dikes* when they cut across other formations. *Sheets* and *sills* are larger bodies of molten rock injected parallel to the structure of the overlying rocks. If weak overlying beds bulged upward as the magma came in, a lens-shaped body, called a *laccolith,* is created. When cooling takes place at these greater depths, the magma may already be partly solid; perhaps it moved as a mush of crystals floating in a liquid, like half-frozen milk. The crystals could have formed somewhere on the upward journey, or possibly have started to grow in the magma chamber itself. Even when no crystals have a head start, cooling proceeds more slowly than it would on the surface, and the crystal grains get a chance to grow a little larger than in lava-flow basalts.

Porphyry (Pl. 3): Porphyries are like a frozen rock mush, with isolated crystals of some mineral, commonly feldspar, embedded in the finer-grained ground mass of igneous rock. Often the feldspar *phenocrysts* show signs of growth over a long period of time from solutions that have changed successively in composition. Such examples are helpful in tracing the history of rocks, and give support to a theory that all igneous rocks can be derived from a single magma, for the remaining liquid can leak away at different stages during the separation of earlier-forming crystals, and the final rocks, though all formed from one original magma, will differ, since each will be made up from the elements that were still mobile and able to escape from the hardening mass. Feldspar, quartz, pyroxene, and olivine all — at one time or another — have been found as phenocrysts in porphyry. The solidified rock may be known as a rhyolite porphyry or a basalt porphyry.

Diabase (Pl. 3): Usually the dark minerals form first and the later-growing feldspar grains fill in the remaining space. Sometimes, however, the feldspar may start to grow first and form lathlike crystals, and the dark minerals then fit themselves in around them. This texture is known as diabasic and is a common traprock type.

The Plutonic Rocks

We cannot positively distinguish between the coarse-textured rocks that were once actually molten and the similar-appearing rocks that many geologists now think were formed by an atom by atom replacement of continuously solid rocks. It is safer to group them all under the term *plutonic rocks*. Probably many were completely molten, for some granites very clearly have been squeezed into spaces in other rocks. Their chemical and mineral compositions wholly parallel those of the eruptive rocks we have described above; the chemically identical groups differ only in grain size. There are many more varieties of plutonic rocks named, however, without a specific fine-grained equivalent for each, but in any case we would not recognize so many different combinations in the field.

Granite (Pls. 1, 2): This, with all its closely related species, is the commonest of the coarse-grained group. It is composed of quartz and orthoclase feldspar, with usually a few grains of a dark mineral. Grain size may range from ⅟₁₆ to ½ in. (1 mm–1 cm) or more. *Pegmatite* is the name for a very coarse granite (see Pls. 5, 6, and p. 24), in which a grain may be several feet across. The dark mineral may be mica, amphibole, or pyroxene. Quartz may average about 27%; the mica and dark minerals, 3 to 10%. If albite feldspar is also present and even more abundant than the orthoclase, the rock is called a *soda-granite*. But when the albite feldspar has more than a one-tenth content of calcium feldspar molecules, anorthite — making it another plagioclase feldspar — we then would call it a *quartz monzonite*. It is not necessary, nor even desirable, for the collector to learn the special variety names. Unless he can give the rocks the detailed microscopic study required to make certain of an exact name, "granite" is sufficient.

Granites are usually light in color, and individual mineral grains can be distinguished easily. They may be gray, white, pink, black, and yellow-brown. Because they are resistant rocks they frequently form prominent landscape features (Stone Mountain, Georgia). Monumental and building stone quarries often work in granite, and the mineral collector should look there for small pegmatites, crystal-lined cavities, and for seam surfaces that may have been coated with crystals during the late stages in the crystallization of the granite. *Syenite* (Pls. 3, 4) is like granite, except that it lacks the free silica (quartz), but it finds less use as a building stone.

Diorite (Pl. 4): Diorite is a darker rock than granite as a rule, though its texture and its occurrence are similar. Like granite, diorite is a group name for granite-textured rocks rich in plagioclase and almost without quartz. *Soda-diorite* has more of the albite molecule in the feldspar and *lime-diorite* has more of the anorthite molecule. *Anorthosite* is a name given to a diorite that is composed almost entirely of feldspar; occurrences in the Adirondacks and in Labrador of labradorite feldspar rocks are important examples of this type of rock. Quartz may be about 3%, feldspar 75% or more, dark minerals 20% or so, usually amphiboles.

Gabbro (Pls. 1, 2): Gabbro is still lower in silica and darker in color than diorite. Chemically it is the coarse equivalent of diabase. Its feldspar is a plagioclase richer in lime than the feldspars of diorite, and the dark mineral is more often a pyroxene than an amphibole. Olivine may be present.

Peridotite or Pyroxenite (Pl. 4): This is a dark rock composed almost entirely of dark minerals: olivine, or olivine and pyroxene. A pure olivine rock, such as the sandy olivine formation at Webster, North Carolina, is a *dunite,* and a rock of pure pyroxene is a *pyroxenite.* The most famous peridotite is the pyroxene-olivine mixture, now largely altered to serpentine, called *kimberlite* in South Africa. It is the matrix of diamonds, the rock of the "blueground pipes."

The Sedimentary Rocks

As rocks of any sort are exposed on the surface of the earth, the sun and rain, the air and frost start an attack upon them, breaking them down to soil. The jagged mountains of the moon, which has no atmosphere, stand high and sharp today because heat and cold are not enough to tear them down. It takes the oxygen in the air and the water that falls as rain to really destroy rocks and then carry away the pieces. In high mountain regions where the temperatures change rapidly and drastically, fracturing of rocks by freezing is an active cause of rock disintegration. In tropical lowlands temperatures may change little but the chemical alteration by water, oxygen, and soil acids proceeds at a steady pace. The feldspars change to clay, freeing the quartz grains. Groundwater may dissolve the silica or the metal elements and carry them off in the water that seeps through the rocks. Streams running across these disintegrating rocks carry the sand and clay to lower levels. Somewhere the streams stop running and drop their loads. The slower they run the finer the material they still carry, and eventually only minerals that dissolved in the water remain to reach the sea. As we go toward the mouth of a river we find that each successive bed of sediments shows a concentration of like-sized particles. In valleys, in lake beds, or on sea floors, wherever they pile up, we find concentrations of like grains, and in each deposit a horizontal layering, called *stratification.* *Sedimentary rocks* gradually form as these deposits become ever thicker, finally forming rigidly cemented masses. Loose grains are welded together, joined by pressure that locks the grains and by the deposit of a cementing substance at the contact of the grains. Sedimentary rocks lie in thick beds, one after another, often forming deposits thousands of feet thick. Much of the North

American contenent is mantled by sedimentary rocks, now raised again from sea floor, where they were laid down on top of the older crystalline rocks that mark the real crust of the earth.

Deposits may be water-laid, wind-laid, or ice-laid. Recent glaciation has covered the northern parts of North America with unconsolidated mixtures of rocks and clay. Allied layered sand deposits were formed by the water that ran from the melting glacier. None of this debris, such as the mixture of clay and boulders known as *till,* would be considered a rock by the collector, because it is not cemented together into a solid mass. The older sediments, however, have become cemented and are rocks in the usual sense.

Arkose is a rock derived by mechanical disintegration (fragmentation by freezing and warming) of a granitic rock. This may form when the disintegration process has not turned the feldspar into clay. It really amounts to a coarse sandstone, the grains of which are both quartz and feldspar. In the hand specimen, when no evidence of banding (and of the secondary origin) is obvious, a sediment with such fresh feldspar might be mistaken for the far more firmly cemented primary rock, the original granite.

Conglomerate (Pl. 4) is a rock composed of rounded waterworn pebbles, usually of quartz, cemented by the mass of finer material filling the spaces in between. Often there is a contrast in color of the pebbles to that of the matrix, which makes appropriate the name "puddingstone" frequently applied to colorful conglomerates found on Mount Tom and at Roxbury in Massachusetts. Glacial boulders of this formation have been found as far away as Long Island, New York.

Breccia is almost the same as conglomerate, except that its pebbles are more angular in outline and have not been so rounded by water. Breccias may also form well under the surface of the earth, when buried beds of rock are shattered by movements of the crust. The overlying rock pressure will crush the fragments together so that in time they are easily cemented again into a solid mass. Breccia marbles are often seen in decorative stonework.

Sandstone (Pls. 1, 2, 4) is a common rock composed principally of sand grains cemented more or less firmly together. Depending upon the character of the cement, the rock may be white, gray, yellowish, or dark red. Often the cementing material is strongly stained with iron.

Iron oxide is the coloring matter of the brown sandstone of New York City's famous "brownstone fronts." This facing rock came from almost horizontal sandstone beds lying in the Connecticut Valley. Dinosaur footprints have been found in the rocky floor of great sandstone quarries worked for this stone at Portland, Connecticut.

Shale (Pl. 5) is a rock composed principally of clay particles, often with a little sand intermixed. Stream-carried mud will obviously be deposited farther from the shore than stream-carried sand. Shale is built up by successive layers of the finer particles that traveled farther in a quietly flowing stream before settling to the bottom. On the floor of a sea that was slowly deepening we would expect a sedimentary sequence of sandstone beds, overlain by shale, with that in turn mantled by still finer material from clearer water.

Limestone (Pls. 1, 2, 4) is composed of calcium carbonate (calcite) in a very finely granular texture. Some of the lime was chemically precipitated. Other limestone beds represent the accumulation of lime removed from seawater by living organisms. Beds of clean limestone can only form farther out in the sea and in deeper water beyond the distance that stream-borne clay particles and sand can travel. Often remains of the organic life of the sea of the period of the lime deposition are included in the beds. These are fossils.

Dolomite resembles limestone, except that chemically it is richer in magnesia, but it forms under the same conditions and probably represents later alteration of the limestone by seawater.

Salt, Coal (Pl. 5), Oil: *Salt,* is an economically valuable substance associated with sedimentary deposits resulting from some special set of conditions. We have seen in our own lifetime how the level of Great Salt Lake can change as the water source fails. In time, if it wholly evaporates and then becomes buried by later sediments, it would form a typical bed of *rock salt.* Burial protects it from re-solution. *Coal* represents the compaction and partial carbonation of plant remains buried in the same way. *Oil* probably results from similar burial of animal remains in sediments. Adjacent sand formations provide reservoirs into which the oil migrates. The search for oil is also a search for buried structures and formations that might have trapped a pool.

Special Features of Sedimentary Rocks

From their manner of formation by deposition along the shore in mudflats, and on the floor of the sea, sedimentary rocks are likely to enclose foreign substances and characteristic markings that in time will be preserved as rock when the sediments are hardened. These included surface irregularities like ripple marks and raindrop dents; for waves washed seashores and rain showered down millions of years ago just as it does today. Animal remains, shells, and plant remains may become entrapped and preserved, often to their finest detail, in the sediments. Such *fossils* are characteristic of sedimentary rocks, and are best shown in shales and limestones (Pl. 2). The geologist uses them as the guide to tell him the age of the rocks; he knows from the kind of fossils he finds whether a formation is a million years old or a hundred million years old. The study of fossils is a science known as *paleontology* and it can be as complex and as fascinating as mineralogy. Those who live where sediments abound may find that their collection of fossils is more varied than that of their minerals, for in such regions the minerals are likely to be few in number and monotonous in appearance.

The Metamorphic Rocks

The pressure and the heat that accompany deep burial of sedimentary rocks will in time make unstable the oxidized and hydrated minerals that formed on the surface as the primary rocks decomposed and decayed. Heat and pressure create an environment like the original one deep under the crust or in volcanoes, where the primary rock minerals first formed. Eventually the moisture, oxygen, and carbon dioxide that came from the air will again be pressed out of the rocks. The sediments making up the shale, sandstone, and limestone will begin to change. Some minerals — the more drastically changed ones, like the clay of shales — will revert completely to the ancestral mica and feldspar. However, despite the mineral change the rocks still preserve the banding created by their water-laid origin. Sediments are usually a concentration of one or two minerals, in contrast to the heterogeneous character of the original rock. So, though the high-temperature minerals of the crystalline rocks are reborn, the original mixture of minerals has been destroyed. This manifests itself in the new mineral makeup and arrangement of the regionally *metamorphosed* ("changed form") *rocks.*

Slate (Pl. 5) resembles shale, except that it is a first stage in a progressive change of clay back to mica. Small mica flakes have grown along new cleavage surfaces to give the hardened shale a luster not noted in dull earthy shales. The tiny growing mica flakes tend to arrange themselves so that their flat sides lie across the direction of the pressure, with the result that the cleavage of the slate follows the new mica plate direction; that is, at right angles to the squeezing. Often the flakes of slate cut sharply across the original stratified shale bed, whose layering was the prominent structural feature of the sediments.

Phyllite (Pl. 5) is not very different from slate, except that now metamorphism has been more intense and the new mica crystals have grown larger to give a distinct micaceous parting direction to the rock, with a dull micaceous luster. It is hard to draw a line between the slates on the one hand and the phyllites on the other. Though phyllite often shows a wavy rather than a flat surface, it is usually anybody's guess when the mica luster on the cleavage face has become sufficiently pronounced. Phyllite may be greenish, grayish, or reddish, like slate. It is only found in regions of low-grade metamorphism where the crustal buckling has been slight. It will not be found in regions where unaltered sediments prevail.

Schist is the final product of the alteration by heat and pressure alone of a mixture of hydrated and oxidized minerals. Such shales, on complete recrystallization, will compress to a final rock that is predominantly mica in composition (Pl. 5). The mica is especially conspicuous in the direction of the easy fracture, the cleavage direction of the schist. As in the earlier phyllite and slate stages, the mica crystals have arranged themselves so that the flat plates have grown at right angles to the crustal pressure affecting the rock. Often certain typical high-pressure minerals, like garnet, staurolite, andalusite, or kyanite, grow in the mica of the schists. The micaceous banding and the predominance of one mineral makes schist distinct from any primary rock, even though the principal minerals may be identical.

Gneiss (Pls. 1, 2) represents the same intensity of metamorphism as the schist, but in its mineral makeup, mica (or hornblende) is less predominant. Its sedimentary ancestor may be a sandy shale or a shaly sandstone. Fresh granite can also be changed to gneiss by a simple rearrangement of its mica, so that the plates are all aligned in one direction in place of the less conspicuous structure of an ordinary granite. Gneisses, which may be gray to almost white, resemble granites very closely except for this alignment of the mica. An exact line of distinction between gneiss and schist is difficult to draw, for many gneisses look far richer in mica than they truly are, when only a mica-rich parting plane is seen.

Quartzite (Pl. 5) is formed by the metamorphism of sandstone. Since quartz grains are about the same, hot or cold, little change can take place in them. In deep burial and renewed cementation, the sand grains eventually become welded so firmly together that any fracture breaks across the grains, instead of around loosely held surfaces, as in the sandstones. Quartzites are among the hardest and the most resistant of all rocks. They show the same colors as the sandstones: brown, yellow, gray, reddish, or white.

Marble (Pls. 1, 2), like the quartzites, forms in regional metamorphism from another single-mineral sedimentary rock; and like sandstone is a rock in which no major change can take place other than a growth and cementation of the individual crystal units. Marble forms from limestone and dolomite. If the original sediments are fairly pure carbonates, the metamorphic product becomes a coarsely crystalline white or colored marble and may be valued for decorative purposes. The crustal squeezing and heat of regional metamorphism are not always necessary for the recrystallization of a limestone into coarse grains that will take a polish. Occasionally, time and burial with ample circulating groundwater solutions will do the same thing, but in those cases the fossil shells preserved in the original lime sediments persist in the decorative marbles. Such marbles are often buff-colored and their fossils may show as lighter-colored sections of purer calcite.

Contact Metamorphism

Sometimes pressure and heat are not the sole factors in the metamorphism of earlier rocks. The intrusion of a magma with the varied accompanying gases that soak out ahead through the enclosing rock, carrying metallic elements and silica in solution with them, will change simple sediments to a new type of rock and permit the growth of different silicate minerals, like garnet and epidote. Ore minerals — metal sulfides — frequently accompany the economically worthless silicates under *contact metamorphism*. An impure limestone is the most interesting and most easily altered formation, whereas an igneous rock or a gneiss is the least altered, least interesting, and has the least likelihood of fostering an ore deposit.

Hornfels is a compact fine-grained black rock that forms near the line of contact of sedimentary country rocks with an invading magma, where there is often a zoning away from the source of the heat and gases. Under unusual conditions, coarse new mineral crystals may form, and some of the finest of all mineral-collecting localities are such coarsely crystalline contact-metamorphic zones. Altered limestone blocks from Monte Somma, the classic ancestor of Vesuvius, are the finest examples. Here the rising lava has plucked limestone from the walls of its channelway and borne blocks upward to its mouth. In the course of their rise they have been saturated with volcanic gases and solutions, which substituted one element for another, taking a little of this and adding a little of that all the way up. Then they were tossed out onto the surface all done, honeycombed with crystal-lined cavities in which typical contact-metamorphic minerals like vesuvianite, garnet, scapolite, spinel, and all their high-temperature brethren have grown.

Summary of Rock Characteristics

IGNEOUS

Volcanic: Fine-grained, a mixture of unrecognizable minerals; their only inherent structure that of the flow lines in obsidians and rhyolites.

Plutonic: Coarse-grained, without any noticeable structures in the hand specimen, and composed of common identifiable primary minerals (quartz, feldspar, mica, dark minerals).

SEDIMENTARY: Mainly a single, low-temperature mineral; banded, stratified, and often fossiliferous.

METAMORPHIC: High-temperature minerals, like those of the plutonic rocks, but banded, stratified, and, as a general rule, with a concentration of a single mineral in a formation.

Mineral Environments

It is obvious that the earth's mineral-forming environments vary greatly in character. We have only to consider an exploding volcano and to contrast the conditions in its throat with those of a cool quiet cavern. Minerals are forming in each, and we can see that certain minerals are characteristic of a certain set of conditions. A group of secondary minerals that commonly form in igneous rocks, are the hydrous silicates known as the *zeolites*. Close around active volcanoes we may find water-soluble minerals that form at gas vents. In regions of recent volcanism we find minerals composed of elements that remain long in watery solution, traveling far from their source. They separate from the water at low temperatures and pressures. Stibnite and cinnabar are the best known.

Other elements remain close to their plutonic source, if their volatility and solubility are low. Nevertheless, since all magma has some accompanying gases they commonly do travel a short distance into the surrounding rocks and form veins. So we have an important group of high-temperature minerals, which form in deep-seated veins close to the plutonic rocks. The deepest of such veins are not very different from *pegmatite dikes,* which are narrow bands or veins that represent the coarsest closing stages of granite rock formation. At this stage all the volatiles, and all the still uncombined rare elements, are concentrated in a small residual liquid phase. This liquid is very fluid so the rock-making minerals (quartz, feldspar, and mica) can crystallize in coarse masses, often with many rare associated minerals. Beryllium, tin, tungsten, tantalum, fluorine, and boron are such residual rare elements; we find minerals containing them in the granite pegmatites. Sometimes we find that these pegmatites (*simple pegmatites*) were later attacked by solutions containing other rare and more volatile elements, and that the early normal pegmatite minerals (those of granite, as a rule) have given way to feldspars richer in sodium, that lithium has entered into the mica, and that cesium has replaced some of the beryllium in beryl. In the *complex pegmatites* we look for lithium minerals, albite feldspar, and phosphorus or fluorine minerals that we don't find in the simple pegmatites. Pegmatites dikes are commonly quarried for mica or beryllium ore, or for rarer metals. They are among the best places for the mineral collector to visit.

In addition to the pegmatite dikes there are two more examples of late concentrations of water and other volatiles that are likely mineral sources. One is the *miarolitic cavities* in granite, places where gases, instead of escaping out of the magma through a crack, have formed great trapped bubbles, preserved today in the cold granite as short pegmatitic gashes, their central open cavities lined with crystals. When contraction cracks solidified granite into joints and seams before all the gases have escaped, we sometimes find thin crevices sparkling with small and perfect crystals of typical pegmatite minerals. The seam faces of a granite quarry are always worth examining. Sometimes we find several intersecting sets with different types of minerals in each: high-temperature compounds like topaz, beryl, and fluorite in one, low-temperature epidote and zeolites in another, and calcite and sulfides in a third.

When the magma has really cooled and hardened, and all the high-temperature minerals have separated, there appears still to be considerable water-rich solution to escape, and in this solution are dissolved metals, sulfur, silicon, and other elements. As the liquid escapes, the dissolved elements combine and make mineral deposits along the walls of the fissure through which the solution travels. The mineral-filled fissures are *veins*, and the minerals in these veins are often valuable ores. Even the bordering rock may be attacked by solutions escaping from the fissures, and ore minerals are commonly deposited in the *country rock*, replacing more soluble substances which have been dissolved in their place. Experience has brought recognition that certain minerals are found in veins that must have formed close to the magma at great depth and at high temperatures. Tin and tungsten ores, for example, are found with pegmatite minerals like topaz and beryl. Other elements (antimony, arsenic, and mercury ores) travel great distances and are deposited near the surface and at low temperatures. It is desirable to remember, because it will help in identifications, which are the early high-temperature minerals and which are the late low-temperature minerals. The manner of occurrence is noted in the paragraph **Environment** in each of the detailed descriptions. Knowledge of the type of occurrence helps to eliminate minerals that might be confused with others similar in appearance, but which could not possibly occur in the same environment.

Like the rocks, the veins and their mineral-enriched borders are affected by exposure to the work of the air. Sulfides will oxidize and form water-soluble sulfates. Some of these will be carried away in solution, some will sink down to react with deeper fresh sulfides and enrich them by driving out other elements, replacing iron with copper. Sulfides will change to carbonates, silicates, or oxides by reaction with the wall rocks. A whole new group of ore minerals can form, or the surface exposure (outcrop) may be leached of everything but iron oxide or aluminum oxide. Residual deposits of this sort are *laterites* and *gossans;* a pyrite-rich vein may be changed and leached to form an "iron hat" or limonite gossan, though any gold originally in the pyrite will be freed to remain in the gossan.

As rocks disintegrate and wear away, we find some particularly resistant minerals like quartz persisting. Heavy ones like gold and diamonds may stay close to their original source. They lag behind as running water carries off the lighter and smaller particles. They will ultimately form residual "economic" deposits, and represent a concentration of all the heavy minerals of a great thickness of rock left behind during thousands of years of erosion. Diamond-bearing gravels in many parts of the world are thought to have been concentrated and reconcentrated in this way, perhaps through millions of years. We say that they have "weathered."

Some of the metal elements go into solution and are later deposited in the sea. They may be removed from the seawater by sediments as they pile up on the sea floor, or they may be differentially removed by marine life. Trapped solutions of seawater impregnate these sediments and help cement the grains so they become the sedimentary rocks. Later, when they are raised above the sea, surface waters may seep through them, to dissolve and carry away selected elements. Disseminated metallic elements may become concentrated as water seeps through the sediments and sometimes combine with sulfur and separate out in cavities or in crevices to form ore veins. The low-temperature sulfates, sulfides, and carbonates are common in cavities in sedimentary rocks. Limestone quarries are often good collecting localities. In places we have great sedimentary beds of chemical precipitates, formed, like rock salt and gypsum, by the direct evaporation of cutoff estuaries of saltwater. Local reactions in the ocean appear sometimes to have precipitated, by organic means, beds of iron ore and limestone. Boron-rich lakes may evaporate to form beds of borax ores; we can but speculate on the source of the boron.

Cracks, crevices, and caverns in the sedimentary rocks serve as centers for more mineral precipitation. In the sediments we expect veins to be filled with low-temperature minerals like quartz and calcite, and some of the low-temperature sulfides. In caves we get calcite stalactites and gypsum rosettes. Even in fossils we may find quartz or pyrite linings.

Lastly, as sediments are heated and compressed the secondary minerals reverse their course, and revert again to the high-temperature minerals, many of these, obviously, rock-forming minerals. But conditions of stress, the heat and pressure that caused the schists and gneisses to form, also favor the formation of a new group of minerals. This group has come to be recognized as characteristic of highly metamorphosed rocks; they include garnets and the kyanite-staurolite series of the schists. These regionally metamorphosed rocks usually contain mica, and other minerals with a flattened structure. As the rocks are folded, cross (tension) crevices often develop and into them may migrate all the rare scattered elements disseminated through the bordering rock. This is the origin of the famous Alpine crevices that yield so many beautifully crystallized specimens. As magma, with its fluids rich in rare elements, penetrates into a compressed mass of metamorphosed rocks, additional changes in the original rock composition are brought about by the introduction of silica or boron or magnesia. A new series of contact-metamorphic minerals develops, especially in the impure limestones, to give still another mineral-forming environment. These in turn may decay and join the oxidized group, making a different hydrated set of minerals.

The important thing to remember is that there are a great many mineral-forming environments, and each is characterized by its own suite of minerals. Many are mutually exclusive: beryl will not be found in sedimentary rock in Ohio any more than celestite will be found in a New England pegmatite. So the finder of a blue mineral in each of those states has at least one possibility (when he considers color alone) that need not concern him. If this lesson is clearly understood, and if the reader will continue to observe the environment of each mineral he is trying to identify, his problem will be much simpler (see rear endpaper).

3

Physical Properties
of Minerals

THE IDENTIFICATION of minerals by their physical properties alone is entirely practical for many of the minerals included in this book. It is, however, impossible to distinguish all of the known minerals by these methods, and as the beginner becomes more advanced it is increasingly likely that he will encounter minerals that are not mentioned here. It will be necessary for him to enlist the aid of a trained mineralogist or to train himself so that he can use some of the methods of the professional. The value of the physical properties discussed below varies considerably, and their respective importance varies with the individual and the expansion of his experience.

Distinguishing Characteristics

Color: The ability to interpret the significance of various colors in a mineral is a conspicuous example of experience. Color is the first property noted when we look at a mineral. To the novice it is very disconcerting to learn that color is in most cases the result of the inclusion of an accidental impurity, of no significance to a mineral's composition and apparently of extreme variability. On the other hand, the professional relies constantly upon color, for his experienced eye has learned the hues and tints that are characteristic of one or another mineral.

In some cases color is a fundamental property, directly related to the composition. The blue of azurite and the green of malachite are typical colors of copper minerals; so typical that the discovery of blue and green stains on vein outcroppings are the best possible indications to the prospector that the primary vein below contains copper sulfides. In the opaque sulfide minerals with a metallic luster, color is of fundamental importance, and is constant. In the light-colored, transparent, and translucent minerals, color is variable and of lesser importance. Even with these it can be a valuable guide, however, for some minerals never appear in some colors and hence can be eliminated in the search for the identity of an unknown.

Luster: Luster permits a division into two main classes, the metallic and the nonmetallic lusters. The metallic minerals really look metallic (they may be naturally occurring metals, or are metal sulfides) and their color is constant. The range of identifiable colors in the metallic lusters is not great. The nonmetallic lusters have been given many names, most of which are obvious and to be found in any dictionary. A *vitreous* luster means that the mineral looks like glass; "glassy" is an equally good term. Hard minerals with the elements linked closely together in their structure, and some soft minerals containing certain elements like lead, mercury, and antimony, have a brilliant, almost metallic look, as do diamonds, and are said to have an *adamantine* luster. A *greasy* luster is a little less brilliant and less hard-looking than diamond. A still less brilliant luster is thought to be about like that of resin and is known as a *resinous* luster. A *silky* luster indicates a finely fibrous mineral in parallel bands of needles. A *pearly* luster resembles the reflections from the flat surfaces of an iridescent shell, and is to be noted in minerals with incipient cleavage cracks cracks parallel to and below the reflecting surface.

Hardness: The scale of hardness in use among mineralogists is one that was set up by a German mineralogist, Friedrich Mohs, in 1822 and has been followed ever since. It is recognized that it is not an exact mathematical relationship: 10 on the scale is merely a lot harder than 9, just as 9 is somewhat harder than 8, and so on. For this reason fractional hardness, even when expressed in decimals, will only be an approximate determination. For this reason I give fractions rather than decimals. There are instruments that give accurate hardness tests, and they indicate that diamond would be 1000 on a scale reading from 0 to 1000, while corundum (9 on the Mohs scale) would be about 250 and topaz 160.

The Mohs Hardness Scale

1 Talc	6 Feldspar
2 Gypsum	7 Quartz
3 Calcite (rhomb face)	8 Topaz
4 Fluorite	9 Corundum
5 Apatite	10 Diamond

The mineral with the higher number can scratch anything beneath it or equal to it in hardness. In other words, glass will scratch glass or anything softer. If we can scratch something with quartz but not with feldspar, and that something will scratch feldspar (and naturally not scratch quartz), we say it has a hardness of $6\frac{1}{2}$.

Hardness is usually different in different crystal directions; diamonds are hardest parallel to the octahedron face and cannot be cut in that direction at all. In some minerals this difference is pronounced, as with: calcite, whose base can be scratched with the fingernail even though the cleavage rhombohedron is too hard; phosgenite, whose prism direction can be scratched with the fingernail and the direction across it cannot; and kyanite, whose prism direction can be scratched with a knife, though the direction across is too hard.

We have a few handy implements that will help us if a hardness scale is not available. The fingernail is a little over 2, a copper penny about 3, a steel knife just over 5, glass about 5½, and a good steel file about 6½.

Specific Gravity: This means the weight of a substance in relation to the weight of the same volume of water. A substance with a specific gravity of 2.5 would be 2.5 times as heavy as the same volume of water. It is an important property of minerals and one that becomes evident when we handle many specimens and come to think of them individually as heavy or light in relation to others of about the same size that we have held in hand.

Gravity determinations are made by weighing a substance in air and then suspending it in water and weighing it again. Care should be observed to make sure that the mineral is pure and not mixed with any other substance. It would be well to practice with a scale and make the arrangement for weighing in water with a few known pure samples before attempting an unknown mineral.

To make the calculation, we weigh the substance first in air on an apparatus all set up so that a second lower pan is already in water and balanced before anything is put on either side. We then weigh the substance in the lower pan in water and get a second figure (Fig. 5). The weight in water is then subtracted from the weight in air. This gives us a number that represents the weight of the water pushed out of the way by the stone as it went into the water. This is of course the volume of the stone ×1 — the specific gravity of water. If we divide the weight of the whole stone

Fig. 5 Arrangement for determining specific gravity

by the weight of the water that represents its volume (in other words, the loss of weight when the mineral is weighed in water the second time) we get the specific gravity, or the number of times more the stone weighs than the same amount of water. For example:

Weight in air	23.67 grams
Weight in water	16.95 grams
Loss of weight	6.72 grams

Weight in air 23.67
Divided by   6.72 the loss of weight
Equals   3.52 the specific gravity

There are various other methods for determining specific gravity. High-density liquids that match the density of the unknown, special scales, or water-filled bottles called pycnometers may be used, but all are more complicated or more expensive than the simple balance the amateur can rig up for himself.

Streak is the color of the mineral powder. It is best seen on a white unglazed porcelain tile, obtainable from plumbers. Since the tile has a hardness of about 7, minerals of greater hardness will not make a colored streak. However, for these minerals, particularly the black ones, it is possible to see the color of the powder on bruises, or actually to crush some into powder. It will be found that lighter hues show in the powder of many black minerals (those that are not truly black and opaque but only look so because of their grain size and opacity).

Fracture: An unimportant term referring to the character of a broken surface. Most minerals have an uneven fracture, or an irregular grainy fracture, or a curving, shelly, glasslike break known as a *conchoidal* fracture. Most substances have one or the other as a constant property.

Metal tends to tear and leave small jagged points that catch the flesh as the hand is brushed across them. This is known as a *hackly* fracture, and is usually well shown in copper specimens of the Michigan Upper Peninsula type, where the copper is disseminated in rhyolite. Minerals with a pronounced elongation and cleavage are said to have a splintery fracture, but this is rather forseeable and meaningless.

Cleavage: The tendency of a mineral to break in smooth flat planes is known as cleavage and it is obviously a fundamental property of a mineral, since it is related to the atomic arrangement of the crystal. It is, of course, related to the crystal symmetry of the mineral: a cubic mineral, like sphalerite or fluorite, may have a dodecahedral (12-sided) or octahedral (8-sided) cleavage, while a monoclinic or triclinic crystal will probably have only pinacoidal (one-direction) or prismatic (two-direction) cleavages. Cleavage is one of the most important properties for identification.

Parting: This resembles cleavage except that it is present only in some specimens and cannot take place between random atom planes. It occurs only in certain parallel, but spaced, planes. These are likely to be planes of weakness in the crystal, perhaps because of the presence of a disoriented sheet of atoms in a twin orientation; often seen in Iceland spar calcite and ruby corundum.

Translucency: Minerals range from transparent to opaque. Almost any translucent mineral can under ideal circumstances be nearly or entirely transparent. Hence it is redundant to say that a mineral is transparent to translucent; obviously if it is transparent under some conditions, it will, because of inclusions or flaws, usually be translucent at best. Opaque minerals, on the other hand, include only the sulfides and oxides as a general group; a thin enough splinter will usually show some light transmission. This is related to streak — to the color of the powder, which will be truly black only in the case of the really opaque minerals.

Fluorescence and Phosphorescence: The property of changing invisible ultraviolet light or X-ray beams to visible light is the property known as fluorescence. In some cases the light continues for an interval after the stimulating source is turned off. This is phosphorescence. Phosphorescence is rarer than fluorescence. Not all specimens of a fluorescent mineral will fluoresce; it depends upon the impurities present. Some localities are noted for the abundance of fluorescent minerals (Franklin, New Jersey; Langban, Sweden).

There are several other luminescent effects shown by minerals which are of interest. Some minerals give small flashes of light when stroked with a metal point: sphalerite and corundum may show this *triboluminescence,* as it is called. The sparking is also seen in rock crystal as it is sawed.

Thermoluminescence, or glowing as low heat is applied, is a property shown by fluorite and some calcite.

Other Phenomena: *Pyroelectricity* and *piezoelectricity* are phenomena shown by some minerals, notably tourmaline and quartz. Temperature or pressure changes cause the minerals to acquire an electrical charge, positive and negative poles, as they are warmed and cooled or pressed. This may be demonstrated by dusting the cooling or warming crystal with a dust of red lead and sulfur which has come through a thin silk screen. A simple bellows and screen can be made by placing two layers of a nylon stocking over the end of a rubber bulb filled with a mixture of about 2 parts of red lead to 1 of sulfur. The dust particles receive electrical charges as they pass through the screen and settle on the appropriate ends of the charged crystals, the sulfur receiving a negative charge and settling on the positive end of the crystal and the red lead receiving a positive charge and going to the negative end of the crystal. Though rarely made by amateur collectors, the demonstration is so spectacular that it should be

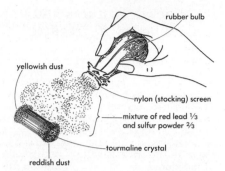

rubber bulb

yellowish dust

nylon (stocking) screen

mixture of red lead $\frac{1}{3}$
and sulfur powder $\frac{2}{3}$

tourmaline crystal

reddish dust

Fig. 6 Piezoelectricity testing device
For best results, puff gently, from a distance of several inches.

tried. The apparatus described above is inexpensive and simple
to make (Fig. 6).

Percussion figures are 6-rayed stars shown by the micas when
they are struck a light single blow by a sharp-pointed needle. The
rays of the star naturally follow crystal directions in the mica.

Asterism is a 6-rayed star shown by some minerals when they
are polished so that a point source of light can be seen through
them, or when they are cut into a sphere so that reflections from
a light can be seen from microscopic inclusions that are arranged
parallel to crystal directions. Rose quartz, some grayish pegmatite
quartz, and corundum (star sapphires) are the best examples of
this phenomenon. It may often be seen on looking at a distant
light through a cleavage sheet of phlogopite mica.

Adularescence or *labradorescence* is a bluish sheen ("Schiller")
seen in some feldspars (moonstone and labradorite) when the light
is reflected at the correct angle. It is caused by a microscopic-scale
intergrowth of light-disturbing planes.

Pleochroism is shown by colored transparent or translucent
crystals of one of the noncubic symmetry groups. Light passing
in one direction is absorbed differently from light traveling in
another direction, so that there is a difference in color in the two
directions. In a few minerals like tourmaline, cordierite, and
andalusite, this color change may be so pronounced that it alone
is a useful guide to identification. In many cases it is a help in
identification, since it shows that the mineral cannot belong to
the cubic group, even though no crystals are present. A small
splinter may be held in front of a Polaroid sheet that has been
cut and mounted in glass in a way that places their two vibration
directions at right angles to each other. As the translucent splinter
is moved back and forth across the dividing line the change in
color will be apparent.

Mineral Textures and
Outlines of Aggregates

Mineral Surfaces

When minerals solidify in open cavities without interference from other solid substances or from each other, they usually assume the shapes known as crystals, discussed in the next chapter. The rate at which crystals grow, the abundance of growing centers, and the nature of the solutions from which they are forming determine whether a single mineral or a mixture of minerals will crystallize, how large the crystals will be, and whether they will form scattered individual crystals or continuous crusts. Such a crystallized crust is known as a *druse;* it may be composed of numerous extremely minute points or of fewer larger crystals. Quartz druses are very common; quartz should be considered the most likely mineral whenever a shining crystal crust is seen. Usually only the points of the crystals will show; the prism faces do not develop well under these conditions (see descloizite, Pl. 29).

Sometimes the crystals are smaller and needlelike. Then they may not end in crystal planes but in a smoothly rounded surface, which may be described under various names, depending upon the size of the individual knobs. The term *botryoidal* (grape-like) is used when the knobs are rather small. *Reniform* (kidney-like) and *mammillary* are equally descriptive terms for larger rounded surfaces (see hematite, Pl. 15).

Various, but always obvious, terms are used to describe other growth habits which may be encountered in minerals. A branching treelike growth may be called *dendritic;* such a pattern is seen in moss agates and in manganese oxide stains on rock seams, often mistaken for fossil plant impressions. Small spheres are called *globular,* slender hairs are *acicular,* hanging masses are *stalactitic* and a regular pattern, like bridge girders, is *reticulated.*

Rock and Mineral Textures

When it does crystallize, the mass of a solidified mineral (away from the possibly freely grown surface) obviously develops under conditions of interference from other growing crystals. The coarseness of the texture will depend upon the same factors that determine the character of the free-growing surface, with more importance in these cases (since we often deal here with direct crystallization of a molten mass) on the viscosity of the solidifying liquid and the rate of cooling. Molten magma that comes to the surface as lava and cools quickly solidifies rapidly. The same magma deep underground cools and solidifies slowly. Fewer centers of crystallization develop when the cooling is slower, and the crystals have a chance to grow larger before they encounter the next growing crystal. In this way we develop *crystalline* textures, which may be fine or coarse, depending on the growth conditions. They are revealed on a broken face by the character of the surface. Most minerals break more easily in one direction than in another; so a break produces an uneven plane integrating the cleavage and easy fracture directions of each of the constituent grains. When we examine such a broken surface we can see if the individual grains are coarse or fine: if it is *coarsely crystalline* or *finely crystalline*. We can also see if the individual crystals are more or less equal in their length and breadth, or if they are elongated in one direction. Various descriptive terms have been applied to such crystalline masses, determined by the characteristics of the mineral grains composing them. They may be *foliated, micaceous,* or *lamellar* if they are tabular in habit and have micaceous cleavages. Needles may be *fibrous, acicular,* or *hairlike*. If the needles have no parallel arrangement but interlock, like the hairs that make up felt, we call the texture *felted;* this texture in jade explains its unusual strength.

Sometimes the crystalline structure is so fine that the individual grains cannot be seen with the naked eye. In this case we call it microscopically crystalline, or *cryptocrystalline*. Nevertheless, it does not mean that the substance is not crystallized; though undetectable except by X-ray, the atomic structure of the grains is the same as in those of the coarsest aggregate. The chalcedony division of quartz has such a cryptocrystalline texture. If a substance is really not crystallized, and gives no regular pattern even in an X-ray diffraction photograph, we call it *amorphous* (without form). Some minerals — but surprisingly few — come in this group, which includes opal and some of the hydrous silicates and oxides. Many substances long considered to be amorphous have been found, since the advent of X-ray studies, to be crystalline after all. Volcanic glass (obsidian) is made of lava that cooled so quickly no crystals developed; it, too, is amorphous.

Compaction

The crystalline mass varies in its resistance to fracture, and various terms have been applied to describe this. If it is very resistant to a separation of the individual grains it is called *compact*. This may be carried to the extreme that we find in quartzite, the metamorphosed sandstone, where the cementation between the grains is such that the rock in breaking actually breaks across the sand grains rather than around their surfaces. In granite the fracture is always through the grains, which are so interlocked that they cannot easily be separated. Other granular rocks may crumble more readily, however; some marbles break easily into little individual cleavage rhombohedrons, and for this reason are worthless as building stones. Olivine rocks (*dunites*) are particularly *friable;* as in some sandstones, the grains shower out when the finger is rubbed across them. Massive minerals with elongated or flattened crystals may break easily into a mass of splinters or plates.

Crystal Classifications

THE SMOOTH-FACED angular shapes assumed by minerals in solidifying from a molten state or in separating from solutions in open
spaces, where they are free to adopt any shape normal to them,
is known as a *crystal.* The external shape so assumed is related
to an internal arrangement of atoms. The smooth surfaces that
bound the crystal, called *faces,* are directly related to the internal
arrangement and their importance (size) to the frequency of the
atoms in the different planes. Other properties of minerals, like
the cleavage already mentioned, are also related to this three-
dimensional atomic pattern. The physicist is now much concerned
with crystals, and this group of scientists has modified the term
crystal to denominate only the internal atomic arrangement without regard to the related surface planes required by the mineralogist and by the classic origin of the word. The presence of external
faces means nothing to an X-ray beam, which pierces a crystal
like a stream of water striking a picket fence, and reflects, like
the water, from occasional planes.

To the mineral collector and expert in field identification, nevertheless, the crystal form is of paramount importance, and a well-
developed crystal is usually sufficiently characteristic to allow
identification from its shape alone. The angles between related
sets of crystal faces are different for many species of minerals, and
minerals can be identified by the careful measurement of the
critical angles on an instrument called a *goniometer.* Since this
is time-consuming and there are easier methods, it is not generally
used as a tool for identification.

Many find *crystallography* the most difficult aspect of mineral
study. The memorizing of all of the *crystal classes* would, indeed,
be rather difficult; but it should be remembered that mineral
representatives of over half of the classes are rare or unknown,
and that the crystal *system* alone is enough for identification when
it is considered along with the other characteristics.

The *crystal system* will be one of six, and the systems are defined
by the relative lengths and inclinations of imaginary internal lines
that run from opposite face centers, parallel to edges of the faces.
For a discussion of the elements of a crystal, let us take a simple
cube and study all its inner connections.

The *axes* are lines running from the center of each face to the
center of the opposite face. As we can see, in a cube there would
be 3 such lines: they are parallel to the corner edges, they intersect in the center at right angles, and they are all equal in length
(Fig. 7).

Next we might run imaginary lines to the corners. These are not parallel to the edge intersections, so they are not the crystal axes. However, if we pick a cube up by two opposite corners and turn it one-third of the way around, we see the cube with a set of faces in exactly the same position as they were before we turned it. Another third of a rotation repeats this experience, and after a third turn of 120°, we have the top back where it started. Though this may not be a crystal axis, it certainly is an axis on which the crystal can be turned to repeat itself without changing its true appearance; in other words, an *axis of symmetry* (Fig. 8), and in this case, it is an axis of *threefold* symmetry. If we were to pick the crystal up between fingers placed in the center of opposite edges, instead of corners, we would find that we would have to give a full half turn before the crystal appeared to reassume its original position. These, then, would be axes of *twofold* symmetry (Fig. 9). In a cube there would be 6 of these, with 4 of the *threefold* symmetry and the 3 crystal axes, which would have *fourfold* symmetry (Fig. 10).

If our cube were of wood and we were to saw it diagonally through the center, we could have two halves, each of which, if placed upon a mirror, would give us back the appearance of the whole cube (Fig. 12). We could also divide the cube in the middle of the face and get the same effect. These then are *planes of symmetry,* and in a cube there are 9 of these (Fig. 11).

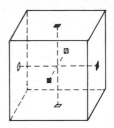

Fig. 7 Cube with 3 principal axes

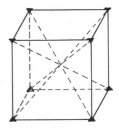

Fig. 8 Corner axes of 3-fold symmetry

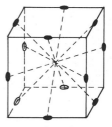

Fig. 9 Axes of 2-fold symmetry

Lines connecting the centers of any like pairs of faces would intersect at a central point. As long as you have opposing pairs of faces on several sides you would have such an intersection of connecting lines and the crystal would have a *center of symmetry.*

We have now reviewed all the symmetry elements of a cube, the crystal system that has the largest number of these elements and the highest symmetry. To sum up, then, we call the system in which this type of crystal occurs, a *cubic* system and define

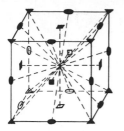

Fig. 10 Cubic axes of symmetry

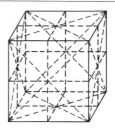

Fig. 11 Planes of symmetry

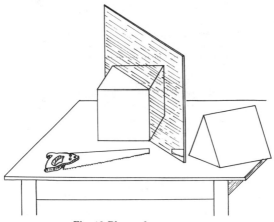

Fig. 12 Plane of symmetry

it as characterized by the possession of *3 equal axes at right angles* to each other. The crystal axes are the basis of the systems; the other elements are not invariable. The fundamental cube has, in addition, 4 axes of *threefold* symmetry, 6 axes of *twofold* symmetry, 9 planes of symmetry, and the *center* of symmetry.

There are some modifications we can now impose on our fundamental cube. We might cut off each corner of the cube, a little at first (Fig. 13) then all the way to the center of each face (Fig. 14). Now we find ourselves with an 8-faced form, a double pyramid, but it still has all the symmetry elements it had when it was a cube. So we can infer that a crystal shaped like this 8-faced form also belongs in the cubic system. This is called an octahedron. Suppose we were to erect a low 4-faced pyramid on each of the faces of the cube, we would then have a 24-faced form, a tetra[4]-hexa[6]hedron (Fig. 15). In the same way we can imagine 3 faces on the octahedron, a trisoctahedron (Fig. 16). So all of

Fig. 13 Cube with octahedral corner truncations

Fig. 14 Octahedron, related to same axes as the cube

Fig. 15 Tetrahexahedron

Fig. 16 Tetragonal trisoctahedron, or "trapezohedron"

these different-looking crystals (and we can get combinations of them too) still fit into our simple cubic system, all with 3 axes of equal length at right angles to each other.

There are 6 crystal systems, and the 32 crystal classes are subdivisions of these. The names of the systems refer to their appearance and their axes, and once learned are easy to remember. The classes depend upon the other symmetry elements present. In some crystals, for example, the top and bottom of the crystal are different, so there is no center of symmetry or horizontal plane of symmetry. Some of the axes of symmetry will also be missing, though the crystal axes must remain.

The symbols, known as Hermann-Mauguin symbols, describe the classes and are derived from the symmetry axes of each class.

The Crystal Systems

A. Cubic or Isometric System (Greek for "equal measure")

In this group the axes are equal in length and at right angles to each other. There are various symmetry classes, keeping the same equal axial ratio but losing some of the elements of symmetry:

1. Hexoctahedral

$$\frac{4}{m}\,\overline{3}\,\frac{2}{m}$$

(common: fluorite, garnet, etc.)

3 (crystal) axes of 4-fold symmetry
4 (diagonal) axes of 3-fold symmetry
6 (diagonal) axes of 2-fold symmetry
9 planes of symmetry
center of symmetry

2. Diploidal

$$\frac{2}{m}\,\overline{3}$$

(pyrite, cobaltite)

4 (diagonal) axes of 3-fold symmetry
3 (crystal) axes of 2-fold symmetry
3 axial planes of symmetry
center of symmetry

3. Tetrahedral	4 (diagonal) axes of 3-fold symmetry
(Hextetrahedral)	3 (crystal) axes of 2-fold symmetry
$\overline{4}$ 3 m	6 diagonal planes of symmetry
(tetrahedrite, sphalerite)	

4. Gyroidal	3 (crystal) axes of 4-fold symmetry
4 3 2	4 (diagonal) axes of 3-fold symmetry
(cuprite, sal ammoniac)	6 (diagonal) axes of 2-fold symmetry

5. Tetartohedral	4 (diagonal) axes of 3-fold symmetry
(Tetartoidal)	3 (crystal) axes of 2-fold symmetry
2 3	
(rare in nature)	

B. Tetragonal System (*tetra,* Greek for "four," referring to the square cross section)

This system resembles the cubic except that one of the axes, one that is always placed vertically as we look at (*orient*) the crystal, is longer or shorter than the other two. This change in the axes means that there is now a fixed vertical direction, and the crystal may not equally well be turned to bring a side up, as in the cubic system. The definitive forms are the upright ones — the prisms — which are vertical and are said to be *first* or *second order,* depending on whether a face cuts one horizontal axis and is parallel to the other or whether each face cuts both axes at an equal distance from the center (Fig. 17). The top and bottom pair of faces is known as the *basal pinacoids.* Intermediate truncating faces are bipyramids (in the classes that are alike at top and bottom; otherwise simply pyramids), and they too may also be first or second order.

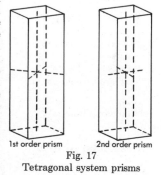

1st order prism   2nd order prism
Fig. 17
Tetragonal system prisms

Eight-faced prisms are known as *ditetragonal prisms,* the adjoining angles in a cross section are unlike, which helps to distinguish them from a combination of first- and second-order prisms. When only one of a ditetragonal pair is preserved, as in Class 8 (or Class 15 in the hexagonal system), it is known as a *third-order form* (see Fig. 19).

6. Ditetragonal bipyramidal

$$\frac{4\ 2\ 2}{m\ m\ m}$$

(zircon, vesuvianite, cassiterite, rutile)

1 vertical axis of 4-fold symmetry
4 horizontal axes of 2-fold symmetry
1 horizontal plane of symmetry
4 vertical planes of symmetry
  center of symmetry

7. Ditetragonal pyramidal

4 m m

(no common mineral)

1 vertical axis of 4-fold symmetry
4 vertical planes of symmetry

8. Tetragonal bipyramidal

$$\frac{4}{m}$$

(scheelite, scapolite)

1 vertical axis of 4-fold symmetry
1 horizontal plane of symmetry
center of symmetry

9. Tetragonal pyramidal
4

(wulfenite)

1 vertical axis of 4-fold symmetry

10. Ditetragonal alternating
(Tetragonal scalenohedral)

$\overline{4}$ 2 m

(chalcopyrite)

3 axes of 2-fold symmetry
2 vertical diagonal planes of
  symmetry

11. Tetragonal trapezohedral
4 2 2

(phosgenite)

1 vertical axis of 4-fold symmetry
4 horizontal axes of 2-fold symmetry

12. Tetragonal alternating
(Tetragonal bisphenoidal)

$\overline{4}$

(no common mineral)

1 vertical axis of 2-fold symmetry

C. Hexagonal System

This system with 3 horizontal axes intersected at right angles by 1 vertical axis is the most complicated of all because of the confusion that results from the very common subdivision in which alternate faces have not formed. This results in a threefold instead of a sixfold symmetry. It is known as the *rhombohedral division* of the hexagonal system, and has sometimes been placed in a separate group called the *trigonal system* with axes that parallel the rhombohedron edges. Since the relationship of the rhombohedral division to the hexagonal system is the same as the sphenoidal or tetrahedral classes in the first two systems, it does not seem logical to follow the trigonal system further. For mathematical reasons it is sometimes preferred, but it only makes the subject unnecessarily difficult.

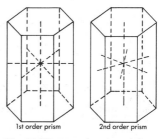

1st order prism   2nd order prism

Fig. 18 Hexagonal system prisms

In the hexagonal system we visualize 3 horizontal axes of equal length, intersected at right angles by a fourth that is longer or shorter. The fully developed forms would be 6-sided prisms or bipyramids of either a first or second order, as in the tetragonal system, depending upon whether 2 or 3 of the horizontal axes were cut (Fig. 18).

There is also a 12-faced form, which is merely a doubling of the 6 faces, called the *dihexagonal prism* (or dihexagonal bipyramid). By alternate development and suppression of one side or the other of these dihexagonal faces, we get a skewed 6-faced form (as in apatite), called the third order, just as in the tetragonal system (Fig. 19).

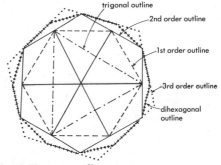

— — — — =1st order outline
———— =2nd order outline
+ + + + + + =dihexagonal outline
·············=3rd order outline
—·—·— =trigonal outline

trigonal outline
2nd order outline
1st order outline
3rd order outline
dihexagonal outline

Fig. 19 Hexagon outlines

13. Dihexagonal bipyramidal

$$\frac{6\ 2\ 2}{m\ m\ m}$$

(beryl)

vertical axis of 6-fold symmetry
6 horizontal axes of symmetry
6 vertical planes of symmetry
horizontal plane of symmetry
center of symmetry

14. Dihexagonal pyramidal

6 m m

(zincite, greenockite)

vertical axis of 6-fold symmetry
6 vertical planes of symmetry

15. Hexagonal bipyramidal   vertical axis of 6-fold symmetry
$$\frac{6}{m}$$ horizontal plane of symmetry
                                    center of symmetry

(apatite, pyromorphite,
vanadinite)

16. Hexagonal pyramidal   vertical axis of 6-fold symmetry
6

(nepheline)

17. Hexagonal trapezohedral   vertical axis of 6-fold symmetry
6 2 2   6 horizontal axes of 2-fold symmetry

(quartz — high tempera-
ture)

In the two trigonal classes of the hexagonal division, the vertical axis has a threefold rather than a sixfold symmetry, but, unlike the rhombohedral division, which follows, in the ditrigonal bipyramidal class there is a horizontal plane of symmetry. The trigonal pyramidal class, which lacks the horizontal plane of symmetry, is logically placed in the rhombohedral group; but since there is no known mineral with this class of symmetry, argument here about its proper position in a classification is purely academic.

18. Ditrigonal bipyramidal   vertical axis of 3-fold symmetry
$\overline{6}$ m 2   3 horizontal axes of 2-fold symmetry
(benitoite)   3 vertical planes of symmetry
                                   horizontal plane of symmetry

19. Trigonal bipyramidal   vertical axis of 3-fold symmetry
$\overline{6}$ horizontal plane of symmetry

(no mineral representative)

The rhombohedral division may be compared with the tetrahedral class of the cubic system and the sphenoidal classes of the tetragonal system; for the rhombohedron, the major form of the division, is developed by the dominant growth of every other face, alternating from top to bottom of the crystal. A simple rhombohedron has 6 faces. With 90° angles it would be a cube stood on its corner, the vertical axis coming out the point, if external form were the only criterion for crystal classification. In the normal orientation of the rhombohedral division,

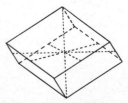

Fig. 20 Rhombohedron axes

the horizontal axes are regarded as coming out the center of each of the equatorial edges (Fig. 20). Because of the alternate-face growth, it differs from the trigonal class (benitoite) by lacking the horizontal plane of symmetry even in the classes with like faces above and below the center.

20. Rhombohedral holohedral (Hexagonal scalenohedral)

$$\bar{3}\,\frac{2}{m}$$

(calcite, hematite, corundum, etc.)

vertical axis of 3-fold symmetry
3 horizontal axes of 2-fold symmetry
3 vertical planes of symmetry (not on the horizontal axes, but between them)
center of symmetry

21. Rhombohedral hemimorphic (Ditrigonal pyramidal)

3 m

(tourmaline)

vertical axis of 3-fold symmetry
3 vertical diagonal planes of symmetry

22. Rhombohedral tetartohedral (Rhombohedral)

$$\bar{3}$$

(phenakite, willemite, dioptase, dolomite)

vertical axis of 3-fold symmetry
center of symmetry

23. Trapezohedral (Trigonal trapezohedral)

3 2

(quartz, cinnabar)

vertical axis of 3-fold symmetry
3 horizontal axes of 2-fold symmetry

24. Rhombohedral tetartohedral
Hemimorphic = Trigonal pyramidal)

3

(no common mineral)

vertical axis of 3-fold symmetry

D. Orthorhombic System

This system is a return to our uncomplicated 3 axes at right angles to each other, now with the variant that all are of unequal length. Obviously there must be a longest, a shortest, and an intermediate axis. To set up properly (orient) an orthorhombic

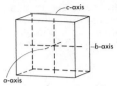

Fig. 21 Orthorhombic system axes and pinacoids

crystal, we place vertically what is commonly the longest direction (the c-axis), and direct the shortest axis (the a-axis) toward us. The intermediate axis running from left to right then becomes the b-axis (Fig. 21). As with bases in the tetragonal and hexagonal systems, the face pairs paralleling each other at opposite ends of the axes are the pinacoids, known respectively as basal, front, and side, or *basal, macro-* and *brachypinacoids* (remember: b-pinacoid equals the brachypinacoid). Vertical sets of 4 faces cutting the 2 horizontal axes are the *prisms* (they are often striated parallel to their length), and similar but horizontal sets of 4 faces cutting the vertical axis and one or the other horizontal axis (like a roof) are the *macro-* and *brachydomes*. Faces cutting all 3 are, as in the other systems, pyramids and bipyramids.

25. Orthorhombic bipyramidal

$$\frac{2\ 2\ 2}{m\ m\ m}$$

(barite group, sulfur, topaz, staurolite, andalusite, olivine, etc.)

3 crystal axes of 2-fold symmetry
3 axial planes of symmetry
center of symmetry

26. Orthorhombic pyramidal

m m 2

(hemimorphite, bertrandite)

vertical axis of 2-fold symmetry
2 vertical planes of symmetry

27. Orthorhombic sphenoidal
(Rhombic bisphenoidal)

2 2 2

(no common mineral)

3 crystal axes of 2-fold symmetry

E. Monoclinic System

Having exhausted the possible variations of 3 axes at right angles, the next mathematical possibility is to reduce the symmetry by inclining one of the axes to the plane of the other two, which remain at right angles. The setting up of such a crystal inclines the tilted axis toward the observer, this is the *clino-axis* or a-axis (Fig. 22). The other two axes lie in a vertical plane at right angles to that defined by the a and c axes. Either the b-axis

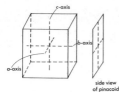

Fig. 22 Monoclinic system axes and pinacoids

or the *c*-axis may be the longer, but the *b*-axis will be one of twofold symmetry and the *a–c* plane will be the only plane of symmetry. The forms are the same as those of the orthorhombic system, except that the macrodomes become, for obvious reasons, *clinodomes*. The pyramids will be "front" or "back," however, so there are only 4 faces in the bipyramid of the full symmetry class.

28. Monoclinic normal (Prismatic) $\dfrac{2}{m}$ (gypsum, spodumene, ortho- clase, chondrodite, epi- dote, etc.)	horizontal axis of 2-fold symmetry vertical plane of symmetry (with 2 crystal axes) center of symmetry
29. Monoclinic hemimorphic (Sphenoidal) 2 (no common mineral, but sugar is a familiar exam- ple)	horizontal axis of 2-fold symmetry
30. Monoclinic hemihedral (Domatic) m (no common mineral)	vertical plane (with *a–c* axes) of symmetry

F. Triclinic System

The last possible variation we can imagine with our 3 unequal axes is to have all 3 inclined at some angle other than 90° (Fig. 23). Since an unsymmetrical set of axes like this can have symmetry only with pairs of faces, the domes, prisms, and pyramids of the other systems are now represented by 2 faces only, which are top and bottom and front and back, to the right and the left, as the case may be. The center of symmetry is the only element of symmetry left, and when it is present it makes the triclinic crystal of the normal class. The triclinic system is the most difficult to work out mathematically. Lacking in its hemihedral class any element of symmetry at all, it is from the standpoint of the

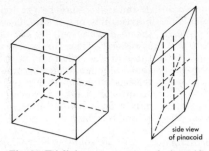

side view
of pinacoid

Fig. 23 Triclinic system axes and pinacoids

mathematician the easiest and most simply understood system.
On the other hand, since the recognition of symmetry and the
proper setting up of crystals is the chief joy of the study of this
aspect of minerals, it is the least satisfying to the collector.

The names of forms revert to those of the orthorhombic system.
Since all are inclined, there would be no point in a clinodome or
clinopinacoid in this system. Any axis can be made the vertical
one. Only the X-ray crystallographer can finally determine the
proper orientation of the group, though the axial ratios determined
by the older methods often coincide with those of the modern
X-ray crystallographer.

31. Triclinic normal   center of symmetry
    (Pinacoidal)
       $\overline{1}$
    (axinite, pyroxenes, and pla-
       gioclase feldspars)

32. Triclinic hemihedral   no symmetry
    (Pedial)
        1
    (no common mineral)

Other Forms and Phenomena

Twinning in Crystals

Since crystals often grow close together, an intergrowth of two
individuals is common. Sometimes the contact plane is a prominent plane in both crystals, and the two individuals are symme-

trically arranged either side of it. When this is suspected and the plane is a frequently observed face, or when we find many identical intergrowths paired on a less common plane, we speak of the doubling as *twinning*. Twins are often marked by re-entrant angles between the two halves. Common types of twinning are sometimes known under the name of a mineral that often intergrows in this fashion. Twinning involves a different orientation of the crystal segments and should not be confused with stepped, parallel growths.

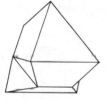

Fig. 24 Spinel twin

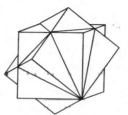

Fig. 25 Penetration twin of fluorite

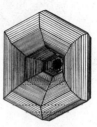

Fig. 26 Rutile "sixling"

In the cubic system we have the contact twinning on an octahedral face, which produces a crystal with a flattened triangular outline known as *spinel twinning* — frequent in spinel (Fig. 24), of course, and in diamond.

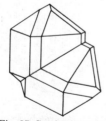

Fig. 27 Cassiterite twin

Two individuals may penetrate each other and corners of one may protrude from faces of the other individual. This is known as *penetration twinning,* often present in cubic fluorite (Fig. 25) and pyrite.

In the tetragonal system we find a repeated twinning in rutile which may make a complete wheel of geniculated ("kneelike") twins (Fig. 26). Cassiterite intergrows in the same fashion so that the re-entrant angle is a good guide to the mineral (Fig. 27).

In the hexagonal system we find calcite contact twins in many different arrangements, and cinnabar in penetrations like fluorite. We also find attractive penetration twinning in phenakite.

The orthorhombic system commonly has a penetration twinning of three individuals on a prism plane ("trilling"), so that the impression of a hexagonal crystal is developed. This is typical in aragonite and chrysoberyl (see Pls. 22 and 18).

Monoclinic crystals often form contact twins on the back pinacoid, as in the fishtail gypsum crystals (Fig. 28). The repeated twinning of the triclinic feldspar is common enough to serve as

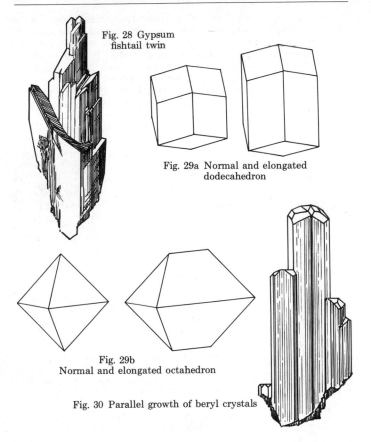

Fig. 28 Gypsum fishtail twin

Fig. 29a Normal and elongated dodecahedron

Fig. 29b
Normal and elongated octahedron

Fig. 30 Parallel growth of beryl crystals

an identification characteristic when the parallel lines are observed on the cleavage faces (see oligoclase, Pl. 35).

Distorted Crystals

The development of crystals is seldom perfectly symmetrical, and we often find greatly elongated crystals of one system resembling those of another. Experience in setting up crystals is the only guide to the recognition of these distorted crystals; an elongated dodecahedron may look like a rhombohedral mineral with a combination of the prism and rhombohedron (Figs. 29a, b). A study of the character of the faces will help in this respect. Prism faces are often striated differently from the terminal faces. If both have the same luster and markings, a distorted crystal should be suspected.

Parallel Growths

It is easy to confuse stepped and parallel growths with twin-nings. Unless a definite re-entrant is seen, with simultaneous reflections from the two individuals on *unlike* faces, the proba-bility is that the group in question is a parallel growth rather than a twin (Fig. 30). This one distinction creates more disagreements among collectors than any other aspect of crystallography.

Crystal Habit

Crystals usually show several different sets of crystal faces, the groups called "forms" in the crystallography discussion. Any crystal can only show the forms of its system. Cubic-system minerals can only have cubes, octahedrons, dodecahedrons, tetra-hexahedrons, trapezohedrons, and the like. They cannot have pinacoids, pyramids, or prisms, which are the forms of another system. Usually a crystal shows a combination of several forms — such as a cube with its corners cut by the octahedron faces, and perhaps with its edges cut off by dodecahedrons (Fig. 31). However, crystals of the same mineral may sometimes be dominantly cubic (Fig. 32) and at other times dominantly octa-hedral (Fig. 33). This is known as *habit,* and we speak of low-temperature (of formation) fluorite as having a cubic habit and high-temperature fluorite as having an octahedral habit. High-temperature calcite is commonly tabular. The study of crystal habit is still in its fundamental stages but is a fascinating branch of crystallography. Temperature, pressure, composition of the mineral-depositing solutions, and variations in their concentration may all play a part in determining the final outline of the crystal. We also find, from the study of ghostlike earlier growth stages delineated by a band of impurities within the crystal (and known

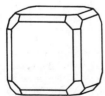

Fig. 31 Combination crystal (fluorite)

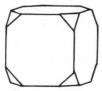

Fig. 32 Crystal habit dominantly cubic

Fig. 33 Crystal habit dominantly octahedral

Fig. 34 Phantom calcite showing habit change with later growth: a prismatic habit replacing an earlier scalenohedral termination

as "phantoms"), that the habit of a crystal may have changed during its growth (Fig. 34).

Pseudomorphs

Occasionally we encounter the misleading situation of one mineral with the crystal outline of another, as a result of having taken in some fashion the place of the original crystal. The simplest way in which this can happen is the change, by simple weathering, of pyrite (iron sulfide) to limonite (hydrous iron oxide). Garnets may be similarly altered. A more complex change takes place when hot solutions alter garnet to chlorite. These are known as *pseudomorphs* (*pseudo* from "false," *morph* meaning "form").

There are several types of such pseudomorphs, and a rather complex series of names has been developed to specify the type of change in each case. The first described are by simple alteration. Crusts may form over crystals, and some call these coatings "pseudomorphs by incrustation." Sometimes an entirely new substance may take the place of the old mineral, as in the serpentine casts of quartz from Bavaria or the Cuban quartz alterations of fluorite.

Paramorphs are special cases where there is no real change in composition but where the mineral has simply rearranged its atoms into a different configuration that no longer coincides with the original crystal outline. Rutile paramorphs after brookite are common at Magnet Cove, Arkansas.

More often we have a slight substitution of elements, as in the change of the blue copper carbonate (azurite) to the more stable green copper carbonate (malachite) or hydrous gypsum replacing water-free anhydrite.

Lastly, we have the case of a mineral simply filling in a space left by the disappearance of the earlier mineral, as in the quartz casts of glauberite at West Paterson, New Jersey. Then there are those objects with no orientable shape — since they are not regulated by crystal laws — which preserve only the form of an empty space lined by crystals; they are often considered pseudomorphs themselves, but really are only pseudo-pseudomorphs!

The Chemical Classification
of Minerals

IN CHAPTER 2 we learned what a mineral is: that it is a kind of naturally occurring chemical compound and that it is composed of various chemical elements. One of the best known of these chemical compounds, ordinary table salt, might be taken as an example. Table salt is a combination of two elements, sodium and chlorine. Sodium is a metallic element and chlorine is gaseous at normal temperatures. We manufacture pure table salt, but we make it from the mineral halite by simply freeing the halite from the various impurities that commonly occur with it in nature. We never find pure sodium in nature, nor do we find pure chlorine. Both of these elements are always combined with something else, since they are too "active" chemically to exist by themselves. Sodium can combine with many different elements, but only particular ones, elements of a metallic type, customarily combine with nonmetallic elements to form what are known as salts. The "salt-forming" elements form acids with hydrogen, such as those used for testing (see p. 11). Consequently, aside from a few native elements that can exist in nature either because of their relative inactivity or unusual conditions, all minerals are salts of one sort or another.

Since there are some 1500 to 2000 recognized minerals, of which almost 270 are individually described in this book, it is necessary to arrange them in some kind of classification. Several approaches to this goal of simplification have been tried. Most recently, an attempt has been made to arrange them by their crystal structure without letting the traditional chemical composition be the determining criterion. Nevertheless, the chemical classification to be found here has best stood the test of time and, with modifications and minor rearrangements, is generally accepted by professional mineralogists. The present classification is that used in the Seventh Edition of *Dana's System of Mineralogy,* which places the silicates last.

The properties of the elements in the natural chemical compounds give the minerals immediately recognizable characteristics in some cases, so that the problem of their specific identification is greatly simplified. The field expert can usually guess the chemical group to which a mineral belongs from its associates in the field (see pp. 24–27, 54–56, and back endpaper) and from the obvious physical properties described below and in the general summary introducing each chemical class in Part II of this book. In other cases it may be sufficient to make a single chemical test to distinguish two groups that sometimes look alike, as for example the carbonates and the sulfates. In general the following rules for the recognition of chemical classes will prevail.

The Elements

Native elements — elements in a free, uncombined state — are not common. With a few exceptions they are not found as natural minerals. Among the *nonmetallic* solid elements we have sulfur and the two forms of carbon (diamond and graphite). These are fairly unmistakable, even though their appearance has little in common. There are a few more elements, known as *semimetals,* which have some characteristics (their chemical activity) but not others (like malleability) in common with the metals. The metals are the most numerous of the native elements. It is their malleability — that is, the way they can be flattened and shaped by hammering — together with their metallic appearance, that makes them easy to recognize. A yellow native metal that can be flattened by hammering can only be gold.

Sulfides and Sulfosalts

Most of these look metallic and all but one or two are soft. The appearance of the nonmetallic sulfides is rather consistent, so they should give little difficulty. In addition, they are usually associated with their metallic-looking relatives in ore veins. Practically all are brittle and the metallic crystals shatter to a dark or black powder when struck by a hammer. All are heavy. The nonmetallics may have a white or light-hued powder (streak).

Oxides and Hydroxides

The very unlike minerals that fall into this category can be further grouped by common characteristics. There are some that are original rock minerals which, since they are oxides, are very resistant to further change by the air's oxygen ("weathering"). The group includes some very heavy rock and ore-vein minerals; those free from water (anhydrous) are relatively hard. Water-free species are usually primary — formed directly from molten rocks, a melt, or from hot, watery (hydrothermal) solutions. Other oxides, those that form on the surface by weathering and many of which contain water, are more likely to be soft. Often they are red, brown, or black, the typical iron and manganese oxide colors. Because of their great variation in appearance, minerals of the oxide group are among the more difficult ones to identify.

Halides

These are compounds of metals with fluorine, chlorine, bromine, and iodine. Many, like halite (rock salt) are water-soluble, and can occur as natural minerals only under unusual conditions. All are light in color when fresh (some of the silver and mercury compounds will darken on exposure to light — whence photography), and many are transparent or translucent. None are hard; many crystallize in the cubic system.

Carbonates

Most of these are translucent to transparent. None are hard; two large groups (the calcite group and dolomite) have a pronounced rhombohedral cleavage. All are more or less readily soluble in acid, freeing bubbles of carbon dioxide as they dissolve.

Nitrates and Borates

Like the halides, most members of this group are very soluble in water and are soft. The exceptions are a few remarkably hard, but very rare, borates, principally occurring in pegmatites. Because of the high solubility, the common borates are restricted to dry countries. They are mainly light-colored and may be transparent.

Sulfates

These can be split into very soluble and rather insoluble ones. The latter, since they contain no water, are called anhydrous. Both types can form in the oxidized portions of sulfide veins, and anhydrous insoluble ones, like barite, also form with the ores. The several copper sulfates are typically high-colored greens and blues. All sulfates are soft; the pure ones are translucent to transparent. Many of the group are extremely insoluble. The formation of hydrous calcium sulfate (gypsum) needles in an acid solution is one indication of the presence of a sulfur atom when we are testing unknown minerals.

Phosphates, Vanadates, and Arsenates

All these are soft and often highly colored. Most of the vanadates and arsenates occur in oxidized zones of ore bodies and are secondary, or weathering, minerals. However, apatite (calcium phosphate) occurs as a primary mineral. It is widely distributed in igneous rocks in microscopic grains, and is considered the likely source of the phosphorus for secondary phosphates. Most are fairly soluble in acid and all can be dissolved after fusion with sodium carbonate. This solution then gives a good phosphorus test (see pp. 62, 66).

Tungstates, Molybdates, and Uranates

This catchall group of soft, heavy, and often colorful ores has few individual members. Each of the common ones has a distinctive appearance or characteristic, so that their recognition is easy.

Silicates

This group, which probably includes half of all known minerals, is the most difficult. Silicates are not easily soluble in acid and many leave a skeletal silica outline of the grain when the compound is dissolved in a salt of phosphorus bead. Some are very hard and are infusible and insoluble. Their specific gravity ranges from fairly light to intermediate; they are never very heavy. Their luster is commonly glassy; most crush to a light powder even though the specimen is black. Their occurrence is chiefly as components of rocks, as segregations in rocks, or as druses of crystals lining cavities in rocks. The greater number of the hard silicates are primary minerals, not products of weathering. Secondary silicates are usually water-containing, and most of these will form a gel in a small quantity of hydrochloric acid, particularly after the blowpipe fusion that we find possible when we heat hydrous silicates.

THE CHEMICAL ELEMENTS AND THEIR SYMBOLS

Aluminum....	Al	Chromium....	Cr	Hydrogen	H
Antimony.....	Sb	Cobalt	Co	Indium	In
Argon..........	A	Columbium*..	Cb	Iodine..........	I
Arsenic	As	Copper.........	Cu	Iridium	Ir
Barium	Ba	Dysprosium ..	Dy	Iron	Fe
Beryllium.....	Be	Erbium	Er	Krypton.......	Kr
Bismuth.......	Bi	Europium.....	Eu	Lanthanum...	La
Boron..........	B	Fluorine.......	F	Lead............	Pb
Bromine.......	Br	Gadolinium...	Gd	Lithium	Li
Cadmium	Cd	Gallium........	Ga	Lutecium......	Lu
Calcium	Ca	Germanium...	Ge	Magnesium ...	Mg
Carbon	C	Gold............	Au	Manganese....	Mn
Cerium	Ce	Hafnium	Hf	Mercury.......	Hg
Cesium	Cs	Helium	He	Molybdenum.	Mo
Chlorine.......	Cl	Holmium......	Ho	Neodymium..	Nd

* In Europe columbium is known as niobium and its symbol is Nb.

Neon............	Ne	Rubidium.....	Rb	Thorium.......	Th
Nickel..........	Ni	Ruthenium ...	Ru	Thulium.......	Tm
Nitrogen.......	N	Samarium.....	Sm	Tin	Sn
Osmium	Os	Scandium.....	Sc	Titanium......	Ti
Oxygen	O	Selenium......	Se	Tungsten......	W
Palladium.....	Pd	Silicon	Si	Uranium	U
Phosphorus...	P	Silver...........	Ag	Vanadium.....	V
Platinum......	Pt	Sodium	Na	Xenon	Xe
Potassium.....	K	Strontium.....	Sr	Ytterbium	Yb
Praseodymium	Pr	Sulfur..........	S	Yttrium	Y
Radium........	Ra	Tantalum.....	Ta	Zinc	Zn
Radon	Rn	Tellurium.....	Te	Zirconium.....	Zr
Rhenium......	Re	Terbium.......	Tb		
Rhodium......	Rh	Thallium......	Tl		

6

Tests, Techniques, and Tips

Fusibility

The ease with which the different minerals will fuse, and the nature of the product of their melting, is the basis for the beginner's primary tests. Most of the sulfides melt easily and often a malleable metallic bead can be recovered. The members of the other groups are usually less fusible and the results accordingly less satisfactory. The first test of an unknown sulfide is to place it on charcoal and melt it, or try to melt it. With the other classes a sometimes easier method is to hold a flake or a splinter in the flame of the blowpipe or Bunsen burner and see if a thin edge will fuse.

With so many variably fusible minerals, a scale of fusibilities has been propounded which assigns a sequence of numbers, up to six for bronzite (a variety of pyroxene whose splinters barely melt on the edge in the hottest flame). Many minerals are quite infusible. Because the numbers are rather meaningless, only simple descriptive terms have been used here, such as "fuses easily," "with some difficulty," "with great difficulty," and so on.

In fusing, the minerals may melt easily to a clear or to a bubbly glass, turn black, or become magnetic. For any mineral with an unusual or characteristic behavior, an attempt has been made to give special mention of the distinctive response. Sometimes the mineral may swell, or send up little horns like a Fourth of July "snake," or open out like leaves of a book (exfoliate). A few minerals glow (phosphoresce) before getting hot enough to become incandescent. Sometimes the flame around the melted grain will be colored by one of the ingredients. This coloration can often be intensified if a drop of acid is added to the fused mass; a flash of color will be seen as the flame first hits the melt.

The easily fused minerals and the ones that are suspected of being sulfides can be placed in a split-pea-sized depression in a charcoal block and blasted with the blowpipe. Many of the sulfides will give off fumes and deposit colored rings around the grain. Details of the tests will be found in the mineral descriptions; but the phenomena to be observed include such things as a garlic smell (arsenic) or, around the edge of the heated area, a yellow coating that turns white on cooling (zinc).

Often a metal bead can be recovered by intensely heating the fused mineral grain in the reducing flame. Sometimes this can be obtained directly; at other times something to aid the separation — a flux (like sodium carbonate), which will remove the sulfur and keep the metal from oxidizing — must be added to the mineral grain. The bead is recovered by pounding up the fused mass, and the color of the metal will usually show what the metallic element was. The malleability or flattening of the bead by the pounding shows it to be a metal. When the presence of iron is suspected, test the bead for magnetism.

If the mineral tends to fly apart as the flame hits it (decrepitates) and will not stay on the charcoal, overcome the difficulty by crushing the mineral to a powder and then blowpiping the powder. It may sometimes be necessary to moisten the powder with saliva to help the particles stick together on the charcoal. Sometimes a splinter can be held in the Bunsen flame for a gentle heating to overcome the tendency to decrepitate, before putting the mineral on the charcoal for final melting. The grain, or powder, can also be heated in a Pyrex test tube, or closed tube, until it stops popping. Single crystal fragments are more likely to decrepitate than fine-grained masses of the same mineral. Crushing is best accomplished in the *mortar,* the most suitable type consisting of a steel cup with a piston nesting in a steel ring that fits closely into the hole. Hammer this with some force and the loose steel collar will prevent the mineral grains from flying out on the rebound. An agate mortar and pestle will serve for more easily crushed grains; here, too, a small, loose metal collar surrounding the pestle will prevent escape of the grains as they break.

In some cases fusion will be impossible. We can still make tests on these fragments. Sphalerite, for example, does not fuse, but if it is heated, then touched with the cobalt nitrate solution, and heated again, it will assume a greenish color that is indicative of the zinc it contains.

Flame Tests

Flame tests are indirectly related to the melting tests, for blowpipe flame colorations are often seen during the fusing of such minerals as the copper sulfides. An added drop of acid may create a brief brilliant flash of color. The usual flame colors can be obtained better in other ways. The most frequent procedure is to insert the platinum wire in a powder of the unknown mineral that has been moistened with nitric acid. Introduce this carefully at the edge of the Bunsen flame, where it will flare in a flash of color, sometimes very distinctively. Copper colors it blue-green, strontium red, calcium orange-red, potassium light violet, lithium red, and so on (see Table I, p. 66). Concentrated solutions of the minerals in acid into which the platinum wire is dipped will also give the typical flame colors. There are two hazards in this test. Arsenic in a mineral reacts with the platinum of the wire to make a brittle compound. If there is any possibility that arsenic is present, the unknown grain should be heated for a long time by the blowpipe ("roasted") before crushing it for use on the platinum wire (arsenic volatilizes easily). Secondly, the sodium in the salts used in bead tests is very persistent on the wire, and gives a yellow hue to the flame. It may also be in the mineral and can mask the color of another element present. (Blue filter glasses are sold which filter out the yellow sodium light and transmit the other colors, but their use requires some experience.) Flame colors may be best observed if you work in a poor light.

Bead Tests

These are made with a platinum wire looped at the end. Small containers with borax ($Na_2B_4O_7 \cdot 10H_2O$), salt of phosphorus (microcosmic salt, $HNaNH_4PO_4 \cdot 4H_2O$), sodium fluoride (NaF) or lithium fluoride (LiF) are most convenient for use. The wire is heated in the flame to red heat and dipped, still hot, into the reagent. Some powder clings to the wire, which is then returned to the flame to melt the white powder to a clear glass. It may be necessary to return to the powder well several times before the loop is filled out with a plump bead. Borax swells into great "worms" as it melts, and finally shrinks to almost nothing as it clears.

The unknown mineral, or the residue of a fused bead from the charcoal, is then crushed in the steel mortar and spilled out onto a convenient, flat, unburnable surface. The bead is heated and pressed onto one or two of the grains, which will cling to it, and returned to a flame (the blowpipe is usually the most efficient method of heating). As the bead melts again, the glowing grains will be seen to dissolve in the clear red liquid; swirling and twisting rapidly, they soon disappear completely. On cooling, if enough of the mineral has been added and if it contains an element that gives a good color, a beautifully tinted bead is to be seen. In many cases the bead hue depends upon the location of the bead in the flame during the heating; for it may be held either in the oxidizing or the reducing part of the flame. Both hues should be observed. A few minutes of reheating in the other part of the flame is enough to reverse the oxidized or reduced condition of the metal.

As usual, a few cautions should be observed. We have noted before that if there is any possibility of arsenic being present the mineral should be throughly heated on the charcoal to drive out the last arsenic traces before it is placed on the platinum wire. It is easy to get too much of the unknown powder in the bead and to end with a black mass. This can be corrected by crushing the opaque bead on the steel mortar edge and introducing a small fragment into a new bead. This usually reduces the concentration down to a point where the bead is transparent. The overdarkened bead can also be removed from the wire loop by heating it red-hot and quickly snapping it off onto the table top. The hot bead will burn anything it strikes, so be careful not to let it fall on anything that can be damaged. The residue left on the wire will probably tint a new bead enough to give a good test. When the test is finished, the wire can be cleaned by snapping it off in the same way. One of the best cleaning methods is to make successive fresh beads until they come out completely colorless. The platinum wire used for the beads should probably be restricted to bead tests without trying to use it also in flame tests, since the sodium in the borax and salt of phosphorus is very persistent and is difficult to remove completely from the wire. It is better to have two wires for the different tests. Bead hues are given in Tables IIa and IIb (pp. 66–67).

The silicates often become partially dissolved in the salt of phosphorus but leave a ghostlike outline of their original shape. This silica skeleton is a good indication of the silicate group.

Tube Tests

Open and closed tubes have some, but not great, use in blowpiping, mainly in testing the sulfides. The results depend upon the deposition of sublimed oxides or of the separated portions of the unknown metals or compounds on the cooler walls of the container. Hold the open tube over the flame at a slight slant to permit the passage of a current of air over the grain being tested. Coatings of oxides will be deposited on the glass above the mineral grains in cooler areas, and in some cases several successive bands of increasingly volatile compounds will be observed. The diameter of the glass tubing used for open tubes may very profitably be somewhat greater than that of the closed tubes, perhaps by $\frac{5}{16}$ in. (8–9 mm) to ensure a good current of air. Pyrex glass is useful but not essential. Heating should not be hastened, or the air supply may be insufficient and the effects obtained like those of the closed tube.

The technique of closed-tube testing is similar, though a different type of sublimate is usually obtained. Water drops may indicate a hydrous mineral. Etching of the glass may suggest the presence of fluorine. If moisture is suspected, it is wise first to heat the tube enough to dry out the air in it before testing for water in the mineral. The typical sublimates of the open and closed tube are listed in Tables IIIa and IIIb (p. 67–68).

Wet Tests in Test Tubes

As a last resort it often becomes necessary to dissolve some of the unknown fragments, or some of the charcoal block residue, in an acid, then try to identify some elements (qualitative analysis). A few reactions are critical, and such tests are essential with minerals for which blowpipe tests will not work. The titanium in ilmenite, for example, must be identified by first dissolving the mineral in a fusion of sodium carbonate and then dissolving the mixture in concentrated hydrochloric acid. When this solution is boiled with zinc or tin (a small sliver of the metal dropped in the test tube will do), it turns blue-violet if titanium is present.

Copper gives acid solutions a greenish color, and the addition of ammonia will turn them blue. Silver in nitric acid solutions precipitates in a white curdy mass if hydrochloric acid is added. If sulfur is suspected, a few drops of a solution of calcite in hydrochloric acid should be added to the nitric acid solution, and small needles of hydrous calcium sulfate (gypsum in nature) will form (precipitate). The addition of a grain of potassium iodide to a weak nitric acid solution of a lead mineral will cause a sparkling yellow precipitate to form. Phosphorus and arsenic may also show up as dustlike yellow grains, but the sparkling spangles of the lead compound are unmistakable. These and other special tests will be found under the appropriate mineral descriptions.

Fluorescence and Phosphorescence

For some time the property of glowing with visible light under the bombardment of invisible rays like X-rays and ultraviolet light, or glowing in the dark after exposure to a source of such invisible radiation or to sunlight, has excited the interest of mineral collectors. This has resulted in special fluorescence displays in many museums and in fluorescence becoming a spectacular toy of the amateur. It had little practical application until it was used as a method for prospecting for scheelite, the fluorescent ore of tungsten. Many other minerals are fluorescent and phosphorescent, but usually this property is not constant enough for it to have much value in testing.

In preparing this book I found, nonetheless, that the ultraviolet light could in some cases be of real testing value after roasting or blowpiping of the specimen. Further work along these lines should be done; the amateur collector has an opportunity here to make a real contribution to mineral-testing techniques by investigating fluorescence in a serious way along the lines suggested throughout the mineral descriptions. Much celestite is naturally fluorescent yellow-green; it was found by experiment that all celestite tested became brilliantly fluorescent and phosphorescent yellow-green after roasting. Barite is only occasionally fluorescent, but all barite tested was found to be fluorescent yellow-orange after roasting. Hence, with the two similar minerals we have only to roast an edge in the flame to red heat, briefly, allow the specimens to cool, and examine them with our ultraviolet light. The yellow-green one will be celestite, the yellow-orange one barite.

There are innumerable tests of this type described throughout the mineral descriptions.

The serious mineral collector should by all means supply himself with one or two ultraviolet lights. The ultraviolet spectrum is a long one, ranging from light with wavelength just beyond the wavelength of visible light to very short rays near the X-ray end of the light spectrum. Different sources of ultraviolet light produce either shortwave ultraviolet or longwave ultraviolet. Longwave ultraviolet lights are cheaper, but fewer minerals respond to them. Some minerals respond to one or the other; others respond to both long- and shortwave ultraviolet light, but their responses may be different. Sicilian aragonite, for instance, is a beautiful brilliant pink under the longwave ultraviolet, with a weak greenish phosphorescence after the exposure; and a medium-intensity greenish white with a bright greenish-white phosphorescence under the shortwave ultraviolet light. Scheelite is negative under longwave ultraviolet and bright blue under shortwave.

Shortwave ultraviolet light is said to have a wavelength of about 2500 angstrom units (or Å, a measure of wavelength of light: 6700 angstrom units is the wavelength of red light; around 4300 angstrom units is the wavelength of visible violet light). Shortwave ultraviolet is best produced by a mercury-vapor light, operating in an evacuated fused-quartz tube, and covered by a filter that shuts out the visible light. Longwave ultraviolet lights, 3000 to 4000 angstrom units, are available in many forms, though the cheapest, like the "black lights" and argon bulbs that sell for less than a dollar, have little value except for very fluorescent minerals such as some of the uranium compounds.

And so the mineral collector is well advised to purchase some sort of ultraviolet light. It makes an impressive spectacle for his friends and it has a very real value as a testing tool.

A Suggested Testing Procedure

The matter of mineralogy is of worldwide occurrence. Aside from locality emphasis, any mineralogical text is international. The laws of physics and chemistry operate everywhere: under identical conditions, the same compounds are invariably produced. So instead of the hundreds of thousands of species with which the entomologist must concern himself, the mineral collector has only about 2000 natural compounds, and of these only 200 can be considered at all common. The problem for the average collector, then, simmers down to which one of 200 possibilities he has. Ordinary physical description, such as environment, color, hardness, and crystal shape, eliminates nine-tenths of what is left, so at the end there are only half a dozen or fewer likely possibilities.

A simple test or two is then sufficient for a final identification. Since the problem is that of separating 1 out of 2 or 3 instead of 1 from 2000, it is practical to make far more use of such primitive elementary tests as the addition of a drop of cobalt nitrate to the surface of a melted mass than is usually suggested in books for beginners.

For more advanced collectors, identification by sight of the common minerals becomes a matter of habit, and then recourse would be made to the more complete series of books listed in the Annotated Bibliography at the back of this *Field Guide*.

The collector should not expect to be able to identify every specimen. In the first place, there probably are eight times as many known minerals as are included here; and inevitably even a complete beginner will encounter some of them when he collects at a good locality. For these he should have no hesitation about enlisting the aid of an expert until he himself attains that status. In the second place, all minerals are not under every circumstance identifiable by simple means. Just as the botanist does not attempt to identify plants without a flower, so might the mineral collector recognize that he too has limitations. A poor, uncrystallized mineral grain may not be identifiable by only a few of its physical properties. Nor has such as uncharacteristic specimen any merit in a collection, unless one begins to specialize and wishes, for example, to collect all possible mineral species from a particular locality.

Let us assume, then, that you have been out collecting somewhere and have secured an attractive specimen that seems worth adding to your collection. You are uncertain of its identity. How can you go about finding out what it is with the help of this book?

Many of the specimens you find will be crystallized. After you have worked with this book for a while you will come to know crystals so well that you will be able to orient them and recognize their crystal system with very little trouble. In many cases you will not regard a specimen as worth collecting unless it is in well-formed, distinctive crystals.

You probably will know in what type of locality you have been collecting: a limestone quarry, a pegmatite dike, an ore deposit, or a granite quarry. You will have observed that certain mineral groups are more likely in one type of deposit than another. If there is any doubt of this in your mind you have only to look over the first boldface subheading under each mineral species, **Environment.** Even if you have not collected the specimen yourself, you can often guess by the associated minerals from what kind of formation it comes. It is this information obtainable from the associated minerals that makes a matrix specimen so much more valuable scientifically than a loose, unattached crystal.

The first step, then, is to look at the specimen carefully, determine its environment and, if possible, its crystal system. You will incidentally observe other physical properties such as color, luster, cleavage, and (should the unknown constitute a major part of the specimen) its specific gravity.

The next step is to make some tests: first the least destructive and simplest, and ones that will give the chemical class as readily as possible. Probably the very first test you will want to make is for hardness, trying the specimen with a knife to see whether or not it can be scratched. If it cannot be scratched you would immediately assign it as most likely a silicate; if it can be scratched it probably belongs to one of the other groups. (There are a few hard oxides and other compounds, but they are comparatively few and you will soon come to know them.)

If you can scratch it, you note whether or not there is a good cleavage. If there is a good rhombohedral cleavage, or something that looks as if it might be rhombohedral, you should suspect a carbonate and try the mineral with a drop of hydrochloric acid. When this test is positive you can easily run down the individual mineral from the carbonate mineral descriptions in the book. If it is negative, you should suspect a sulfate first and make the blowpipe tests (and test for resultant fluorescence if you have an ultraviolet light) and other tests suggested previously in this chapter. If it is highly colored, look among the phosphates and arsenates. If it is metallic in luster, look for it among the sulfides. Memorize the outstanding characteristics of each mineral group that you find summarized in Chapters 5 and 6 under the group names and in the group descriptions throughout Part II.

If the mineral is too hard to scratch, or can be scratched only with difficulty, you have a hard oxide or a silicate. The hard oxides are few in number and are easily recognized by the crystals, which are usually present. If it is a silicate, the problem is much more difficult, for many silicates do not fuse readily, and the elements usually contained in them — calcium, magnesium, iron, potassium, sodium, and others — often give no simple chemical or blowpipe reactions. Fusion, or attempted fusion on charcoal, is recommended. Many of your final determinations will be made by a process of elimination; you will just have to try tests for suspected minerals suggested under the subheading **Tests** in the mineral descriptions, and then see how they work out.

The experienced chemist and the well-qualified amateur with a chemical background can work out an analytical procedure that will enable him to run down almost any mineral. Once the material is put into solution the analytical procedure is much like that followed in a good chemistry course in high school. O. C. Smith's *Identification and Qualitative Chemical Analysis of Minerals* gives an excellent analytical procedure, but this type of mineral identification is usually a later step in the study of minerals. It must be confessed that most mineral identification is done by sight, experience, reading, examination of collections of others, and one or two simple and definitive tests; perhaps the hardness, or streak test, or fluorescence gives the answer. Running a mineral down by a long series of tests, like the identification of a plant by botanical keys, is difficult, time-consuming, and no more necessary for the collector who has had a little experience than is the key in *Gray's Manual of Botany*.

TABLE I. Flame Tests

Flame Coloration or Flash	Element
(Violet) Red	strontium
Bright red	lithium
Orange-red	calcium
Yellow-orange	sodium
Yellow-green	barium
Green	boron
Emerald-green (intense)	copper
Bluish green (pale)	phosphorus
Greenish blue	antimony
Bluish white	arsenic
Blue	tellurium
Violet	potassium

TABLE IIa. Borax Bead Tests

Oxidizing Flame Color		Reducing Flame Color		Element
Hot	*Cold*	*Hot*	*Cold*	
Pale yellow	colorless to white	brown	brown to black	molybdenum
Pale yellow	colorless to white	gray or yellow	brownish	titanium
Yellow to orange	yellow to brown	pale green	green	uranium (fluorescent)
Yellow	green	green	green	chromium
Yellow	green	brown to gray-green	yellow to green	vanadium
Green	blue	colorless to green	opaque red-brown	copper
Blue	blue	blue	blue	cobalt
Yellow to orange	greenish to brown	bottle-green	paler bottle-green	iron
Violet	reddish brown	opaque gray	opaque gray	nickel
Violet	reddish violet	colorless	colorless	manganese

TABLE IIb. Salt of Phosphorus Bead Tests

Oxidizing Flame Color		Reducing Flame Color		Element
Hot	*Cold*	*Hot*	*Cold*	
Yellowish to green	colorless	dirty green	yellow-green	molybdenum
Pale yellow	colorless	yellow	pale violet	titanium
Yellow	yellow-green	light gray-green	green	uranium (fluorescent)
Reddish to gray-green	yellowish green to green	red to gray-green	green	chromium
Yellow	greenish yellow	brown to gray-green	green	vanadium
Dark green	greenish blue	brownish green	opaque red	copper
Blue	blue	blue	blue	cobalt
Yellow to brown-red	brownish yellow	red or yellow to green-yellow	pale violet	iron
Reddish to brown-red	yellow to reddish yellow	reddish to brownish red	yellow to reddish yellow	nickel
Pale yellow	colorless	greenish to dirty blue	greenish blue	tungsten
Insoluble white skeleton in clear bead				silica

TABLE IIIa. Open-Tube Tests

Sublimate(s)	Gases	Element
White powder (yellowish when hot)	dense white fumes	antimony
White minute sparkling crystals	garlic odor	arsenic
Brown (hot) and yellow (cold)		bismuth (oxide)
White powder that fuses to yellow drops, nonvolatile		bismuth (sulfide)
White powder that fuses to yellow drops		lead
Silver droplets (or gray film) (rub with needle to make into droplets)		mercury
Network of slender crystals, yellow (hot) and white (cold)		molybdenum
White powder that fuses to yellow drops		tellurium

TABLE IIIb. Closed-Tube Tests

Sublimate(s)	Element
White needle crystals that will melt	antimony oxide
Black (hot) and reddish-brown (cold) film	antimony sulfides and sulfosalts
Brilliant black; gray and crystalline at lower end	arsenic (metal and arsenides)
White, crystalline	arsenic oxide
Deep red to black liquid (hot); reddish-yellow solid (cold)	arsenic sulfides and sulfosalts)
Black, turning red when rubbed	mercury sulfide
Water drops on cool part	hydrous mineral

TABLE IV. Fusibility

Typical Minerals	Standard Scale	Behavior	Description in Mineral Text Section
Stibnite	1	melts easily in any flame	fuses very readily
Natrolite Chalcopyrite }	2	melt in any flame	fuse easily
Almandine	3	melts with difficulty in alcohol flame	fuses
Actinolite	4	no fusion in alcohol flame, thin splinters melt to globule in gas flame	fuses with some difficulty
Orthoclase	5	gas flame rounds thin edges	almost infusible
Bronzite	6	gas flame barely rounds thinnest edges	melts only on thinnest edges in gas flame
Topaz	infusible	no rounding of any sort	infusible

PART II

*Mineral
Descriptions*

Mineral Descriptions

The Elements

NOT MANY ELEMENTS are found in their uncombined or pure states. Usually there are too many other substances present at the time of their formation with which they can combine. Most of those found either do not form oxides or do so only at high temperatures. They form into three major groups: the metals, the semimetals, and nonmetals.

The Metals

The metals are most readily identified by their color and malleability (which means that they can be deformed by pounding without crumbling).

GOLD Au Cubic — hexoctahedral $\frac{4}{m}\overline{3}\frac{2}{m}$ **Pl. 8**

Environment: In quartz veins and in stream deposits.
Crystal description: Most often in octahedral crystals, with or without other faces. However, clusters of parallel growths distorted into feathery leaves, wires, or thin plates are most common.
Physical properties: Rich yellow to silvery yellow. *Luster* metallic; *hardness* $2\frac{1}{2}$–3; *gravity* 19.3. Very malleable and ductile.
Composition: Gold, usually alloyed with silver. The higher the silver content, the paler the color.
Tests: Fuses readily on charcoal, drawing into golden button. Pure gold is soluble in aqua regia; silver-rich gold is soluble in other acids.
Distinguishing characteristics: Confused with metal sulfides, but distinguished from them by softness and malleability. Microscopic brown mica flakes, which may be seen in streams or in mica schist, are distinguished by the blowpipe test or by crushing the mica plates with a needle.
Occurrence: The inertness of gold and its great density make it concentrate in streambeds, either in small flakes or in larger

nuggets, from which it may be recovered by panning. It is of very wide occurrence, originating most often in quartz or sulfide veins, from which it is freed by the destruction of the enclosing rock in the weathering process. Nuggets are more rounded the farther they have traveled from their source. Mines in quartz veins often produce rich specimens of the quartz-gold mixture, "picture rock." Sometimes cavities yield well-crystallized pieces. Gold is also found in brown iron-stained rock, freed from the associated sulfides that have oxidized and weathered away. Some gold deposits can be worked profitably even when yielding only a few dollars in gold to the ton. Hence, any specimen showing visible gold is very rich. Beautifully crystallized gold specimens have been found all over the world. California, Australia, and Hungary are famous for specimens, but in all likelihood some of the best were smelted for their metal; when intrinsic values are high it is rare to find minerals in their natural state, be they metal or gemstones.

SILVER   Ag   Cubic — hexoctahedral $\dfrac{4}{m}\,\overline{3}\,\dfrac{2}{m}$ **Pl. 8**

Environment: In ore veins.
Crystal description: In cubic or octahedral crystals, but either is uncommon; more often it forms long distorted wires. The Kongsberg (Norway) crystals — among the best — may be pseudomorphs after the sulfide mineral argentite.
Physical properties: Fresh surface bright white, usually blackened by tarnish. *Luster* metallic; *hardness* 2½–3; *gravity* 10.0–11.0. Very malleable and ductile.
Composition: Silver, usually fairly pure.
Tests: Pure Ag fuses readily on charcoal to a white button. Impurities tend to make melting more difficult. Dissolves in nitric acid, giving curdy precipitate on the addition of hydrochloric acid.
Distinguishing characteristics: No other white malleable metal, soluble in acid, is likely to be encountered. Lead is softer and grayer; platinum is harder and insoluble; the white sulfides are brittle.
Occurrence: In Mexico and Norway in veins with calcite and silver sulfides; often in wires and in good crystals. In n. Canada and Czechoslovakia with uranium ores (pitchblende) and in Michigan in pure masses with the native copper, forming aggregates known as "halfbreeds." Native silver is not the most important source of silver; the silver minerals with which it is commonly associated, as at Cobalt, Ontario, are more abundant. Many lead ores contain valuable percentages of silver.

COPPER   Cu   Cubic — hexoctahedral $\dfrac{4}{m}\,\overline{3}\,\dfrac{2}{m}$ **Pl. 8**

Environment: In the upper levels of copper sulfide veins and in some types of volcanic rock.

Crystal description: Usually in distorted, often rounded, complex crystals, with cubes, dodecahedrons, and octahedrons predominant. Often in hackly masses without recognizable crystal forms.

Physical properties: Copper color. *Luster* metallic; *hardness* $2\frac{1}{2}$–3; *gravity* 8.9. Malleable and ductile.

Composition: Fairly pure, often alloyed with small amounts of silver, arsenic, iron, etc.

Tests: Small bits fuse on charcoal to black-coated copper button; malleable, soluble in acids, giving greenish solutions. Colors flame blue-green.

Distinguishing characteristics: Green and blue stains on rock outcrops, known as "copper blooms," are a guide to copper and its associated minerals. They will almost always be noted in the field. The malleability and the color are the distinguishing characteristics.

Occurrence: Since weathering processes free copper from its primary ore, chalcopyrite, it is likely to be found in the cap rock of copper-bearing sulfide veins, particularly in arid climates. Native copper is also found in ancient lava flows. It is abundant in this form only in n. Michigan, where copper has been deposited in a thick series of flows, and this is the only place where all the copper is in the uncombined, native, state. Great masses found in these deposits were hard to remove because of their size and the difficulty of breaking them up. Nuggets from this deposit carried south by the glacier were scattered across the north-central states, and were used by the Indians for the manufacture of copper artifacts. Native copper was once found in Chessy, France, and Cornwall, England.

MERCURY   Hg   Hexagonal — rhombohedral $\overline{3}$

Environment: Often in volcanic regions, in low-temperature veins.

Crystal description: This is the only metal liquid at normal temperatures. It does not become solid until the temperature falls to $-40°$F, which equals $-40°$C. Hence, we only find it in nature in the form of liquid metallic drops or as thin metallic films on small cavities and surfaces of rocks.

Physical properties: Silvery white. *Luster* metallic; *gravity* 13.6. Liquid.

Composition: Mercury, sometimes with a little silver.

Tests: Volatilizes (disappears as fumes) under a blowpipe; dissolves in nitric acid.

Distinguishing characteristics: The liquid droplets cannot be confused with anything else. The silvery films are more confusing but can easily be burned off with a blowpipe. The associations are important.

Occurrence: Native mercury is almost invariably associated with the red sulfide of mercury, cinnabar. It may be found in cavities and fissures in cinnabar-impregnated rocks. It sometimes forms as a result of the weathering of cinnabar, which leaves cavities lined with drops and films of mercury. Mercury and cinnabar will be found in rocks of regions where there has been some volcanic or hot-spring activity, but the deposits may be some distance from the igneous source.

Found in the U.S. in California, Oregon, Texas, and Arkansas. The most notable occurrences are the Almadén (Spain) and the Idrija (Yugoslavia) cinnabar mines. It is never an ore alone, but often enriches the mercury sulfide ores.

PLATINUM   Pt   Cubic — hexoctahedral $\frac{4}{m}\overline{3}\frac{2}{m}$

Environment: Mainly in grains and nuggets in sands and gravels.
Crystal description: Crystals (octahedrons and cubes) are rare. Usually it is found in the form of thin scales or grains.
Physical properties: Light gray-white. *Luster* metallic; *hardness* $4-4\frac{1}{2}$; *gravity* 14.0–19.0 (the pure metal is 21.5); *fracture* hackly; *cleavage* none. Malleable and ductile; sometimes magnetic.
Composition: Usually very impure, most commonly mixed with iron, also alloyed with other members of its chemical group: iridium, osmium, rhodium, and palladium (hence, the great range in specific gravity).
Tests: The high gravity, color, and malleability are characteristic, coupled with its infusibility and its insolubility in acid.
Distinguishing characteristics: Few substances will be confused with it. The magnetism of the iron-rich nuggets would confuse the finder if it were not for platinum's high gravity, the malleability, and insolubility.
Occurrence: Chiefly found in placer deposits, sometimes associated with gold. Its primary occurrence is usually in basic igneous rocks; commonly in olivine rocks known as dunites, olivine pyroxenites, or gabbros. The best crystals have come from the Urals, in slightly waterworn shapes. Colombia and Alaska are other important placer sources.
Interesting facts: A very important metal for chemical uses, because of its insolubility and high melting point and its ability to bring about a chemical reaction without entering into it itself (a catalyst). It is used in this way in the manufacture of sulfuric acid and in automobile antipollution devices.

IRON   Fe   Cubic — hexoctahedral $\frac{4}{m}\overline{3}\frac{2}{m}$ **Pl. 9**

Environment: In meteorites and rarely in basalt.
Crystal description: Practically unknown in crystals, and rare except in meteorites. Sometimes found in large masses dissemi-

nated through rock, sometimes in placers in nuggets (josephinite, a nickel-iron alloy).

Physical properties: Steel-gray. *Luster* metallic; *hardness* 4–5; *gravity* 7.3–7.8; *fracture* hackly; *cleavage* cubic, also has distinct partings parallel to the cube and dodecahedron. Magnetic.

Composition: Iron, usually with some nickel. In meteorites nickel may be abundant.

Tests: Magnetic, easily soluble in acids with rusty residue on evaporation.

Distinguishing characteristics: Native iron is so rare that its few sources are well known. Masses of iron from slag are often mistaken for meteorites. A suspected meteorite should be tested for nickel (see millerite, p. 87), after the presence of iron has been shown by a magnet or a compass. A polished surface is then acid-etched to bring out a crystal pattern, known as Widmanstaetten lines, for final confirmation.

Occurrence: Because of the easy oxidation, native iron is naturally most uncommon. It has been found in disseminated grains in a basalt in Bühl, northwest of Kassel, Germany, and in masses of considerable size once thought to be meteorites at Disko I., Greenland. Iron-nickel alloys are found in gold placers in New Zealand, Oregon, and British Columbia. Native iron is found in meteorites, which range from pure metal to stone with small percentages of metal. The nickel content roughly determines the crystal texture and the pattern that is brought out by the etching with dilute nitric acid.

Interesting facts: Tremendous numbers of meteorites fall daily; few reach the earth, and fewer yet are found. The iron meteorites are the rarer type but are more often recognized than the stones. There is usually a crust on a fresh meteorite, from the melting of the surface during its fall. In their passage through the air, meteorites are never actually melted; they never contain cavities, enclose pebbles, or make casts of objects they hit. They are most often confused with concretions of various sorts, with pyrite balls, and with corroded rocks; but none of these are ever magnetic.

The Semimetals

This group of native elements is distinguished from the true metals because its members are not malleable and ductile like the metals. It includes, among other elements, arsenic, antimony, and bismuth.

ARSENIC As Hexagonal — scalenohedral $\overline{3}\frac{2}{m}$ **Pl. 9**

Environment: In ore veins in crystalline rocks.

Crystal description: Crystals, almost unknown, are rhombo-hedrons resembling cubes. The commonest appearance is in rounded mammillary or botryoidal crusts or granular masses.
Physical properties: White. *Luster* metallic; *hardness* $3\frac{1}{2}$; *gravity* 5.7; *fracture* uneven; *cleavage* basal (rarely seen, since crystals are rare). Brittle.
Composition: Arsenic, usually relatively pure, sometimes with a little antimony.
Tests: It is tin-white in color, brittle, and volatilizes completely under the blowpipe, giving off a garlic odor and not melting.
Distinguishing characteristics: Can be confused with an-timony (which melts) and with the antimony-arsenic compound allemontite (which gives off white arsenic fumes and forms a metallic globule that takes fire and burns). The color and total volatilization distinguishes it from most other similar sub-stances.
Occurrence: In metal ore veins, but not common. Most collec-tion specimens are the botryoidal crusts from Saxony. In France it was found at Ste-Marie-aux-Mines, Alsace. It has been found in masses in Arizona. Small balls of crystals are found in a decomposed rhyolite in the Akadani Mine, Fukui Prefecture, s. Honshu, Japan. Allemontite (AsSb) occurs in veins but is not infrequent in pegmatites.

TELLURIUM Te   **Pl. 9**
Hexagonal — Trigonal trapezohedral 3 2
Environment: Medium-temperature veins, often associated with gold ores, sometimes alone.
Crystal description: Massive, often in large segregations with columnar structure, occasionally in free-growing slender crys-tals.
Physical properties: Tin-white. *Luster* metallic; *hardness* $2-2\frac{1}{2}$; *gravity* 6.1–6.3; *fracture* uneven; *cleavage* prismatic good, basal poor. Brittle.
Composition: Native tellurium, sometimes with a little selen-ium, iron, and, in telluride occurrences, gold and silver.
Tests: Volatilizes rapidly and completely on charcoal under blowpipe flame, with a blue flame coloration.
Distinguishing characteristics: Its behavior on the charcoal is distinctive; sylvanite would leave a metallic bead.
Occurrence: Massive tellurium and veins of tellurium have been found in n. Mexico, where it has altered to form, among other minerals, poughite (yellow), $Fe_2(TeO_3)_2(SO_4) \cdot 3H_2O$; and in Lincoln Co., Nevada. The best American crystals are from Colorado, where tellurium has been found at Cripple Creek in Teller Co. and in several other Colorado gold-mining areas.

The Nonmetals

SULFUR S Orthorhombic — bipyramidal $\frac{2}{m}\frac{2}{m}\frac{2}{m}$ **Pl. 8**

Environment: Chiefly associated with volcanic rocks, though the major commercial deposits are in sedimentary rocks and are derived from the breakdown of sulfates like gypsum or come from H_2S.

Crystal description: All low-temperature natural crystals are orthorhombic. Remelted sulfur crystallizes in an unstable form in the monoclinic system. Well-formed translucent crystals are common in the sedimentary occurrences, usually steep bipyramids, sometimes tabular. Irregular skeletal crystals are characteristic of the volcanic localities. Often in crusts without individualized crystals.

Physical properties: Light yellow when pure, sometimes amber when stained with hydrocarbons; some slaglike volcanic specimens are reddish from selenium contamination or grayish from arsenic contamination. *Luster* resinous; *hardness* 2; *gravity* 2.0–2.1; *fracture* conchoidal; *cleavage* basal, prismatic, and pyramidal. Brittle.

Composition: Sulfur but often contaminated with clay or bitumen. Volcanic sulfur may contain selenium, arsenic, etc.

Tests: Melts at 108°C and burns with a blue flame and acrid fumes of SO_2. Insoluble in water and acids, dissolves in carbon disulfide.

Distinguishing characteristics: There are few minerals with which it would be confused. The ease of melting and the burning will readily distinguish it from any other substance.

Occurrence: Sulfur is a characteristic deposit of the late stages of volcanic activity. In Middle and South America it has been quarried from the craters of volcanoes that are, or have been thought to be, extinct. Small sulfur crystals will be found in cavities in some weathered sulfides. In galena it is associated in cavities with anglesite. It is constantly forming in crusts of small crystals at a fumarolic deposit south of San Felipe, Baja California. The economically important deposits in Sicily and along the Gulf Coast, however, appear to have formed from gypsum (calcium sulfate) through a chemical reaction. The best specimens come from the Italian sulfur mines, where well-formed crystals up to 6 in. (15 cm) or more in length are found. Probably comparable ones occur in Louisiana and Texas, but because of the method of mining (the Frasch process of melting sulfur from the deeply buried rocks with superheated steam and piping the liquid sulfur to the surface), the only crystals available come from the diamond-drill well cores. Large amounts of sulfur are extracted from high-sulfur fuel oils in the refining process. Crystals have also been found in an asphaltic deposit in n. Italy, in a sulfur deposit in France at Malvesi, near Narbonne, with gypsum at Bex, Switzerland, near Cadiz, Spain, and in limestone in Michigan.

Interesting facts: Sulfur is of great economic importance in fungicidal plant sprays, the vulcanization of rubber, and the production of sulfuric acid. It is a poor conductor of electricity and with friction becomes negatively charged. The warmth of the hand will cause crystals to expand at the surface and crack. Specimens should be kept out of sunlight and handled as little as possible.

DIAMOND   C   Cubic — hextetrahedral $\overline{4}$ 3 m   **Pl. 9**

Environment: Commonly in alluvial deposits probably derived from dark plutonic rocks, where they are primary.

Crystal description: Most often in brilliant, commonly well-formed, octahedrons. The cube faces are never smooth; though unmistakable, they are always uneven but still lustrous. Hex-octahedrons usually almost spherical, with curved faces. Also in balls with a radiating structure, known as ballas, and in black compact masses known as carbonado. Flat triangular crystals are usually spinel-twinned octahedrons known to the diamond trade as "macles."

Physical properties: White, or tinted, gray to black. *Luster* adamantine; *hardness* 10; *gravity* 3.52; *fracture* conchoidal; *cleavage* perfect octahedral, poor dodecahedral. Brittle; often fluorescent.

Composition: Carbon.

Tests: Infusible, insoluble. Burns at high temperatures.

Distinguishing characteristics: The submetallic (adamantine) luster is unmistakable when combined with the crystal form and hardness. The quartz pebbles with which it is most often confused, because they too will scratch glass, are wholly different in luster.

Occurrence: In alluvial deposits the harder and heavier diamonds have survived when the parent rock has weathered and been worn away. They are mined from the original rocks only in Siberia, South Africa, and in Arkansas. They occur in a basic plutonic rock in cylindrical, more or less vertical, plugs known as "pipes." Sporadic diamonds found in the e. U.S., in California, and in glacial deposits in the North indicate that there may be other, still unrecognized, diamond-bearing formations. Alluvial localities are numerous. In recent years Siberia has become an important source.

Interesting facts: Only about 20% of the diamonds found are said to be suitable for gem use; the balance are used in industry for tools and dies, or crushed to a fine abrasive powder. The difference in hardness between diamond (10) and corundum (9) is far greater than that between the other intervals in the Mohs scale.

GRAPHITE C   Pl. 9

Hexagonal — Dihexagonal bipyramidal $\dfrac{6\ \ 2\ \ 2}{m\ m\ m}$

Environment: Mainly in metamorphic rocks.
Crystal description: Isolated crystals are thin plates, usually in marbles, with rhombohedral faces on the edges. Commercial deposits are veinlike masses of solid material, or abundant plates disseminated through rock.
Physical properties: Black. *Luster* submetallic; *hardness* 1–2; *gravity* 2.3; *streak* black; *cleavage* perfect basal. Flexible inelastic flakes; greasy feel; stains the fingers; completely opaque.
Composition: Carbon.
Tests: Infusible, insoluble.
Distinguishing characteristics: Can only be confused with molybdenite, which shares its softness and greasy feel but is soluble in nitric acid and gives off fumes under the blowpipe flame.
Occurrence: Most frequently observed in schist and as isolated, well-formed but tiny black crystals in an impure marble, associated with other minerals like spinel, chondrodite, and pyroxene; apparently the result of the metamorphism of the organic material in the limestone. Around Ticonderoga, New York — where it was formerly mined for use in lead pencils — it also occurs in thin veins. Madagascar and Sri Lanka (Ceylon), where it forms large pure masses in thick veins, are the most important occurrences. European localities include Bohemia, Bavaria, and Styria (Austria); there were important deposits in Siberia.
Interesting facts: Its Old World name, plumbago (black lead), comes from its use in lead pencils. It is also used as a lubricant and as a refractory in crucibles. It is an outstanding example of the relation of internal atomic arrangement to physical properties. Carbon, with a spacing that gives it a gravity of 2.3, is opaque and one of the softest minerals. The diamond, which is the same element in a closer spacing with a consequent specific gravity of 3.5, is transparent and the hardest substance known.

The Sulfides and Sulfosalts

This group of compounds of the metallic and submetallic elements with sulfur is economically of great importance because many of the metal ores belong to this group. Most of them are easily recognized by their metallic luster. Brittleness distinguishes them from the native metals. Few of them stand up well to atmospheric weathering; usually they alter to secondary ore minerals and are not encountered in mines until the lower levels are reached. They may be subdivided into the simple compounds of a metal element with sulfur, the *sulfides*, and into compounds of a metal element with sulfur plus a semimetal (As, Sb, or Bi), known as the *sulfosalts*.

The Sulfides

ARGENTITE Ag_2S Cubic — hexoctahedral $\dfrac{4}{m}\,\overline{3}\,\dfrac{2}{m}$ **Pl. 9**

Environment: In fairly low-temperature ore veins formed at some distance from the primary source.

Crystal description: Frequently occurs in poorly formed, dull, black crystals, usually cubic, but often so distorted and branching that it is difficult to recognize their faces. Commonly massive.

Physical properties: Dark lead-gray. *Luster* metallic, usually tarnished a dull black; *hardness* $2-2\frac{1}{2}$; *gravity* 7.3; *fracture* subconchoidal; *cleavage* poor cubic and dodecahedral. Like lead, can be cut by a knife (sectile).

Composition: Silver sulfide (87.1% Ag, 12.9% S).

Tests: Blowpipe fuses it into a bead on charcoal, which in an oxidizing flame gives silver button. Tests for silver then apply.

Distinguishing characteristics: Sectility distinguishes it from other sulfides, particularly galena (which shows better cleavage). Grayer color distinguishes it from native silver; colorless HNO_3 solution distinguishes it from chalcocite; copper nitrate solution is green.

Occurrence: Argentite is the most important primary ore of silver. Of common occurrence in veins with native silver. Fine crystals are found in Mexico, in Saxony, at Kongsberg, Norway, and at Cobalt, Ontario. There are no good commercial occurrences remaining in the U.S.

Interesting facts: Argentite has a cubic structure only at temperatures above 180°C. This indicates that it must have formed at temperatures higher than 180°C. Actually all Ag_2S specimens are acanthite (orthorhombic Ag_2S) and are pseudomorphs after the original cubic argentite.

CHALCOCITE Cu_2S **Pl. 10**

Orthorhombic — bipyramidal $\dfrac{2}{m}\,\dfrac{2}{m}\,\dfrac{2}{m}$

Environment: Usually secondary, in ore veins and disseminated deposits.

Crystal description: Commonly massive; crystals are infrequent. The angles are often close to 60° and some crystals may look 6-sided. Elongated prisms are often twinned in geniculated (kneelike) pairs.

Physical properties: Dark lead-gray (specimens in collections usually become coated with a soft brown-black film; see under marcasite, p. 95). *Luster* metallic; *hardness* $2\frac{1}{2}$-3; *gravity* 7.2-7.4; *fracture* conchoidal; *cleavage* poor prismatic. Moderately sectile.

Composition: Cuprous sulfide (79.8% Cu, 20.2% S).

Tests: Powder when moistened with HCl on platinum wire colors flame bluish green (Cu). Careful blowpiping with gas flame will produce a copper bead. Soluble in nitric acid, giving green solution that becomes blue on addition of ammonia.

Distinguishing characteristics: Usually associated with copper minerals, it is less sectile than argentite and gives easy copper tests. The gray color distinguishes it from the related copper sulfides.

Occurrence: Chalcocite is an important ore of copper. It is sometimes primary, and sometimes secondary (when associated with chalcopyrite, bornite, and covellite). A high-temperature, primary, cubic form of Cu_2S is known as digenite, and was abundant at Butte, Montana. Chalcocite's most frequent occurrence is the result of a process known as *secondary enrichment* by solutions descending from oxidizing copper iron sulfides near the surface. Some of the lower-grade copper sulfides and copper iron sulfides are enriched in copper, the sequence being from primary chalcopyrite ($CuFeS_2$), through bornite (Cu_5FeS_4), and covellite (CuS), to chalcocite (Cu_2S). It is found in fine crystals in sulfide veins in Cornwall, England, at an ancient mine in Bristol, Connecticut (the best American occurrence), and at Butte, Montana, where digenite also occurs in 1-2 in. (2.5-5 cm) crystals. French localities include Cap Garonne in Var, Garde-en-Oisans (Isère), Giromagny (Belfort), and Framont (Alsace). Its French name is chalcosine.

BORNITE Cu_5FeS_4 **Pl. 10**

Cubic — hexoctahedral $\dfrac{4}{m}\overline{3}\dfrac{2}{m}$

Environment: Commonly disseminated in igneous intrusives as a primary mineral. Also in copper ore veins, both as a primary and secondary mineral.

Crystal description: Crystals rare and poor, usually in intergrown clusters and always small. As a rule bornite is massive and compact.

Physical properties: Bronze, but the metallic luster rapidly to purple after a freshly broken surface is exposed. *Hardness* 3; *gravity* 4.9-5.4; *fracture* uneven; *cleavage* poor octahedral. Brittle.

Composition: Sulfide of copper and iron (63.3% Cu, 11.1% Fe, 25.6% S).

Tests: Fuses to a brittle magnetic globule on charcoal. Dissolves in nitric acid and gives a copper coloration to the solution.

Distinguishing characteristics: Could be confused with pyrrhotite, but it gives the copper tests, and requires roasting to become magnetic. Niccolite is similar in color, but is nonmagnetic and remains so despite roasting. The purple tarnish is also characteristic. Bornite occurs with the other copper sulfides and is an important ore of copper. It has been found in fair crystals at Cornwall, England, at Charrier, near La Prugne, France, and at Bristol, Connecticut. However, at the economically important localities in Arizona it is massive, and intimately intergrown with chalcopyrite and chalcocite.

Interesting facts: Its characteristic and colorful tarnish has given rise to the old miner's term "peacock ore" and its French name erubescite, although most dealers' "peacock ore" actually is chalcopyrite that has been treated to make it colorfully iridescent.

GALENA   PbS   Cubic — hexoctahedral $\dfrac{4}{m}\overline{3}\dfrac{2}{m}$ **Pl. 8**

Environment: In ore veins, in igneous and sedimentary rocks, and desseminated through sediments.

Crystal description: Crystals very common, usually cubic, sometimes octahedrons. They may also show combinations of several forms of the cubic system. Frequently in granular masses, often very fine-grained or fibrous.

Physical properties: Lead-gray. *Luster* metallic; *hardness* $2\frac{1}{2}$–$2\frac{3}{4}$; *gravity* 7.4–7.6; *fracture* even (rarely seen); *cleavage* perfect cubic; occasional octahedral parting. Brittle.

Composition: Lead sulfide (86.6% lead, 13.4% sulfur). Often contains silver, arsenic, antimony, and other impurities.

Tests: Fuses on charcoal, with yellow coating around the bead, and can be reduced to lead. Makes cloudy solution in nitric acid, with sulfur and lead sulfate separating out.

Distinguishing characteristics: The cubic cleavage, with the lead-gray metallic color and luster, is characteristic. Might be confused with dark sphalerite, in which case the light streak of the latter would permit a distinction. Other similar sulfides have good cleavages in a single direction, but not in 3 directions. The blowpipe reactions will help in very fine-grained (and deceptive) varieties.

Occurrence: The chief ore of lead. It is found in medium and low-temperature ore veins in which open cavities are frequent; hence, crystals are common and well developed. Unfortunately, their faces are usually dull. Commonly associated with the sulfides sphalerite, pyrite, and chalcopyrite, and with quartz, siderite, dolomite, fluorite, calcite, or barite as worthless associates (gangue minerals). This same mineral association occurs in both sedimentary rocks and igneous rocks.

Fine distorted crystals have been found in Germany, and good examples in France, Yugoslavia, and elsewhere in Europe. The Joplin District of Missouri, Kansas, and Oklahoma is notable for its crystals; usually cubes, sometimes cubo-octahedrons with octahedral growths on the faces. Cen. Missouri is a recent source of relatively shiny cubic crystals. Spinel-twinned cubo-octahedral crystals seem to be characteristic of a good Mexican (Naica) occurrence. There are so many occurrences of fine examples of this mineral that it is futile to attempt to list more. **Interesting facts:** Through alteration, galena produces many other lead minerals like anglesite, cerussite, and phosgenite. It often contains enough silver to make it also an important ore of that mineral. It is commonly thought that galena with flaky curving cleavage planes — irregular rather than smooth, often slightly tarnished — is likely to be higher in the silver impurity.

SPHALERITE ZnS   **Pl. 8**
Cubic — hextetrahedral $\overline{4}$ 3 m

Environment: In sulfide ore veins in all rock classes.
Crystal description: Tetrahedral crystals very common, sometimes so completely developed as to look octahedral. Cube, dodecahedron, and tristetrahedron faces also present, the latter often rounded so that it is difficult to distinguish the faces. Also stalactitic, granular, and massive.
Physical properties: Colorless (very rare) through yellow to red-brown and black. *Luster* adamantine to resinous; *hardness* $3\frac{1}{2}$-4; *gravity* 3.9-4.1; *fracture* conchoidal; *cleavage* perfect dodecahedral. Brittle; transparent to opaque; interesting luminescent effects (see below); fluorescent occasionally.
Composition: Zinc sulfide (67.0% Zn, 33.0% S with varying amounts of iron and manganese, and other elements).
Tests: Practically infusible on charcoal, but gives coating around chip, which is yellow when hot and white when cold. Touched with cobalt solution, the yellow coating becomes green in the reducing flame. The addition of Na_2CO_3 facilitates this test. Dissolves in HCl with bubbles of H_2S (rotten-egg smell).
Distinguishing characteristics: When it is very black its high luster gives it a resemblance to galena, but the streak and the blowpipe tests suffice for this distinction. Resembles some siderite, but can be distinguished by remaining nonmagnetic after heating and by its higher gravity. The characteristic luster and association with pyrite and galena generally serve to identify sphalerite.
Occurrence: Same as galena, with which it is usually associated. Localities are almost too numerous to mention, but the

gemmy, transparent light yellow to red Santander (Spain) masses are notable. Joplin crystals range from black and dull irregular giants to minute red ("ruby jack") incrustations. The palest U.S. specimens are from Franklin, New Jersey, in light yellow-green crystals. Trepča, Yugoslavia, has become an important source of good "black jack" specimens.

Interesting facts: Sphalerite is the principal primary ore of zinc. It alters to hemimorphite, smithsonite, and willemite. The impurities gallium, indium, and cadmium make it also the chief ore of those metals. Its cleavage and luminescence make it of considerable mineralogical interest. It is the best example of dodecahedral cleavage, and with care perfect dodecahedrons can be cleaved out. Sometimes it fluoresces orange in ultraviolet light. Fluorescent sphalerite also shows the remarkable phenomenon of *triboluminescence;* that is, it emits flashes of orange light on being lightly stroked with a hard substance like a knife or a stone. Rare-gem collectors treasure fiery brilliants that may be cut from the light-hued Picos de Europa, Santander (Spain) specimens.

CHALCOPYRITE $CuFeS_2$ **Pl. 10**
Tetragonal — scalenohedral $\overline{4}\ 2\ m$

Environment: Common in sulfide veins, and often disseminated through igneous rocks.

Crystal description: The characteristically sphenoidal crystals of chalcopyrite resemble tetrahedrons. Crystals are common; often they are large, but the faces usually are somewhat uneven and tarnished in brilliant iridescent hues. Usually massive.

Physical properties: Golden. *Luster* metallic, often with iridescent tarnish; *hardness* $3\frac{1}{2}$–4; *gravity* 4.1–4.3; *fracture* uneven; *cleavage* 1 poor (and rarely noted). Brittle.

Composition: Sulfide of copper and iron (34.5% Cu, 30.5% Fe, 35% S).

Tests: On charcoal fuses to magnetic black globule; touched with HCl, tints flame with blue flash. Solution with strong nitric acid is green; ammonia precipitates red iron hydroxide and leaves a blue solution.

Distinguishing characteristics: Confused with gold, but is brittle, gives black streak, and dissolves in acid. Distinguished from pyrite by ease of scratching, and by copper tests. The color is slightly more yellow than that of pyrite. Pyrite will frequently show striated cubes or pyritohedrons, whereas chalcopyrite, if not massive, is in characteristic sphenoidal crystals.

Occurrence: The most important copper ore. Widely distributed and may be found in all types of unweathered occurrences. Often associated with other copper minerals: pyrite, sphalerite, galena, and pyrrhotite. The economically important "porphyry coppers" of Bingham (Utah), Ely (Nevada), and Ajo (Arizona) are low-grade disseminations in igneous rocks.

The best crystals are from: Cornwall, England; Akita and Tochigi Prefectures, Japan; French Creek, Pennsylvania; and several Colorado localities. Often crystallized in parallel growths on and through crystals of sphalerite in the Joplin District. 6 in. (15 cm) giant crystals were found in Freirina, n. Chile. Abundant in n. Mexico, where there is a good source of large crystals.

Interesting facts: Chalcopyrite is the primary mineral that by alteration and successive enrichment with copper produces the series starting with chalcopyrite and going through bornite (Cu_5FeS_4), covellite (CuS), chalcocite (Cu_2S), and ending rarely as native copper (Cu). Its structure is so closely related to that of sphalerite it forms intergrowths with that mineral, and small, isolated, free-growing crystals perched on crystals of sphalerite are all parallel. The same face on all the chalcopyrites gives simultaneous reflections.

GREENOCKITE CdS   **Pl. 10**
Hexagonal — Dihexagonal pyramidal   6 m m
Environment: In traprock cavities and in ore veins.
Crystal description: Crystals small, complex, and very interesting for their hemimorphic hexagonal development. Very rare, however; usually manifest as a yellow dusting over other minerals, especially sphalerite and calcite.
Physical properties: Yellow to brown or red. *Luster* adamantine to resinous; *hardness* $3-3\frac{1}{2}$; *gravity* 4.9–5.0; *fracture* conchoidal; *cleavage* good prismatic and poor basal. Brittle; transparent to translucent.
Composition: Cadmium sulfide (77.8% Cd, 22.2% S).
Tests: In closed glass tube the yellow powder turns red when hot and back to yellow or brown when cool. Gives a reddish-brown coating on charcoal in the reducing flame. Soluble in HCl, giving hydrogen sulfide gas.
Distinguishing characteristics: Likely to be mistaken for sphalerite when in crystals, but can be distinguished by its crystal form and by the closed-tube test. The yellow films might be confused with uranium minerals, but the association with zinc minerals should suffice for correct identification.
Occurrence: Crystals are very rare, and were first found at Greenock, Scotland, in cavities in traprock, associated with prehnite. The largest are not much over $\frac{1}{4}$ in. (6 mm) long. A few crystals have been found in the Paterson (New Jersey) traprock area. Orange-red microscopic crystals were described from Llallagua, Bolivia, associated with pyrite and tin ores. Yellow films are common in the Joplin area, in the Illinois-

Kentucky fluorite region, and are the yellow pigment of some Arkansas smithsonite.

Interesting facts: It is the only ore of cadmium, but that metal is recovered only as a by-product of lead and zinc refining. The cadmium is separated in the purification of the other metals. Unusual electronic properties make its artificial manufacture of some interest.

PYRRHOTITE $Fe_{1-x}S$ **Pl. 10**
        Pseudohexagonal (several polymorphs)

Environment: Widespread in many types of occurrences.

Crystal description: Crystals usually tabular, their commonest form being hexagonal plates. Its general occurrence, however, is massive and granular.

Physical properties: Bronze. *Luster* metallic; *hardness* 4; *gravity* 4.6–4.7; *fracture* subconchoidal; *cleavage* none, but crystals commonly show a basal parting. Brittle; magnetism varies from strong to negligible.

Composition: Ferrous sulfide (approximately 60.4% Fe, 39.6% S). There is a slight deficiency of Fe in this mineral, which makes it unstable and easily decomposed. The x in its formula ranges from 0.0 to 0.2.

Tests: Fuses easily to black magnetic mass; dissolves readily in HCl, producing hydrogen sulfide (rotten-egg smell).

Distinguishing characteristics: The magnetic character of its powder is usually sufficient to distinguish it from anything similar in color (fresh bornite and niccolite) and from pyrite and chalcopyrite.

Occurrence: Pyrrhotite is a common mineral of magmatic segregations and high-temperature ore veins. It also occurs in pegmatites and in contact-metamorphic deposits. Good crystals have been found in Rumania, showing a laminated vertical development (deep, discontinuous, horizontal grooving) and concave basal faces. The largest crystals of good form have come from the San Antonio mine at Aquiles Serdán (formerly Santa Eulalia), Chihuahua, Mexico. Well-formed platy crystals were found in a pegmatite at Standish, Maine. Morro Velho, Brazil's deep gold mine in Minas Gerais, is the source of small sharp hexagonal plates that are perched on calcite rhombs. The main ore body at Sudbury, Ontario, is pyrrhotite, and the ore minerals pentlandite (an iron-nickel sulfide) and chalcopyrite are embedded in it. It tends to crumble in collections.

Interesting facts: Meteorites contain the closely related non-magnetic mineral troilite (FeS), which is regarded as a balanced ferrous sulfide. Pyrrhotite's structure has been repeatedly studied, and most examples prove to be mixtures of hexagonal and monoclinic lattices. Those with less sulfur are likely to be hexagonal; those with great sulfur excesses, monoclinic. Heating to 350°C makes all fully hexagonal.

NICCOLITE NiAs   **Pl. 10**

Hexagonal — Dihexagonal bipyramidal $\dfrac{6\ 2\ 2}{m\ m\ m}$

Environment: In ore veins with silver; also copper and nickel arsenides and sulfides.

Crystal description: Crystals rare, poor, and small. Also massive and in reniform crusts.

Physical properties: Copper-colored. *Luster* metallic, tarnishing black; *hardness* 5-5½; *gravity* 7.8; *fracture* uneven; *cleavage* none. Brittle.

Composition: Nickel arsenide (43.9% Ni, 56.1% As). Arsenic sometimes replaced in part by antimony. (Nickel antimonide is breithauptite.)

Tests: On charcoal gives fumes with faint arsenic (garlic) odor and fuses to bronzy, metallic globule. Gives nickel test with dimethylglyoxime (pink needles in ammonia-neutralized acid solution). Dissolves in nitric acid to form clear green solution with black residue.

Distinguishing characteristics: The copper color is characteristic. It may be confused only with the related breithauptite (NiSb), from which it can hardly be distinguished, especially since niccolite often contains some antimony. Most frequently associated with silvery white, massive smaltite.

Occurrence: Niccolite is a relatively rare mineral, but because of its occurrence with related ore minerals, it too is a valuable ore of nickel. Usually massive in veins with the other minerals and best observed in polished specimens.

Free-growing crystals are rare and usually represented in collections only in specimens from Germany, either from Reichelsdorf or Eisleben. Niccolite and breithauptite occur in large masses at Cobalt, Ontario, usually intimately associated with smaltite, chloanthite, and silver.

Interesting facts: This mineral, known to the old German miners as *Kupfernickel* (copper nickel), gave the element its name. *Nickel* was a disparaging name for imps (see cobaltite, p. 94).

MILLERITE NiS   **Pl. 11**

Hexagonal — Hexagonal scalenohedral $\overline{3}$ m

Environment: In limestone and dolomite, sometimes in ore veins.

Crystal description: Its common name, "capillary pyrites," aptly describes the hairlike crystals. Very rarely coarse enough to show the hexagonal outline. Also in crusts with columnar fracture.

Physical properties: Brass-yellow. *Luster* metallic; *hardness* 3-3½; *gravity* 5.3-5.6; *fracture* uneven; *cleavage* 2 rhombohedral. Brittle.

Composition: Nickel sulfide (64.7% Ni, 35.3% S).

Tests: Fuses easily on charcoal in the reducing flame to a black magnetic bead. Gives nickel test (pink solution) with dimethylglyoxime in nitric acid solution that has first been neutralized with ammonia.

Distinguishing characteristics: The golden capillary crystals could only be confused with capillary tourmaline or rutile, neither of which would fuse on charcoal, nor would they be found in the same associations. The nickel test would distinguish it from similarly colored sulfides.

Occurrence: Millerite is sometimes used as an ore of nickel, when found in minor quantities in association with other metallic sulfides in veins, as in Germany. It is widely distributed through limestones, particularly near St. Louis, Missouri, and Keokuk, Iowa. At these places it is found in cavities lined with crystals of calcite, dolomite, and fluorite, in cobwebby masses or in slender radiating bundles of hairs. It is interesting to speculate that the original source of this nickel might be meteoritic.

COVELLITE CuS   **Pl. 11**

Hexagonal — Dihexagonal bipyramidal $\dfrac{6\ 2\ 2}{m\ m\ m}$

Environment: In enriched portions of copper sulfide veins.

Crystal description: Thin platy hexagonal crystals, usually standing on edge. Often their basal pinacoids are coated with a secondary chalcopyrite or are so tarnished that the blue color does not show. Also massive intergrown plates, with the space between filled in with chalcocite.

Physical properties: Blue, usually tarnished purple to black. *Luster* metallic; *hardness* $1\frac{1}{2}$-2; *gravity* 4.6; *cleavage* basal; plates flexible but not elastic. Sectile; translucent blue-green in very thin plates.

Composition: Cupric sulfide (66.4% Cu, 33.6% S).

Tests: Blue flakes catch fire and burn with blue flame before melting. Further blowpiping melts them to a bead, at first with some boiling and bubbling.

Distinguishing characteristics: Platy appearance is characteristic. The blue color should not be confused with the iridescent film common on chalcopyrite and bornite. Always associated with other copper minerals.

Occurrence: A rare mineral; possibly always a secondary alteration product except for an occurrence of small crystals around a fumarole at Vesuvius. The largest sheets came from Sardinia, but their edges were poorly formed. The sharpest, best-developed, and unmistakably hexagonal plates are those from Butte, Montana. At Kennicott, Alaska, it was found in rich blue masses in a lathlike texture, with chalcocite.

Interesting facts: Covellite is a valuable ore of copper, but good specimens are relatively rare. It is one of the most beautiful examples for the study of polished specimens under the microscope in polarized light. The laths are intergrown in a felted mass; as the specimen is rotated, the color of each plate changes from light to dark blue and back again.

CINNABAR HgS   **Pl. 12**
                Hexagonal — Trigonal trapezohedral 3 2
Environment: In shallow veins and rock impregnations.
Crystal description: Well-individualized crystals rare, crystallized crusts and complex intergrowths fairly common. Twinned intergrowths of steep rhombohedrons found at several localities. Also massive, powdery, and granular, sometimes in capillary needles.
Physical properties: Bright red to brick-red. *Luster* adamantine; *hardness* $2\frac{1}{2}$; *gravity* 8.1; *fracture* subconchoidal; *cleavage* very perfect prismatic. Translucent to transparent.
Composition: Mercury sulfide (86.2% Hg, 13.8% S).
Tests: Volatilizes completely on charcoal. In open tube produces sulfur fumes; forms black ring and above this a thin deposit of metallic droplets. This "mercury mirror" can be resolved into larger drops by scratching over its surface with a needle.
Distinguishing characteristics: Likely to be confused with realgar, cuprite, and possibly "ruby jack" sphalerite or hematite. Easily distinguished by the open-tube test.
Occurrence: Cinnabar, the chief ore of mercury, is deposited by hot ascending solutions near the surface of the earth and far removed from their igneous source. It is associated with native mercury, stibnite, realgar, opal, quartz, and barite. The richest occurrences are in Yugoslavia, Spain, and Italy. Good crystals of the penetrating rhombohedron type have been found in the U.S.S.R., Hunan Province, China, and at Kirby, Pike Co., Arkansas. Waterworn cinnabar nuggets are found in the Tempati River, Surinam. American deposits are not extensive; the best are in California. Smaller ones have been found in Nevada, New Mexico, and Texas.

REALGAR AsS   Monoclinic — prismatic $\dfrac{2}{m}$ **Pl. 12**
Environment: In low-temperature veins.
Crystal description: Good crystals fairly common, usually prismatic; also massive.
Physical properties: Orange-red. *Luster* resinous; *hardness* $1\frac{1}{2}$–2; *gravity* 3.4–3.5; *fracture* subconchoidal; *cleavage* perfect side and fair basal. Sectile; translucent to transparent.
Composition: Arsenic sulfide (70.1% As, 29.9% S).

Tests: Fuses easily, melting to shiny mass, spreading and completely volatilizing with the characteristic garlic odor. Makes red deposit shading to orange and yellow on walls of closed tube, with yellow fumes escaping from the end.

Distinguishing characteristics: It could be mistaken for cinnabar; blowpipe and closed-tube tests would show the differences. Often associated with yellow orpiment.

Occurrence: Not a common mineral, but an important ore of arsenic. Usually in rich veins, as at the Getchell gold mine in Nevada, with calcite and yellow, micaceous orpiment. Like stibnite and cinnabar, it is a late magmatic mineral associated with hot springs. It is often associated with colemanite, as at Boron, California, and Bigadiç, Turkey. Large isolated single crystals have been found in marble pockets, as in Carrara, Italy, and Binnatal, Switzerland.

Excellent, old-time crystal specimens are those of Transylvania, Rumania. Rich masses and well-developed crystal pockets are found in the U.S. at Getchell Mine, Nevada, and the Reward Mine, King Co., Washington.

Interesting facts: A very unstable mineral, easily affected by light, so most museum specimens crumble to an orange dust after a few years of display. Storage in darkness delays the deterioration, but even this will not indefinitely preserve specimens; seemingly other factors, like exposure to air or release of pressure, play a part. The ancient Chinese apparently admired its red hue and used small fragments for carvings, though these artifacts now are badly affected by time. Most of our good crystals are obtained by dissolving calcite-filled veins in HCl to expose the arsenic sulfide crystals (realgar and orpiment) lining the walls.

ORPIMENT As_2S_3 Monoclinic — prismatic $\dfrac{2}{m}$ **Pl. 12**

Environment: Always associated with realgar in low-temperature veins.

Crystal description: Always well crystallized, though often in compact masses characterized by micaceous yellow flakes. Free-growing crystals relatively rare; usually they form as crystalline crusts, the individuals being difficult to orient.

Physical properties: Orange-yellow to yellow to brown on crystal surfaces other than the cleavage direction. *Luster* resinous to pearly; *hardness* $1\frac{1}{2}$–2; *gravity* 3.4–3.5; *cleavage* perfect micaceous, side pinacoidal. Sectile; flexible but inelastic cleavage flakes; translucent to transparent.

Composition: Arsenic trisulfide (61% As, 39% S).

Tests: Same as for realgar (above).

Distinguishing characteristics: Unlikely to be taken for any other mineral. The cleavage distinguishes it from sulfur without resort to blowpipe tests. The association with realgar and stibnite eliminates other yellow minerals like uranium minerals (autunite) and greenockite.

Occurrence: In the U.S.S.R. and Macedonia, orpiment sometimes forms large mica-like cleavable masses. Good crystals from Rumania and Lucéram (s. France), and unusually large isolated ones at Mercur, Utah. Rich masses, mixed with realgar, lie all about the dumps at the old Getchell gold mine (Nevada), their weather-affected surfaces looking greenish yellow, whereas the realgar dust is orange. Fine brownish resinous crystal crusts have been found in Peru, in Iran at Valilo, and at Ahar, in Azerbaijan.

Yellow hairs on calcite found at Manhattan, Nye Co., Nevada, were long thought to be orpiment too, but are now identified as a new mineral, also found in Japan, named wakabayashilite ($As_{10}SbS_{18}$).

Interesting facts: Like realgar, it is unstable in light. Though less vulnerable than realgar, it tends to dull and develop a white film in museum collections, presumably of oxidation, and in time it loses most of its beauty. The usual color of the front and top crystal faces is more of a brownish orange, very different from the color of a fresh cleavage surface, an orangish yellow. The red and yellow arsenic sulfide mixture is very decorative, but its poisonous character and tendency to disintegrate make it unsatisfactory for the interior design trade, though it is widely sold for such uses.

STIBNITE Sb_2S_3 **Pl. 11**

Orthorhombic — bipyramidal $\dfrac{2}{m}\dfrac{2}{m}\dfrac{2}{m}$

Environment: In low-temperature veins and rock impregnations. Associated with arsenic and antimony minerals.

Crystal description: Usually in well-formed crystals, sometimes very large and solid (Japan), at other times slender and fragile. Fibrous, massive, bladed, or granular.

Physical properties: Steel-gray. *Luster* metallic; *hardness* 2; *gravity* 4.5–4.6; *fracture* subconchoidal; *cleavage* perfect side pinacoid. Sectile.

Composition: Sulfide of antimony (71.7% Sb, 28.3% S).

Tests: Melts to a liquid, spreads out and completely volatilizes on charcoal, making a white coating around grain and weakly coloring the blowpipe flame white. Dissolves in hot concentrated HNO_3 and slowly forms a white precipitate on addition of water.

Distinguishing characteristics: Distinguished from lead-bearing sulfosalts by the lack of a lead coating (yellow) on the charcoal and by the complete volatility. Distinguished from bismuthinite by its lower gravity, watery fusion on charcoal, and more rapid volatilization.

Occurrence: An ore of antimony. Like realgar and orpiment, a late low-temperature deposit of hot solutions, often associated with the arsenic minerals and cinnabar. The finest crystals are brilliant needles over a foot long (30 cm) from the Ichinokawa Mine, Iyo Province (now Ehime Prefecture), n. Shikoku I., Japan. Next in quality and in moderate abundance are stubbier, bluntly terminated 1 or 2 in. (2.5–5 cm) crystals in radiating clusters from Baia Sprie (Felsöbanya), Rumania. The best U.S. crystals have been found at Manhattan, Nye Co., Nevada. Large crystals, almost comparable to those of Japan, have been found in Huarás, Peru. Giant ocherous pseudomorphs, now two Sb oxides — cervantite (Sb_2O_4?) and stibiconite [$Sb_3O_5(OH)$] — give promise of some eventual fine stibnites from Mexican sources.

Interesting facts: Stibnite is the outstanding example of a mineral with the property of well-developed gliding planes; so well developed that many of the crystals found in nature are bent, or soon become bent, without fracturing. The atoms will glide a definite distance in the basal plane, and then stop.

BISMUTHINITE Bi_2S_3 **Pl. 11**

Orthorhombic — bipyramidal $\frac{2}{m}\frac{2}{m}\frac{2}{m}$

Environment: Pegmatites and high-temperature ore veins.

Crystal description: Rare in free-growing needlelike crystals. Commonly in embedded masses with a bladed or fibrous structure. Large altered crystals show that it can grow larger, but no unaltered giants have been found.

Physical properties: Steel-gray. *Luster* metallic; *hardness* 2; *gravity* 6.4–6.5; *fracture* brittle or splintery; *cleavage* perfect side pinacoid. Slightly sectile.

Composition: Sulfide of bismuth (81.2% Bi, 18.8% S).

Tests: Fuses easily and volatilizes very slowly, forming dark gray globules surrounded by thin yellow sublimate. The powder dissolves easily in hot concentrated nitric acid, forming yellow spongy insoluble residue (sulfur).

Distinguishing characteristics: Can be confused in massive form with stibnite and the sulfosalts. Complete volatilization under the blowpipe separates it from the sulfosalts, and the formation of a spherical globule instead of a watery liquid distinguishes it from stibnite.

Occurrence: Bismuthinite is an ore of bismuth, much like stibnite in appearance. Also precipitated from igneous solutions but not usually associated with the arsenic-antimony suite. Minute ribbonlike crystals found around fumaroles in the Lipari Is. are in part bismuthinite and partly galenobismutite ($PbBi_2S_4$), first named cannizarite when the unbismuthinite-like

needles were all thought to be a new mineral. The richest
occurrences are in Bolivia, in the tin-tungsten veins. A frequent
pegmatite mineral, large masses have been found in quarries at
Bedford, Westchester Co., New York, and in Boulder Co., Colorado. Pseudomorphs 2 ft. (61 cm) long of a bismuth carbonate
(bismutite) after bismuthinite crystals have been found in
northern Brazil.

PYRITE FeS_2 Cubic — diploidal $\dfrac{2}{m}\overline{3}$ **Pl. 11, 13**

Environment: All classes of rocks, and all types of veins.
Crystal description: Often crystallized, most frequently in
striated cubes, less commonly in pyritohedrons or octahedrons.
Massive pyrite is common.
Physical properties: Light yellow. *Luster* metallic; *hardness*
6–6½; *gravity* 5.0; *fracture* conchoidal; *cleavage* none. Brittle.
Composition: Iron sulfide (46.6% Fe, 53.4% S).
Tests: Fuses easily. Becomes magnetic and gives off SO_2 fumes.
Insoluble in HCl, but a fine powder will dissolve in concentrated
HNO_3.
Distinguishing characteristics: The tarnished sulfide might
be confused with chalcopyrite, but its great hardness is distinc-
tive. It is yellower and more slowly soluble in nitric acid than
marcasite, giving a clear solution. It is harder than gold, and
very brittle.
Occurrence: A frequent associate of all sorts of metal ores.
In addition, it forms concretionary masses in sedimentary rocks.
It is common in coal, and in slates and other metamorphic
rocks. Daisylike disks with coarser cube "petal" rims were found
in the Dallas–Fort Worth airport construction. It is so often
mistaken for gold that it is popularly known as "fool's gold."
Fine specimens have been found throughout the world; one
could not do the mineral justice in a short list. Particularly
notable are the large well-formed crystals from Leadville,
Colorado, the complex and perfect crystals from Rio Marina
on the island of Elba, and the well-developed crystal groups
from Park City, Utah. Misshapen octahedral crystals containing 0.2% arsenic were found at French Creek, Pennsylvania.
Peru, in both Quiruvilca and Cerro de Pasco, yields outstanding
octahedral crystals. Many Mexican occurrences have been
reported. Highly modified crystals in fine clusters are typical
of Oruro and Colavi, Bolivia. "Cathedral" pyrite is a name given
to large Leadville (Colorado) cubes with Gothic arch patterns
on their faces. Falun, Sweden, yielded a pyrite rich in cobalt.
Interesting facts: Pyrite was once important as a source of
sulfur for the manufacture of sulfuric acid, and could be again.
It is frequently rich in gold values and therefore may be an
important ore of gold.

COBALTITE CoAsS Cubic — tetartoidal 2 3 **Pl. 13**

Environment: In sulfide veins with other cobalt and nickel ores, and disseminated in metamorphic rocks.

Crystal description: Crystals, often well formed, in cubes and pyritohedrons resembling pyrite. Also granular, massive.

Physical properties: Tin-white. *Luster* metallic; *hardness* $5\frac{1}{2}$; *gravity* 6–6.3; *fracture* uneven; *cleavage* good cubic. Brittle.

Composition: Cobalt sulfarsenide (35.5% Co, 45.2% As, 19.3% S).

Tests: Fuses on charcoal with difficulty after powdering; granules magnetic, giving off sulfur and faint arsenic fumes. Grains partially dissolve in warm nitric acid, giving clear pink to red solution; residue remains metallic in luster.

Diagnostic characteristics: The tin-white color, coupled with the cubic or pyritohedral crystal form, is unmistakable. Cobaltite is harder and has a less even cleavage than galena.

Occurrence: An ore of cobalt but a rare mineral. Large — 1 in. (2.5 cm) or more — well-formed pyritohedral crystals are found at Tunaberg, Sweden, and Skutterud, Norway. Granular masses are found in veins at Cobalt, Ontario, mixed with, and hard to distinguish from, the white cobalt and nickel arsenides.

Interesting facts: Cobalt gets its name from the word "kobold" (German, *Kobalt*) given to imps that were supposed to live underground and tease the miners; today we might call them gremlins.

LOELLINGITE FeAs$_2$

Orthorhombic — bipyramidal $\dfrac{2\ 2\ 2}{m\ m\ m}$

Environment: High-temperature and medium-temperature veins, and (the iron-rich variety) in pegmatites.

Crystal description: Small crystals of a prismatic habit. Commonly massive or in thin veinlets.

Physical properties: Tin-white. *Luster* metallic; *hardness* 5–$5\frac{1}{2}$; *gravity* 6.2–8.6; *fracture* uneven; *cleavage* basal.

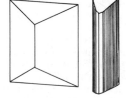

Composition: Diarsenide of iron, sometimes plus cobalt and nickel; only the iron end-member of this series exists as a mineral. Small quantities of nickel and cobalt may be present, making the varieties nickelian and cobaltian loellingite. Arsenic totals about 68%.

Tests: Fuses with difficulty to a magnetic globule, giving off white arsenic oxide fumes (garlic odor) on charcoal. Dissolves in nitric acid to form a clear yellow solution, which may be colored pink or pale greenish if notable quantities of cobalt or nickel are present. See other tests under skutterudite (p. 99). **Distinguishing characteristics:** Very difficult to distinguish from arsenopyrite, which it resembles in appearance and occurrence, but loellingite gives no sulfur test (see arsenopyrite, p. 96). Indistinguishable from the skutterudite, safflorite [(Co, Fe)As$_2$], and rammelsbergite groups without X-ray tests (but these are rare vein minerals not found in pegmatites). **Occurrence:** Loellingite is a rare mineral in the U.S. except in some of the New England pegmatites, where it forms metallic stringers in garnet or phosphates. Crystals are found at Franklin, New Jersey. Massive loellingite or rammelsbergite (NiAs$_2$) was one of the cobalt ores at Cobalt, Connecticut, in a high-temperature vein. It has been reported from Gunnison Co., Colorado, and Alexander Co., North Carolina. It is more abundant abroad, where good crystals were found in Norway, Sweden, and Finland. Pegmatitic loellingite is also found in Brazil.

MARCASITE FeS$_2$ **Pl. 13**

Orthorhombic — bipyramidal $\dfrac{2\ 2\ 2}{m\,m\,m}$

Environment: Sedimentary rocks and low-temperature veins.
Crystal description: Crystals tabular, parallel to a horizontal axis. However, usually grown together in curving or cockscomb-like groups. Also in concretionary masses with radiating structure and botryoidal or reniform crusts.
Physical properties: Light brass-yellow. *Luster* metallic; *hardness* 6–6½; *gravity* 4.9; *fracture* uneven; *cleavage* poor prismatic. Brittle.
Composition: Iron sulfide (46.5% Fe, 53.5% S).
Tests: The same as pyrite, except that more sulfur is freed in the strong nitric acid solution, leaving it cloudy; some solution takes place in the cold dilute nitric acid, indicated by the immediate formation of bubbles on the grains.
Distinguishing characteristics: Only likely to be confused with pyrite, from which it can be distinguished by greater solubility in cold dilute nitric acid. Generally whiter than pyrite on a fresh surface, and, like it, harder than most other sulfide minerals.
Occurrence: The geological conditions that cause iron and sulfur to combine to form the mineral marcasite are critical; normally pyrite is produced. Marcasite is associated with galena, sphalerite, calcite, and dolomite, as at Joplin, Missouri, and in the Wisconsin lead-zinc region. It is often in spear-shaped intergrowths in clays and marls (though these are often actually pyrite).

Interesting facts: Marcasite specimens almost invariably oxidize in collections, freeing sulfur to form an acid that attacks the labels and trays, and speed the disintegration of the specimens. Often it is intergrown with pyrite, but no satisfactory method of preventing the decomposition has yet been found. It has been suggested that the breakdown is due to revived virulence of a geologically ancient infection of anaerobic bacteria and that thorough sterilization can halt, or slow, the destruction. It is an interesting suggestion and might be profitably investigated further by collectors. Chalcocite seems another likely prospect for such an experiment.

ARSENOPYRITE FeAsS Pl. 13

Monoclinic — prismatic $\dfrac{2}{m}$

Environment: High-temperature veins, pegmatites, and sometimes disseminated in crystalline (igneous) rocks.

Crystal description: Pseudo-orthorhombic, commonly in distinct crystals, elongated parallel to a horizontal axis, like marcasite, or vertically. Often forms solid masses.

Physical properties: Silver-white. *Luster* metallic; *hardness* $5\frac{1}{2}$–6; *gravity* 5.9–6.2; *fracture* uneven; *cleavage* prismatic. Brittle.

Composition: Iron sulfarsenide (34.3% Fe, 46.0% As, 19.7% S). Often intergrown with loellingite, an iron arsenide, and rammelsbergite.

Tests: Arsenic (garlic) smell is noted immediately after fracturing with hammer blow. On charcoal gives white fumes and leaves black magnetic mass or, after long blowpiping, a globule. Decomposed by nitric acid, leaving spongy sulfur mass. Sulfur test can be obtained by fusing with sodium carbonate, crushing on silver disk, and wetting. Tarnished spot proves sulfur.

Distinguishing characteristics: Distinguished from the white nickel arsenides by a sulfur test and by negative results in a nickel test. Crystals are common enough to be a guide in its identification.

Occurrence: Arsenopyrite is an ore of arsenic, usually a by-product of other mining operations. Good crystals were common in the Freiberg (Germany) nickel-silver mines, in the Cornwall and Bolivian tin mines, and in the Iname Mine, Aichi Prefecture, Japan. The Panasqueira (Portugal) arsenopyrites are among the best found; 12 in. (30 cm). Long nail-like crystals were typical of low-temperature deposition in a Japanese locality (Obira mine, Kyushu I.). Trepča, Yugoslavia, and Zacatecas, Mexico, are other noteworthy localities. A massive vein of arsenopyrite was mined in Edenville, New York.

Interesting facts: Often found in pegmatites in crystals and associated with garnet and the phosphates. Loellingite sometimes takes the place of arsenopyrite, as at Franklin, New Jersey. The cobaltiferous variety, danaite, in which cobalt may take the place of as much as 9% of the iron, is named for J. Freeman Dana of Boston, not for the famous mineralogist James D. Dana.

MOLYBDENITE MoS_2 Pl. 13

Hexagonal — Dihexagonal bipyramidal $\dfrac{6\ \ 2\ \ 2}{m\ m\ m}$

Environment: Disseminated in igneous rocks and pegmatites.
Crystal description: Crystals are common, sometimes well developed but usually misshapen, since they are tabular and bend easily. Also, in small irregularly shaped flakes; rarely finely granular.
Physical properties: Lead-gray. *Luster* metallic; *hardness* 1–1½; *gravity* 4.7–4.8; *streak* gray on paper; *cleavage* perfect micaceous basal. Laminae flexible, but not elastic; greasy feel; sectile.
Composition: Molybdenum disulfide (60.0% Mo, 40.0% S).
Tests: Under the oxidizing flame gives sulfur fumes on charcoal and colorful coatings around the assay; red near the assay; yellow, cooling to white farther away. The white coating touched by the reducing flame becomes azure-blue.
Distinguishing characteristics: Can only be confused with graphite, which is blacker. The blowpipe test is extremely easy and characteristic. A violet color is seen between the slightly divided cleavage flakes of molybdenite.
Occurrence: Molybdenite becomes an ore of molybdenum at Climax, Colorado, and Bingham Canyon, Utah, where small flakes are abundantly scattered through the porphyry. The best specimens are the large plates from Deepwater, New South Wales, associated with quartz. Good crystals, embedded in granitic rock or quartz, are fairly common. Chelan, Washington, is a notable example for these.
Interesting facts: Molybdenite, though seldom seen in rocks, may be the primary source of molybdenum, from which secondary molybdenum minerals (molybdates) are formed as a result of weathering. However, although unrecognizable as a mineral, there appears to be an amorphous, easily oxidized molybdenum sulfide that decomposes readily and on any drying redeposits as a water-soluble blue film giving inky tints to the rock at the Marysvale (Utah) and Lakeview (Oregon) uranium workings, to cite two localities. Called ilsemannite, a solution of this Mo-oxide could be a most important source of the Mo needed for wulfenite formation, the origin of which has always been something of a mystery. Powellite is often in platy pseudomorphs after molybdenite, penetrating the cleavage plates of the original crystals.

CALAVERITE	$AuTe_2$	
SYLVANITE	$(Au,Ag)Te_2$	**Pl. 12**

Monoclinic — prismatic $\dfrac{2}{m}$

Environment: Low-temperature ore veins.

Crystal description: Crystals common, but usually deeply striated and difficult to orient; elongated parallel to a horizontal axis. Commonly twinned. Also granular and massive.

Physical properties: Pale brass-yellow to silver-white. *Luster* metallic; *hardness* $2\frac{1}{2}$; *gravity* 8.2 (sylvanite)–9.3 (calaverite); *fracture* uneven; *cleavage* none (sylvanite has a side pinacoid cleavage). Brittle.

Composition: Telluride of gold and of silver (44.03% Au, 55.97% Te). Calaverite becomes sylvanite when 13.4% of the gold is replaced by silver.

Tests: Gives blue tint to flame on charcoal, eventually leaves gold button. Higher silver content of sylvanite makes bead whiter.

Distinguishing characteristics: The deeply striated elongated crystals are unmistakable. The gold bead is easy to obtain and can hardly be misidentified.

Occurrence: Calaverite is a rare mineral, but it is an important ore of gold in: Kalgoorlie, Western Australia; Calaveras Co., California; and Cripple Creek, Colorado.

In the veins it is associated with sylvanite, tellurium, quartz, and fluorite. Sylvanite is also found in Transylvania, Rumania. Large crystals were found at Vahatala, Fiji.

Interesting facts: Calaverite and sylvanite are closely related minerals. The blister-gold specimens sold in Colorado as natural gold are actually examples of these two ores that have been roasted to drive off the tellurium and bring the gold to the surface. The structure of these minerals has proved one of the most tantalizing problems that the X-ray mineralogists have encountered. The conclusion is that they are actually triclinic and twinned.

Higher Arsenides of Cobalt, Nickel, and Iron

This group of minerals includes varieties that are related chemically and can be divided into two isomorphous series on the basis of their crystal structure. They have recently been clarified and the names simplified, replacing some that will be found in the older literature. "Isomorphous series" is a term appearing frequently in mineralogy, and it describes a series of structurally (and crystallographically) alike minerals that contain mixtures of two or more of the metallic elements in a chemical combination, any of which may be more abundant. The pure compounds — the salts with only one of the two or more metal elements possible — are called the end-members of the series.

SKUTTERUDITE $(Co,Ni,Fe)As_3$

Isometric — diploidal $\dfrac{2}{m}\overline{3}$

Environment: This series occurs in medium-temperature veins, associated with silver and related cobalt and nickel minerals.
Crystal description: Usually massive and granular. Crystals may develop, particularly on surfaces in contact with calcite vein filling, but they are dull and uneven. Cube and octahedron commonest, sometimes dodecahedron and pyritohedron.
Physical properties: Tin-white. *Luster* metallic; *hardness* $5\frac{1}{2}$-6; *gravity* 6.1–6.8; *fracture* granular; *cleavage* none. Brittle.

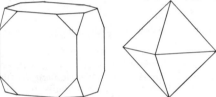

Composition: Triarsenide of cobalt, nickel, and iron; this series was formerly known under the name smaltite-chloanthite and considered to be completely isomorphous with a third iron triarsenide. Recent studies indicate that only the cobalt triarsenide actually exists in a pure state and that cobalt, iron, and nickel are always present in the others. This suggests that skutterudite should be the name for the high cobalt end-member (formerly smaltite), and the others should be known (depending upon their composition) as nickelian skutterudite (instead of chloanthite) and ferroan skutterudite (instead of the discredited "arsenoferrite"). Arsenic amounts to 75% of the weight; the balance is made up by the metals.
Tests: Fuses on charcoal, giving an arsenic (garlic) odor and forming magnetic ball. Cobalt-rich skutterudite ball dissolves in nitric acid to form a pink solution. Iron and nickel are usually present, however, in sufficient quantity to mask the color. Tests on analyzed samples showed that a nitric acid solution of (cobalt) skutterudite neutralized by ammonia becomes red-violet and a red-violet precipitate settles out. A nickel skutterudite under the same conditions gave a blue-violet solution and a pale green precipitate. The rare ferroan skutterudite gives a strong brown iron-hydroxide precipitate that will mask either of the other elements.

Distinguishing characteristics: Likely to be confused with arsenopyrite, which gives no cobalt or nickel test; with cobaltite and a series of diarsenides (loellingite and rammelsbergite), which cannot be distinguished by the methods described here.
Occurrence: In North America this series is abundant and of great economic importance at Cobalt, Ontario, but is rare elsewhere and important only in Germany, France, Spain, Morocco, and Chile. In recent years, the best crystals have been the highly cobaltian skutterudites of Bou Azzer, Morocco.
Uses: Valuable ores of cobalt and nickel.
Interesting facts: The weathering of this group of minerals results in the formation of pink and green secondary minerals (erythrite and annabergite) on outcrops and near the surface. These colors are good guides to the presence of minerals of this and the related group. They are rarely pure and commonly have zones of different compositions so that it is impossible to get a pure sample for testing.

The Sulfosalts

This is a group of sulfide minerals in which antimony, arsenic, or bismuth join with a truly metallic element to form a double salt. For simplicity the formula can be divided into the two sulfide combinations that make up the mineral. Since there are many combinations of the identical elements in different proportions, each making a different mineral, we usually require some additional data, such as crystal form, to make positive identifications. Often even the qualitative analysis from blowpipe and chemical tests will be insufficient. Many of the sulfosalt minerals are relatively rare, so fortunately their identification is a problem not often encountered. Also, their crystals are not infrequent, since all are relatively low-temperature and pressure minerals, and we can usually use the crystals to confirm a tentative identification. Without the crystals we cannot make a positive identification in many cases, but must turn the specimen over to the X-ray mineralogist.

Some series are more common than others. There are, for instance, several similar lead antimony sulfides, but the lead arsenic sulfides are rarer, fewer, and different in structure. Arsenic can be present in the predominantly antimony-bearing minerals and antimony in the arsenic-bearing minerals, but not to the unlimited extent of an isomorphous series.

POLYBASITE $(Ag,Cu)_{16}Sb_2S_{11}$ **Pl. 13**

Monoclinic — prismatic $\frac{2}{m}$

Environment: Low-temperature silver-bearing veins.

Crystal description: Flat pseudohexagonal plates, with pseudorhombohedral faces on the edges. Base commonly triangularly striated parallel to 3 of the face edges. Also massive.

Physical properties: Iron-black. *Luster* metallic; *hardness* 2–3; *gravity* 6.0–6.2; *fracture* uneven; *cleavage* perfect basal. Brittle; deep red and translucent in thin splinters.

Composition: A silver antimony sulfide, in which the copper may substitute to about 12%. An average composition might run about 65% Ag, 9% Cu, 10% Sb, 15% S, and about 1% As.

Tests: Fuses easily, drawing into a shiny, dark metallic globule that dulls on cooling. Partly malleable, then crushes to powder. Good white antimony sublimate. Acid solutions show silver test.

Distinguishing characteristics: The crystal form is the best guide to this mineral after the silver is identified. Crystals might be mistaken for hematite, but softness and the easy fusibility would soon show them to be something different. The streak is darker. Specular hematite would be weakly magnetic and the crystals sharper and more lustrous.

Occurrence: Polybasite occurs with other silver antimony sulfides. Often an important ore of silver, for it has been abundant in Mexico and fairly common in the German silver districts. Outstanding specimens have not been found in the U.S., but small quantities occur in many mines in Colorado, Idaho, Montana, and Nevada.

Interesting facts: Its similarity in appearance to crystals of the hexagonal system suggests that at some temperature (that of its formation) it inverts to the higher-symmetry group.

STEPHANITE Ag_5SbS_4 **Pl. 14**

Orthorhombic — pyramidal m m 2

Environment: Low-temperature silver veins.

Crystal description: Usually recognized by its crystals, which are common, well formed, and occasionally large. Short-prismatic to tabular crystals, sometimes intergrown to produce apparently hexagonal shapes. Also massive and disseminated.

Physical properties: Iron-black. *Luster* metallic; *hardness* 2–2½; *gravity* 6.2–6.3; *fracture* subconchoidal to uneven; *cleavage* 2 poor. Brittle. Tends to become dull black in a collection.

Composition: Silver antimony sulfide (68.5% Ag, 15.2% Sb, 16.3% S).

Tests: Fuses easily, drawing into a shiny gray globule, which dulls on cooling and assumes tarnish. White antimony sublimates form around the assay.

Distinguishing characteristics: Identified first by blowpiping as a silver antimony sulfide, it then usually can be specifically identified by its good crystal shape.

Occurrence: Stephanite is associated with other sulfides (galena, sphalerite, argentite, native silver, tetrahedrite, pyrite), the ruby-silvers (proustite and pyrargyrite) and the gangue minerals (quartz, barite, siderite, calcite, and fluorite).

Fine examples have come from Mexico, where it formed crystals several inches across. It was also found in Saxony (East Germany), the Harz, Cornwall, and Bolivia. The chief U.S. occurrence is now exhausted, since it was one of the important silver ores of the famous Comstock Lode in Nevada. It is still sparsely found in Colorado and California, and in Canada at Cobalt and South Lorrain, Ontario.

PYRARGYRITE Ag_3SbS_3 **Pl. 14**
Hexagonal — Ditrigonal pyramidal 3 m
Environment: Low-temperature silver veins.
Crystal description: Often well crystallized; being hemimorphic, the upper faces differ from those of the lower end, although since they are seldom doubly terminated it is not usually apparent. Most often terminated with gently sloping rhombohedron faces. Steep scalenohedral faces less common. Also massive.
Physical properties: Deep red to almost black. *Luster* adamantine; *hardness* $2\frac{1}{2}$; *gravity* 5.8–5.9; *fracture* conchoidal; *cleavage* 2 rhombohedral (1 good). Brittle.
Composition: Silver antimony sulfide (59.9% Ag, 22.3% Sb, 17.8% S). Surprisingly low in As, even though it occurs with proustite.
Tests: Fuses readily into round shiny globule. Antimony sublimate forms white ring close to assay, best seen immediately after first melting. Continued heating makes dull gray malleable button, which gives good test for silver (hydrochloric acid added to nitric acid solution).
Distinguishing characteristics: Usually the crystal form and dark red color are a sufficient guide. Pyrargyrite could be confused with dark proustite, but the antimony sublimate around the pyrargyrite button shows the difference.

Cuprite gives copper tests, zincite is infusible. In general, the mineral associations suggest silver minerals whenever we encounter pyrargyrite or proustite.
Occurrence: Pyrargyrite is a late mineral in the silver veins, and probably is also formed secondarily. Specimens are usually characteristic of the early stages of a silver-mining operation. It is sometimes an important ore of silver. Although fine specimens are often destroyed to recover their silver value, the specimen value as a rule is much greater. The best examples have come from Germany, in the Harz and Saxony. In France good crystals were found at Ste-Marie-aux-Mines, Alsace, and at Chalanches, Isère. Some Mexican mines, as at Guanajuato, have enough pyrargyrite for it to be an ore. It is not abundant in the U.S.
Interesting facts: It is known as dark ruby-silver ore and it

is distinguished as a rule by its color from the light ruby-silver ore, proustite. Like the latter, on exposure to light it has a tendency to form a dull oxidized coating that dims its luster. If the specimen can stand it, a light brushing with soap and water will remove most of the coating. A quick dip in a silver-cleaning solution has been found effective but may be risky.

PROUSTITE Ag_3AsS_3 **Pl. 12**
    Hexagonal — Ditrigonal pyramidal 3 m
Environment: Low-temperature silver veins.
Crystal description: Crystals common, usually steeper rhombohedrons than in pyrargyrite, or in scalenohedrons truncating trigonal prisms. Also massive. Trillings frequent in Chañarcillo crystals (Chile).
Physical properties: Light to dark red. *Luster* adamantine; *hardness* 2–2½; *gravity* 5.6–5.7; *fracture* conchoidal; *cleavage* distinct rhombohedral. Brittle; translucent to transparent.
Composition: Silver arsenic sulfide ($3Ag_2S \cdot As_2S_3$: 65.4% Ag, 15.2% As, 19.4% S). Antimony sometimes present to about the same extent — to 3% — that arsenic is present in pyrargyrite.
Tests: Fuses at once into globule on charcoal, giving abundant arsenic (garlic) fumes, coloring flame around assay white, and forming no deposit close to the globule. Malleable dull gray button, formed after long blowing, dissolves in nitric acid and gives silver test when hydrochloric acid is added.
Distinguishing characteristics: Can be mistaken for pyrargyrite, but is usually lighter in color. Other red minerals, with their distinctions, are listed under pyrargyrite (preceding).
Occurrences: Proustite is a late primary or a secondary mineral in the veins. The finest crystals ever found came from Chañarcillo, Chile. Some of these are in long crystals, many of which are trillings. They may be over 4 in. (10 cm) long and about ½-¾ in. (1–2 cm) across, and are bright red. The little-known Keeley Mine (South Lorrain, Ontario) crystals were also outstanding. Darker but well-developed crystals came from the Harz and Saxony. It is an important ore mineral in Mexico, and although occasionally noted in the U.S. it is usually rare. Good crystals have been found in Niederschlema, near Schneeberg, East Germany.

TETRAHEDRITE $(Cu,Fe)_{12}Sb_4S_{13}$ ⎫
TENNANTITE $(Cu,Fe)_{12}As_4S_{13}$ ⎬   **Pl. 14**
           Cubic — hextetrahedral $\overline{4}$ 3 m
Environment: Usually medium- and low-temperature ore veins.
Crystal description: Tetrahedrite commonly well crystallized in sharp, distinct, well-formed tetrahedrons; tennantite less well developed, and often more cubic in habit. Also massive.

Physical properties: A gray to iron-black. *Luster* metallic; *hardness* 3–4½ (tennantite harder); *gravity* 4.6–5.1 (tetrahedrite denser); *cleavage* none; *fracture* subconchoidal to uneven. Brittle; some specimens of tennantite translucent deep red in thin splinters.

Composition: Copper, iron antimony, and arsenic sulfide; really a whole series of related minerals (isomorphous series) with antimony and arsenic end-members. Copper is the predominant metal, but zinc, mercury, silver, and lead can also enter into the composition. Tetrahedrite (the antimony-rich member) is far more common than tennantite.

Tests: Easily fused, with arsenic or antimony fumes, or both, plus sulfur. Fused globule dissolved in nitric acid gives good red-brown precipitate with ammonia (Fe), and blue (Cu) color to solution. Lead and silver can be shown to be present by adding hydrochloric acid to the nitric acid solution. The blue-green solution turns greener and a white precipitate forms. These tests should suffice; normally crystals are enough, when visible.

Distinguishing characteristics: When crystals are present, they are the best guide. Failing these, the problem becomes more difficult, since there are many gray metallic sulfides with which these two can be confused. Detection of copper, iron, lead, and silver should permit running tetrahedrite-tennantite down by elimination. The subconchoidal, brilliant fracture, lack of cleavage, and comparative hardness are all significant.

Occurrence: Tetrahedrite is one of the commonest and economically the most important of the sulfosalts. Often an important ore of copper, and usually to be found in typical copper ore associations. Fine glossy crystals, probably the best in the U.S., have come from Bingham Canyon, Utah. It is found in many European localities (in Germany, England, and Czechoslovakia) and in some of the famous South American copper mines (Cerro de Pasco, Casapalca, and Morococha, Peru).

Tennantite is much rarer. The best-formed and multifaced crystals have come from the isolated sulfide pocket occurrence at Binnatal, Switzerland (binnite). It is also found in many U.S. mines, where it is difficult to distinguish from the tetrahedrites found in other sections of the same veins. Tsumeb, South West Africa, has become an important locality with sharp 1 in. (2–3 cm) tetrahedrons. An occurrence in Zacatecas, Mexico, of like-sized crystals first called tennantite turned out to be a mixture of the two (tennantite and tetrahedrite) grown over crystals of chalcopyrite that are scattered over a crystallized quartz crust.

ENARGITE Cu_3AsS_4 **Pl. 14**
Orthorhombic — pyramidal m m 2
Environment: Medium-temperature ore veins.

Crystal description: Crystals common, usually prismatic, with several grooved, almost curving, prisms, and a flat truncating base. Sometimes tabular; also massive and granular.

Physical properties: Gray-black to iron-black. *Luster* metallic; *hardness* 3; *gravity* 4.4–4.5; *fracture* uneven; *cleavage* perfect prismatic. Brittle.

Composition: Copper arsenic sulfide (48.3% Cu, 19.1% As, 32.6% S), but up to 6% antimony can take the place of arsenic. The far rarer arsenic equivalent is known as famatinite and has a redder tint on a polished surface.

Tests: Fuses on charcoal (with the sublimates and odor of S, Sb, and As), leaving a bead that can produce, with borax fluxes and great care, a copper bead. Touched with hydrochloric acid the melted bead will show a blue Cu flame; or in a nitric acid solution plus ammonia will give the Cu blue color.

Distinguishing characteristics: The crystals are typical, and may resemble those of manganite, but the blowpipe reactions will show the difference. It is difficult to distinguish from many related minerals, though the tests for As and Cu separate enargite from minerals lacking those elements.

Occurrence: Enargite is an important ore of copper and is usually associated in ore deposits with other copper minerals and sulfides. It is frequently in well-crystallized specimens, and individual crystals may be 1 in. (2–3 cm) long.

An abundant ore in the sulfide part of the great Chuquimata copper deposit (Chile). Butte, Montana, is the most important locality in the U.S., but it is also found in Colorado, Utah, and California. Microscopic crystals have been found at Picher, Oklahoma, perched on $\frac{1}{4}$ in. (5 mm) chalcopyrite crystals. 2–4 in. (5–10 cm) long crystals have been found in n. Peru at Quiruvilca. Good $1\frac{1}{2}$ in. (4 cm) crystals are found in Japan at the Kaize-mura Mine, Nagano Prefecture.

Interesting facts: Enargite was originally thought to be isomorphous (antimony present to any amount in place of arsenic) with the antimonial equivalent famatinite. It is now known to be different in structure. Famatinite (Cu_3SbS_4) has a cubic structure. At Morococha, Peru, the ore seems to be transformed upward from enargite at the base of crystal crusts into a pinkish gray, a seemingly dimorphous cubic equivalent without distinct cleavage planes called luzonite. Luzonite crystals have been found at the Teine Mine, Sapporo, Japan, and in Taiwan at the Chinkuashih Mine.

BOURNONITE $PbCuSbS_3$ **Pl. 14**

Orthorhombic — bipyramidal $\frac{2\ 2\ 2}{m\ m\ m}$

Environment: In medium-temperature ore veins, full of open cavities.

Crystal description: A popular mineral among collectors for its large interestingly intergrown crystals, which produce a radiating (cogwheel) effect. Usually in short-prismatic, tabular crystals, sometimes several inches across. Also massive.

Physical properties: Black to grayish black. *Luster* metallic-adamantine; *hardness* $2\frac{1}{2}$–3; *gravity* 5.8–5.9; *fracture* subconchoidal to uneven; *cleavage* 1 good, 2 less good at right angles to it. Brittle.

Composition: Lead and copper sulfantimonide ($2PbS \cdot Cu_2S \cdot Sb_2S_3$: 13.0% Cu, 42.5% Pb, 24.7% Sb, 19.8% S; some As can take the place of Sb).

Tests: Fuses easily to a silvery, metallic globule with first a white and then a yellow coating around the assay. Decomposed by nitric acid, giving a solution that is weak blue-green in color (Cu), which becomes cloudy with a white precipitate of S and Pb, and a skeletal yellow residue of S.

Distinguishing characteristics: The crystals are very typical, and usually show the intergrowth known as twinning. When crystals are not present, difficult to identify positively.

Occurrence: One of the commonest of the sulfosalt group, and open cavities (vugs) are unusually frequent in bournonite-bearing veins. Its associates are galena, sphalerite, tetrahedrite, chalcopyrite, pyrite, siderite, quartz, and barite. Particularly good specimens came from Germany, both from Neudorf in the Harz and from Horhausen, Rhein province. Large crystals were found in Cornwall, and crystals up to 4 in. (10 cm) across have come from Bolivia. In Japan, the Chichibu Mine, Saitama Prefecture, is a good crystal source. In the U.S. good crystals have been found with pyrite and siderite at Park City, Utah, in Yavapai Co., Arizona, and in Colorado and Montana.

Interesting facts: Bournonite is known as *Radelerz* (wheel ore) by German miners and in Cornwall under the equivalent term "cogwheel ore." The striking crystal outline seems to have caught the fancy of miners and collectors alike the world over, and examples of the Cornwall Herodsfoot Mine "cogwheels" command premium prices. The world's finest museum examples will be found in London and Truro, Cornwall.

BOULANGERITE $Pb_5Sb_4S_{11}$ **Pl. 14**

Monoclinic — prismatic $\dfrac{2}{m}$

Environment: Medium- and low-temperature ore deposits.

Crystal description: Long prisms to fibers, deeply striated. Also in solid feathering masses.

Physical properties: Bluish lead-gray. *Luster* metallic; *hardness* $2\frac{1}{2}$–3; *gravity* 5.7–6.3; *cleavage* 1 good, parallel to the elongation (none across, thin fibers flexible, unlike jamesonite). Fibrous, splintery.

Composition: Lead antimony sulfide ($5PbS \cdot 2Sb_2S_3$: 55.4% Pb, 25.7% Sb, 18.9% S).

Tests: Decrepitates, then melts easily into flattened bubbly mass that clings to charcoal. Acid reactions are like those of jamesonite, except that solution takes longer.

Distinguishing characteristics: Almost indistinguishable from similar species, all known as "feather ores," except by X-ray pattern or by a quantitative analysis. In contrast to jamesonite, boulangerite fuses with decrepitation, forming a spreading, frothing, spongy mass. Jamesonite fibers are more brittle than those of boulangerite. Both tend to alter into a yellow-brown pseudomorphous mass called bindheimite $[Pb_2Sb_2O_6(O,OH)]$.

Occurrence: Boulangerite is associated in veins with other lead sulfosalts, and with stibnite, sphalerite, galena, quartz, and siderite. It occurs at many localities in Europe as well as in Peru and Mexico. In the U.S. solid plumose (feathering) masses are found in Stevens Co., Washington. In Idaho, Colorado, and Nevada similar examples occur with other ores, but it is not abundant in this country. Common in loose hairs resembling the usual jamesonite in Zacatecas, Mexico.

MIARGYRITE AgSbS$_2$ Monoclinic — prismatic $\dfrac{2}{m}$ **Pl. 15**

Environment: Low-temperature silver-bearing veins.

Crystal description: Usually small black striated crystals of complicated form, and difficult to orient. Also massive.

Physical properties: Iron-black to steel-gray. *Luster* metallic; *hardness* 2–2½; *gravity* 5.1–5.3; *streak* cherry-red; *fracture* subconchoidal; *cleavage* 3 poor. Brittle; translucent red in thin splinters.

Composition: A silver antimony sulfide. Some arsenic may replace the antimony. The arsenic equivalent (smithite) is very rare, however, and has only been found at Binnatal, Switzerland.

Tests: Fuses easily into elongated, flattened, black globule, with heavy antimony sublimate. On prolonged blowing it "boils" and sinks farther into charcoal. Gives silver test in acids.

Distinguishing characteristics: The red streak and the acid silver test eliminate all minerals but pyrargyrite. Behavior differences before the blowpipe and the complex crystals of miargyrite make distinguishing these two minerals easy.

Occurrence: A rare mineral, never forming large crystals; but it is of some silver ore importance in Germany — in Saxony and the Harz — and in Mexico. In silver-bearing veins it is associated with polybasite, stephanite, proustite, and pyrargyrite, as well as with native silver and argentite. Good specimens have been found in the San Juan district of Colorado, in Idaho, and in some quantity in California (Randsberg district).

JAMESONITE $Pb_4FeSb_6S_{14}$ **Pl. 15**

Monoclinic — prismatic $\dfrac{2}{m}$

Environment: Low- to medium-temperature ore veins.

Crystal description: Almost always finely fibrous, sometimes in loosely matted hairs. Also in solid feathering masses.

Physical properties: Dark gray. *Luster* metallic; *hardness* $2\frac{1}{2}$; *gravity* 5.5–6.0; *cleavage* across the elongation. Brittle.

Composition: Lead, antimony, iron, sulfide ($4PbS \cdot FeS \cdot 3Sb_2S_3$: 50.8% Pb, 29.5% Sb, 19.7% S). Also some Zn and Cu, and small percentages of Ag and Bi.

Tests: Fuses easily and almost disappears, leaving coating of yellow to white sublimates around the assay which form a magnetic crust. Pulls together more than boulangerite. Soluble in hot HCl, with smell of H_2S (rotten-egg smell). A strong solution in hydrochloric acid frees a white flaky precipitate (lead chloride) as the acid cools. Weaker solutions may become only cloudy or even remain clear.

Distinguishing characteristics: Difficult to distinguish from related minerals. Plumosite ($Pb_5Sb_6S_{14}$), meneghinite ($Pb_{13}Sb_7S_{23}$), boulangerite ($Pb_5Sb_4S_{11}$), zinkenite ($Pb_6Sb_{14}S_{27}$) lack the Fe but are very similar in appearance, except that jamesonite fibers are more brittle. The Germans call the latter group the flexible "feather ores." They might be mistaken for some of the manganese oxides, but the form of occurrence and the blowpipe tests should separate these.

Occurrence: Jamesonite occurs with lead ores, locally, and is commercial ore when it is mixed with other metal ores. Příbram in s. Bohemia and Baia Sprie (formerly Felsöbanya) in Rumania are important Old World localities. Cornwall was the source of good matted-hair specimens. In the U.S., Colorado is an abundant source of feather ores, since felted masses of a mixture of zinkenite and jamesonite were formerly found. Idaho, Utah, Nevada, and California have reported occurrences. Usually it is in solid plumose masses, sometimes in slender hairs on crystal cavity surfaces. However, in Noche Buena, Zacatecas, Mexico, the jamesonite looks more like tiny stibnites, and the boulangerite forms as hairy masses.

The Oxides

Compounds of the metallic elements with oxygen are placed in this group. Most of them have simple crystal structures and simple chemical compositions. Because of their uncomplicated chemistry the relationships between them are more obvious than in most groups. Water is a mineral (and a rock) that is often considered with this group but, abundant as it is, it hardly requires further mention in a practical book such as this.

In general, the oxide minerals are most varied in their physical properties. The group includes very soft and very hard minerals, minerals that are transparent and minerals that are opaque. Some of the rarest gems and some of the most abundant ores are simple oxides. Some metals, like silver and gold, do not combine chemically with oxygen, and therefore have no representatives in this group. Lead oxides are very rare, but the oxide of tin is the only abundant compound in which this metal is found in nature. The primary oxides form deep in the crust, most often when liquid rock is solidifying. The commonest oxides, however, are those that form from other minerals (such as the sulfides) on weathering at the surface, to constitute great "rust" blankets protecting the still fresh underlying rocks. The minerals of the latter type often contain water as well as the oxygen and are soft; all of the really hard oxides are the primary ones. Quartz was formerly considered an oxide, but because of its internal crystal structure and the physical properties it is now placed with the silicates.

CUPRITE Cu_2O Cubic — gyroidal 4 3 2   **Pls. 12, 15**
   Environment: Oxidation zone of copper sulfide ore bodies.
   Crystal description: Crystals commonly cubes and octahedrons and combinations of these forms. Frequently in needle-like, red, distorted cubes; sometimes in parallel growths, coating cavities in limonite (chalcotrichite). Also massive and scattered throughout limonitic rocks, or in red coatings on native copper crystals.
   Physical properties: Red to dark red. *Luster* adamantine: *hardness* $3\frac{1}{2}$–4, *gravity* 5.8–6.1; *fracture* conchoidal; *cleavage* poor octahedral. Brittle; translucent, transparent.
   Composition: Cuprous oxide (88.8% Cu, 11.2% O).
   Tests: Fuses on charcoal and easily reduced to copper bead. Dissolves in acid, giving a blue copper color, and colors (green) blowpipe flame.
   Distinguishing characteristics: Distinguished by crystal shape and copper tests from the ruby-silvers. The blowpipe tests for copper and sulfur also distinguish it from cinnabar, realgar, and zincite. Rutile is usually too dark and brown and has a hardness of 6–6.5. There are almost invariably other copper minerals associated with cuprite.
   Occurrence: An important secondary ore of copper. It forms near the surface during the oxidation and enrichment of copper sulfide ore bodies as a result of weathering. Minerals of similar origin are its usual associates: native copper, malachite, azurite, and limonite. This group reaches its best development in desert

country, where oxidation has been deep. Often it seems to be characteristic of the deepest oxidation zone, with cuprite just above the enriched sulfides. Native copper is often adjacent to the cuprite in such deposits and frequently the cuprite has grown on the copper surface. It is a common mineral of wide distribution. Only a few localities can be mentioned. The most complex crystals came from Cornwall. The Chessy (France) malachite-coated octahedrons are common in large collections (see azurite, p. 158). Sw. U.S. has been the chief American source of fine specimens, especially the Copper Queen Mine at Bisbee, and at Clifton, Arizona. Chalcotrichite has been found at Bisbee, Morenci, and Jerome, Arizona. Tsumeb, South West Africa, is a late entrant in the important-locality list. Australia has had several good occurrences, including Cobar and Broken Hill (New South Wales), Burra-Burra and Wallaroo (South Australia). Giant 2 in (5 cm) crystals, coated with malachite and gemmy within, forming model-like dodecahedral crystals perched on quartz crusts, have been found at the Ongonja Mine, South West Africa.

Interesting facts: Cuprite belongs to an uncommon class of the cubic system, and its crystals sometimes show the required rare faces. Since it is invariably a secondary mineral, the best specimens must be found in the early stages of a mine's development.

ZINCITE ZnO   **Pl. 20**
        Hexagonal — Dihexagonal pyramidal 6 m m

Environment: A mineral of one locality — a metamorphosed weathered ore deposit.

Crystal description: Crystals rare, always pyramidal, showing interesting hexagonal hemimorphism, usually lying sidewise on a fissure in a calcite vein. Also in solid masses and in calcite in rounded club-shaped masses with distinct partings.

Physical properties: Orange-yellow to deep red. *Luster* subadamantine; *hardness* 4; *gravity* 5.4–5.7; *streak* orange-yellow; *fracture* conchoidal; *cleavage* prismatic (plus a basal parting). Brittle; translucent to transparent.

Composition: Zinc oxide (80.3% Zn, 19.7% O). Some Mn present, except in synthetic crystals.

Tests: Infusible on charcoal, but the assay on heating turns black — and on cooling regains the original color. Eventually acquires coating of yellow- (hot) white (cold) zinc oxide which turns green in oxidizing flame after touch of cobalt nitrate solution. This test is improved by crushing and mixing with sodium carbonate. Soluble in acids.

Distinguishing characteristics: The infusibility, plus the zinc test on charcoal, plus solubility in nitric or hydrochloric acid will give a positive identification. The crystals, when present, help; but the most important aspect of all is its invariable association as a reddish-orange mineral with black magnetic franklinite, greenish willemite, and white calcite.

Occurrence: This mineral would not be included here were it not once of considerable economic importance as an ore of zinc at Sterling Hill and Franklin, New Jersey; this is the only important locality. It occurs there in red grains and masses in a white, highly fluorescent calcite, associated with willemite and franklinite. It is the most abundant red Franklin mineral and, hence, is always easily identified in the ore mixtures that are typical of the Franklin specimens. It has been reported in Poland, Tuscany, Spain, and Tasmania.

Interesting facts: Manganese is believed to cause the red color. Synthetic crystals are light yellow to colorless to pale blue. Some form accidentally from smelter fumes (and examples were marketed as "willemite from Algeria") but they can be grown by hydrothermal methods and from a vapor.

MASSICOT PbO

Orthorhombic — Rhombic bipyramidal $\dfrac{2}{m}\dfrac{2}{m}\dfrac{2}{m}$

Environment: Oxidized zones of lead deposits.

Crystal description: Artificial crystals only; natural occurrences are earthy to scaly.

Physical properties: Sulfur to orpiment yellow, sometimes with reddish tint, due to minium (Pb_3O_4) impurity. *Luster* greasy to dull; *hardness* 2; *gravity* 9.7; scales flexible but not elastic; *cleavage* several. Thin scales transparent.

Composition: Lead oxide (82.83% Pb, 7.17% O).

Tests: Fuses easily to form a yellow glass.

Distinguishing characteristics: Association with galena is the best guide. Its fusibility without burning like sulfur or giving off arsenic fumes like orpiment should identify it.

Occurrence: Massicot is a secondary mineral, forming like the red litharge and minium on the alteration of galena. Usually forms a scaly coating or pulverulent film on corroded cavities in that mineral. Litharge (also PbO) has been described as forming the red edge of the massicot scales. Bright red, earthy minium forms scattered crusts on galena or on rock a little farther from the immediate vicinity of the fresh lead sulfide.

Probably far commoner than generally supposed, but dismissed by most mineral collectors as a thin dull coating marring the beauty of their specimens. It is found in the old slags of the Greek lead workings at Lavrion, Greece. In Sardinia and in Germany and Hungary it is associated with galena. In Mexico it is reported to occur in deposits from the two great volcanoes. It has been reported from many U.S. localities, especially in Colorado at Leadville (a source of good minium, too), and in Nevada and California. In Missouri near Potosi, it has been found in the galena associated with the barite of the "tiff" diggings. Bright red masses of minium (Pb_3O_4) from Broken Hill, New South Wales, were the result of a fire and, though of questionable legitimacy as minerals, are the best specimens available to collectors.

CORUNDUM Al_2O_3 Pl. 15

Hexagonal — scalenohedral $\overline{3}\,\dfrac{2}{m}$

Environment: Plutonic, pegmatitic, and metamorphic rocks.
Crystal description: Six-sided crystals, sometimes elongated into tapering bipyramids, or sharp prisms, but also in scaly 6-sided plates. The metamorphic occurrences have large embedded crystals, showing series of parallel striations, like the plagioclase feldspars. May be in fine-grained black disemina-tions with magnetite (emery).
Physical properties: Colorless, brown, black, yellow, red, blue, violet. *Luster* adamantine; *hardness* 9; *gravity* 3.9–4.1; *fracture* conchoidal or uneven; *cleavage,* none, but well-devel-oped partings on rhombohedral planes and sometimes on the base; breaks into sharp fragments (brittle), but often is very tough. Transparent to translucent; often triboluminescent, and fluorescent orange, yellow, or red.
Composition: Aluminum oxide (52.9% Al, 47.1% O).
Tests: Infusible and insoluble.
Distinguishing characteristics: Resembles many silicate minerals. The fine parallel rulings on parting faces are distinc-tive and might result in a confusion with some feldspars. It often shows color bands and bronzy luster on basal planes. The great hardness is diagnostic; since it is harder than any other natural mineral except diamond, a hardness test should suffice. The crystal form and the high gravity (higher than in most silicates) are also distinctive, when they can be observed or determined.
Occurrence: Usually characteristic of rocks lacking or poor in silicon oxide, with which presumably the aluminum oxide would combine to form another mineral if it were available. Found in igneous rocks, particularly nepheline syenites, as an acces-sory. Also found in pegmatites, in schists that were formed by a regional metamorphism of sediments accompanied by an intro-duction of alumina-bearing solutions, and in metamorphosed limestones. Associated with spinel, kyanite, garnet, and high-calcium feldspars.

It is an important industrial abrasive and refractory, but also has many gem varieties. There are numerous localities, so only a few of the important ones can be mentioned. The gem gravels of Sri Lanka (Ceylon), which were derived mainly from pegmatites, are rich in corundum, including many with gem tints. Large blocks and crystals of corundum have been mined in Africa, Brazil, and Madagascar. Some of the South African crystals are particularly well formed and may be very large. The rubies and sapphires of Burma occur in crystals in a metamorphosed limestone, and many are recovered as residual remnants in the earth just at the top of the solid rock. Tanzania, along the Umba River, is becoming an important source, where the corundum crystals occur in vermiculite (hydrated mica) dikes and as red plates (ruby) in green zoisite (Longido Hills).

The U.S. occurrences are as large crystals and masses in Georgia and North Carolina, together with a few rubies and sapphires. In Montana it is found near Helena in waterworn pebbles in terrace gravel bars by the Missouri River and at Yogo Gulch as flat, blue, gemmy crystals in a dark-colored fine-grained igneous dike. In California small but well-formed crystals have been found in Riverside, San Bernardino, and San Diego Cos. Emery has been mined at Peekskill, New York, and Chester, Massachusetts.

Interesting facts: The gem colors are caused by minor metal oxide impurities. Ruby, for example, is colored by chromium oxide. Corundum is often fluorescent, glowing red or orange in ultraviolet light, and some is strongly triboluminescent, giving orange flashes when it is sawed or hammered.

Corundum has proved easy to synthesize, except that very high temperatures are involved. It crystallizes at once on the solidification of molten alumina. This has led to the mass production of synthetic jewelry stones by simple melting of a suitably pigmented powder in an oxyhydrogen flame and allowing the hot rain to build up a stalagmite, known as a "boule," which is then cut up into decorative stones. Invented by a French chemist in 1891 who claimed to "reconstruct" rubies, it is known now as the Verneuil process. Lately, rubies have also been grown by hydrothermal methods, crystallized from molten solutions, and "pulled" from pots of fused alumina.

HEMATITE   Pl. 15

Fe_2O_3 Hexagonal — scalenohedral $\overline{3}\frac{2}{m}$

Environment: A common substance of general occurrence.
Crystal description: A mineral of widely varied appearance. Thick tabular crystals with rhombohedrons and scalenohedrons sometimes bordering a base. Also thin flat scales, which may be intergrown into "iron roses." Low basal rhombohedrons often merged into a curved surface to make thin lenticular scales. Also in mammillary or reniform radiating growths, sometimes in micaceous black schistlike rocks, and in soft, red earthy masses of "paint ore."

Physical properties: Red or black. *Luster* earthy or metallic; *hardness* 1–6½; *gravity* 4.9–5.3; *streak* bright to dark red; *fracture* conchoidal to uneven; *cleavage* none, but rhombohedral and sometimes basal parting. Compact varieties brittle; excessively thin plates translucent and red. Usually slightly magnetic.

Composition: Iron (ferric) oxide (70.0% Fe, 30.0% O).

Tests: Infusible on charcoal, but becomes strongly magnetic. Soluble in concentrated HCl.

Distinguishing characteristics: The red streak is the most important test in distinguishing dark compact varieties of hematite from limonite. The crystallized "specular" varieties (specularite) are similarly differentiated from ilmenite and magnetite. The hardness, infusibility, and magnetism after roasting distinguish it from black sulfides and sulfosalts. Behavior under the blowpipe also distinguishes the soft red varieties from cinnabar, cuprite, minium, and the like. There are some hydrous red iron oxides that are often confused with hematite; lepidocrocite [FeO(OH)] is the most important.

Occurrence: The most important ore of iron. It occurs in tremendous beds of sedimentary origin, altered and enriched by subsequent solutions after being laid down. Small black scales have been found around gas vents on lava flows near volcanoes (Vesuvius and Alaska). Massive black beds and scaly schistose hematite rocks are found in metamorphosed sedimentary formations, and hematite crystals may form in rocks of contact metamorphism. Red hematite commonly forms in the soil as the result of weathering of other iron-bearing minerals, and is responsible for the red coloration of many sedimentary rocks. Hematite has formed important secondary ore deposits after iron sulfides (as in Missouri). It is also a primary mineral in veins cutting igneous rocks. It is even suggested that at Los Lagos, Chile, there may have been a lava flow that was pure iron oxide, part of which crystallized as hematite, part as magnetite.

The most spectacular large crystals of hematite — flat plates 6 in. (15 cm) or more across — have been found in metamorphosed Brazilian sediments. Many attractively crystallized specimens of rhombohedral habit, often with an iridescent tarnish, come from the island of Elba, Italy. The famous "iron roses" from crystal-lined pockets in the Alps are unmatched elsewhere. Cumberland, England, produces small specular crystals, and the best examples of the interesting reniform knobs — "kidney ore" — of reddish-black splintery ore.

For all of its great iron deposits, the U.S. has not produced many spectacular specimens. The Mesabi Range of Minnesota yields only small crystals, and the softer Clinton Red Beds of Alabama have no crystals. The micaceous schistlike Michigan hematite is brilliant and typical of that occurrence. In its many varieties hematite is one of the commonest minerals we are likely to encounter.

ILMENITE $FeTiO_3$ Hexagonal — rhombohedral $\overline{3}$ **Pl. 15**
Environment: In metamorphic and plutonic rocks and in pegmatites.
Crystal description: Equidimensional to tabular, and down to fine, scaly crystals. Also compact, massive, or granular; and as a black sand.
Physical properties: Black to brownish black (geikielite) and deep red (pyrophanite). *Luster* metallic to submetallic; *hardness* 5–6; *gravity* 4.1–4.8; *streak* black to brownish red to ocher-yellow; *fracture* conchoidal to subconchoidal; *cleavage* none in ilmenite (rhombohedral in geikielite and pyrophanite). Brittle; ilmenite is weakly magnetic.
Composition: An iron titanium oxide; related to hematite except that half of the iron has been replaced by titanium; manganese and magnesium can also take the place of the remaining iron (then the minerals are known respectively as pyrophanite ($MnTiO_3$) and geikielite ($MgTiO_3$). Normal ilmenite has 36.8% Fe, 31.6% Ti, 31.6% O.
Tests: Infusible on charcoal, but splinter held in forceps will be slightly rounded on edges in hottest blowpipe flame. Best test is titanium coloration: after fusion in borax and repowdering, the pulverized mineral is partially dissolved in hot concentrated HCl; the acid is then filtered, leaving a clear yellow solution that, after boiling with tinfoil (real tin), becomes very pale blue or violet. Since this is difficult to observe, it is best to use a very strong solution.
Distinguishing characteristics: Color of the streak distinguishes it from hematite, the lesser magnetism from magnetite, the great hardness from the black sulfosalts, and the magnetism from brookite or rutile. Columbite and tantalite are much heavier, but may require a chemical or specific gravity test.
Occurrence: Ilmenite is a common accessory grain in basic igneous rocks, and the grains are often concentrated in sands resulting from rock destruction by weathering. Fine sharp crystals have been found in a pegmatite at Kragerø, Norway. Flat plates are common in U.S. pegmatites, as at Bedford, Westchester Co., New York.

In the U.S. it is mined at Sanford Lake in the Adirondacks, where it forms great masses but no good crystals. Occurrences at Lake Allard, Quebec, are of great economic importance, for titanium has become a valuable commercial metal. The magnesian ilmenite, geikielite, has been found in waterworn pebbles in the gem gravels of Sri Lanka (Ceylon) and in grains in the marble of Riverside, California. The manganese ilmenite, pyrophanite, has been found in small red tabular crystals in Sweden and in a rock in Brazil.

Interesting facts: Important as a source of white titanium oxide now, the principal pigment for paint. Technological progress has made fabrication of titanium metal a practical and commercial operation, and there are a number of uses for this lightweight yet strong metal. The titanium content that long made ilmenite worthless as an iron ore has now become the more valuable constituent.

BIXBYITE $(Mn,Fe)_2O_3$ Cubic — diploidal $\frac{2}{m}\bar{3}$ **Pl. 16**

Environment: Volcanic rocks and metamorphic manganese deposits.

Crystal description: Perfect, shiny, cubic crystals with modified corners; may be half an inch (1 cm) on an edge, or larger. Also granular, mixed with other manganese ores.

Physical properties: Black. *Luster* metallic; *hardness* 6–6½; *gravity* 4.9–5.1; *streak* black; *fracture* irregular; *cleavage* octahedral (cubic in Patagonian crystals). Brittle.

Composition: Iron manganese oxide; iron can substitute for the manganese up to about 59% Fe_2O_3, or so little that it is nearly pure Mn_2O_3.

Tests: Fuses with some difficulty, forming (in the high Fe varieties) a magnetic globule. Partly soluble in HCl, freeing acrid vapors of Cl.

Distinguishing characteristics: A rare mineral, the crystals from known localities are easy to identify by their shape. The granular material is identifiable only by X-ray methods. A manganese test would indicate the presence of this element. The associated and similar silicate braunite (Mn_7SiO_{12}) and hausmannite ($MnMn_2O_4$) are infusible; most of the other Mn minerals are softer, fibrous or columnar, or lack crystal form entirely.

Occurrence: Bixbyite is of ore abundance and valuable for its manganese only when mixed with other manganese ores. The most interesting mineralogical occurrence is that of the Thomas Range, Utah, where it is found in cavities in a light gray altered rhyolite, associated with topaz, pink beryl, and quartz — the result of deposition from volcanic gases that penetrated and altered the rock. It has been reported from Patagonia in larger and more highly modified crystals. Several localities in New Mexico and one in n. Mexico yield small crystals much like those of Utah. Found with other manganese ores in India, Sweden, and South Africa.

Interesting facts: Though actually too rare to warrant inclusion here, it is nevertheless a popular and desirable mineral for collectors; and probably is more abundant than generally realized.

RUTILE TiO$_2$ **Pl. 16**

Tetragonal — Ditetragonal bipyramidal $\dfrac{4\ \ 2\ \ 2}{m\,m\,m}$

Environment: In plutonic and metamorphic rocks, often in seams in such rocks.

Crystal description: Crystals common, most frequently long striated prisms that sometimes are hairlike. Often twinned into bridge-girderlike lattices or into 6- or 8-sided forms known as sixlings or eightlings (Fig. 26, p. 49).

Physical properties: Black in large crystals, golden to reddish brown in capillary needles or thin, flat crystals. *Luster* metallic-adamantine; *hardness* 6–6½; *gravity* 4.2–4.3; *streak* light brown; *fracture* subconchoidal to uneven; *cleavage* basal and prismatic. Brittle; translucent to transparent and deep red-brown in thin pieces.

Composition: Titanium oxide (60.0% Ti, 40.0% O).

Tests: Infusible and insoluble in acid. Can be made soluble by fusing with borax powder, then test for Ti by dissolving the mixture in HCl, filtering and boiling the yellow solution with tinfoil (real tin) to produce faint blue or violet color (see ilmenite, p. 115).

Distinguishing characteristics: Difficult to confuse with other minerals, especially after a test for magnetism (negative) and for Ti. Crystals so common they are easy to identify. The waterworn crystals have an adamantine luster but a bruised look which gives them a sort of light-colored "skin" that is easy to recognize. Black to reddish-brown adamantine crystals may be recognized by their striated prisms or geniculated twins. Distinguished from cassiterite (gravity 6.8–7.1) by its lesser "heft."

Occurrence: Common in embedded crystals in gneiss or schist, in pegmatites, and free-growing in veins of the alpine type. Since it is also a hard, heavy, and common accessory mineral of primary rocks, it occurs in alluvial concentrations of heavy sands.

Large black shiny crystals, more or less equidimensional, are found in a quartzite at Graves Mountain, Georgia, associated with kyanite and lazulite. Beautiful reticulated growths of slender crystals were found in open seams in North Carolina at Hiddenite. Fine oriented growths of flat reddish rutile needles on hematite plates are common among the Swiss "iron roses." Perfect eightlings and rutile replacements of brookite (TiO$_2$) crystals (paramorphs) are common at Magnet Cove, Arkansas. Slender red-brown hairs of rutile penetrate quartz crystals — by replacement — to form rutilated quartz, also known as "flèches d'amour" or "Venus hairstone." Brazil, Switzerland, the U.S. (West Hartford, Vermont, and Alexander Co., North Carolina) have produced fine specimens of this growth of rutile and quartz.

Interesting facts: Rutile is used as an ore of titanium and of purified titanium oxide. It has been synthesized in commercial-size crystals by the Verneuil process (see corundum, p. 112). Color of pure, wholly oxidized material is a pale yellow, almost white; the less oxidized is darker, blue to black. Free Ti may be a partial cause of the dark color of most rutile, though an invariable Fe impurity no doubt shares the responsibility.

Oriented growths of rutile within the crystal network of other minerals are common. Oriented three-dimensional sets of rutile hairs cause the streaks of the stars seen in star quartz and star corundums.

PYROLUSITE MnO_2 **Pl. 16**

Tetragonal — Ditetragonal bipyramidal $\dfrac{4\ 2\ 2}{m\ m\ m}$

Environment: Secondary manganese deposits and secondary veins.

Crystal description: Rarely in prismatic or stubby well-formed crystals. Sometimes in fibrous crystals and often in fibrous masses that are pseudomorphous after other manganese oxides. Also massive, fibrous; and as black powdery to granular masses.

Physical properties: Steel-gray to iron-black. *Luster* metallic; *hardness* $6-6\frac{1}{2}$ (for crystals) to as little as 2 (for massive material); *gravity* 4.4–5.0; *streak* black (soft material blackens the fingers); *fracture* uneven; *cleavage* prismatic. Brittle.

Composition: Manganese dioxide (63.2% Mn, 36.8% O), often with a small amount of water, heavy metals, phosphorus, and other elements.

Tests: Infusible on charcoal; dissolves in HCl with the evolution of Cl, an acrid gas. Borax bead test is easy, showing in the oxidizing flame a fine amethystine color. (Avoid getting too much and having a black bead.)

Distinguishing characteristics: Sooty-black character of the streak and the manganese tests prove presence of manganese, but it is virtually impossible to tell one Mn oxide mineral from another without distinct crystals, except by X-ray tests. "Pyrolusite" is a safe name for any fibrous-looking mass of black manganese oxide needles or for the black powdery alterations of other manganese minerals.

Occurrence: Pyrolusite is the commonest and most important secondary ore of manganese. It forms under conditions of oxidation, either from primary manganese minerals like the carbonate rhodochrosite, the silicate rhodonite, and the numerous manganese phosphates or as direct deposits from cold groundwaters in bogs and on the sea floor. It is usually the mineral that makes the fernlike markings commonly observed along rock fissures. These are known as dendrites, and are often mistaken for fossil ferns. Localities for pyrolusite are hardly worth mentioning since the mineral is so widespread. Good specimens are found in some of the Minnesota and Michigan iron ores.

CASSITERITE SnO_2 **Pl. 16**

Tetragonal — Ditetragonal bipyramidal $\dfrac{4\ \ 2\ \ 2}{m\ m\ m}$

Environment: Pegmatites and high-temperature veins.

Crystal description: Commonly in well-formed crystals, sometimes prismatic (Cornwall), even needlelike (Cornwall and Bolivia), but more often bipyramidal. Frequently twinned, showing the characteristic re-entrant angle of a twin crystal. Also in red-brown, fibrous, banded crusts ("wood-tin"), in waterworn gray pebbles with a greasy luster ("stream-tin"), and in granular masses.

Physical properties: Light yellowish to red-brown to black, usually banded within a single crystal. *Luster* adamantine to greasy; *hardness* 6–7; *gravity* 6.8–7.1; *streak* nearly white; *fracture* subconchoidal to uneven; *cleavage* poor prismatic. Brittle; transparent to translucent.

Composition: Tin oxide (78.6% Sn, 21.4% O); usually with a fair amount of iron and sometimes some tantalum, which substitutes for the tin.

Tests: Infusible. Slowly becomes coated with gray or silvery film of tin metal on standing in cool dilute hydrochloric acid with strip of zinc (cut from casing of dry-cell battery).

Distinguishing characteristics: The light streak, high gravity, and high hardness rule out most similar minerals. The HCl test for tin then eliminates the rest. Might be confused with black tourmaline (which is much lighter), with rutile or columbite-tantalite (make the tin test), and with magnetite (try for magnetism). Some cassiterite is very black, so tests are sometimes essential. Color banding across the broken crystals and the light true color (despite a black exterior appearance) are very typical.

Occurrence: The most important ore of tin. Occurrence is limited to high-temperature veins, associated with tungsten ores, and with silicate gangue minerals; in pegmatites it is an important accessory. Often found in streambeds as waterworn pebbles; in Cornwall these were mined before the veins were. In fumarole deposits (Durango, Mexico) it has formed on rhyolite flow rocks.

Good crystals come from Cornwall, where it has been mined since Roman days. Bohemia and Saxony have important high-temperature vein occurrences. Alluvial deposits — which are still worked in China, in West Malaysia, and in Indonesia — are among the most important economic occurrences. In Bolivia beautiful specimens are found in association with a variety of minerals. In the U.S., cassiterite occurs in pegmatites (of no commercial value) though vein deposits in Virginia and California have been unsuccessfully worked. The small red-brown botryoidal masses of "wood-tin" found attached to rhyolite (and broken loose in placer washings in Durango, Mexico) are very different from the other tin varieties; but once seen they are easily recognized.

ANATASE TiO$_2$ Pl. 16

Tetragonal — Ditetragonal bipyramidal $\dfrac{4\ 2\ 2}{m\,m\,m}$

Environment: In seams and silicate veins, probably formed at fairly low temperatures.

Crystal description: Several habits, but always crystallized. Steeply pyramidal, pseudo-octahedral or tabular, often very complexly modified.

Physical properties: Blue, light yellow to brown. *Luster* adamantine to submetallic; *hardness* 5½–6; *gravity* 3.8–3.9; *streak* white; *fracture* subconchoidal; *cleavage* perfect basal and pyramidal. Brittle; translucent to transparent.

Composition: Titanium oxide (60.0% Ti, 40.0% O) like rutile, except that its atomic structure, and therefore its crystal form, is different.

Tests: Same as for rutile (p. 117).

Distinguishing characteristics: Usually the crystal form is sufficient. Might be confused with some of the octahedral minerals like microlite, which is generally far heavier. It is safest to get the Ti coloration test (see ilmenite, p. 115).

Occurrence: Anatase is most frequent in vein- or fissure-type deposits of the alpine variety. Of value only to collectors, because of its rarity, but holds great scientific interest. Steep blue-black bipyramids occur on quartz in the French Alpine region. Modified pseudo-octahedral brown crystals occur on the gneiss in fissures in the Binnatal area, Switzerland, and at Spissen, where some of the largest-known crystals occur: steep ditetragonal bipyramids as much as ½ in. (1 cm) tall. 3-cm crystals have been found at Gieserntal. It is found in Brazil on some of the quartz of the veins of the Diamantina district, often altered to rutile if the crystals were not encased in and protected by the quartz. Waterworn, gemmy, tiny deep blue tabular crystals have come from diamond washing in Minas Gerais, Brazil. Anatase is not common in the U.S. The largest crystals (blue) have been found in Gunnison Co., Colorado. Small steep bipyramids were found in calcite-filled quartz veins in a quarry at Somerville, Massachusetts. Waterworn crystals were found in gold washings in North Carolina, and minute steep bipyramids on mica flakes in Lincoln Co., North Carolina.

Interesting facts: Anatase is the second of 3 titanium oxides (with rutile, brookite), all chemically alike but distinguished by their crystal symmetries. Probably rarest of the three, and supposedly the one deposited at the lowest temperature. It is also the most readily altered of the titanium oxides.

BROOKITE TiO_2 **Pl. 16**

Orthorhombic — Rhombic bipyramidal $\dfrac{2}{m}\dfrac{2}{m}\dfrac{2}{m}$

Environment: Silica-bearing veins deposited by hot solutions.
Crystal description: Always crystallized; usually thinly tabular parallel to a side pinacoid and then elongated and striated vertically. More equidimensional at Magnet Cove, Arkansas.
Physical properties: Red-brown to black. *Luster* adamantine to submetallic; *hardness* $5\frac{1}{2}$-6; *gravity* 3.9-4.1; *streak* white to gray or yellowish; *fracture* subconchoidal to uneven; *cleavage* poor prismatic and basal. Brittle; translucent to opaque.
Composition: Titanium oxide (60.0% Ti, 40.0% O).
Tests: Same as for rutile (p. 117).
Distinguishing characteristics: The crystals — brown elongated flat plates often variegated in color with black corners — are very typical in their association with quartz in veins. There are not many minerals with which it can be confused, and none of those will give a Ti test.
Occurrence: Brookite is another of the titanium oxide group (with rutile and anatase) forming under special conditions at relatively low temperatures. Found also as detrital grains in sandy sediments — grains reported apparently to have grown larger after their deposition in sand, presumably fed by cool solutions percolating through the rocks.

The Swiss occurrences are among the best, yielding very thin crystals, almost an inch (better than 2 cm) long and clearly showing the red-brown color. A well-known English occurrence is the long-exhausted quartz vein with embedded typical brookite plates at Tremadoc, Wales.

It is not uncommon in similar environments in the U.S., but the outstanding American occurrence is in untypical crystals in the quartzite at Magnet Cove, Arkansas. Abundant, black, more or less equidimensional crystals — 1 in. (2 cm) or so across at their best — dot a corroded, rusty quartz at this locality. Typical thin plates have been found with the quartz at Ellenville, New York, associated with chalcopyrite. Brookite is likely to be encountered in any anatase occurrence, as in Somerville, Massachusetts. Small crystals were in the "sand" in the bottom of an amethyst pocket near Butte, Montana.

TUNGSTITE $WO_3 \cdot H_2O$ (?)   Orthorhombic (?)
Environment: A secondary mineral, derived from the alteration of tungsten minerals.

Crystal description: Sometimes in small scaly crystals; more often a pulverulent yellow coating or film on other tungsten minerals.

Physical properties: Yellow-earth colors. *Hardness* $2\frac{1}{2}$; *gravity* 5.5 (?); *streak* yellow, powdery; *cleavage* 2 (usually not visible).

Composition: Probably a tungsten oxide with water; analyses have shown about 75% WO_3.

Tests: Infusible, but blackens before the blowpipe. Insoluble in acids.

Distinguishing characteristics: Could be mistaken for several other earth-yellow minerals like greenockite, uranium minerals, and limonite, but its insolubility and infusibility will distinguish it from them. Always associated with tungsten minerals, especially huebnerite and wolframite.

Occurrence: Tungstite is very closely associated with, and usually forms coatings on, wolframite and huebnerite. It sometimes colors scheelite yellow or greenish, and is a helpful guide in the recognition of tungsten deposits. Found near the surface wherever tungsten ores occur. Cornwall produced it at one time and more recently Bolivia has yielded some fine coatings. It can still be found at the old Trumbull occurrence in Connecticut, from which it was first described. Veins of huebnerite in North Carolina (Vance Co.) liberally showed coatings of tungstite. Fine examples come from the Spanish wolframite mines near Ciudad Rodrigo.

Interesting facts: Though a rare mineral of no commercial value because of its scarcity at most localities, it is important as a good guide to tungsten ore. This relationship is frequent in minerals and often requires the inclusion of some rare species even in a limited mineral list.

URANINITE UO_2 Cubic — hexoctahedral $\frac{4}{m}\overline{3}\frac{2}{m}$ **Pl. 17**

Environment: Pegmatites and medium-temperature veins.

Crystal description: Two types of this material are distinguished: crystals known as uraninite and a botryoidal variety with a radiating structure, known as pitchblende. The crystals are cubes, octahedrons, and dodecahedrons. The botryoidal type is more abundant, but found at fewer localities.

Physical properties: Steely to velvety or brownish black. *Luster* submetallic, pitchlike, greasy, or dull; *hardness* 5–6; *gravity* 6.4–9.7; *streak* brownish black, grayish, or olive-green; *fracture* conchoidal or uneven; *cleavage* none. Brittle; opaque.

Composition: Uranium dioxide; plus many other elements derived from the spontaneous breakdown of the uranium, the end-products of the series being helium and lead.

Tests: Infusible. Readily soluble in nitric and sulfuric acids, more slowly in hydrochloric. A drop of concentrated nitric acid left to dry on uraninite (free of calcite) evaporates to leave a fluorescent spot. The powder treated with a drop of nitric acid dries to a brilliantly fluorescent dot. Borax, sodium, and lithium fluoride beads are brilliantly fluorescent in ultraviolet light.

Distinguishing characteristics: Crystal form distinctive, but in rock it might be mistaken for microlite (which gives no fluorescent bead or test), magnetite (magnetic), and spinel (much lighter), among the cubic-system minerals. Other black minerals that might give trouble include tourmaline and cassiterite (light streak), columbite, tapiolite, and tantalite (no U test), and a whole series of dark, primary uranium-bearing minerals which would be hard to distinguish. Any one of the uranium minerals placed on a photographic film in the dark for about 24 hours would make self photographs.

Occurrence: Uraninite is a constituent of pegmatites; pitchblende is a vein mineral. The pegmatite occurrences are widespread but are economically of little importance. In these it is commonly altered to an orange and yellow, amorphous, greasy material (known as gummite) that sometimes surrounds a residual core of fresh black uraninite.

The important sources of uranium ore are the vein deposits, which have been subdivided into several types. Typical of the best are the silver-pitchblende veins of Jáchymov, Czechoslovakia, and Great Bear Lake, Northwest Territories.

Good crystals and dendrites, altered in part to gummite, have come from the American pegmatites in New England and North Carolina. An unusual calcite pegmatite at Wilberforce, Ontario, has provided the largest known crystals, some of which reach 3 in. (7.5 cm) on a cubic edge. Usually uraninite crystals are small.

Pitchblende in the U.S. has come only from Colorado, but rich, important veins are worked at Great Bear Lake in Canada.

Interesting facts: Once considered almost worthless, pitchblende came into economic consideration first as a source of radium; with the atomic age it became about the most sought-after mineral in the world. Small quantities of uranium are widely distributed. It has long been used as a measure of geologic time. Uranium atom after uranium atom transforms itself to lead, releasing helium. Now that the rate of radioactive decay is known, an analysis of the amount of lead or helium compared to the remaining uranium immediately gives the time that has elapsed since the mineral came into being in the place where it was found. The only weak point in these analyses, which give the earth an indicated age of at least 500,000,000 years, is an uncertainty about the possibility of a partial escape of some of the elements.

GUMMITE   U oxides, plus H_2O (?)   **Pl. 20**

Environment: Pegmatite veins and pitchblende deposits.

Crystal description: Appears amorphous and never in crystals, though under the microscope in crossed polarized light it is sometimes doubly refracting (and therefore must be crystallized).

Physical properties: Orange-red to grayish yellow. *Luster* greasy to waxy; *hardness* $2\frac{1}{2}$–5; *gravity* 3.9–6.4; *cleavage* none. Brittle. Not really a mineral but a mixture of several different uranium oxides, silicates, and salts.

Composition: Uranium oxides plus water, a stage in the alteration of uraninite by oxidation and hydration. All of the fission products of uranium — lead, radium, helium — are present, plus uranium and various impurities.

Tests: See uraninite (preceding); the fluorescence test of the evaporated nitric acid solution described there, is a new and good test for some uranium minerals. The fluorescent residue can be obtained with other minerals, so it only proves presence of uranium.

Distinguishing characteristics: Always in pseudomorphs after uraninite, and the primary mineral is often still present in part. Color and luster both typical and not likely to be confused with any other mineral. Usually not fluorescent (the yellow sometimes is), but will make self photographs on film.

Occurrence: A secondary mineral; a late stage in the alteration of uraninite by oxidation and hydration. It commonly forms attractive dendritic growths in feldspar, pseudomorphous after uraninite. An intermediate brown stage (noted at Spruce Pine, North Carolina) lies between the colorful gummite and the fresh black uraninite and is known as clarkeite. The whole series of minerals that make up these crusts of alteration are ill defined and need further study.

It is common in pegmatites at some localities, though unknown at others. Brilliant red-orange gummite has been found in Rajputana (now approximately Rajasthan and Ajmer) in India. It is one of the ores in Zaïre (Belgian Congo) and is found as a pseudomorph after pitchblende in Bohemia and Saxony. The bright orange part is principally curite (a lead uranate named for the discoverers of radium), together with becquerelite (a calcium uranate), and yellow soddyite (a hydrous uranium silicate). In the U.S. the best specimens are the large heavy masses found in North Carolina in Mitchell Co., and the brilliant dendrites of the Ruggles Mine at Grafton, New Hampshire. Not common in the weathered ores of Great Bear Lake, Northwest Territories. It is predominantly a denizen of pegmatites, since the uraninite from which it forms is a pegmatite mineral. Black nodules with colorful rims occur in India and Argentina (Angel Mine).

BRUCITE $Mg(OH)_2$ **Pl. 17**

Hexagonal — scalenohedral $\bar{3}\,\dfrac{2}{m}$

Environment: Veins in serpentine and magnesite and basic rocks.

Crystal description: Most often in free-standing but ill-defined poor crystal plates; also foliated, massive, and fibrous.

Physical properties: Pearly white to pale green, yellow, or blue. *Luster* pearly and waxy; *hardness* $2\frac{1}{2}$; *gravity* 2.4; *cleavage* micaceous. Plates flexible, nonelastic, and sectile; transparent. Fluoresces blue.

Composition: Magnesium hydroxide (69.0% MgO, 31.0% H_2O).

Tests: Infusible but glows brightly in the flame. Soluble in acids.

Distinguishing characteristics: Harder than talc but a little softer than mica. The less cleavable plates are inelastic. Gypsum is far less soluble in acids. The fluorescence is probably diagnostic in most cases.

Occurrence: Brucite is derived from the enclosing serpentine through alteration by hot watery solutions and is a common constituent of such hydrothermal veins in basic rocks. Also in flakes scattered through marbles, derived from periclase (MgO). The world's outstanding occurrences are American. Large crystals were found in the old Tilly Foster iron mine at Brewster, New York, and comparable specimens came from Texas, Lancaster Co., Pennsylvania, where crystals 7 in. (19 cm) across were found. Long fibers of brucite resembling asbestos are found in the Quebec asbestos mine at Asbestos. Light blue-green veins are occasionally intersected at the Gabbs (Nevada) magnesite mine.

MANGANITE MnO(OH) Monoclinic — prismatic $\dfrac{2}{m}$ **Pl. 17**

Environment: Veins and with manganese ores, forming at higher temperatures than the other manganese oxides.

Crystal description: Usually crystallized, often in well-developed striated prisms commonly terminated by a horizontal base (looks orthorhombic). May be large, an inch (3 cm) or more; often in closely grown crusts of small crystals.

Physical properties: Steel-gray to iron-black. *Luster* submetallic; *hardness* 4; *gravity* 4.2–4.4; *streak* reddish brown (nearly black); *fracture* uneven; *cleavage* perfect side, poor prismatic and basal. Brittle; translucent (red-brown) in very thin splinters.

Composition: Basic manganese oxide (62.4% Mn, 27.3% O, 10.3% H_2O).

Tests: Same as for pyrolusite (p. 118).

Distinguishing characteristics: Crystals resemble some entirely different minerals, like enargite and some black silicates, but can be distinguished from these by the blowpipe reactions, solubility and dark streak, and association with pyrolusite. The coarse crystals help to distinguish it from other Mn minerals, but X-ray tests are often necessary. Frequently alters to masses of parallel fibers of pyrolusite; hence, a paramorph.

Occurrence: Since manganite's associations often suggest the presence of low-temperature hot solutions, it is a somewhat different type of occurrence from that of the other secondary manganese minerals. Its associates, along with some other manganese minerals, are barite, calcite, and siderite. It is also found in secondary deposits, and consequently can be associated with pyrolusite, limonite, and psilomelane.

The best crystals are from a famous occurrence at Ilfeld in the German Harz mining district. Fine U.S. specimens have come from an iron mine at Negaunee, Michigan, where the crystals line cavities in the iron ore. It is not uncommon elsewhere but is difficult to recognize.

PSILOMELANE $(Ba,H_2O)_4Mn_{10}O_{20}$ Orthorhombic   **Pl. 17**
  Environment: Secondary manganese oxide deposits.
  Crystal description: Crystals not known; found in stalactitic, reniform, botryoidal, and mammillary masses and crusts, and may also be earthy.
  Physical properties: Iron-black to steel-gray. *Luster* dull to submetallic; *hardness* 5–6, but often very soft; *gravity* 3.3–4.7; *streak* black to brownish black; *fracture* smooth to conchoidal; *cleavage* none. Brittle to powdery.
  Composition: A basic oxide of barium with 2 valences of manganese (approximately 16% BaO, 80% MnO and MnO_2, and 4% H_2O, with various other impurities).
  Tests: Same as for pyrolusite (p. 118).
  Distinguishing characteristics: This is the usual name applied to the black, noncrystalline-looking manganese masses commonly found associated with more definitely crystallized pyrolusite and manganite.
  Occurrence: Like pyrolusite a purely secondary mineral. Formerly considered common, but current recognition that true psilomelane is a barium-bearing manganese oxide has reduced its abundance as a species and narrowed the field of occurrence. The presence of barium is difficult for the amateur to ascertain. "Wad" is the name given to an ill-defined group of hard amorphous-appearing manganese oxides with water. They are mixtures of the barium-bearing psilomelane with other related minerals.

BAUXITE $Al(OH)_3$ plus Al and H_2O Amorphous   **Pl. 17**
  Environment: Weathered surface deposits.
  Crystal description: Amorphous to microcrystalline. Usually

massive; sometimes in little spherical brown masses in matrix (pisolitic); more often like a hard clay. Diaspore sometimes makes fine light purple crystals at Chester, Massachusetts.

Physical properties: White to dark red-brown. *Luster* dull; *hardness* 1–3; *gravity* 2.0–2.5; *fracture* earthy.

Composition: "Bauxite" is a group term, like "limonite" and "gummite," widely accepted and used to describe a mixture of more or less hydrated aluminum oxides but now no longer used as a proper mineral name. The specific minerals are gibbsite [$Al(OH)_3$], boehmite [$AlO(OH)$], and diaspore ($HAlO_2$). In the common mixture any crystals will be microscopic and probably indistinguishable; thus the word is still useful.

Tests: Infusible and insoluble; is colored blue when moistened with cobalt nitrate and heated by the blowpipe flame.

Distinguishing characteristics: Much like a clay, though most bauxite is perhaps a little harder than the usual clays. Sometimes in nodules with sparkling shrinkage cavities lined with tiny crystals. The pisolitic types are easier to spot.

Occurrence: Bauxite is the chief ore of aluminum. It is a secondary mineral resulting from the leaching of silica from clay minerals, clayey limestones, or low-silica igneous rocks, commonly under conditions of tropical weathering. This explains the geographical distribution of aluminum ores, most of which are found in the tropics, and some of which are residual from earlier geological periods when climates were different. Abundant in Jamaica, in Brazil, Surinam, and French Guiana in South America, in Alabama, Georgia, and Arkansas in the U.S., and in France and Hungary in Europe.

GOETHITE $HFeO_2$ Pl. 17

Orthorhombic — Rhombic bipyramidal $\frac{2}{m} \frac{2}{m} \frac{2}{m}$

Environment: Secondary oxidized deposits, sometimes in low-temperature veins.

Crystal description: Small, black, shiny, equidimensional crystals rare. Commonly in slender flattened plates, velvety surfaces of needles, and occasionally in brilliant rosettes of radiating plates. Also fibrous-massive with reniform surfaces; compact or earthy.

Physical properties: Brilliant black to brownish black (crystals) to brown to yellow (fibrous varieties). *Luster* adamantine-metallic to silky; *hardness* 5–5½; *gravity* 3.3–4.3; *streak* brownish yellow to yellow; *fracture* uneven; *cleavage* side pinacoid. Brittle; translucent in thin splinters.

Composition: Hydrogen iron oxide (62.9% Fe, 27.0% O, 10.1% H_2O).

Tests: Gives off water in closed tube and turns to hematite. Practically infusible on charcoal, but becomes magnetic.

Distinguishing characteristics: Distinguished from hematite by its streak and from limonite by its structure (silky, fibrous, radiating). The magnetism after heating distinguishes it from most other similar minerals.

Occurrence: After hematite, goethite is the most important ore of iron. Many substances formerly regarded as limonite are now recognized as having a definite goethite structure. In veins it forms crystals in the late stages, and thus becomes an accessory mineral of ore deposits (fluorite, barite, and hematite). Also (and more important economically), it is a secondary mineral formed under weathering conditions from sulfides and siderite. It is deposited as "bog iron ore," and forms residual brown iron ores in the sw. U.S., in Missouri, and in Cuba.

Widespread in Germany, France, and England in crystallized specimens and often in pseudomorphs after pyrite crystals. In the U.S. the best specimens are the radiating terminated crystal clusters from the pegmatite pockets of the Florissant region, Colorado. Good fibrous specimens are found in the iron mines of Michigan and Minnesota. Often seen as tiny brownish tufts on and in quartz crystals, in drusy veins and quartz crystal-lined geodes.

LIMONITE $FeO(OH) \cdot nH_2O$ Amorphous   **Pl. 18**
Environment: Secondary deposits resulting from weathering.
Crystal description: Amorphous, in botryoidal and reniform crusts, stalactites; earthy and powdery. Without internal structure, most of the fibrous-looking material formerly called limonite is now considered goethite.
Physical properties: Brown-black to ocher-yellow. *Luster* glassy to dull; *hardness* to $5\frac{1}{2}$; *gravity* 2.7–4.3; *streak* brown to yellow; *fracture* conchoidal to earthy; *cleavage* none. Brittle.
Composition: Various hydrous ferric oxides; of indefinite composition.
Tests: Same as for goethite (preceding).
Distinguishing characteristics: It is essentially the same as goethite, but it does not show goethite's fibrous or silky appearance on a fresh break. Distinguished from its manganese counterpart, wad, by the streak, and the magnetism after heating.
Occurrence: Limonite is the coloring matter of soils, forming from iron minerals at surface temperatures as the rocks weather. It stains weathered rocks, forms dendrites on rock seams, and colors moss agates. Soluble in several acids; oxalic is one of the best for cleaning limonite-stained crystals. Alters to hematite quite easily through a loss of water. With slightly higher temperatures, soils are red not brown.

"Limonite" is a usefully ambiguous term, best retained for use when we are speaking of unidentified hydrous iron oxides or mixtures of several.

SPINEL MgAl₂O₄ Cubic — hexoctahedral $\frac{4}{m}\overline{3}\frac{2}{m}$ **Pl. 18**

Environment: Plutonic, pegmatitic, and metamorphic rocks.
Crystal description: In octahedrons, with cube and dodeca-hedron truncations rare. Often two halves are intergrown (twinned) with the second half rotated 180°, forming a flat triangle and having re-entrant angles beneath each of its corners. Also in irregular embedded grains, and coarsely granular.
Physical properties: Black, dark green, red, blue, violet, orange-brown, lilac, or white. *Luster* glassy: *hardness* 7½–8; *gravity* 3.5–4.1; *fracture* conchoidal; *cleavage* none, but poor octahedral parting. Brittle; transparent to opaque; red and lilac varieties fluorescent red or yellow-green.
Composition: Magnesium aluminum oxide (28.2% MgO, 71.8% Al₂O₃); but in this formula magnesium can be wholly or partly replaced by iron, zinc, or manganese, making a series of related minerals with different names. The zinc spinel (gahnite) is the commonest of these; hercynite, the iron spinel, and galax-ite, the manganese spinel, are rarer.
Tests: Infusible, insoluble.
Distinguishing characteristics: Usually distinguished by its crystal shape and hardness, and often by its color and twinning. Magnetite is magnetic, chromite is heavier, garnet is fusible, zircon and microlite are heavier.
Occurrence: Spinel, like corundum, is a mineral of meta-morphosed limestones and low-silica pegmatites, and con-sequently it is commonly associated with corundum. Sometimes forms a gemstone, but Sri Lanka (Ceylon) is almost the sole important source of gemmy material. Fine large black crystals have come from Madagascar.

The largest American crystals, which are over 4 in. (10 cm) on an edge, came from a lost locality near Amity, New York. Spinel is common in the metamorphosed limestones of the New York–New Jersey highlands belt, with corundum, diopside, graphite, chondrodite, and phlogopite. Fine blue crystals are found near Helena, Montana.

Gahnite, dark green zinc spinel, occurs with garnet at Charle-mont, Massachusetts, in good crystals decorated with triangular markings. Also found at Spruce Pine, North Carolina, where it sometimes forms transparent, bright green but very flat crys-tals in the mica plates. Gahnite is also found at Franklin, New Jersey.

Galaxite forms small black grains with garnets near Galax, in North Carolina, on Bald Knob.
Interesting facts: Red spinel, though little known, is a valua-ble jewelry stone, and was often confused with ruby. A famous crown jewel of Great Britain, the Black Prince's Ruby, is such a spinel.

MAGNETITE $FeFe_2O_4$ Pl. 18

Cubic — hexoctahedral $\frac{4}{m}\bar{3}\frac{2}{m}$

Environment: Plutonic, pegmatitic, and metamorphic rocks, and sands.

Crystal description: Usually in octahedrons, commonly striated with triangular markings on the octahedron faces. Dodecahedron modifications common. Since these faces are usually built up of heavy octahedron striations, the dodecahedron is striated lengthwise. Cubic faces rare; commonly massive or granular.

Physical properties: Black. *Luster* metallic; *hardness* 6; *gravity* 5.2; *streak* black; *fracture* subconchoidal to uneven; *cleavage* none, but sometimes an octahedral parting. Brittle; magnetic; sometimes a natural magnet (lodestone).

Composition: Ferrous and ferric iron oxide (72.4% Fe, 27.6% O); also written $FeO \cdot Fe_2O_3$. Other elements — magnesium, zinc, and manganese (rarely nickel) — can substitute in part for the first (the FeO, or ferrous) Fe, while small amounts of aluminum, chromium, manganic Mn, and vanadium can replace part of the second (the Fe_2O_3, or ferric) Fe. This permits a whole series of related minerals to which different names have been given, but magnetite is by far the most important.

Tests: Naturally magnetic; further tests unnecessary.

Distinguishing characteristics: The magnetism (and frequent polarity) distinguishes it from most other similar minerals. The streak is blacker than that of ilmenite; it is brittle and much lower in gravity than ferrian platinum or the native iron-nickel compounds. Zinc-rich magnetite (franklinite) is less magnetic.

Occurrence: An important ore of iron. A widespread accessory mineral forming small grains in igneous rocks, which, after weathering, are often concentrated into black beach sands (once used in the U.S. Senate as ink-blotting sand). Sometimes magnetite is concentrated by magmatic processes into solid ore deposits, rich enough to mine. In metamorphic rocks it may form fine crystals. Also found well crystallized in pegmatites and high-temperature veins.

A very common mineral, so widespread that only a few U.S. localities need be mentioned. Fine crystals have come from French Creek, Pennsylvania, from Port Henry and Brewster, New York, and from the zinc mines at Franklin, New Jersey (franklinite). It is embedded in chlorite schist at Chester, Vermont, with fine pyrite crystals. Good irregular lodestone masses are found at Magnet Cove, Arkansas, and good clusters of crystals occur in Millard Co., Utah. Crystals of magnetite may be several inches across, but most are smaller; an inch or so (2 or 3 cm) is the usual size. Pseudomorphs of hematite after magnetite are common. Many of the best clusters of magnetite crystals, like those from Pelican Point, Salt Lake, Utah, or Durango, Mexico, are now actually composed of hematite, give a red streak, and are only weakly magnetic. They are called martite.

Interesting facts: Early magnets were made by striking the iron with the natural lodestone magnet whose properties have intrigued men for generations. Like garnet and spinel, magnetite is often found in thin crystals in mica sheets and can be identified by its color (black and opaque usually, sometimes gray) and by regular partings parallel to the crystal outline which produce tiny cracks in the plate. A light viewed through such a crystal held close to the eye will appear to be surrounded by rays, resembling the asterism described under phlogopite (see p. 247).

CHROMITE $FeCr_2O_4$ Pl. 18

Cubic — hexoctahedral $\dfrac{4}{m}\,\overline{3}\,\dfrac{2}{m}$

Environment: Magmatic segregations and in basic rocks.

Crystal description: Octahedral crystals usually small and inconspicuous. Generally massive and granular.

Physical properties: Black. *Luster* submetallic; *hardness* $5\frac{1}{2}$; *gravity* 4.1–4.9; *streak* brown; *fracture* uneven; *cleavage* none. Brittle, sometimes slightly magnetic.

Composition: A ferrous chromic oxide (68.0% Cr_2O_3, 32.0% FeO).

Tests: Infusible on charcoal, but gives green color to cooled borax beads.

Distinguishing characteristics: Distinguished from magnetite by its weak magnetism and from spinel by its dark streak and lesser hardness. Commonly associated with green minerals (uvarovite garnet) and purple chlorite.

Occurrence: Chromite is the only ore of chromium, and a valuable refractory. Sometimes found as isolated crystals in veins in or scattered through serpentine; but the economically important occurrences are in podlike segregation lenses in altered basic rocks. It is also sparsely disseminated through basic rocks as an accessory mineral. Crystals almost 1 in. (2 cm) long have been found in Sierra Leone and lately in Brazil.

Minute crystals are found in the serpentines near New York City (Hoboken and Staten I.), in Maryland, and in pyrrhotite at Outokumpu, Finland, together with the rare (found only there) rhombohedral equivalent of hematite, eskolaite (Cr_2O_3). Small economically workable deposits have been found in Maryland, North Carolina, and California. The U.S.S.R., Africa, Turkey, Brazil, Cuba, and New Caledonia have commercially important deposits that can be worked for ore.

Interesting facts: Although today the U.S. produces very little chromite, for many years a mine in Maryland was the world's only producing locality. At that time it was used solely as a pigment and for tanning. To date there has been no such thing as a really good mineral specimen of chromite, relatively abundant though it is.

CHRYSOBERYL $BeAl_2O_4$ **Pl. 18**

Orthorhombic — Rhombic bipyramidal $\dfrac{2\ 2\ 2}{m\ m\ m}$

Environment: Pegmatite dikes.

Crystal description: Rare in simple orthorhombic crystals, elongated prismatically and tabular parallel to the b-axis. Commonly twinned, usually 2 in a flat wedge-shaped pair, showing a V marking on the broad face; but sometimes 3, intergrown to produce pseudohexagonal trillings.

Physical properties: Gray, greenish yellow, yellow, brown, blue-green (becoming violet-red in artificial light in the variety alexandrite). *Luster* glassy; *hardness* $8\frac{1}{2}$; *gravity* 3.5–3.8; *fracture* conchoidal to uneven; *cleavage* 3 fair and 1 easy parting along twin boundaries. Brittle; transparent; alexandrite is fluorescent red.

Composition: Oxide of beryllium and aluminum (19.8% BeO, 80.2% Al_2O_3).

Tests: Infusible, insoluble.

Distinguishing characteristics: Best distinguished by its extreme hardness, just beneath that of corundum. Always in crystals, usually embedded in mica, feldspar, or quartz, but breaking free and then showing the V striations on the broad face. Only beryl, with which it is often associated, presents a likely possibility for confusing the two, but chrysoberyl has a higher luster and is denser. Golden beryl loses its color on heating, chrysoberyl does not.

Occurrence: A relatively rare mineral, but one of considerable importance as a gem mineral. It can occur only in pegmatite dikes and (in U.S.S.R.) in the bordering schists. At Takowaja, U.S.S.R., it is associated with emerald and phenakite in 4 in. (10 cm), 6-sided flattened twins of the green variety, alexandrite. Larger but similar green-brown twins with deeper re-entrants are found in Brazil. It is also found in single crystals and in gemmy waterworn pebbles in Brazil and Sri Lanka (Ceylon). In Tanzania and at Carnaiba, Brazil, alexandrite-type trillings are associated with emerald in typical mica schist associations.

In the U.S., large 7 in, (18 cm) crystals in a pegmatite in Boulder Co., Colorado. In New England at several localities in Maine — especially Ragged Jack Mountain, Peru — and at

Haddam Neck, Connecticut. A few crystals were found in building excavations in New York City.

Interesting facts: Chrysoberyl frequently contains parallel, needlelike inclusions of microscopic size, which reflect a streak of light when such a stone is cut in a rounded shape. This is known as chatoyancy, and the resultant gemstone is known as a cat's-eye. Cat's-eyes come from Sri Lanka and Brazil; with alexandrites they make extremely expensive chrysoberyl gems. A bright yellow-green color is highly valued in the clear gem varieties.

MICROLITE $(Na,Ca)_2Ta_2O_6(O,OH,F)$ **Pl. 18**

Cubic — hexoctahedral $\dfrac{4}{m}\,\overline{3}\,\dfrac{2}{m}$

Environment: Pegmatite dikes and in small crystals disseminated throughout large calcite-rich intrusive masses only recently recognized as magmatic in origin and known as carbonatites.

Crystal description: Usually octahedral, commonly with corners modified. Pyrochlore crystals rarer and smaller than those of microlite. Also in earthy alterations of a light cream color.

Physical properties: Yellow, yellow-brown to almost greenblack. *Luster* resinous; *hardness* 5–5$\frac{1}{2}$; *gravity* 4.2–6.4; *streak* white, yellowish or brownish; *fracture* subconchoidal to uneven; *cleavage* none, but octahedral parting (often well developed). Brittle; translucent to transparent.

Composition: A complex oxide of tantalum (with some columbium), with sodium, calcium and oxygen, hydroxyl (OH), and fluorine. The columbium (niobium) equivalent is rare and known as pyrochlore $(NaCaCb_2O_6F)$, which gives its name to a mineral group, of which microlite is now considered only one member.

Tests: Usually infusible, sometimes can form with difficulty a slaggy mass. Insoluble in nitric and hydrochloric acids, but decomposes in strong sulfuric acid. Light brown crystals turn almost white after heating and then fluoresce red.

Distinguishing characteristics: Sometimes closely resembles other rare-earth minerals from which it is not easily differentiated. The crystals help when visible. Black varieties may resemble uraninite, but they are lower in density and only slightly radioactive; the green varieties resemble gahnite (spinel) but are denser. Specimens from the old known localities are easy to tell, but a new occurrence might be difficult to spot.

Occurrence: Microlite is sometimes an ore of tantalum. It was named for the small size of its original (Massachusetts) crystals, but subsequently crystals over 6 in. (15 cm) cross were found at Amelia, Virginia. It is quite common in the U.S. but rare in Europe. Good dark octahedral crystals are found in the New

England pegmatites (Portland and Haddam Neck, Connecticut, and in Maine). Large yellow-brown or green-brown crystals are common at the Rutherford and Morefield Mines, Amelia, Virginia. It has been mined in Dixon, New Mexico, where light yellow grains are disseminated through violet lepidolite, sometimes in considerable abundance. Green crystals were found at Topsham, Maine, and at Equador, near Parelhas in ne. Brazil. It is reported as a secondary mineral as an alteration product of simpsonite (AlTaO) in Australia, and of tantalite in Brazil.

COLUMBITE   (Fe,Mn)(Cb,Ta)$_2$O$_6$ ⎫
TANTALITE   (Fe,Mn)(Ta,Cb)$_2$O$_6$ ⎭   **Pl. 19**

Orthorhombic — Rhombic bipyramidal $\dfrac{2}{m}\dfrac{2}{m}\dfrac{2}{m}$

Environment: Pegmatite dikes.

Crystal description: Always in crystals or crystal aggregates. Sometimes in well-formed rectangular crystals ranging from very thin to almost equidimensional. Parallel ("graphic") growths in quartz or feldspar have been noted.

Physical properties: Black to red-brown and colorless. *Luster* submetallic to resinous; *hardness* 6; *gravity* 5.2–8.0; *streak* black to brown to white; *fracture* uneven; *cleavage* front and side pinacoid. Brittle; opaque to translucent or transparent.

Composition: The two names are applied to the end-members of a continuous mineral series ranging from an almost pure columbate (niobate) of iron and manganese to an almost pure tantalate of iron and manganese. The columbium (niobium) or tantalum oxide will range from 78% to 86%. Niobium (Nb) is the European equivalent of the American name, columbium.

Tests: Infusible and insoluble. Some varieties (Fe-rich) weakly magnetic.

Distinguishing characteristics: These are best recognized by the high gravity of the tantalum-rich varieties. The fracture faces are commonly iridescent, bluish. In their occurrence they can be confused with magnetite (but are less magnetic), with uraninite (but are not radioactive), with black tourmaline or cassiterite (but are higher in gravity), and wolframite (which has a more perfect cleavage). Columbite and tantalite are separated on the basis of density; tantalite begins about 6.6 specific gravity.

Occurrence: This pair is found only in pegmatites or in gravels derived from pegmatites. They are the chief ores of columbium and tantalum. The representative in some pegmatites will be high in Cb and in others it will be richer in Ta. Both minerals may be present in a single pegmatite when there is a long series of stages of rare mineral deposition. These are common and widespread minerals, found in commercial quantities in Africa,

Australia, and Brazil. In all of these localities they are also recovered from alluvial deposits, where they have been washed out of decomposing pegmatites. They are commonly associated with cassiterite and with rare-earth minerals.

Fine crystals, up to several inches in length, have been found in the New England pegmatites. Small manganotantalites or manganocolumbites are often associated with the secondary albite feldspar cleavelandite at such pegmatites as Newry, Maine, and Amelia, Virginia. This type is brown and translucent. A white bismuth and antimony-bearing variety, resembling cerussite in appearance, has been found in Brazil and Mozambique.

Fine crystals have been found in: North Carolina around Spruce Pine; New Mexico; the Black Hills, in heavy masses; and the Pikes Peak district of Colorado.

Interesting facts: Columbite often forms in parallel crystal growths with a related mineral, samarskite (next); the great resistance of columbite to alteration makes the columbite area look blacker and fresh on the brown weathered samarskite.

Particularly good examples of this association have come from the Divino de Ubá pegmatite in Minas Gerais, Brazil.

SAMARSKITE   Pl. 19
$(Y,Er,Ce,U,Ca,Fe,Pb,Th)(Cb,Ta,Ti,Sn)_2O_6$

Orthorhombic — Rhombic bipyramidal $\dfrac{2\ 2\ 2}{m\,m\,m}$

Environment: Pegmatite dikes.

Crystal description: Crystals usually embedded in rock and consequently difficult to see. Best obtained when weathered out. Usually prismatic, in quartz or feldspar, showing a rectangular cross section an inch or more (2 or 3 cm) across. Also massive and partly shattered.

Physical properties: Velvety black (on a fresh break). *Luster* vitreous to resinous; *hardness* 5-6; *gravity* 4.1-6.2; *streak* reddish brown to black; *fracture* conchoidal; *cleavage* 1 poor. Brittle; thin edges translucent.

Composition: An extremely complex mixture of rare-earth elements with columbium and tantalum oxide. The last two account for about half of the weight.

Tests: In closed tube it rapidly crumbles to black powder. Splinter edges usually split away, but if preheated in closed tube they will fuse to a black glass in the blowpipe. Gives fluorescent bead with sodium fluoride.

Distinguishing characteristics. Rather difficult to tell from related and associated species, but the fracture, color, and gravity mark it as one of the rare-earth group. More specific identification requires tests not practical to describe in a short *Field Guide.*

Occurrence: Like its rare-mineral associates, samarskite is exclusively a mineral of pegmatites, usually forming roughly crystallized shapes, with no free-growing faces. At the few localities where it is abundant, has some potential value as a source of the rare elements contained. Crumbles with weathering, so ordinarily not found in alluvial deposits.

Originally found in the Urals in a pegmatite rich in rare earths; later it also turned up in Norway and Sweden. The most abundant specimens have come from a weathered pegmatite very rich in rare-earth minerals at Divino de Ubá, Minas Gerais, Brazil, where it formed parallel growths of columbite associated with monazite and euxenite (another black lustrous mineral of about the same composition). Surface of these crystals coated with a yellow-brown oxidation film. Samarskite is not common in the U.S. It is found in Mitchell Co., North Carolina, in large, poorly formed crystals, and in small quantities in Maine, Connecticut, and Colorado.

The Halides

This is a group of soft minerals, many very soluble in water and some of them of considerable economic importance. The best known is common salt. Some, because of the ready solubility, are very rare; others, like salt, are so abundant that they are common despite their solubility. The water-soluble members of the group are easily recognized by their crystal form and taste. They can be confused only with a few water-soluble sulfates or the very rare nitrates, which will also taste when touched by the tongue but which are very different in crystal form. The water-insoluble ones discussed here crystallize (with but a few exceptions) in the cubic system, and the cube is the prevailing crystal form present.

HALITE   NaCl   Cubic — hexoctahedral $\frac{4}{m}\overline{3}\frac{2}{m}$ **Pl. 19**

Environment: Dried lakes in arid climates; sedimentary beds.
Crystal description: Commonly in cubic crystals, often distorted with hopperlike depressions in each cube face; also massive and granular, like marble; sometimes in large, cleavable, single crystal masses.
Physical properties: Colorless, white, sometimes reddish (from impurities) or blue (see **Interesting facts**). *Luster* glassy; *hardness* $2\frac{1}{2}$; *gravity* 2.1–2.6; *fracture* conchoidal; *cleavage* perfect cubic. Brittle; transparent; water-soluble, sometimes red fluorescent.
Composition: Sodium chloride (39.4% Na, 60.6% Cl).

Tests: Readily soluble in water; tastes salty. Colors flame yellow (sodium).

Distinguishing characteristics: The salty taste should be enough. Distinguished from other salty-tasting minerals by the sodium flame (sylvite is KCl) and from some water-soluble sulfates by the perfect cubic cleavage.

Occurrence: Halite sometimes forms white crusts around gas vents in volcanic regions; but the important occurrences that would classify it as a one-mineral rock are the sedimentary beds interstratified with other sediments, formed in ancient geological time by the evaporation of closed saltwater basins. These rock-salt strata are associated with gypsum and other sedimentary formations. Salt layers may flow under pressure and squeeze up through weak places, making pluglike formations of solid salt (salt "domes" of the Gulf Coast). Salt is recovered by mining, or by introducing water to dissolve the salt beds and pumping this brine up through wells from the depths.

Salt formations are worldwide. The best-known European deposits are at Stassfurt, East Germany, in Galicia, Poland, and in the Salzkammergut, Austrian Tyrol. In the U.S. halite is mined in New York State, Michigan, New Mexico, and Louisiana; and it is obtained as brine in New York State, Kansas, and elsewhere. Good crystals form on the surface of evaporating dry lakes, as at Great Salt Lake, Utah, and in Death Valley, California. A pink coloration in Searles Lake (California) halite crystals is owed to an algae that grows in brine.

Interesting facts: Halite (especially the Stassfurt and New Mexico occurrences) sometimes shows an intense blue to violet color, which forms clouds and irregular patches. This is thought to be attributable to free sodium, or colloidal sodium, combined with natural irradiation and some heat of burial. When such a specimen is dissolved in water, the solution remains colorless, and so is any salt that may be recrystallized from such a brine.

SYLVITE   KCl   Cubic — hexoctahedral $\frac{4}{m}\frac{-}{3}\frac{2}{m}$ **Pl. 20**

Environment: Sedimentary salt beds, volcanic fumaroles.

Crystal description: Like halite, but the cubes are much more frequently modified by octahedron faces, which may even be dominant. Like halite, massive and cleavable.

Physical properties: Same as halite in color and luster. *Hardness* 2; *gravity* 2.0; *fracture* conchoidal; *cleavage* cubic. Brittle; transparent; water-soluble.

Composition: Potassium chloride (52.4% K, 47.6% Cl). Some Na may be present.

Tests: More bitter taste than halite. When Na is not abundant the violet K flame is readily seen, but it may be masked by the Na.

Distinguishing characteristics: Distinguished from halite by the taste and the flame test. The crystals commonly show octahedral faces (rare in halite). In the mined occurrences, sylvite is frequently colored red by hematite inclusions, though there seems no genetic reason for it.

Occurrence: Sylvite forms layers like halite, but it is more soluble than that compound. Consequently the sylvite beds will usually lie above the halite in the sedimentary deposit series, since it is one of the last minerals to come out of an evaporating salt lake. It is much rarer than halite. Good specimens come from Stassfurt, East Germany, and from New Mexico.

Interesting facts: Both sylvite and halite are said to be very diathermanous, which means being transparent to heat waves, which act like light waves penetrating a transparent substance, passing easily through it without being absorbed and without warming the mineral itself. It is of economic importance as a major source of potash for fertilizer.

CERARGYRITE AgCl $\Big\}$
BROMYRITE AgBr $\qquad$ **Pl. 19**

Cubic — hexoctahedral $\dfrac{4}{m} \, \bar{3} \, \dfrac{2}{m}$

Environment: The weathered, secondary zone of ore deposits.

Crystal description: Cubic crystals fairly common, often embedded in white clayey material. Also in massive crusts, sometimes with a columnar structure.

Physical properties: Almost colorless to greenish gray or gray (darkening to violet-brown in light). *Luster* adamantine; *hardness* 1–1½; *gravity* 5.5; *fracture* conchoidal; *cleavage* none. Very sectile.

Composition: Silver chloride (60% to 75% Ag, the balance is Cl or Br in varying proportions, making a perfect series). Embolite [Ag(Cl,Br)], Pl. 19, is intermediate between the two end-members.

Tests: Fuse easily on charcoal, flattening out in a layer of silver. Gray mass then tested by its malleability or by solution in nitric acid, with a curdy precipitate forming on the addition of hydrochloric acid.

Distinguishing characteristics: Given the weight, waxy look, and high sectility, there are few minerals with which these could be confused other than the mercury chloride (calomel). The blowpipe production of the metallic silver settles that problem.

Occurrence: Cerargyrite and bromyrite are secondary silver minerals that form as a result of the surface oxidation of silver ores; most often in regions of deep weathering where there is an abundance of chlorine and bromine; and so in desert climates. Once an important ore of silver at some localities, as Leadville, Colorado; San Bernardino Co., California, and at Treasure Hill in Nevada. Important elsewhere in Mexico, Peru, and Chile. Like many minerals, these two practically exist only as relics of the past. There are no longer any unexploited ore veins near enough to the surface and rich enough to provide, ever again, good examples of these minerals. Yellow $\frac{1}{4}$ in. (6-7 mm) crystals can still be found in the unmined gossan at Broken Hill, New South Wales.

Interesting facts: The highly sectile character and waxy or hornlike appearance has given this mineral the popular name "horn silver." Specimens should be kept away from light to prevent their darkening.

SAL AMMONIAC NH_4Cl **Pl. 19**
Cubic — gyroidal (?) 4 3 2 (?)

Environment: Volcanic fumarole deposits.

Crystal description: Usually in octahedral, cubic, or dodecahedral crystals, or combinations of these faces. Also in fragile white crystalline crusts.

Physical properties: White to yellow. *Luster* glassy; *hardness* $1\frac{1}{2}$-2; *gravity* 1.5; *fracture* conchoidal; *cleavage* 1 poor. Brittle; transparent; water-soluble.

Composition: Ammonium chloride (33.7% NH_4, 66.3% Cl).

Tests: Volatilizes and sublimes on charcoal, and creeps up on walls of closed tube. Soluble in water, tastes bitter. Curdy white precipitate forms (proving Cl) when silver nitrate crystal is dropped in distilled water solution of sal ammoniac.

Distinguishing characteristics: Its manner of occurrence is typical; a test for chlorine and the volatility, together with the absence of sodium or potassium flame coloration, are usually sufficient.

Occurrence: Sal ammoniac is of very limited occurrence, since it is a mineral that characteristically forms only at gas vents around active volcanoes or at fissures on fresh lava flows. Ammonium chloride vapor is bluish; the mineral forms without a liquid stage as a sublimate around the orifices from which the gas is actually escaping, and usually at relatively high temperatures, possibly 400°-500°F (250°-300°C). Vesuvius is one of the oldest and most productive localities, but fine crystals, up to $\frac{3}{8}$ in. (1 cm) across formed during the eruption of Paricutín in Mexico in the mid-40s. Crusts of free-standing crystals were particularly characteristic of the early stages of a cycle of activity, when gas was abundant.

Interesting facts: Sal ammoniac is made artificially as a vapor by blowing ammonia fumes across hydrochloric acid, and this method is often used to make a dull white coating on objects to be photographed.

It is so soluble in water that it will only be found on hot lava rocks immediately after its formation, before rain has a chance to wet the matrix and dissolve it.

CALOMEL HgCl   Pl. 21

Tetragonal — Ditetragonal bipyramidal $\dfrac{4}{m}\dfrac{2}{m}\dfrac{2}{m}$

Environment: Mercury deposits.

Crystal description: Usually in crystals, often minute and coating other minerals. Most often tabular, sometimes pyramidal. Commonly in skeletal parallel growths rather than good individual crystals.

Physical properties: White, grayish, or yellowish (darkening on exposure to light). *Luster* adamantine; *hardness* 1–2; *gravity* 6.5; *fracture* conchoidal; *cleavage* 2 (1 good). Sectile; translucent; fluorescent red.

Composition: Mercurous chloride (85.0% Hg, 15.0% Cl).

Tests: Completely volatilizes on charcoal, without melting.

Distinguishing characteristics: The sectile character and the adamantine luster distinguish it from everything but the silver halides. Silver minerals fume and melt but do not volatilize completely on the charcoal, leaving instead a flattened silver residue. In an Hg association the fluorescence is significant.

Occurrence: A relatively rare mineral, associated with other mercury minerals, probably always secondary and late in the mineral sequence. It will be found in small brilliant crystals in cavities, associated with cinnabar and often perched on crystals of that mercury ore. Found in U.S. at Terlingua, Texas, and near Murfreesboro, Arkansas; in Europe, at various cinnabar localities.

Related species: Nantokite (CuCl; copper chloride) and almost as rare marshite (CuI; copper iodide) are the only colorless or white copper minerals. Both are tetrahedral. Marshite forms triangular lustrous tetrahedral crystals at Chuquicamata, Chile, and was formerly found at Broken Hill, New South Wales. Near Chuquicamata in a new mine tunnel orange incrustations of marshite, catalyzed by iron rails and bolts, are forming from the drainage waters.

Marshite is colorless to pale yellow when fresh, as a rule, but seems to turn coppery on exposure to light and air. Iodine vapors emanate when a sealed marshite container is opened, and can be smelled; perhaps free copper remains to give the color noted in older exposed specimens.

FLUORITE CaF$_2$ Cubic — hexoctahedral $\dfrac{4}{m}\bar{3}\dfrac{2}{m}$ Pl. 20

Environment: Sedimentary rocks, ore veins, and pegmatites.

Crystal description: Most commonly in cubes, less often in octahedrons, occasionally in complex combinations. Sometimes forms twin intergrowths with a second individual, whose corners project from each cube face (Fig. 25, p. 49). Also massive and fine-grained.

Physical properties: Colorless, black, white, brown, and all spectral and pastel intermediates. *Luster* glassy; *hardness* 4; *gravity* 3.0–3.3; *fracture* conchoidal; *cleavage* perfect octahedral. Brittle; transparent; thermoluminescent and often fluorescent.

Composition: Calcium fluoride (51.1% Ca, 48.9% F).

Tests: In closed tube or test tube, often becomes phosphorescent on light heating (this thermoluminescence must be observed in the dark). Fuses on charcoal with a little difficulty. Powder mixed with sulfuric acid and boiled in glass test tube etches (frosts) the glass surface to just above the solution.

Distinguishing characteristics: The perfect cleavage and the hardness are distinctive. Often fluorescent (usually blue) under ultraviolet light. Harder than calcite, and commonly more attractively colored (and does not bubble when a drop of hydrochloric acid is placed on it). Much softer than quartz. Its powder does not dissolve in nitric acid, as apatite's does.

Occurrence: A common vein or gangue mineral, and often accompanies the ore minerals. It frequently forms in low-temperature deposits; its crystals are often found in cavities in sedimentary rocks. The crystal shape (habit) is influenced by the temperature of formation. Octahedral and complex crystals are usually considered characteristic of high-temperature fluorite; cubic crystals prove a low-temperature occurrence. The important and commercial deposits are mainly low-temperature ones; the octahedral high-temperature Alpine crevice and pegmatite occurrences are seldom of economic importance. Fluorite is used as a source of fluorine for hydrofluoric acid, for the manufacture of milk glass, as a flux for the steel industry, and in the refining of aluminum.

It is one of the most popular minerals among collectors because of the beauty of specimens. Widespread in occurrence. The most attractive examples are the very fluorescent cubic crystals from Cumberland, England. Cornwall crystals are often more complex and have greater interest; Germany produces several types of crystals, including vein material of both cubic and octahedral habit. Pink Göschenen (Switzerland) octahedrons are greatly sought after. The octahedral face is usually dull, the cubes are often very shiny. Dodecahedral edge truncations on deep purple cubes characterize the La Collada (Asturias, Spain) fluorites.

Fluorite is an abundant and important economic mineral in the U.S. in the Illinois-Kentucky field (cubic crystals in sedimentary beds and veins), at Westmoreland, New Hampshire (beautiful green octahedrons), and in New Mexico (pale blue cubes), to mention a few localities. Common in limestone pockets in the Midwest, as at Clay Center, Ohio (brown crystals fluorescing yellowish). Mexico has become the leading producer. Músquis, in Coahuila, has fine light purple specimens. At Naica, it is a gangue mineral, but the exquisite modifications on the light-hued crystals make them the modern equivalents of the 19th-century Cornwall crystals.

Interesting facts: "Fluorine" and "fluorescence" are two words derived from the name of this mineral. The brilliant colors of some fluorites are attributed to hydrocarbons; they can be removed by heat. Only the softness prevents widespread use for jewelry. The Chinese make many fluorite carvings, which are marketed under the misleading name of "green quartz." Transparent colorless pieces have great value in the manufacture of optics, for which purpose it is now crystallized synthetically.

ATACAMITE $Cu_2Cl(OH)_3$ **Pl. 20**

Orthorhombic — bipyramidal $\dfrac{2}{m}\dfrac{2}{m}\dfrac{2}{m}$

Environment: Weathered, secondary ore deposits in dry climates.

Crystal description: Usually in small thin prisms. Sometimes in tabular form, when it resembles brochantite or antlerite; also fibrous, massive, granular, and as sand.

Physical properties: Deep emerald-green. *Luster* glassy; *hardness* 3–3½; *gravity* 3.8; *fracture* conchoidal; *cleavage* side pinacoid. Brittle; transparent.

Composition: Basic copper chloride (74.3% Cu, 13.0% Cl, 12.7% H_2O).

Tests: Fuses easily, giving continuously a bright blue flame like that normally seen briefly after a touch of hydrochloric acid. Will finally yield copper bead. Easily soluble to a green solution in nitric acid and gives Cl test (with silver nitrate), leaving a blue solution above the white precipitate.

Distinguishing characteristics: Resembles malachite (but in dissolving does not effervesce) and some copper phosphates and sulfates (which do not so readily give the blue copper flame without HCl, nor do they give a Cl test).

Occurrence: A rare copper mineral of wholly secondary origin; results from the alteration, usually under arid conditions, of copper sulfide minerals through weathering. Common under the extreme conditions of continuous dryness of the South American west coast in Chile (the Atacama Desert). The best crystals, nevertheless, came from South Australia. Small needles have been found at Vesuvius in a fumarole deposit. The U.S. has produced a few examples at several western localities — including San Manuel, Arizona — but it is probably often unrecognized, being confused with similar-appearing and commoner minerals. Among the popular minerals sought by competitive collectors, good examples are likely to be high-priced.

Interesting facts: In South America it is a copper ore when mined with other copper-bearing minerals. Once in demand as a sand for ink-drying (before we used blotters); the supplies for this were commonly imported by the British from Chile.

CRYOLITE Na_3AlF_6 Monoclinic — prismatic $\dfrac{2}{m}$ **Pl. 21**

Environment: Pegmatite dikes.

Crystal description: The monoclinic crystals are usually in subparallel growths on a solid cryolite surface (this is practically a one-locality mineral) and look like cubes, sometimes with apparent octahedral truncations. Also massive.

Physical properties: White or colorless. *Luster* glassy or greasy; *hardness* $2\frac{1}{2}$; *gravity* 2.9–3.0; *fracture* uneven; *cleavage* none, but pseudocubic partings. Brittle; translucent.

Composition: Fluoride of sodium and aluminum (32.8% Na, 12.8% Al, 54.4% F).

Tests: Fuses very easily on charcoal with a yellow (sodium) coloration of the flame. Bead that forms is clear when hot, white when cold, and fluoresces blue-green in shortwave ultraviolet light.

Distinguishing characteristics: Specimens of the one important locality should be easily recognized. Failing that, the fusion test is sufficient.

Occurrence: A strange mineral, and surprisingly uncommon in nature. The only important locality was a unique now worked-out pegmatite in Greenland, where the cryolite formed great solid masses, sometimes with fissures lined with crystals of cryolite or of some other related mineral. Embedded in it, and common in cryolite specimens, are chalcopyrite, siderite, and galena. It was mined for use as the solvent of bauxite aluminum ore, for the electrolytic recovery of aluminum. The U.S. occurrence in Creede, Colorado, is of little importance. Cryolite is made artificially from fluorite for the same use.

Interesting facts: This mineral has a very low ability to bend light (refraction); it is close to water in that respect. Consequently, cryolite powder put in water comes so close to the liquid in its refraction of light that the powder becomes almost invisible.

The Carbonates

These constitute an important and abundant group. Good examples are common and many are of considerable economic importance. One member of the group, calcite, is sufficiently abundant to fulfill that part of a rock definition which says it must "constitute an important part of the earth's crust." Carbonates form in various ways: as primary minerals, separating both from hot solutions freshly springing from inside the earth, and from cold solutions on the surface, near the surface, or from the very ocean itself. The carbon dioxide (CO_2) of the air combines with water (H_2O) to form a mild acid — carbonic acid (H_2CO_3) — which attacks the surface minerals. Some of the elements dissolve, often to reappear in a solid form as carbonates. This corrosion by carbonic acid is one of the principle mechanisms in the chemical weathering of rocks. The same attacker alters many of the metal ores, the sulfides, when they are exposed at the surface. When such ore deposits are in rocks that are predominantly carbonates like limestones (calcium carbonate), we often find the metals concentrated and immobilized as carbonates in the upper, weathered, ore zones.

There are two great crystallographically alike groups in the carbonates, in which several elements can mutually replace each other to yield two series of minerals whose precise identification may be difficult. One compound, calcium carbonate, is common to both, but otherwise the two series do not overlap. The first series, with rhombohedral crystals, is known as the calcite group, and the second, with orthorhombic crystals, as the aragonite group. Although their structures are different, they have some properties in common.

All of the carbonates are soft, all of them are light-colored and translucent to transparent, all are soluble in acid (some dissolve more easily than others) as bubbles of CO_2 escape. They are predominantly, but not exclusively, secondary in origin.

Calcite Group

The compositions of this group have been depicted with a triangle, the corners of which were labeled respectively $CaCO_3$ (calcite), $MgCO_3$ (magnesite), and $FeCO_3$ (siderite). Mineral names have sometimes been given to intermediate members of the group, as will be seen. Pure calcium, iron, or magnesium carbonates are uncommon, but we can usually say that a specimen has predominantly one or another composition and therefore give it a name which is close enough. However, in recent years analyses have shown that all possible combinations of these elements with manganese, zinc, and cobalt cannot exist in nature, and the old simple explanation is no longer accurate. Although the elements can replace each other to a limited extent, it would be misleading to illustrate them with a triangular diagram, implying that any area of the triangle might be occupied by an example. Some writers call the entire group either calcite or brownspar, including

in the latter magnesite, siderite, rhodochrosite, and smithsonite.
All of the members of this group belong to the rhombohedral
division of the hexagonal system, and have excellent rhombohedral cleavage. Crystals and crystalline masses are common.
All have strong double refraction (best shown by the doubling
of lines or dots seen through a clear cleavage of "Iceland spar"
calcite). And of course all dissolve in hydrochloric acid, which
sometimes must be heated, with the release of bubbles (CO_2 gas).

CALCITE $CaCO_3$ **Pls. 21, 22**

Hexagonal — Hexagonal scalenohedral $\bar{3}\frac{2}{m}$

Environment: All types of occurrences and with all classes of
rocks.

Crystal description: Often crystallized, extremely varied in
appearance, from tabular (rare) to prismatic or needlelike.
Scalenohedrons and rhombohedrons commonest. Also microcrystalline to coarse.

Physical properties: Colorless, white, pale tints. *Luster*
glassy; *hardness* 3 (cleavage face); *gravity* 2.7; *fracture* conchoidal; *cleavage* rhombohedral. Brittle; transparent to translucent; often fluorescent, red, pink, yellow; phosphorescent,
briefly orange-red at Franklin, New Jersey; also persistent blue.
Sometimes thermoluminescent.

Composition: Calcium carbonate (56.0% CaO, 44.0% CO_2; Mn,
Fe, and Mg may partially replace Ca).

Tests: Easily scratched; dissolves in cold dilute hydrochloric
acid with effervescence. (Simply place drop of acid on specimen,
avoiding good crystal faces, since the acid destroys the lustrous
surface.)

Distinguishing characteristics: The bubbles in acid distinguish it from all other minerals with prominent cleavages, even
the other carbonates (which do not dissolve quite so readily in
cold acid). Aragonite dissolves as easily, but has a different
crystal form and no cleavage. When heated, aragonite crumbles
to powder and loses its fluorescence. Even when not previously
fluorescent, calcite usually becomes so after heating.

Occurrence: One of the commonest of minerals, forming in
veins as a gangue mineral, precipitating from seawater to build
up limestones, and secondarily from solution and redeposition
in limestones and other rocks. Localities are far too numerous
to list; crystals may be flat plates 1 ft. (30 cm) across (Palm
Wash, California), steep golden scalenohedrons 2 ft. (61 cm) long
(Missouri-Kansas-Oklahoma lead district), or transparent
masses a foot (30 cm) through (Iceland — the original Iceland
spar). Marble, cave formations, travertine, and onyx are all
calcite varieties. Oolitic calcite sand forms on the shores of
Great Salt Lake.

Interesting facts: Calcite is frequently fluorescent; a small amount of manganese is enough to make it glow red under some wavelengths of ultraviolet light. Flawless transparent calcite is used in optical instruments, especially in geological (polarizing) microscopes. Calcite has a well-developed gliding plane — a knife edge can be pressed into the obtuse recessed edge of the cleavage rhomb and a section will glide forward to create the effect of a twin crystal. This is easy only with the clear Iceland spar, or optical type. Most calcite is white, though various impurities may tint it almost any color, even black. Since it is a common late-vein mineral, the removal of calcite by dissolving it away with a weak acid (hydrochloric or acetic — used very weak to avoid damaging anything else) often exposes well-formed crystals of other minerals.

Calcite is much softer on the base than on its cleavage face. Though it is No. 3 on the Mohs scale, it can be scratched with the fingernail on the basal plane (about $2\frac{1}{2}$). The hardness of 3 is found on the rhombohedron cleavage face.

MAGNESITE $MgCO_3$ **Pl. 21**

Hexagonal — Hexagonal scalenohedral $\overline{3}\frac{2}{m}$

Environment: Associated with serpentine and in sedimentary beds.

Crystal description: Usually in dull white microcrystalline masses. Has been described in small prismatic needles but has now been found in large transparent Iceland-spar-like crystals and cleavages. Also coarsely granular, like a marble.

Physical properties: White, colorless, light tints. *Luster* glassy to dull; *hardness* $3\frac{1}{2}$–5; *gravity* 3.0–3.2; *fracture* conchoidal to smooth; *cleavage* rhombohedral. Brittle; transparent to translucent.

Composition: Magnesium carbonate (47.6% MgO, 52.4% CO_2), often with some iron and calcium.

Tests: The tongue adheres to the porcelaneous material. Dissolves with bubbles in hot hydrochloric acid.

Distinguishing characteristics: The white, dull, fine-grained porcelaneous masses can be identified by their behavior in acid. Both the marble-grained and the recently discovered transparent rhombs can be confused with calcite or dolomite but are heavier and make no response to cold hydrochloric acid.

Occurrence: Usually results from a hot-water (hydrothermal) alteration of serpentine, which creates solid white veins in the parent rock. Small free-growing crystals were found in serpentine fissures on Staten I., New York. Huge quantities of the dull white material have been mined as sources of magnesia and magnesium in Washington and California. Good crystals have been found associated with strontianite and dolomite at Oberndorf, Styria (Austria), in a magnesite quarry.

Currently a marble-like variety with very coarse grain is being exploited in Brazil. This deposit is the source of large Iceland-spar-like crystals and cleavages occurring in cavities in the bed with quartz and other minerals. This stratified deposit probably represents a final stage in a magnesia-enrichment process that takes place in nature, changing limestones into dolomites.

SIDERITE $FeCO_3$ **Pl. 21**

Hexagonal — Hexagonal scalenohedral $\overline{3}\,\dfrac{2}{m}$

Environment: Sedimentary formations, ore veins, and pegmatites.

Crystal description: Most commonly in rhombohedrons, often very acute, sometimes in scalenohedrons. Massive, in granular, crystalline cleavable aggregates, and earthy. Sometimes in fibrous radial knobs (sphaerosiderite) and in saddle-shaped rhombohedrons like dolomite.

Physical properties: Brown, white to gray. *Luster* vitreous to pearly; *hardness* $3\frac{1}{2}$-4; *gravity* 3.8-3.9; *fracture* conchoidal; *cleavage* rhombohedral. Brittle; transparent to translucent.

Composition: Iron carbonate (62.1% FeO, 37.9% CO_2), usually with some magnesium and calcium replacing part of the iron.

Tests: Fragments become magnetic after being heated on charcoal, and dissolve in hot acid with effervescence.

Distinguishing characteristics: Ease of scratching and the cleavage show it to be a carbonate; and usually the brown color, which is often only a thin surface layer, suggests iron carbonate. The magnetism after heating is then sufficient.

Occurrence: Very common in low- and medium-temperature ore veins, in which it is often associated with calcite, barite, and the sulfides. Also characteristic of sedimentary rocks, where it frequently forms concretionary masses ("clay ironstone"). Sometimes used as an ore of iron (France and Germany). Also in pegmatites associated with phosphates.

Some of the best crystals are from the Cornwall mines, where they show quite a variety of forms. Allevard, France, and Erzberg, Styria (Austria), are notable as a source of clusters of crystals. Panasqueira, Portugal, and the Morro Velho mine at Nova Lima, Minas Gerais, are also outstanding sources of specimen crystals. Large brown embedded cleavages are associated with the Greenland cryolite. At many localities in the U.S., including the old mines at Roxbury, Connecticut (where it forms great cleavable masses and free crystals, often altered to limonite), in Vermont, in New York State, in New England pegmatites, and in good crystals in Colorado in ore veins. As a rule siderite crystals are not large, but very large, if dull, crystals have lately been found at St. Hilaire, near Montreal, Quebec. To date, there is really no outstanding U.S. occurrence.

Interesting facts: It is not surprising that siderite, since easily altered, is commonly changed to limonite pseudomorphs which preserve the original shape of the crystal.

RHODOCHROSITE $MnCO_3$ Pl. 22

Hexagonal — Hexagonal scalenohedral $\overline{3}\frac{2}{m}$

Environment: Ore veins and metamorphic manganese deposits.

Crystal description: Most often in rhombohedrons (sometimes very steep), and also in scalenohedrons. Granular, massive, and in rounded spherical and botryoidal crusts.

Physical properties: Deep rose-pink to pale pink, gray, or brown. *Luster* vitreous to pearly; *hardness* $3\frac{1}{2}$–4; *gravity* 3.4–3.6; *fracture* conchoidal; *cleavage* perfect rhombohedral. Brittle; transparent to translucent.

Composition: Manganese carbonate (61.7% MnO, 38.3% CO_2; with any or all of the following present: iron, calcium, magnesium, zinc, and cobalt).

Tests: Dissolves slowly in cold and rapidly in warm hydrochloric acid with effervescence. Powder colors borax bead violet in oxidizing flame (test for Mn).

Distinguishing characteristics: The cleavage and hardness (and acid test) show it to be a carbonate of this group. The borax bead test shows it to be a manganese mineral and eliminates about everything else. Pink color the best guide.

Occurrence: Rhodochrosite is usually a gangue mineral of copper and lead ore veins, but sometimes it occurs, like siderite, in pegmatites. At Butte, Montana, it was an ore of manganese. Commonly alters to black manganese oxides on weathering, and the black stains are very apparent on the containing rocks. Good specimens not common. Fine crystals have come from several mines in Colorado, where it forms deep pink rhombohedral crystals up to several inches (10 cm) across, associated with pyrite, fluorite, quartz, and ore sulfides. Butte produces rhombohedral and scalenohedral crystals to 1 in. (2.5 cm) as well as solid cleavable and granular masses, always paler than the Colorado material, of a milky-pink color. Pegmatite rhodochrosite is often grayish or brownish. Botryoidal masses and scalenohedral crystals — secondary in character, for they incrust limonite — have come from Germany (where it has been called *Himbeerspat,* or "raspberry spar"). "Rosinca" is a name applied to an Argentine occurrence of pink crusts used for decorative purposes. Good but often thinly quartz-coated crystals have come from Cananea, Mexico. Hotazell, South Africa, has produced some gemmy $\frac{1}{2}$–$\frac{3}{4}$ in. (1–2 cm) crystals of unusual quality which can perhaps be regarded as the most spectacular specimens for collectors.

SMITHSONITE $ZnCO_3$ Pl. 22

Hexagonal — Hexagonal scalenohedral $\overline{3} \dfrac{2}{m}$

Environment: Secondary (weathered) zone of zinc ore deposits.

Crystal description: Crystals normally indistinct and rounded, usually dull, rounded rhombohedrons, sometimes rounded scalenohedrons. Also thick radiating botryoidal and mammillary crusts, with a crystalline surface (usually blue), brown dull crusts, and earthy masses ("dry-bone ore"). Larger, steep rhombohedral, and almost gemmy crystals have lately been turning up in Africa.

Physical properties: White, yellow (from Cd), greenish or bluish (from Cu), or pink (from Co). *Luster* subadamantine to vitreous; *hardness* 5; *gravity* 4.3–4.4; *fracture* conchoidal; *cleavage* rhombohedral, often curving spherically. Brittle; translucent.

Composition: Zinc carbonate (64.8% ZnO, 35.2% CO_2), usually with some of the Zn replaced by Fe, Mg, and Ca; Cd, Cu, and Co may be present.

Tests: Only good test is in closed tube, when the white material is coated with film that is yellow when hot and white when cold. Grain heated on charcoal, touched with cobalt nitrate and reheated, gives good green (Zn) color.

Distinguishing characteristics: Cleavages and crystal shape show it to be a carbonate, as does its bubbling in hot hydrochloric acid. The hardness is unusual for a carbonate, and the gravity is high. Crusts sometimes resemble prehnite, which is harder and does not dissolve in acid. Might also be confused with chrysocolla-stained (but much harder) quartz, or hemimorphite crusts (Sardinia and Mexico).

Occurrence: In its best development, a mineral of dry climates formed in limestone regions from primary zinc sulfides by weathering. Sometimes an important ore of zinc, as at Leadville, Colorado, where its ore value was overlooked for years.

The most beautiful solid specimens are the thick blue-green crusts from the Kelly Mine, Magdalena, New Mexico. This material was once marketed for a jewelry stone under the name "bonamite." Similar but thinner crusts were found in Lavrion, Greece, and in the Barranca de Cobre, Mexico, where some are pink. Large pale pink, green, and blue crystals are common only at Tsumeb, South West Africa, but only white ones have flat faces. The largest single crystals are those of the Broken Hill Mine in Zambia. Steep, to 2 in. (3–5 cm), clear yellow rhombohedrons. Yellow, greenockite-stained "turkey-fat ore" crusts and stalactites come from Arkansas and Sardinia. Most common type is the hard, porous, dull, bonelike mass known as "dry-bone ore."

Plates

Plate 1

COMMON ROCKS

(hand specimens)

These examples are trimmed into the 3 × 4 × 1½ in. (7 × 10 × 4 cm) pillow outlines considered most convenient for student use.

1. Granite   p. 17
   San Diego County, California

2. Gabbro   p. 18
   San Diego County, California

3. Granitic gneiss   p. 22
   San Diego County, California

4. Sandstone   p. 19
   Santa Barbara County, California

5. Dolomitic marble   p. 22
   Placer County, California

6. Limestone   p. 20
   Santa Barbara County, California

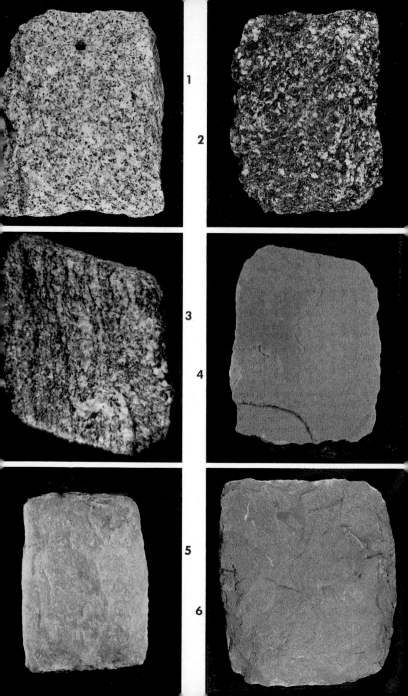

Plate 2

COMMON ROCKS

(close-up view to show life-size grains)

1. Granite   p. 17
   Quartz (white), orthoclase
   feldspar (pink), and mica
   (silvery gray) are combined
   in this typical example.
   Westerly, Rhode Island

2. Gabbro   p. 18
   Black pyroxene and white
   albite feldspar compose
   this rock.
   *Salem Neck, Salem, Mas-
   sachusetts*

3. Gneiss with feldspar   p. 22
   "eye"
   Almost granite-like, the
   streaked mineral pattern
   shows this to be a metamorphic rock.
   *Westchester County, New
   York*

4. Red sandstone   p. 19
   The weakly cemented sand
   grains are principally
   quartz, stained and cemented with iron oxide.
   *East Longmeadow, Massa-
   chusetts*

5. Marble: dolomitic   p. 22
   Recrystallized by heat and
   pressure, the grains of this
   marble are relatively
   coarse and the stone can be
   polished for decorative use.
   The Bronx, New York City

6. Limestone with   p. 20
   fossils
   Fine-grained deep-sea sediments commonly preserve
   the shapes of prehistoric
   life forms.
   Near Cincinnati, Ohio

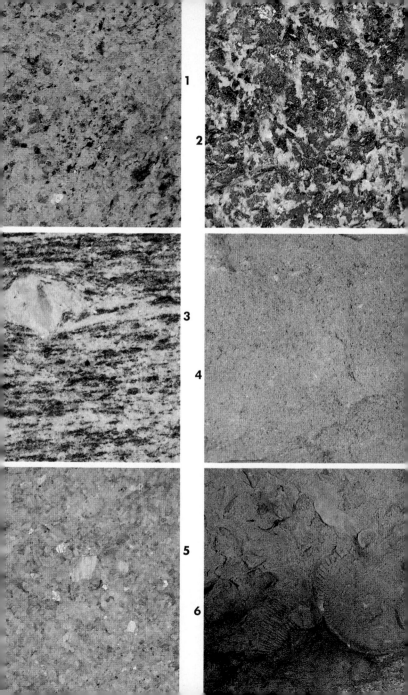

Plate 3

IGNEOUS AND PLUTONIC ROCKS

(hand specimens)

1. Rhyolite   p. 15
This example shows clearly the flow lines that are sometimes characteristic of this fine-grained volcanic rock. It probably flowed sluggishly and was rather thick and viscous.
Colorado

2. Obsidian   p. 14
The shelly fracture and vitreous luster of this black natural glass may be seen in this example, along with a few streaks of lava that had begun to crystallize into a fine-grained rock.
Wyoming

3. Porphyry   p. 16
An early growth of coarse feldspar crystals while the magma was still underground is revealed by the texture of this rock, in which we see the feldspar blades embedded in a dark, fine-grained mass.
Colorado

4. Diabase   p. 16
It is difficult to see the whole mass of elongated feldspar crystals making this dark rock a diabase. They suggest that in this type of rock the feldspars start to form early, before the darker minerals, a reverse of the usual situation.
Minnesota

5. Syenite   p. 17
The light-colored rock consists mainly of potash feldspar, without the quartz grains that would make it a granite. Some syenites are very dark, but all show less mottling than the granites they resemble.
Ontario

6. Basalt   p. 16
It is easy to see how this dike of basalt squeezed its way in between the walls of coarse granitic rock long after that was cool and probably many geological periods later.
Minnesota

Plate 4

PLUTONIC AND SEDIMENTARY ROCKS

(hand specimens)

1. Diorite   p. 17
The darker color, yet granitic look and texture of diorite is well shown in this example. The dark minerals form a greater total of the whole.
Massachusetts

2. Peridotite   p. 18
Olivine-rich rocks are seldom fresh and unaltered; hence, they are not as dark as one would expect. "Blueground" looks very light indeed at the African diamond mines, because the dark minerals are mainly changed to serpentine, which is much lighter in color.
Quebec

3. Nepheline syenite   p. 17
Although it contains no quartz, most rocks of nepheline syenite are very pale in color, for both the feldspar and the nepheline are often white. Almost pure white examples have been used in glassmaking.
Ontario

4. Conglomerate   p. 19
The rounded pebbles to be found in a darker mass of sand and gravel give this stone its common name "puddingstone."
Massachusetts

5. Sandstone   p. 19
Coarse or fine sand cemented together but showing easy fracture around the grains and usually along definite beds makes sandstone one of the easiest rocks to identify. Fine-grained volcanics sometimes resemble it, but if one is out collecting it will be evident whether the area is sedimentary or igneous.
Connecticut

6. Limestone   p. 20
Limestone varies greatly, from soft, poorly compacted masses filled with fossils and some mud to hard, white or gray compact stones that are used for lithographic reproduction of pictures. This soft fossiliferous limestone is typical of many beds. Not infrequently, perfect fossil forms weather free and can be picked off the little pedestals of rock residue on the surface of the outcrop.
Missouri

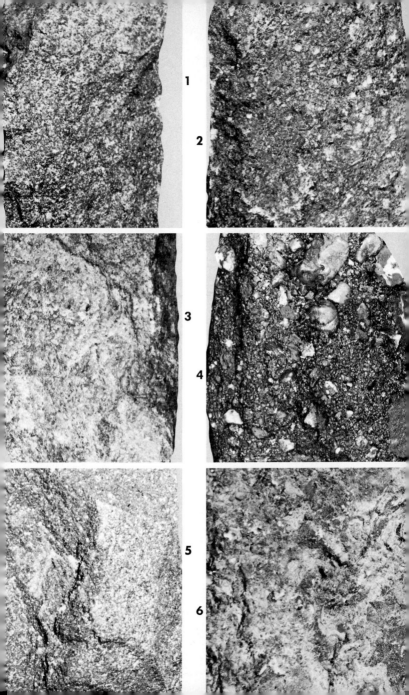

Plate 5

SEDIMENTARY AND METAMORPHIC ROCKS

(hand specimens)

1. Shale   p. 19
The thin layers and the fine
clayey material that com-
pose shale are very characteristic, but its color may
vary from black to white,
with grays, dark reds, and
greens very common. Fos-
sils, often of leaves and
plant remains, are frequent.
Illinois

2. Coal   p. 20
Coal is very distinctive, and
no trouble to identify. A
flame across its edge soon
gives a coal smoke smell
that is unmistakable. Soft
coal becomes anthracite
when it is squeezed during
mild metamorphism of the
country rocks.
Pennsylvania

3. Slate   p. 21
Shale turns to slate in the
early stages of metamor-
phism and though it still
looks much like shale, it is
harder and breaks with a
splintery fracture at right
angles to the direction of
pressure. The color, the
luster, and the grain size are
still about the same as in
the shale.
Maryland

4. Phyllite   p. 21
Greater metamorphism
forms small mica flakes
along the fracture surfaces
of slate, and often crumple
the layers a little, so that
there is a wavy surface of
fracture.
Vermont

5. Quartzite   p. 22
Sandstone becomes so
tightly cemented together
that the grains no longer
separate on fracture but
break right through.
Quartzite still may look
about the same after metamorphism, but it is a very
solid, very durable rock.
Wisconsin

6. Mica schist   p. 22
Intense metamorphism of a
shaly rock has developed
large mica flakes that characterize a typical schist.
Often, when we break such
a rock parallel to the banding, we see only mica; the
quartz and feldspar show
only when it breaks the
other way.
New York

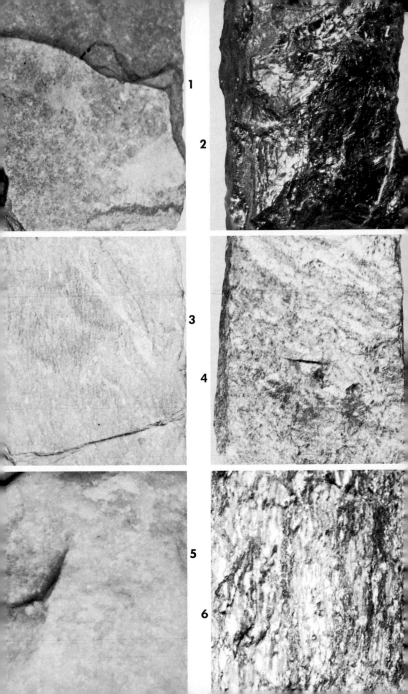

Plate 6

COLLECTING LOCALITIES

1. Kinkel Quarry, Bedford, N.Y., in the late 1930s   p. 284

A group of collectors, members of the New York City Mineral Club, the country's oldest, on an outing. Most serious collectors join clubs in their communities for fellowship and education. Groups can usually arrange visits to localities that will normally not be open to individuals. Collectors should be careful to observe scrupulously any restrictions on collecting and behavior requested by the authorities who grant the permit. Due caution should be exercised at all times. No responsible collector can expect someone else to insure his safety, and a careless accident can result in the closing of a locality to all visitors. Be responsible, and blame no one but yourself if you get hurt!

2. The Harding Mine, Dixon, New Mexico   p. 259

This combination of an open pegmatite quarry and an underground mine shows many of the characteristics of a typical complex pegmatite. The coarse spodumene crystals, standing like fence pickets in the quartz along the wall, show how much larger the crystals that grow in these coarse, volatile-rich magma phases are than those found in a granite. The waste dumps of such a quarry are likely to contain many interesting minerals. The Harding Mine is famous as a source of specimens of pink muscovite, lepidolite, microlite (one of the economic minerals for which it was worked), and flat beryl (a second economic ore) crystals, as well as the pictured spodumene.

Plate 7

COLLECTING LOCALITIES

Now the victim of urban sprawl, this was a typical crushed-rock quarry in a metamorphosed diorite. Calcite-filled seams could once be etched out to reveal brilliant little babingtonite crystals, and pegmatitic phases in the rock contained crystals of epidote, titanite, orthoclase, and other minerals.

Heavy blasting produces highly shattered rock masses and weak walls. Collectors clambering around tumbled masses of rock should keep clear of dangerous overhangs and precariously balanced blocks. Quarries are no place for unsupervised children and irresponsible adults. Keep clear of all quarry machinery—many quarry operators' complaints are of damage to idle equipment during the weekend.

This giant open pit is typical of modern mines. Emphasis today is on large, low-grade deposits that can be worked on an enormous scale, and as the old-time high-grade ore bodies are exhausted we can expect more of the giant open-cut mines. Specimens will still be found, for even low-grade bodies contain stringers of richer ore.

At Chuquicamata, where the climate is extremely dry, there are many interesting secondary minerals that have been formed and concentrated by the sparse, but rich, supergene waters that have leached the upper layers and redeposited copper minerals a few hundred meters deeper. When permission to enter such a mine can be obtained, the collector has some of his best opportunities. Underground mines refill mined-out stopes with waste rock and fewer and fewer dumps are formed. Often the only source of specimens are miners; it is to be hoped that one day the operators themselves will appreciate the specimens they daily destroy and salvage a few for collectors.

Plate 8

ELEMENTS AND SULFIDES

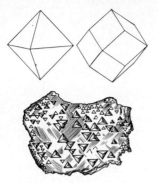

1. Gold in quartz   p. 71
Nevada County, California

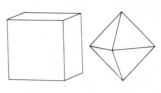

2. Silver   p. 72
Kongsberg, Norway

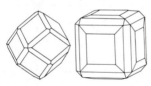

3. Copper   p. 72
Keweenaw County, Michigan

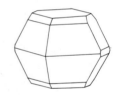

4. Sulfur   p. 77
Agrigento, Sicily

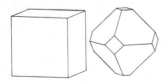

5. Galena on dolomite   p. 82
Central Missouri lead district, Reynolds County, Missouri

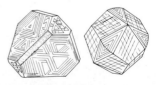

6. Sphalerite ("ruby jack")   p. 83
Joplin District, Missouri-Kansas-Oklahoma

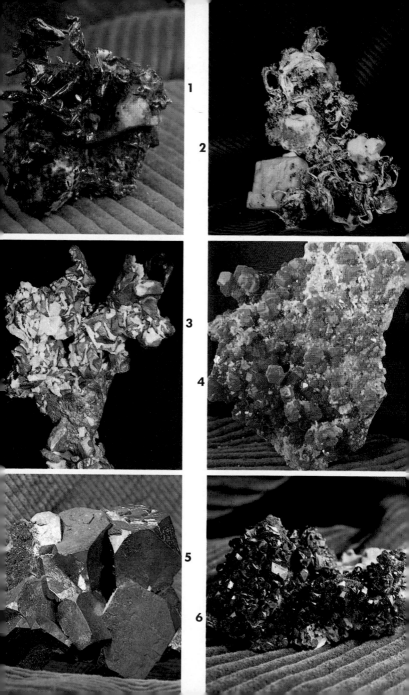

Plate 9

ELEMENTS AND SULFIDES

1. Native iron meteorite   p. 74
   Structural pattern brought
   out by acid etching (Widmanstaetten lines)
   El Capitan, New Mexico

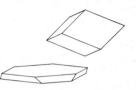

2. Native arsenic   p. 75
   Příbram, Czechoslovakia

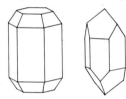

3. Native tellurium   p. 76
   Boulder County, Colorado

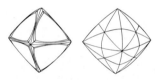

4. Diamond crystal in   p. 78
   blue ground
   South Africa

5. Graphite vein   p. 79
   Buckingham, Quebec

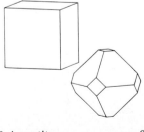

6. Argentite   p. 80
   Guanajuato, Mexico

Plate 10

SULFIDES

1. Chalcocite   p. 80
   Cornwall, England

2. Bornite   p. 81
   Cornwall, England

3. Chalcopyrite   p. 84
   Cornwall, England

4. Greenockite   p. 85
   Bishopton, Scotland

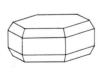

5. Pyrrhotite   p. 86
   *Aquiles Serdán, (Santa
   Eulalia), Chihuahua,
   Mexico*

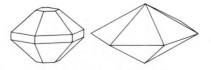

6. Niccolite   p. 87
   Sangerhausen, Saxony

Plate 11

SULFIDES

1. Millerite   p. 87
   St. Louis, Missouri

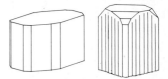

2. Bismuthinite   p. 92
   Llallagua, Bolivia

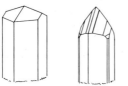

3. Stibnite   p. 91
   *Ichinokawa Mine, Iyo (now
   Ehime Prefecture), Shikoku
   I., Japan*

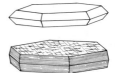

4. Covellite   p. 88
   Butte, Montana

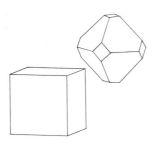

5. Pyrite cubic crystals   p. 93
   Leadville, Colorado

6. Pyrite pyritohedrons   p. 93
   Park City, Utah

Plate 12
SULFIDES, TELLURIDE, SULFOSALT, OXIDE

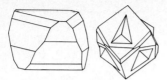

1. Cinnabar crystals   p. 89
   Hunan Province, China

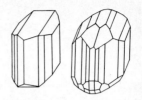

2. Realgar   p. 89
   Getchell Mine, Nevada

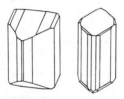

3. Orpiment with   p. 90
   realgar
   Getchell Mine, Nevada

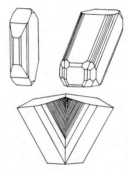

4. Calaverite with   p. 98
   sylvanite
   Cripple Creek, Colorado

5. Proustite   p. 103
   Chañarcillo, Chile

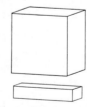

6. Cuprite: variety   p. 109
   chalcotrichite
   Bisbee, Arizona

Plate 13

SULFIDES

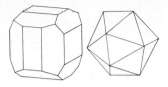

1. Cobaltite   p. 94
   Tunaberg, Sweden

2. Arsenopyrite   p. 96
   Trepča, Yugoslavia

3. Marcasite   p. 95
   *Joplin District, Missouri-
   Kansas-Oklahoma*

4. Marcasite-Pyrite   p. 95
   "dollar"
   Sparta, Illinois

5. Molybdenite   p. 97
   Wakefield, Quebec

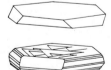

6. Polybasite   p. 100
   Arizpe, Sonora, Mexico

Plate 14

SULFOSALTS

1. Stephanite   p. 101
   Arizpe, Sonora, Mexico

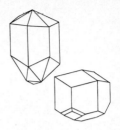

2. Pyrargyrite   p. 102
   Harz Mountains, Germany

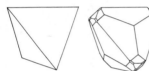

3. Tetrahedrite   p. 103
   Capnic, Rumania

4. Enargite   p. 104
   Butte, Montana

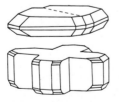

5. Bournonite   p. 105
   Cornwall, England

6. Boulangerite   p. 106
   Nerchinsk, Siberia

Plate 15

SULFOSALTS AND OXIDES

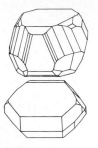

2. Jamesonite p. 108
Tuscany, Italy

1. Miargyrite p. 107
Zacatecas, Mexico

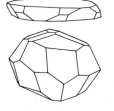

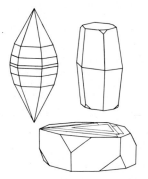

3. Cuprite in limonite p. 109
Cornwall, England

4. Corundum crystals p. 112
in matrix
*Macon County, North Caro-
lina*

5. Hematite: kidney p. 113
ore
Cumberland, England

6. Ilmenite p. 115
Alexandria, New Hampshire

Plate 16

OXIDES

1. Bixbyite crystal on   p. 116
   topaz
   Thomas Range, Utah

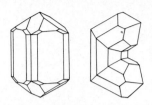

2. Rutile: large crystal   p. 117
   Lincoln County, Georgia
   Left: sixling
   Parkesburg, Pennsylvania

3. Pyrolusite   p. 118
   Lake County, New Mexico

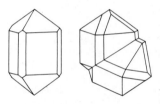

4. Cassiterite   p. 119
   Slavkov, Czechoslovakia

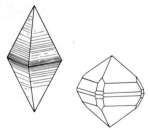

5. Anatase   p. 120
   Tavetsch, Switzerland

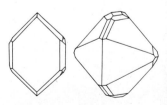

6. Brookite   p. 121
   Tremadoc, Wales

Plate 17

OXIDES

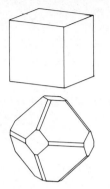

1. Uraninite   p. 122
   Chinkolobwe, Zaïre

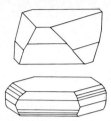

2. Brucite   p. 125
   Lancaster County, Pennsylvania

3. Manganite   p. 125
   Ilfeld, The Harz, Germany

4. Bauxite   p. 126
   Bauxite, Arkansas

5. Psilomelane   p. 126
   Iserlohn, Westphalia, Germany

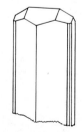

6. Goethite   p. 127
   Negaunee, Michigan

Plate 18

OXIDES

1. Limonite: stalactitic   p. 128
   Hardin County, Illinois

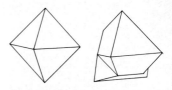

2. Spinel   p. 129
   Sterling Hill, New Jersey

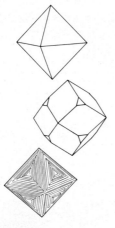

4. Chromite   p. 131
   Siskyou County, California

3. Magnetite   p. 130
   *Tilly Foster Mine, Brewster,
   New York*

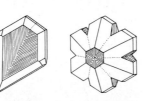

5. Chrysoberyl   p. 132
   Greenwood, Maine

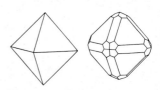

6. Microlite   p. 133
   Left: In lepidolite
   Dixon, New Mexico
   Right: In cleavelandite
   Amelia, Virginia

Plate 19

OXIDES AND HALIDES

1. Left: Columbite-
   Tantalite   p. 134
   Right: Manganotantalite
   Rio Grande do Norte, Brazil

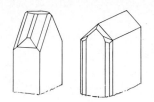

2. Samarskite   p. 135
   Mitchell County, North Carolina

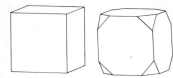

3. Halite   p. 136
   Kalucz, Poland

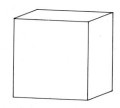

4. Cerargyrite   p. 138
   Leadville, Colorado

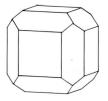

5. Embolite-Bromyrite   p. 138
   Broken Hill, New South Wales

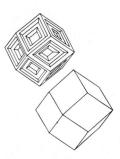

6. Sal Ammoniac   p. 139
   Paricutín Volcano, Michoacán, Mexico

1
2
3
4
5
6

Plate 20

OXIDES AND HALIDES

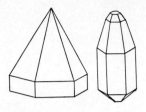

1. Zincite p. 110
   Franklin, New Jersey

2. Gummite p. 124
   Orange and yellow, with brown cyrtolite (a zircon variety) embedded in feldspar. The original dendritic uraninite crystals are preserved now as gummite
   Ruggles Mine, Grafton, New Hampshire

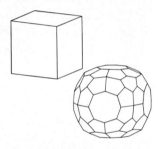

3. Fluorite cubes p. 140
   Bingham, New Mexico

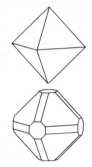

4. Fluorite octahedrons p. 140
   Göschenen, Switzerland

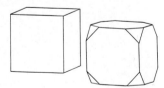

5. Sylvite p. 137
   Carlsbad, New Mexico

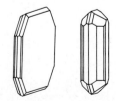

6. Atacamite p. 142
   Moonta, South Australia

Plate 21

HALIDES AND CARBONATES

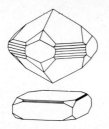

1. Calomel   p. 140
   Terlingua, Texas

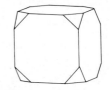

2. Cryolite   p. 143
   Ivigtut, Greenland

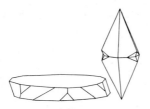

3. Calcite (platy)   p. 145
   Guanajuato, Mexico

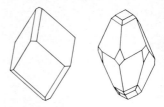

4. Calcite (rhombo-   p. 145
   hedral)
   Transparent calcite cleavage
   rhombs that exhibit double
   refraction in both the image
   doubling and in the escaping
   light rays
   Colorless (Iceland spar): *New
   Mexico*
   Brown: *Chihuahua, Mexico*

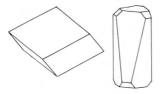

5. Magnesite   p. 146
   Weathered secondary nodule
   and primary crystals
   Brumado, Bahia, Brazil

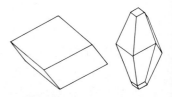

6. Siderite   p. 147
   *Morro Velho, Minas Gerais,
   Brazil*

Plate 22

CARBONATES

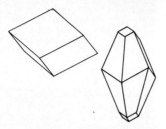

1. Calcite   p. 145
   Gananoque, Quebec

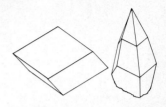

2. Rhodochrosite   p. 148
   Top: *Catamarca, Argentina*
   Bottom: *Emma Mine, Butte,
   Montana*

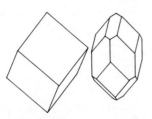

3. Smithsonite   p. 149
   *Kelly Mine, Magdalena, New
   Mexico*

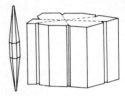

4. Aragonite   p. 150
   Left: Trilling
        Minglanilla, Spain
   Center: *Bisbee, Arizona*
   Right: Pseudomorph after a
   trilling
        Roswell, New Mexico

5. Aurichalcite   p. 156
   Mapimí, Durango, Mexico

6. Malachite   p. 156
   *Burra Burra, South Aus-
   tralia*

Plate 23

CARBONATES

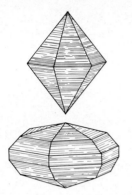

2. Strontianite   p. 152
   Drensteinfurt, Westphalia,
   Germany

1. Witherite   p. 151
   Cave-in-Rock, Illinois

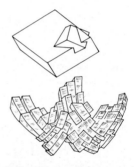

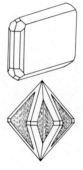

4. Dolomite: curved   p. 154
   crystals
   Picher, Oklahoma

3. Cerussite: twin   p. 153
   growth
   Tsumeb, South West Africa

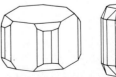

5. Hydrozincite crust   p. 155
   Malfidano, Sardinia

6. Phosgenite   p. 157
   Monteponi, Sardinia

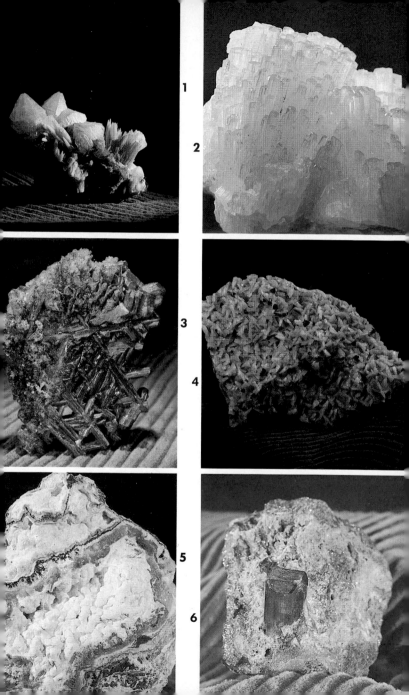

Plate 24

CARBONATE AND BORATES

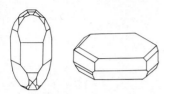

1. Leadhillite   p. 159
   Granby, Missouri

2. Kernite   p. 162
   Boron, Kern County, California

3. Ulexite: image-transmitting fibrous vein material   p. 163
   Boron, Kern County, California

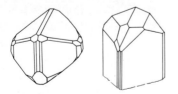

4. Borax: dehydrated crystals, "tincalconite"   p. 163
   Esmeralda County, Nevada

5. Colemanite   p. 164
   Boron, Kern County, California

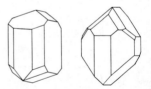

6. Howlite   p. 165
   Tick Canyon, Los Angeles County, California

Plate 25

SULFATES

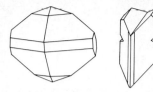

1. Thenardite   p. 166
Soda Lake, San Luis Obispo County, California

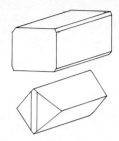

2. Barite   p. 166
Left: *Mapimí, Durango, Mexico*
Right: *Stoneham, Colorado*

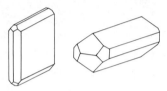

3. Celestite   p. 168
Top left: *Sinaloa, Mexico*
Lower left: *Orangeville, Ontario*
Right: *Woodville, Ohio*

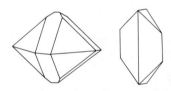

4. Anglesite: forming   p. 169
from galena with "eyes" of
fresh galena
Potosi, Missouri

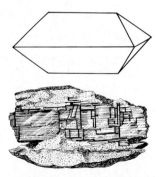

5. Anhydrite   p. 170
Left: *Naica, Mexico*
Right: *Simplon Tunnel, Switzerland*

6. Glauberite   p. 171
San Bernardino County, California

Plate 26

SULFATES AND PHOSPHATES

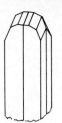

1. Polyhalite: fibrous   p. 172
   vein
   Bad Aussee, Austria

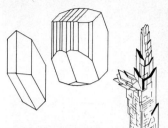

2. Gypsum: p. 172
   cave growth, rose,
   and crystals
   Top pair: *Mammoth Cave,
     Kentucky; Sahara Desert,
     Africa*
   Center: *Salt Plain, Oklahoma*
   Bottom pair: *Mahoning
     County, Ohio*

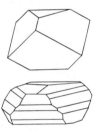

3. Alunite   p. 177
   Marysvale, Utah

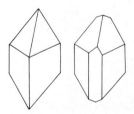

4. Hureaulite   p. 185
   Left: *Mangualde, Portugal*
   Right: *Hagendorf, Bavaria,
     West Germany*

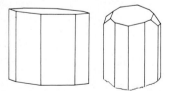

5. Triphylite   p. 181
   *Smith Mine, Chandler's
   Mill, Newport, New Hamp-
   shire*

6. Beryllonite: loose   p. 183
   crystals
   Stoneham, Maine

Plate 27

CARBONATE AND SULFATES

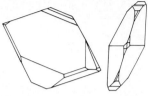

1. Azurite   p. 158
   Bisbee, Arizona

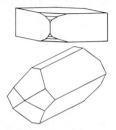

2. Barite   p. 166
   Left: *Superior, Arizona*
   Right: *Chihuahua, Mexico*

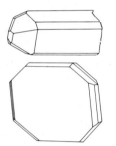

3. Linarite   p. 177
   Bingham, New Mexico

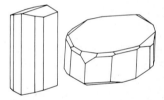

4. Brochantite on   p. 175
   hematite
   *Stanton, Sullivan County,
   Missouri*

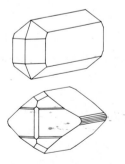

5. Antlerite   p. 176
   Chuquicamata, Chile

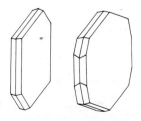

6. Copiapite   p. 179
   Atacama Desert, Chile

Plate 28

SULFATES AND PHOSPHATES

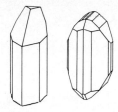

2. Crocoite   p. 180
   Dundas, Tasmania

1. Caledonite   p. 179
   Tiger, Arizona

3. Heterosite (Pur-   p. 182
   purite)
   Solid mass (left) together
   with (right) what was a tri-
   phyllite-laminated intergrowth with another phosphate [graftonite
   $(Fe,Mn,Ca)_3P_2O_8$]
   Grafton, New Hampshire

4. Erythrite   p. 189
   Alamos, Mexico

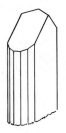

5. Annabergite: variety   p. 190
   cabrerite
   Lavrion, Greece

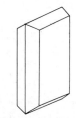

6. Variscite   p. 191
   Nodule with altering borders
   of wardite (blue) and other
   phosphates
   Fairfield, Utah

Plate 29

ARSENATES AND PHOSPHATES

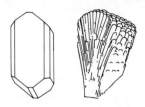

1. Monazite crystals   p. 184
on beryl
Jefferson County, Colorado

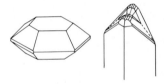

2. Vivianite   p. 188
Mullica Hill, New Jersey

4. Herderite   p. 194
Alexandria, New Hampshire

3. Descloizite   p. 193
Mammoth Mine, Tiger, Arizona

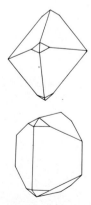

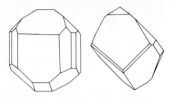

5. Amblygonite   p. 195
Araçuaí, Minas Gerais, Brazil

6. Libethenite crystals   p. 197
on limonite
Liskeard, Cornwall

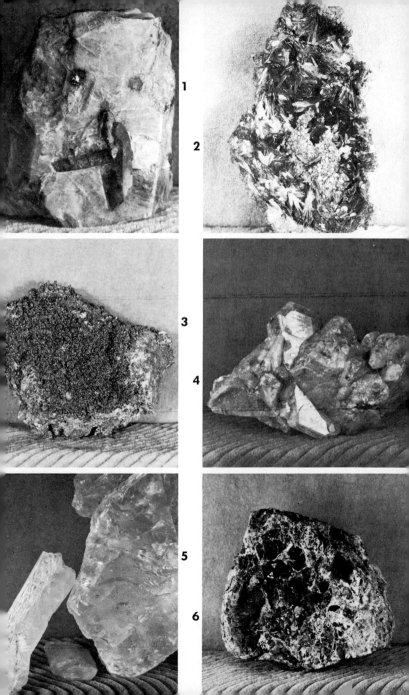

Plate 30

ARSENATES AND PHOSPHATES

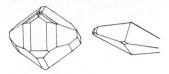

1. Brazilianite   p. 195
Conselheiro Pena, Minas Gerais, Brazil

2. Olivenite   p. 196
·Cornwall, England

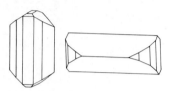

3. Adamite: coarse   p. 198
crystals on limonite
Ojuela Mine, Mapimí, Mexico

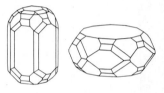

4. Apatite   p. 201
Left: *Bancroft, Ontario*
Center: *Campo Formosa, Bahia, Brazil*
Right: *Cerro de Mercado, Durango, Mexico*

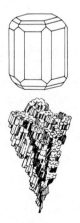

5. Pyromorphite   p. 202
El Horcajo, Spain

6. Mimetite   p. 203
San Pedro Corralitos, Mexico

Plate 31

PHOSPHATES

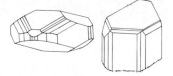

1. Augelite crystals on p. 199
   rock
   *White Mountain, Mono
   County, California*

2. Dufrenite crust (rock- p. 199
   bridgeite)
   Rockbridge County, Virginia

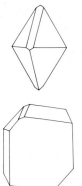

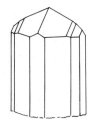

4. Eosphorite p. 207
   Rumford, Maine

3. Lazulite crystals in p. 205
   sandstone
   Graves Mountain, Georgia

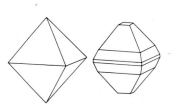

5. Wardite in phosphate p. 208
   nodule
   Fairfield, Utah

6. Wavellite p. 209
   Garland County, Arkansas

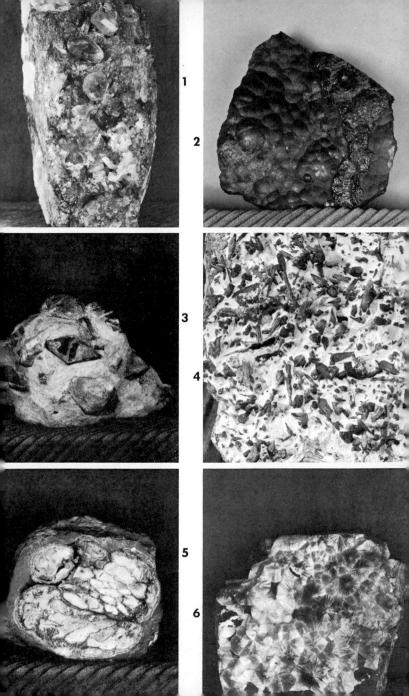

Plate 32

PHOSPHATES TO TUNGSTATES

1. Vanadinite   p. 204
   Mibladen, Morocco

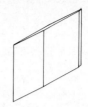

2. Turquoise in trach-   p. 209
   itic rock (= microcrystalline
   syenite)
   Battle Mountain, Nevada

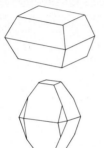

4. Autunite   p. 211
   Urgeiriça, Portugal

3. Torbernite   p. 210
   Left: *Shaba (Katanga),
   Zaïre*
   Right: *Gunnislake, Corn-
   wall, England*

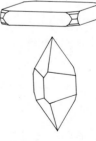

6. Wulfenite   p. 217
   *Los Lamentos, Chihuahua,
   Mexico*

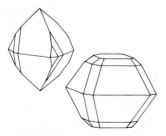

5. Scheelite   p. 215
   *Cohen Mine, Cochise County,
   Arizona*

Plate 33

TUNGSTATES TO SILICATES

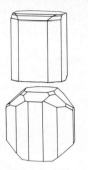

1. Wolframite   p. 213
   Panasqueira, Portugal

2. Wolframite: variety   p. 213
   ferberite
   Boulder County, Colorado

3. Powellite crystal   p. 216
   crust
   Goldfield, Nevada

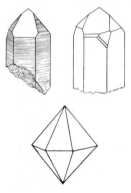

4. Quartz: rock crystal   p. 219
   Mount Ida, Arkansas

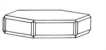

5. Tridymite: twinned   p. 222
   crystals on rock
   Padua, Italy

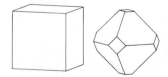

6. Cristobalite: tiny   p. 223
   white crystals on cracks in
   lithophysae in obsidian
   Inyo County, California

Plate 34

SILICATES

1. Quartz: amethyst   p. 219
   crystal
   Guerrero, Mexico

2. Quartz: agate with   p. 219
   crystal border
   Rio Grande do Sul, Brazil

3. Opal   p. 223
   Left: Common green opal
      Bahia, Brazil
   Rear: Precious opal
      Queensland, Australia
   Center: Fire opal
      Querétaro, Mexico
   Right: Hyalite opal
      Canutillos, Bolivia

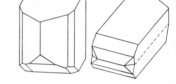

4. Microcline feldspar   p. 226
   ("Amazonstone")
   Crystal Peak, Colorado

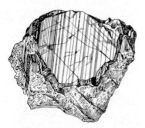

5. Labradorite with   p. 227
   schiller color flash and polysynthetic twin striations
   Lammenpaa, Finland

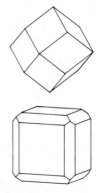

6. Sodalite   p. 230
   *Victoria da Conquista,
   Bahia, Brazil*

Plate 35

SILICATES

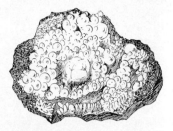

1. Opal: variety   p. 223
   hyalite
   San Luis Potosí, Mexico

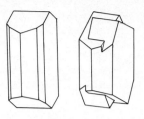

2. Orthoclase crystal   p. 225
   in porphyry
   Robinson, Colorado

3. Albite   p. 227
   Rauris, Austria

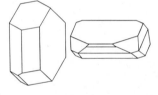

4. Oligoclase: shows   p. 227
   plagioclase twin striations on
   cleavage face
   Bakersville, North Carolina

5. Leucite: crystal in   p. 229
   matrix
   Hot Springs, Arkansas

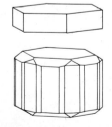

6. Nepheline: large   p. 229
   crystals
   Bancroft, Ontario

Plate 36

SILICATES

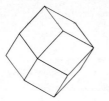

1. Lazurite: "lapis p. 231
lazuli"
Crystal in marble
Koktscha, Afghanistan
Massive type
Lake Baikal, Siberia

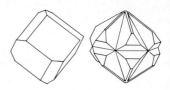

2. Chabazite with p. 234
calcite
Two Islands, Nova Scotia

3. Prehnite p. 244
Paterson, New Jersey

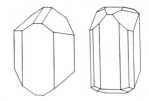

4. Diopside with esso- p. 254
nite garnet
Crystal bundle (rear)
Brompton Lake, Quebec
Long crystal
Val d'Ala, Piemonte, Italy
Short crystal
De Kalb, New York

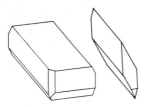

5. Rhodonite p. 259
Crystal in galena
*Broken Hill, New South
Wales*
Massive type
*Los Angeles County, Cali-
fornia*

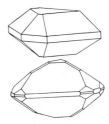

6. Benitoite on white p. 264
natrolite vein
*San Benito County, Cali-
fornia*

Plate 37

SILICATES

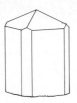

1. Scapolite p. 231
(Wernerite)
Bathurst, Ontario

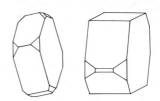

2. Heulandite p. 233
Berufjördhur, Iceland

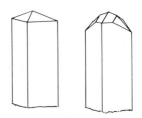

3. Stilbite p. 234
Two Islands, Nova Scotia

4. Natrolite p. 235
Bergen Hill, New Jersey

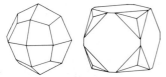

5. Analcime (Analcite) p. 236
Keweenaw, Michigan

6. Cordierite p. 237
Bamle, Norway

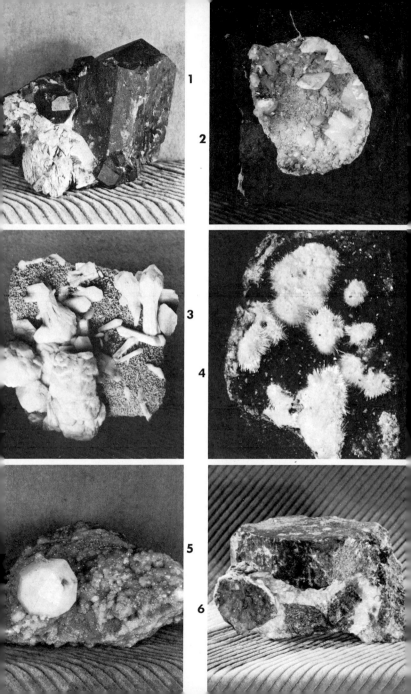

Plate 38

SILICATES

1. Pyrophyllite   p. 238
   Lincoln County, Georgia

2. Serpentine with   p. 240
   asbestos veins
   Williams, Arizona

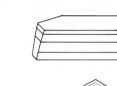

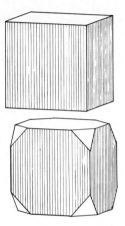

3. Apophyllite   p. 241
   Bergen Hill, New Jersey

4. Chlorite   p. 242
   West Chester, Pennsylvania

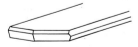

5. Margarite vein   p. 243
   Chester, Massachusetts

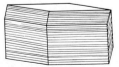

6. Muscovite crystals   p. 245
   with albite
   Chaffee County, Colorado

1

2

3

4

5

6

Plate 39

SILICATES

1. Biotite mica   p. 246
Chester, Massachusetts

2. Phlogopite mica   p. 247
Perth, Ontario

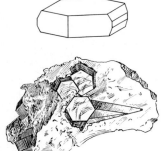

3. Lepidolite mica in   p. 248
curved knob
Auburn, Maine

4. Actinolite   p. 251
Cranston, Rhode Island

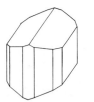

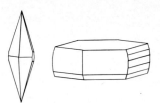

6. Enstatite   p. 253
Baltimore, Maryland

5. Hornblende   p. 252
Sterling Hill, New Jersey

Plate 40

SILICATES

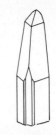

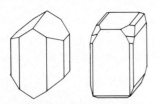

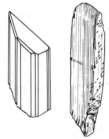

1. Augite crystals in   p. 256
   porphyry
   Fassatal, Austrian Tyrol

2. Acmite (Aegirine)   p. 256
   crystals in rock
   Magnet Cove, Arkansas

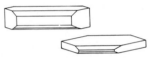

3. Spodumene   p. 258
   Norwich, Massachusetts

4. Wollastonite   p. 260
   Perheniemi, Finland

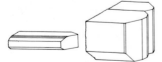

5. Pectolite vein   p. 261
   Bergen Hill, New Jersey

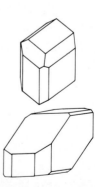

6. Babingtonite   p. 262
   Westfield, Massachusetts

Plate 41

SILICATES

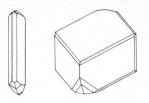

1. Neptunite   p. 263
   San Benito County, California

2. Chrysocolla   p. 263
   Bagdad, Arizona

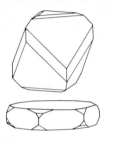

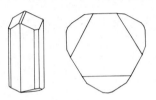

4. Tourmaline: variety   p. 266
   elbaite
   Minas Gerais, Brazil

3. Eudialyte   p. 265
   Kola Peninsula, U.S.S.R.

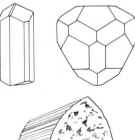

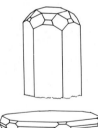

6. Beryl in white   p. 267
   quartz
   Minas Gerais, Brazil

5. Tourmaline: variety   p. 266
   schorl with typical cross section (left)
   Haddam, Connecticut

Plate 42

SILICATES

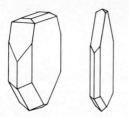

1. Hemimorphite   p. 269
   Aquiles Serdán (Santa Eulalia), Chihuahua, Mexico

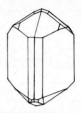

2. Euclase   p. 286
   Left row: *Rio Grande do Norte, Brazil; Tanzania; Chivor, Colombia*
   Right row: *Minas Gerais, Brazil*

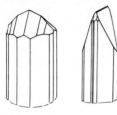

3. Danburite   p. 271
   Charcas, San Luis Potosí, Mexico

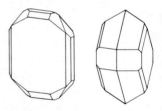

4. Olivine grains in   p. 272
   basalt "bomb"
   San Carlos, Arizona

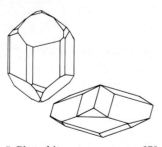

5. Phenakite   p. 273
   Left: on quartz
   Florissant, Colorado
   Right: *São Miguel de Piraçicaba, Minas Gerais, Brazil*

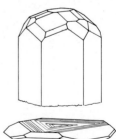

6. Willemite: variety   p. 274
   troostite crystals in calcite
   Franklin, New Jersey

Plate 43

SILICATES

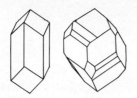

1. Dioptase with calcite   p. 275
   Tsumeb, South West Africa

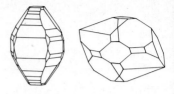

2. Humite (-Chondrodite): brown crystal in marble   p. 276
   Northern New Jersey

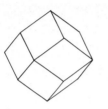

3. Garnet: variety almandine crystals in mica schist   p. 277
   Wrangell Island, Alaska

4. Garnet: variety grossular   p. 277
   Jeffrey Quarry, Asbestos, Quebec

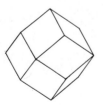

5. Garnet: variety uvarovite on chromite (with purple kaemmererite)   p. 277
   Jackson, California

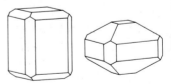

6. Vesuvianite (Idocrase)   p. 280
   Center: *Lake Jaco, Morelos, Mexico*
   Left: *Sanford, Maine*
   Right: Massive "Californite" type
   British Columbia

Plate 44

SILICATES

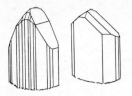

1. Zoisite   p. 281
   Wardsboro, Vermont

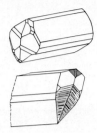

2. Epidote   p. 282
   *Guadalupe Island, Baja
   California*

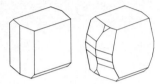

3. Allanite (Orthite)   p. 283
   with radiating cracks in the
   feldspar around the allanite
   rods
   *Brooklyn-Battery Tunnel,
   New York City*

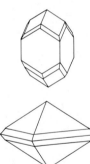

4. Zircon   p. 284
   Brudenell, Ontario

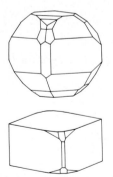

5. Datolite crystals   p. 285
   in traprock
   Paterson, New Jersey

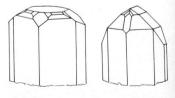

6. Topaz   p. 287
   Minas Gerais, Brazil

Plate 45

SILICATES

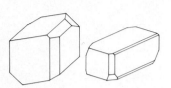

1. Axinite   p. 288
   Left: *Victoria da Conquista Bahia, Brazil*
   Right: *Le Bourg-d'Oisans, Dauphiné, France*

2. Andalusite   p. 289
   Left: *Delaware County, Pennsylvania*
   Right: Variety chiastolite *Lancaster, Massachusetts*

3. Sillimanite: parallel   p. 290
   crystals in rock
   Willimantic, Connecticut

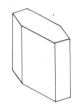

4. Kyanite: blue   p. 291
   crystals in quartz
   Canton, Connecticut

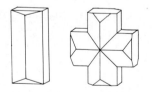

5. Staurolite   p. 292
   Loose crystals
      Taos, New Mexico; Fannin County, Georgia
   In schist
      Mink Pond, New Hampshire

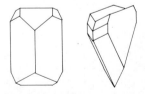

6. Titanite (Sphene)   p. 292
   Capelinha, Minas Gerais, Brazil

Plate 46

PHOTOMICROGRAPHS

by Alan de Haas

Many collectors find greater beauty and crystal perfection in tiny crystals that can best be viewed through the microscope. Much greater symmetry is likely to be present in the smaller crystals. Some minerals are only known as microscopic crystals.

Micromount collectors find this phase of the hobby the most practical because of the small space such a collection occupies, and the far lower cost of acquiring an extensive suite of species.

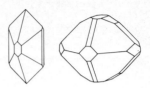

2. Scorodite   p. 192
Brejanca, Portugal
12×

1. Strengite   p. 191
Indian Mountain, Alabama
10×

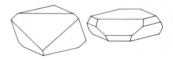

4. Jarosite   p. 178
Coquimbo, Chile
20×

3. Bertrandite twin   p. 270
Portland, Connecticut
40×

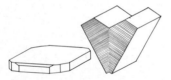

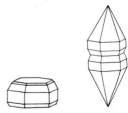

5. Fayalite: tiny crystal in an obsidian lithophysa (see under cristobalite, p. 223)
Coso Hot Springs, Inyo County, California
35×

6. Spangolite twin ($Cu_6AlClSO_{10} \cdot 9H_2O$): a rare and crystallographically unusual copper mineral (not described in the text)
Bingham, New Mexico
40×

Interesting facts: The mineral was named for James Smithson, the Englishman who left money for the establishment of the Smithsonian Institution. It is often known as "calamine" in Europe, a name Americans once applied to the zinc silicate but have now dropped in favor of "hemimorphite."

Aragonite Group

This group of structurally and chemically related orthorhombic carbonates is also characterized by crystal similarities, particularly by a tendency to intergrow with other individuals in clusters of three crystals, assuming a pseudohexagonal appearance. Their cleavage goes from fair to inconspicuous but is never so perfect as that of the calcite group. Like that group, the orthorhombic carbonates have unusually strong double refraction, which may be observed as a conspicuous inner fuzziness in clear members of the family (aragonite and cerussite).

ARAGONITE $CaCO_3$ **Pl. 22**

Orthorhombic — Rhombic bipyramidal $\frac{2}{m} \frac{2}{m} \frac{2}{m}$

Environment: Hot-spring deposits, some ore veins, and sedimentary formations.

Crystal description: Single crystals, most often long slender needles, also in tabular plates. Trillings (3 intergrown individuals) common, looking like short hexagonal prisms, or even hexagonal plates. Re-entrant angle visible in fresh, sharp crystals in the center of each apparent prism of these pseudohexagons, and striations on the apparent base disclose the 3 individuals. Also in crusts and stalactites.

Physical properties: Colorless, white, pale violet, light blue, or light yellow. *Luster* vitreous; *hardness* $3\frac{1}{2}$-4; *gravity* 2.9-3.0; *fracture* subconchoidal; *cleavage* poor, parallel to prism and side pinacoids. Brittle; translucent to transparent, commonly fluorescent and phosphorescent.

Composition: Calcium carbonate, like calcite (56.0% CaO, 44.0% CO_2; with strontium [mossottite], lead [tarnowitzite], and sometimes zinc [nicholsonite]).

Tests: Dissolves with bubbles in cold hydrochloric acid, like calcite. Strong solutions give a precipitate of white needles or granules of calcium sulfate when sulfuric acid is added to the hydrochloric acid solution.

Distinguishing characteristics: Recognizable as a carbonate by its effervescence in hydrochloric acid; as the aragonite group by lack of a conspicuous cleavage; as a calcium carbonate by its sulfate precipitate (only in concentrated solutions) and by the weak red-orange coloration of the flame; and as aragonite by the pink-violet color it assumes when a powder is boiled in a test tube with a cobalt nitrate solution (calcite stays white). Also, it crumbles more on heating than calcite does and loses its fluorescence, whereas calcite tends to remain intact and to gain fluorescence.

Occurrence: Aragonite is far rarer than calcite, apparently being deposited from warmer solutions (but not too warm) than calcite. It is found around hot springs in crusts and thick beds (which are cut as onyx marble). Fine needlelike elongated and pointed crystals were found in the Cumberland (England) iron mines. Good pseudohexagonal trillings common in the Sicilian sulfur mines and as isolated 6-sided rods and plates in central Spain, the former in crystal clusters with sulfur, gypsum, and celestite, the latter with gypsum in red and green shale beds often colored by red-stained clay inclusions. Trillings, and sandy pseudomorphs of this type have been found at Chaves (near Roswell, New Mexico), in s. France, Morocco, and at the Matsushiro gypsum mines, Ota City, Shimane Prefecture, Honshu, in giant spherical masses. Violet pseudohexagonal rods cross gas cavities in basalt at Suzu Gun, Ishikawa Prefecture, in the Noto Peninsula, Japan.

A white coral-like branching growth, called *flos ferri* (iron flowers), has been found in Austrian iron mines (and in New Mexico and Mexico).

Interesting facts: The iridescent inner surfaces of shells (and pearls) are composed of aragonite secreted by mollusks. The light violet cast that is common in some aragonites (those from green shale in Spain and from Japanese basalt) seems to be due to iron plus a natural irradiation. It fades from crystals exposed on outcrops but can be restored by irradiation in the laboratory.

WITHERITE $BaCO_3$ **Pl. 23**

Orthorhombic — Rhombic bipyramidal $\dfrac{2}{m}\dfrac{2}{m}\dfrac{2}{m}$

Environment: Low-temperature lead and fluorite ore veins.

Crystal description: Though orthorhombic it is twinned into pseudohexagonal trillings, most often resembling hexagonal bipyramids. Also in crusts with rounded surfaces; columnar and granular.

Physical properties: White, light yellowish, or gray. *Luster* glassy: *hardness* $3-3\frac{1}{2}$; *gravity* 4.3–4.7; *fracture* uneven; *cleavage* 1 good and 2 poor. Brittle; translucent; commonly fluorescent blue.

Composition: Barium carbonate (77.7% BaO, 22.3% CO_2; may contain some Ca).

Tests: Dissolves readily in hydrochloric acid with effervescence. Slender white needles form as 2:3 HCl acid solution cools, dissolve again on heating or dilution. Even dilute solutions form precipitate of barium sulfate crystals when sulfuric acid is added. A hydrochloric acid solution on a platinum wire placed in the flame gives a yellow-green flash (barium flame).

Distinguishing characteristics: Recognized as a carbonate by its hardness and effervescence in acid. Recognized as witherite by the flame coloration.

Occurrence: Witherite is a surprisingly rare mineral and in its best occurrences accompanies lead ore (galena) in veins. The best specimens, pseudobipyramids, have always come from Cumberland and Northumberland, England. Comparable though generally smaller individual trillings of stubbier habit occur in the s. Illinois fluorite mines. Otherwise it appears to be very rare in the U.S., having been reported only in massive specimens near Yosemite National Park (associated with barite and some rare barium minerals) and at Thunder Bay, Ontario. Possibly it is more common than generally supposed, because usually unrecognized.

Interesting facts: Its rarity can be accounted for in part by the ease with which it can be altered to the very insoluble sulfate, barite. When sulfide minerals weather they produce excess sulfuric acid, which immediately reacts with the soluble witherite, reprecipitating it as barite. At the Illinois locality, however, some of the witherite appears still to be forming at the expense of the calcite rather than forming as barite.

STRONTIANITE $SrCO_3$ **Pl. 23**

Orthorhombic — Rhombic bipyramidal $\dfrac{2\ 2\ 2}{m\ m\ m}$

Environment: Veins or concretions in sedimentary rocks.

Crystal description: Most common formation is in fibrous veinlets. Also in good acicular crystals; its pseudohexagonal intergrowths are the rarest of the aragonite group. Also long needles, massive, and fine-grained.

Physical properties: White or colorless, light green, pink, yellowish, brownish, or gray. *Luster* glassy; *hardness* $3\frac{1}{2}$–4; *gravity* 3.7; *fracture* uneven; *cleavage* 1 good and 1 poor. Brittle; transparent to translucent.

Composition: Strontium carbonate (70.1% SrO, 29.9% CO_2, sometimes with a little Ca).

Tests: Like witherite readily soluble in acid, and concentrated solution forms slender, white, water-soluble crystals on cooling. Precipitates out strontium sulfate crystals when sulfuric acid is added to solutions of medium strength. Strong hydrochloric acid solution gives a brilliant red flash (strontium flame) when a platinum wire dipped in it is thrust into the Bunsen burner flame.

Distinguishing characteristics: Recognized as a carbonate by ease of solution in hydrochloric acid with the release of bubbles and by softness, and as a strontium mineral by the brilliant red flame color.

Occurrence: Strontianite locally was an important source of strontium for use in fireworks and in the refining of sugar. It was mined only in Germany at Drensteinfurt, near Hamm, West Germany, where veins cut shaly limestone beds underlying beet fields. These veins were up to several inches across and contained frequent crystal-lined cavities. They were the source of the best-known specimens, but are now, of course, only of historical interest. Also found in fibrous veins in Germany, England, and the U.S. Sometimes forms nodules in limestone, as at Schoharie, New York, in Pennsylvania, and near Barstow, California. Long, pale pink, loosely aggregated needles and compact masses have been found near Cave-in-Rock, Illinois, associated with fluorite and witherite. Brown-tipped but small elongated trillings coming from Oberndorf, Styria (Austria), are the best recently available specimens.

CERUSSITE PbCO$_3$ **Pl. 23**

Orthorhombic — Rhombic bipyramidal $\dfrac{2\ 2\ 2}{m\ m\ m}$

Environment: Secondary (weathered) zone of lead ore deposits.

Crystal description: Flat plates common only in small crystals; larger crystals, up to 6 in. (15 cm), usually intergrown into skeletal lattices, like bridge girders, or in great V's of 2 individuals grown together. Sometimes intergrows in the 6-sided habit of a pseudohexagonal bipyramid. Also massive, and the fragile fibrous white crusts of loosely consolidated needles.

Physical properties: Colorless, white, light yellow to gray; some African twins are dichroic in yellow and violet. *Luster* adamantine; *hardness* 3-3½; Gravity 6.5-6.6; *fracture* conchoidal; *cleavage* good prismatic. Brittle; transparent to translucent; often fluorescent yellow.

Composition: Lead carbonate (83.5% PbO, 16.5% CO$_2$).

Tests: One of the most interesting minerals for blowpiping. Gentle heat turns it yellow to red-brown as it gets hotter. Cools instantly to faceted crystallized bead. Slight excess of heat starts rapid transformation to lead. Metal bead ejected from crystallizing carbonate bead as it solidifies. Make this test; it is one of the pleasant experiences of blowpipe testing!

Distinguishing characteristics: The luster, high gravity, and light color distinguish it from most minerals, and the manner of occurrence distinguishes it from all but anglesite (lead sulfate) and phosgenite (lead chlorocarbonate). The solubility in nitric acid and the fusion behavior distinguish it from the first, the hardness from the latter.

Occurrence: Cerussite is always a secondary mineral that forms from galena through surface alteration, usually when the veins penetrate limestones or dolomites, the carbonate sedimentary rocks. Naturally, its most frequent and best-developed occurrences are where weathering has penetrated deeply, as in desert country. An important ore of lead.

The best and the largest clear crystals have come from Tsumeb, South West Africa, associated with malachite, azurite, smithsonite, and anglesite. Good examples were found in the upper levels at the Broken Hill mine, New South Wales. In the U.S., mines in the Organ Mountains, New Mexico, produced some large V twins, silky white and rust-stained, associated with spectacular wulfenite, anglesite, and vanadinite. Other occurrences are too numerous to list.

Other Carbonates

DOLOMITE $CaMg(CO_3)_2$ **Pl. 23**
              Hexagonal — rhombohedral $\overline{3}$

Environment: Sedimentary rocks, ore veins in sediments, and — rarely — in metamorphic rocks in higher-temperature surroundings.

Crystal description: Crystals rarer and as a rule smaller than calcite, but may range from prismatic to the usual rhombohedron. In limestone or dolomite beds in pockets, commonly in pearly, pinkish, saddle-shaped, subparallel intergrowths of rhombohedral crystals. As a bedded rock formation, microcrystalline to a coarse marble.

Physical properties: Colorless, white, pinkish, or light tints. *Luster* glassy to pearly; *hardness* $3\frac{1}{2}$–4; *gravity* 2.8; *fracture* conchoidal; *cleavage* rhombohedral. Brittle; transparent to translucent.

Composition: Calcium magnesium carbonate (30.4% CaO, 21.7% MgO, 47.9% CO_2, if the calcium-magnesium ratio is 1:1). It may vary slightly in either direction from this and still be called dolomite, even when some iron has also intruded.

Tests: Like calcite, except that it dissolves very slowly in cold acid, unless powdered first and dropped in test tube with acid. Warming the acid speeds the bubbling.

Distinguishing characteristics: The "pearl spar" white to pinkish crystal intergrowths are readily recognizable. Slow effervescence in cold acid distinguishes it from calcite (rapid) and magnesite (only in hot acid). The intermediate specific gravity will help when a pure piece can be obtained. Seems seldom to be fluorescent.

Occurrence: Far less common than calcite; dolomite rock probably forms by subsequent alteration of a limestone after its deposition. The pearly clusters are especially common in the U.S., in association with galena, sphalerite, and calcite in low-temperature veins (Missouri-Kansas-Oklahoma lead district), and in pockets in limestone or dolomite quarries (Rochester, New York).

Large (several inches) and fine crystals have been found in Switzerland, in pegmatitic seams in North Carolina, and in veins in Colorado. Fine clear Iceland-spar-type crystals, collected in a magnesite quarry at Ergui, near Pamplona, Spain, have provided excellent specimens for contemporary collectors.

Interesting facts: Dolomite differs slightly in its crystal form from the other rhombohedral carbonates and does not occur in scalenohedrons. It is usually early in a mineral series, and directly coats the wall rock, underlying calcite, sphalerite, galena, fluorite, celestite, or gypsum, all of which are likely to be later in the depositional sequence.

HYDROZINCITE   Pl. 23

$$Zn_5(CO_3)_2(OH)_6 \quad \text{Monoclinic} \quad \frac{2}{m}$$

Environment: Secondary (weathered) zone of zinc deposits.

Crystal description: Does not occur in crystals; forms white crusts that coat limonite and secondary zinc minerals with a fibrous or compact layer.

Physical properties: White, light gray, or light yellow. *Luster* dull; *hardness* 2-2½; *gravity* 3.6-3.8; *fracture* irregular; *cleavage* none. Earthy; translucent; brilliant blue fluorescence under ultraviolet light.

Composition: Basic zinc carbonate (75.3% ZnO, 13.6% CO_2, 11.1% H_2O).

Tests: As with smithsonite, a grain heated on charcoal and touched with cobalt nitrate solution assumes a green color on reheating. Dissolves with bubbles in hot hydrochloric acid.

Distinguishing characteristics: Easy effervescence in hydrochloric acid proves it to be a carbonate. Associations often suggest a zinc mineral, and it is almost always brilliantly fluorescent.

Occurrence: Since hydrozincite only forms as a secondary mineral in weathered zinc deposits, it develops best where weathering is deep and long continued. Its best occurrence was in a mine in Spain, where great thick white crusts were found in a cave. Similarly found elsewhere in adjoining sections of Spain. In the U.S. the right conditions are found in the Southwest; it is at its best in New Mexico, in rounded crusts on limonite and hemimorphite. It is popular among collectors for its fluorescence, and is not uncommon on Mexican specimens.

AURICHALCITE $(Zn,Cu)_5(CO_3)_2(OH)_6$ **Pl. 22**
Orthorhombic 2 2 2

Environment: Secondary (weathered) zone of copper zinc ore deposits.

Crystal description: Crystals never well defined, usually in crusts of thin fragile scales.

Physical properties: Pale greenish blue. *Luster* pearly; *hardness* 2; *gravity* 3.5–3.6; *cleavage* micaceous, flexible. Translucent.

Composition: A basic carbonate of zinc and copper (20.8% CuO, 53.2% ZnO, 16.1% CO_2, 9.9% H_2O).

Tests: Infusible on charcoal but colors the flame green. Soluble in hydrochloric acid with effervescence, giving green solution, which turns blue on the addition of ammonia.

Distinguishing characteristics: The soft pale blue-green scales, which dissolve so easily in acid, are unlike those of any other mineral. The occurrence is also significant.

Occurrence: Since aurichalcite forms as a result of weathering in ore bodies rather high in zinc, it is a good guide to zinc ore; less conspicuous when copper predominates. Usually forms soft crusts on limonite, often with calcite, smithsonite, and hemimorphite. It is a minor zinc source when mined with other minerals.

Good specimens have come from several localities in Utah, and it is also found in some of the Arizona, New Mexico, and Mexican copper mines. European localities include the famous Leadhills locality (Scotland) for rare oxide zone minerals, Matlock in Derbyshire, Altai region of the U.S.S.R., Yugoslavia, and Chessy, France.

Interesting facts: The origin of the name has aroused some interest, since it is derived from the ancient name for brass. In truth, the mineral can be considered a natural "brass ore," but it is quantitatively so rare that it is unlikely that it ever served this purpose.

MALACHITE $Cu_2CO_3(OH)_2$ Monoclinic $\dfrac{2}{m}$ **Pl. 22**

Environment: Secondary (weathered) zone of copper ore deposits.

Crystal description: Usually in fibrous and silky crusts and masses, individualized single crystals are rare. When seen they are usually twinned so that a re-entrant angle shows at the top. Also massive and earthy, often as thin films staining rock.

Physical properties: Light to dark green. *Luster* usually silky, crystals vitreous; *hardness* $3\frac{1}{2}$–4; *gravity* 3.9–4.0; *fracture* usually splintery; *cleavage* basal, visible in crystals, sometimes in the crusts. Brittle; translucent.

Composition: Basic copper carbonate (71.9% CuO, 19.9% CO_2, 8.2% H_2O).

Tests: Dissolves readily in hydrochloric acid with the release of bubbles. Gives copper tests: solution color, bead test, copper bead on charcoal, and flame color.

Distinguishing characteristics: The intense green color shows it to be a copper mineral, but, in case of any doubt, a test should be made to make sure that it is not a chromium or nickel green. Likely to be confused with copper sulfates, arsenates, and phosphates, but its effervescence as it dissolves in the hydrochloric acid eliminates them and proves it to be a carbonate.

Occurrence: The commonest and most stable of the secondary ores of copper, always forming near the surface as a result of the weathering of primary copper sulfides. It is so abundant that it constitutes an important ore, frequently associated in the weathered capping over the copper deposit with azurite, cuprite, and native copper.

Malachite usually forms fibrous crusts and masses, and in a very compact form it was extensively used in Russia for carving and mosaics. Since it varies considerably in hardness and may be poorly consolidated, only the hardest masses are suitable for this use. Africa produces this dense material today, although some years ago it was abundant at the famous Copper Queen Mine at Bisbee, Arizona. In most occurrences malachite forms soft, almost velvety crusts of slender needles, stalactites, and stalagmites, frequently alternating with bands of azurite, its constant associate.

Crystals of malachite are rare and small, few are over $\frac{1}{16}$ in. (2 mm) across. The best have come from Germany, Russia, Tsumeb and South West Africa, Zaïre (Belgian Congo), and sw. U.S. Large pseudomorphs composed of radiating velvety malachite needles, which start from several centers in an alteration of the dark blue crystals of azurite, are frequent. Most recently the finest crystals have come from the Ongonja Mine, South West Africa, but previously from other localities, particularly Arizona. A few large pseudomorphs after azurite like those of Tsumeb have been found in Michoacán, Mexico.

PHOSGENITE $Pb_2(CO_3)Cl_2$ **Pl. 23**
            Tetragonal — Tetragonal trapezohedral 4 2 2

Environment: Secondary (weathered) zones of lead ore deposit.

Crystal description: Always in crystals, sometimes in long and slender prisms; but shorter and squarer when large. May be up to 6 in. (15 cm) in length, and several inches across.

Physical properties: Colorless, white, yellowish brown to gray. *Luster* adamantine; *hardness* $2\frac{1}{4}$–$2\frac{3}{4}$; *gravity* 6.0–6.1;

fracture conchoidal; *cleavage* good prismatic, poor basal. Slightly sectile; transparent to translucent; fluoresces a brilliant orange-yellow.

Composition: A chlorocarbonate of lead (81.9% PbO, and about 13% Cl and 8% CO_2).

Tests: Blackens, bubbles, and spreads thinly, fuming and sinking into charcoal and leaving lead bead.

Distinguishing characteristics: Recognized as a carbonate by its bubbles in acid, as a lead mineral by its gravity and the blowpipe tests. Distinguished from cerussite by its tetragonal crystal form and blowpipe behavior. Hardness varies greatly with crystal direction, and the prism face or prism cleavage surface may be scratched by the fingernail (hardness of $2\frac{1}{2}$) parallel to the long (vertical) axis, but not across it.

Occurrence: A rare secondary lead mineral, particularly popular among collectors for its rarity and fluorescence, and sometimes found in good crystals. It forms as a result of the weathering of primary lead ores. Good crystals were found with related secondary minerals at Matlock, England, but the finest locality has proved to be Monteponi in Sardinia, where crystals many centimeters across have been found, derived with anglesite and cerussite from the alteration of a granular galena. More recently obtained at the Mammoth Mine, Tiger, Arizona, and in giant examples at Tsumeb, South West Africa.

Interesting facts: Phosgenite is one of the secondary lead minerals that have formed in gas holes in slag dumped into the Mediterranean by the ancient Greeks in their operation of the mines at Lavrion, Greece.

AZURITE $Cu_3(CO_3)_2(OH)_2$ **Pl. 27**

Monoclinic — prismatic $\frac{2}{m}$

Environment: Secondary (weathered) zone of copper ore deposits.

Crystal description: Commonly crystallized, often in large well-formed, equidimensional, deep blue crystals and in rosette-like aggregates. Also in slender blue needles or hairs. Frequently altered completely or in part to malachite. Commonly forms botryoidal growths like (and interlayered with) malachite, in crusts, stalactites, or stalagmites; and massive and earthy.

Physical properties: Light blue to almost black. *Luster* glassy; *hardness* $3\frac{1}{2}$–4; *gravity* 3.8; *fracture* conchoidal; *cleavage* 1 good and 2 poor. Brittle; transparent in thin chips.

Composition: Basic copper carbonate (69.2% CuO, 25.6% CO_2, 5.2% H_2O).

Tests: The copper-blue color is distinctive. Fuses on charcoal, and with careful treatment will give copper bead in reducing flame. Dissolves in hydrochloric acid with effervescence. Drop of solution on platinum wire gives fine blue copper flame; ammonia added to green acid solution turns it blue.

Distinguishing characteristics: Most other minerals that blue disseminated azurite resembles are harder. Effervescence in acid distinguishes it from other secondary copper compounds (linarite the most likely) for which it might be mistaken.

Occurrence: Azurite forms under conditions that are identical with those of malachite, with which it is always associated. Found in fine crystals at Chessy, France, from which it received its British name chessylite. South Australia and New South Wales gave comparable examples. Sharp brilliant crystals, the finest known and up to 6 in. (15 cm) long, were found at Tsumeb, South West Africa. Clifton and Bisbee, Arizona, are noted for the fine azurite crystals of their early days. Fine malachite pseudomorphs have come from Tsumeb and from Arizona. Although azurite is rarer than malachite, fine occurrences are common and much too numerous to list. Azurite and malachite stains on the rocks have served as valuable prospecting guides.

LEADHILLITE $Pb_4(SO_4)(CO_3)_2(OH)_2$ **Pl. 24**

Monoclinic — prismatic $\dfrac{2}{m}$

Environment: Secondary (weathered) zone of lead deposits.

Crystal description: Usually in plates, which look hexagonal because of a twinning. The base has a pearly luster and on the more prismatic crystals may be concave. Blue or green tints on the summits usually fade downward to white.

Physical properties: White, often tinged with light yellow, blue, or green. *Luster* pearly on the prominent cleavage surface, resinous to adamantine on the others; *hardness* 2.5; *gravity* 6.3–6.4; *fracture* conchoidal; *cleavage* 1 perfect, almost micaceous. Slightly sectile; translucent to transparent; fluoresces orange.

Composition: Basic sulfate and carbonate of lead (82.7% PbO, 7.4% SO_3, 8.2% CO_2, 1.7% H_2O).

Tests: Fuses easily on charcoal and is yellow when hot, white when cool (a sign of lead). Dissolves in nitric acid, forming bubbles, but leaves a residue of white insoluble lead sulfate.

Distinguishing characteristics: It is likely to be confused with other oxidized lead minerals such as phosgenite and cerussite (which dissolve in nitric acid without a sulfate residue) and anglesite (which does not dissolve).

Occurrences: This rare but attractive mineral usually forms crystals, but occurs at few localities. Delicate blue crystals have been found in the Mammoth Mine, Tiger, Arizona, associated with malachite, cerussite, willemite, dioptase, and wulfenite. Fine platy crystals were found in cavities from which galena had been leached at the Beer Cellar Mine, Granby, Missouri. The original occurrence was in the lead district on the northern border of England, and was first described from Leadhills, Scotland, to which it owes its name.

The Nitrates

This is a small and mineralogically unimportant group of minerals, most of which are extremely soluble in water. Hence, we do not find them in ordinary climatic regions; the arid west coast of Chile and some of the dry-lake deposits of California and Nevada are about the total occurrences. All are soft; only one appears to be insoluble in water, and that one is very rare.

SODA NITER $NaNO_3$

Hexagonal — Hexagonal scalenohedral $\overline{3}\frac{2}{m}$

Environment: Residual water-soluble surface deposits in deserts.

Crystal description: Usually in white masses; cavities sometimes have rhombohedral crystals, resembling calcite.

Physical properties: Colorless, white, tinted red-brown, or yellow. *Luster* glassy; *hardness* $1\frac{1}{2}$-2; *gravity* 2.2-2.3; *fracture* conchoidal; *cleavage* perfect rhombohedral. Slightly sectile; transparent to translucent.

Composition: Sodium nitrate (36.5% Na_2O, 63.5% N_2O_5).

Tests: Burns, with spurt of yellow flame when dropped on glowing spot in charcoal. Dissolves in water, tastes cooling to the tongue. Heated in closed tube with potassium disulfate, gives off brown fumes (NO).

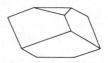

Distinguishing characteristics: The deflagration on coals shows it to be a nitrate, and the yellow color shows the sodium. Could only be confused with halite, which melts on the hot charcoal.

Occurrence: Abundant only in beds — composed principally of gypsum, halite, soda niter, and other related minerals — in the desert western slope of the Andes, n. Chile. Small quantities are reported in some of the dry California lake beds, and in Humboldt Co., Nevada. It is still mined in Chile for use in fertilizers, but the rich masses from the heyday of nitrate mining are now only to be seen sealed up in museum jars.

Interesting facts: Its crystal network is identical in character and dimensions with that of calcite. Soda niter crystals in exact parallel position can be grown on the surface of calcite rhombs from saturated solutions of soda niter. Discarded specimens of this mineral tossed out in a garden led to the discovery of the importance of nitrogen to plant growth.

NITER KNO_3

Orthorhombic — Rhombic bipyramidal $\frac{2}{m}\frac{2}{m}\frac{2}{m}$

Environment: Cavern walls, as an efflorescence. Also in dry soils in the floor of caves but freed only by dissolving it out in water.

Crystal description: Occurs as thin crusts and as silky short fibers on rock surfaces, cavern walls, etc. Never in well-formed crystals (but easily made artificially; hence, data on cleavage, fracture, and tenacity are available).

Physical properties: White. *Luster* glassy; *hardness* 2; *gravity* 2.1; *no fracture* visible in usual occurrences; *cleavage* good. Slightly sectile.

Composition: Potassium nitrate — "saltpeter" (46.5% K_2O, 53.5% N_2O_5).

Tests: Like soda niter, but burns and explodes on hot coals, with violet flame.

Distinguishing characteristics: Behavior on coals distinguishes it from other salts, and the violet flame characterizes it as a potassium mineral.

Occurrence: Niter is found only as an efflorescence which forms on rain-protected surfaces, as in caves and along cliffs, from solutions percolating down through the rocks. Probably of organic origin. Rarer than soda niter but sometimes used as a fertilizer.

Found in the dirt floor of caves in Kentucky and Tennessee, and sometimes in efflorescences along the limestone cliffs.

The Borates

These compounds form an important class of minerals that can be divided into two groups: (1) those of primary origin, forming from igneous sources almost free of water; they are relatively rare and unimportant; (2) the hydrous borates, forming in arid climates from surface solutions; these are locally abundant and are the commercial sources of borax. Hydrous borates are associated with halite, gypsum, and related sulfates. Those of primary origin occur in high-temperature veins and in pegmatites. Some borates are extremely hard, like the almost legendary jeremejevite,

$Al_6B_5O_{15}(OH)_3$, which was recently found (in blue crystals) for the second time (in South Africa); the original occurrence was a 19th-century discovery in Siberia. Although the hardness of water-free borates can reach $7\frac{1}{2}$, the hydrous borates are soft. Some of the artificial water-free boron compounds are among the hardest substances known.

KERNITE $Na_2B_4O_7 \cdot 4H_2O$ **Pl. 24**

Monoclinic — prismatic $\dfrac{2}{m}$

Environment: Buried strata beneath a dry lake bed.

Crystal description: Forms solid veins of large embedded crystals. Specimens are usually elongated fragments, parts of a single crystal, bounded by the cleavage planes of the base and the front faces.

Physical properties: Colorless, but turns white on long exposure to the air. *Luster* glassy, but dulled as the surface alters; *hardness* 3; *gravity* 1.9; *fracture* conchoidal (difficult to see because of the good cleavage); *cleavage* perfect basal and front pinacoid, producing long splinters. Brittle (splintery); transparent when fresh.

Composition: Hydrous sodium borate (51.0% B_2O_3, 22.7% Na_2O, 26.3% H_2O).

Tests: Under the blowpipe reacts like borax, with less swelling.

Distinguishing characteristics: The blowpipe reaction is characteristic, and only resembles that of borax itself. Distinguished from borax by greater hardness, its cleavage, and greater resistance to the chalky alteration.

Occurrence: Kernite was found by a drill hole several hundred feet beneath the surface at Kramer, Kern Co., California, in a great concealed bed, associated with borax and believed to have been derived from borax by the pressure and temperature resulting from the deep burial. It probably occurs elsewhere in many yet undrilled borax deposits, having formed in the same way. The chief source of borax today; an ideal ore, yielding more than its initial weight in product. A little has been found near the surface on the floor of Death Valley — an indication of the summer temperatures that develop there. Also found in Argentina.

Interesting facts: New minerals discovered today usually occur in small quantities and are of no commercial importance. This startling exception was found in 1926 in the process of drilling some prospecting holes at the Kern Co. locality, and it almost immediately became the leading ore of borax. Specimens do not keep well in collections since they usually absorb moisture from the air, which dulls the surface or penetrates cracks and makes the specimen cloudy. It is also a remarkable ore because the crystallization of a water solution yields 1.59 times as much of the desired product, borax, as borax itself.

BORAX $Na_2B_4O_7 \cdot 10H_2O$ **Pl. 24**
Monoclinic — prismatic $\frac{2}{m}$

Environment: Dry lake beds in desert country.
Crystal description: Usually forms crystals, often very large and well formed — but unfortunately they do not keep in the mineral cabinet. Also mixed with other compounds in crusts of various minerals in salt lake beds.
Physical properties: White, colorless, yellowish, grayish, bluish, greenish. *Luster* glassy; *hardness* 2–2½; *gravity* 1.7; *fracture* conchoidal; *cleavage* 3, 1 good. Brittle; transparent to translucent; crystals lose water and turn white.
Composition: Hydrous sodium borate (36.6% B_2O_3, 16.2% Na_2O, 47.2% H_2O).
Tests: Swells and fuses easily to a clear glass sphere that clings to the charcoal, coloring the flame yellow. Water-soluble; tastes sweetish but astringent.
Distinguishing characteristics: Not likely to be confused with any other mineral; characteristic fusion behavior with which the mineral collector is so familiar will distinguish it from most minerals. Rapid whitening of the crystals confirms other tests.
Occurrence: Used from ancient times, and brought to Europe by caravan from the dry lake bed in Tibet where it was found. Extensive deposits of this type are, or have been, worked in California and Nevada. The crystals are loose, fully developed, and often quite large; single crystals to 6 or 7 in. (15 or 20 cm) long and as much as a pound (½ kg) in weight have been recorded. Many are natural, as at Searles Lake, California; others form in sumps during mining operations, as at Boron, California. It is used as a flux, an antiseptic, as a water softener — and in mineralogy for borax beads. Its ancient name is "tincal," a name now applied to the unpurified material (tincalconite).

ULEXITE $NaCaB_5O_9 \cdot 8H_2O$ **Pl. 24**
Triclinic — pinacoidal $\overline{1}$
Environment: Desert borax deposits.
Crystal description: Usually forms soft white cottony masses of loosely intergrown fibrous crystals commonly known as "cotton balls" or "sheet cotton." Also, at Boron, California, in solid veins of parallel fibers, the so-called "television ore."
Physical properties: White. *Luster* silky; *hardness* 2½; *gravity* 1.6. Soft and cottony; translucent fibers in asbestoslike seams.
Composition: Hydrous sodium calcium borate (43.0% B_2O_3, 7.7% Na_2O, 13.8% CaO, 35.5% H_2O).
Tests: Fuses easily to a clear glass, coloring the flame yellow (Na). Glass fluoresces white in longwave ultraviolet, phosphoresces yellow. Slightly soluble in hot water.

Distinguishing characteristics: Fusibility distinguishes it from fibrous asbestos varieties; relative insolubility in water will distinguish it from capillary sulfates or salt.

Occurrence: Ulexite forms in borax deposits and salt beds in loose fragile balls or crusts, often mixed with salt, gypsum, or glauberite. Found in 3–4 in. (7–10 cm) balls in the Mojave Desert of s. Nevada and California. Similar occurrences are found in Chile and Argentina.

Interesting facts: The fibrous compact-vein parallel-fiber ulexite appears to be limited to the deep Boron deposit. It transmits light, and images, along each fiber and presaged the invention of fiber optics by transmitting images along a bundle of such threadlike crystals.

COLEMANITE $Ca_2B_6O_{11} \cdot 5H_2O$ **Pl. 24**

Monoclinic — prismatic $\dfrac{2}{m}$ (?)

Environment: Desert borax deposits.

Crystal description: Commonly in distinct crystals, sometimes thin and platy, more often well developed and more or less equidimensional. Also in granular masses, and lining geodes in beautiful druses.

Physical properties: White or colorless. *Luster* glassy; *hardness* 4–4½; *gravity* 2.4; *fracture* subconchoidal to uneven; *cleavage* perfect side pinacoid. Brittle; transparent; sometimes fluorescent.

Composition: Hydrous calcium borate (50.9% B_2O_3, 27.2% CaO, 21.9% H_2O).

Tests: Decrepitates so violently that it is difficult to fuse on charcoal. Grain in forceps decrepitates but melts with protrusions a little like borax. Colors flame green. Soluble in hot hydrochloric acid, with the precipitation of thin "snowflakes" of boric acid upon cooling.

Distinguishing characteristics: Resembles many other minerals, but its manner of occurrence is a good guide. Then the blowpipe test should prove the identity, for it does not resemble many other borates.

Occurrence: Another of the borate minerals to form in association with borax, ulexite (from which it is believed to have formed), and Tertiary clays in old lake beds in s. California. The most important ore of borax until kernite was discovered. Good specimens have been found in Death Valley at Ryan, California, and in several other borax mining areas in San Bernardino Co., California. Comparable crystals have been obtained in Turkey. Realgar is often an associate, suggesting that volcanic sources were involved in its formation.

Interesting facts: Colemanite specimens in collections have a tendency to collect dust in definite areas on crystal surfaces. Though the reputed crystal symmetry would not permit the compound to be pyroelectric and therefore show positive and negative charges with temperature changes (like tourmaline and quartz), it seems probable that there is some structural lack of symmetry responsible for this. Most specimens in mineral cabinets show this conspicuous dustiness in particular areas; it is sufficiently prevalent to be a distinguishing characteristic.

HOWLITE $Ca_2B_5SiO_9(OH)_5$ **Pl. 24**

Monoclinic — prismatic $\dfrac{2}{m}$

Environment: Desert borax deposits and related formations.
Crystal description: No good crystals visible in its w. U.S. occurrence, which is in the form of white rounded nodules. They make solid compact masses, without marked structure, and their surfaces look like small cauliflower heads. In Nova Scotia some crystal faces have been noted on the surfaces of similar nodules.
Physical properties: White. *Luster* subvitreous or dull; *hardness* $3\frac{1}{2}$; *gravity* 2.5–2.6; *fracture* even; *cleavage* none. Chalky to compact; translucent to opaque; sometimes fluorescent.
Composition: Basic silicoborate of calcium (44.6% B_2O_3, 28.6% CaO, 15.3% SiO_2, 11.5% H_2O).
Tests: Fuses to a clear glass sphere under the blowpipe, but less readily than borax and kernite. Soluble in hydrochloric acid, and with careful evaporation will be found to leave a silica gel on walls of test tube.
Distinguishing characteristics: Fusibility under the blowpipe indicates its borate nature; HCl solubility and its softness distinguish it from a chemically similar mineral (bakerite, hardness $4\frac{1}{2}$) and from datolite (hardness $5\frac{1}{2}$), which is very different in occurrence. Distinguished from the sodium borates by the green (boron) flame coloration and insolubility in water.
Occurrence: Found as nodules embedded in clay of borax deposits in California. Nova Scotia has similar but smaller nodules in gypsum and anhydrite beds.

The Sulfates

This is a widespread and abundant group of minerals that have a few properties in common, making them as a rule easy to classify. All are translucent to transparent; many are very light in color. A few, the sulfates of the common metals, are very soluble in water; some are insoluble in water but soluble in acid, whereas one important group is rather insoluble in the common acids. None are hard, but most are fairly high in specific gravity.
Tests for the group: The powdered mineral is fused with soda

on charcoal to a gray mass. This mass is placed on a silver sheet, crushed, and moistened. Presence of S is proved by appearance of a black stain on the silver when the assay is washed off.

Water-soluble sulfates form a white precipitate of calcium sulfate when a hydrochloric acid solution, in which calcite has been dissolved (calcium chloride), is added to the sulfate solution. The fluorescence of the cooled whitened portion of blowpiped minerals of the barite-celestite-anhydrite series is a new test that should be investigated further by collectors. The fluorescence does not show while the grain is still hot.

THENARDITE Na_2SO_4 Pl. 25

Orthorhombic — Rhombic bipyramidal $\dfrac{2\ \ 2\ \ 2}{m\ m\ m}$

Environment: Dry salt-lake beds in desert climates.

Crystal description: Commonly in intergrown, poorly defined crystal clusters, and difficult to recognize. When distinct: tabular, short-prismatic, or pyramidal. Sometimes in sharp crossed-twin crystals. Also forming beds of solid material.

Physical properties: Colorless to light yellowish or brownish, often clay-filled and gray. *Luster* glassy; *hardness* $2\frac{1}{2}$–3; *gravity* 2.7; *fracture* uneven; *cleavage* good basal. Transparent to translucent; weakly fluorescent (yellow-green under longwave ultraviolet); and phosphorescent.

Composition: Sodium sulfate (56.3% Na_2O, 43.7% SO_3).

Tests: Fuses easily, at first to clear glass (becomes cloudy on cooling and nonfluorescent); then bubbles, spreads flat, fluoresces white in shortwave ultraviolet light. Dissolves readily in water; tastes salty. Water solution precipitates calcium sulfate out of solution made by dissolving calcite in hydrochloric acid.

Distinguishing characteristics: Recognized by the flame coloration (Na), the S test, and ease of solution in water. Confused with other water-soluble minerals like halite, but distinguished from them by S test. Distinguished from glauberite by being completely soluble in very little water.

Occurrence: Thenardite has formed very frequently as the result of evaporation of a salt lake. Known from such occurrences in Spain, Siberia, and the Caucasus. Also found in Africa and in numerous deposits in Chile. The U.S. beds are in Arizona, Nevada, at Searles Lake, San Bernardino Co., and in Soda Lake, San Luis Obispo Co., California.

BARITE $BaSO_4$ Pls. 25, 27

Orthorhombic — Rhombic bipyramidal $\dfrac{2\ \ 2\ \ 2}{m\ m\ m}$

Environment: Sedimentary rocks; a late gangue mineral in ore veins.

Crystal description: Crystals commonly tabular, often very large. Also prismatic, equidimensional, in featherlike groups, concretionary masses, "desert roses," and fine-grained, massive.
Physical properties: Colorless to bluish, yellow, brown, reddish. *Luster* glassy: *hardness* 3–3½; *gravity* 4.3–4.6; *fracture* uneven; *cleavage* perfect basal and prismatic, with a fair side pinacoid. Brittle; transparent to translucent; sometimes fluorescent.
Composition: Barium sulfate (65.7% BaO, 34.3% SO_3).
Tests: Decrepitates, whitens, but fuses only with some difficulty. After intense heating, whitened assay fluoresces, usually bright orange. Gives S test with soda.
Distinguishing characteristics: High gravity in such a light-colored mineral usually sufficiently significant. Distinguished from calcite by insolubility in acid; from feldspar by its softness; from celestite and anhydrite by orange fluorescence after firing and the green flame color; and from fluorite by lack of typical fluorite fluorescence.
Occurrence: Although barite often is an accompanying mineral of sulfide ore veins, it is even more common in sedimentary rocks, where it forms concretionary nodules and free-growing crystals in open spaces. Veins of almost pure barite have been mined in several localities. The finest large barite crystals have come from Cumberland, England; single domatic free-growing crystals may be as much as 8 in. (20 cm) long. The British occurrences are notable for their delicate coloring and well-formed crystals. There are many other fine localities, however. In Baia Sprie (Felsöbanya), Rumania, it is intimately associated with stibnite needles, usually in flat colorless or yellowish crystals. Other occurrences abroad are too numerous to mention.

In the U.S. it is mined in the Midwest, as in Missouri. There white bladed "tiff" masses are found where the soil contacts the undecomposed limestone — the barite having settled as the enclosing rock weathered away. Good white to clear crystals, some a foot (30 cm) long, have also been found in Missouri. It is found in perfect imitative "roses" of a red-brown color and sandy texture near Norman, Oklahoma. Fine crusts of blue crystals are found in veins in soft sediments near Stoneham, Colorado. Great concretions, known as "septarian nodules," found in the Bad Lands of South Dakota contain up to 4 in. (10 cm) fluorescent, transparent, amber-colored crystals in the cracks.
Interesting facts: An important commercial mineral; widely used as a pigment in the preparation of lithopone and as a filler for paper and cloth. Barite "mud" is poured into deep oil wells to buoy up the drilling tools. Several hundred years ago, a massive, concretionary variety of barite from Italy was found to phosphoresce on light heating, and was called "Bologna

stone" from its locale of discovery. It was, of course, of great interest to the alchemists, the founders of chemistry, who were trying to make gold from the base metals.

CELESTITE SrSO$_4$ **Pl. 25**

Orthorhombic — Rhombic bipyramidal $\dfrac{2\ \ 2\ \ 2}{m\ m\ m}$

Environment: Sedimentary rocks; rarely a gangue mineral of ore veins.

Crystal description: Usually in crystals, commonly tabular, resembling barite; also granular and in fibrous veins.

Physical properties: Colorless to white, red-brown, orange, or light blue. *Luster* glassy; *hardness* 3–3½; *gravity* 3.9–4.0; *fracture* uneven; *cleavage* like barite, perfect basal and prismatic and poor pinacoidal. Brittle; transparent to translucent; sometimes fluorescent.

Composition: Strontium sulfate (56.4% SrO, 43.6% SO$_3$).

Tests: Cracks, fuses with difficulty on charcoal. After firing, with whitening of the surface, fluoresces and phosphoresces bright green. Gives S test with silver.

Distinguishing characteristics: Light blue color, which often tints only part of the otherwise white crystal, the best diagnostic point. The flame test can only be confused with that from anhydrite (but Ca much less red than Sr). Similar minerals of other groups can be distinguished by the softness and acid insolubility of the celestite, and the fluorescence after heating.

Occurrence: Only rarely an accessory mineral of ore veins that were formed from warm solutions. Usually found in sedimentary rocks; the best occurrences are in cavities in sandstone or limestone, associated with fluorite, calcite, gypsum, dolomite, galena, and sphalerite. Its color in these occurrences very often is the characteristic blue.

Fine, white, elongated, square crystals, an inch (2–3 cm) or so in length, are abundant in the Sicilian sulfur mines, associated with sulfur. Small blue crystals of similar habit were found on a white calcite at Herrengrund (now Špania Dolina, Czechoslovakia). Large flat white blades are found in England at Yate, Gloucestershire.

The best occurrences appear to be in the U.S. Tremendous crystals were found on Kelleys I., Lake Erie, in a large limestone quarry. Some of these crystals were 6–8 in. (15–20 cm) across. A more recent best locality from the standpoint of abundance is Clay Center, Ohio (another limestone quarry), in which pockets are filled with fine blue-to-white bladed celestite, associated with a brown fluorite and yellowish calcite. Some of the white crystals are very thin and fragile; others are thicker, blue, and resemble barite.

Geodes with large blue crystals much like those from

Kelleys I. are found at Lampasas, Texas. Colorless transparent crystals occur with the colemanite in geodes of the Death Valley area. Orange cloudy crystals are found near Toronto, Canada, and in Colorado. Fine blue crystals are found near Manitou Springs, Colorado, and blue radiating columnar crystal intergrowths were found in the gold mines at Cripple Creek, Colorado. A blue fibrous vein material from Bellwood, Blair Co., Pennsylvania, described in 1791, was the original celestite, the first discovery of this mineral. Brilliant geodes lined with gemmy blue crystals are found in Madagascar.

Interesting facts: The blue of celestite has been attributed to the presence of minute amounts of gold, but irradiation also turns some crystals blue.

ANGLESITE PbSO$_4$ Pl. 25

Orthorhombic — Rhombic bipyramidal $\dfrac{2\ 2\ 2}{m\ m\ m}$

Environment: Secondary (weathered) deposits of lead ore.

Crystal description: Tabular to prismatic crystals, may be elongated in any of the axial directions. Also massive, fine-grained, granular to very compact.

Physical properties: Colorless to white or grayish, or tinted with impurities (red or green). *Luster* adamantine; *hardness* $2\frac{3}{4}$–3; *gravity* 6.4; *fracture* conchoidal; *cleavage* basal and prismatic. Brittle; transparent to translucent; often fluorescent (yellow-orange).

Composition: Lead sulfate (73.6% PbO, 26.4% SO$_3$).

Tests: Fuses very easily, forming white enamel, which is briefly yellow while still very hot. With continued blowpiping in the reducing flame, it boils away in spurts and yields lead bead.

Distinguishing characteristics: Easily recognized as a lead mineral by blowpipe reactions. Distinguished from cerussite and phosgenite by lack of effervescence in acids and its behavior on charcoal.

Occurrence: Anglesite only forms during the alteration by weathering of lead sulfide. The best crystals appear to be associated with granular lead ores rather than ores with large well-formed galena crystals; perhaps this is because the granular galena is more rapidly attacked and the anglesite crystals can grow more rapidly. Usually associated with other lead minerals like phosgenite and cerussite, and with other oxidized-zone minerals like malachite and azurite.

Fine, transparent, well-developed isolated crystals an inch (2–3 cm) or so in size are found in small cavities in the granular galena of Monteponi, Sardinia. Large crystals have been found at Tsumeb, South West Africa (with a secondary copper ore), at Broken Hill, New South Wales (with cerussite), and at Coeur d'Alene, Idaho. Fine crystals were once found with pyromorphite and cerussite at the old Wheatley Mine, Phoenixville, Pennsylvania. Small crystals are common on altering galena with tiny yellow sulfur crystals. Sometimes the massive type will be found as concentric gray to black bands surrounding a nucleus of unaltered galena. Good pseudomorphs of anglesite after cubes of galena have been found in the Joplin (Missouri) District. In an interesting Mexican occurrence, yellowish tabular anglesite crystals are embedded in sulfur. There are numerous other good occurrences, too many to list.

ANHYDRITE $CaSO_4$ **Pl. 25**

Orthorhombic — Rhombic bipyramidal $\dfrac{2\ 2\ 2}{m\ m\ m}$

Environment: Sedimentary beds, gangue in ore veins, and in traprock zeolite occurrences.

Crystal description: Crystals relatively rare, rectangular pinacoidal, or elongated parallel to domes. Also coarse to fine-grained, granular.

Physical properties: Colorless, white, gray, blue, lilac, or tinted with visible impurities. *Luster* glassy to pearly; *hardness* $3-3\frac{1}{2}$; *gravity* 3.0; *fracture* uneven to splintery; *cleavage* 3 good pinacoidal. Transparent to translucent; sometimes fluorescent.

Composition: Calcium sulfate (41.2% CaO, 58.8% SO_3).

Tests: Cracks, decrepitates mildly, and fuses with difficulty on charcoal. Gives good S test with silver. Fluoresces various colors after heating, pink (Balmat, New York), yellow-green (Paterson, New Jersey), or blue-white (Switzerland).

Distinguishing characteristics: The cubic aspect of its cleavage and the S test, coupled with the low specific gravity, make its identification easy. Often associated with gypsum in same specimen.

Occurrence: Anhydrite is surprisingly rare in mineral specimens, probably because it is easily altered to gypsum through hydration. It can be deposited directly from seawater. It is found most frequently in sedimentary rocks, especially with salt beds. The metamorphic rock occurrences were probably derived from recrystallized gypsum.

The best occurrences are European. Highly prized attractive lilac crystals and cleavages were encountered in drilling the Simplon Tunnel in Switzerland. It is abundant in Poland in the salt mines near Kraków, and in East Germany at the Stassfurt mine. In these occurrences usually massive, but may also be in small crystals embedded in water-soluble salts.

The most interesting U.S. occurrence has little anhydrite today. It is only a memory preserved in the form of abundant pseudomorphs of quartz and zeolites, after what must have been long blades of anhydrite, in the Paterson (New Jersey) trap area. Some residual anhydrite, altered in part to white gypsum, has been found; the discovery solved a controversy about the origin of the rectangular voids. Clear crystals (usually very small) have been found in salt-well residues in Louisiana. No larger microscopic colorless crystals of anhydrite can be recovered from halite that was caught up in a pegmatitic intrusion encountered in the zinc mine at Balmat, New York, and a violet anhydrite is associated with it in the bounding dike. The best U.S. crystals up to now probably occur in the cap rocks of the salt domes, and are encountered by drilling in the Louisiana-Texas sulfur area. Naturally, specimens from this source are limited. However, anhydrite is an important gangue mineral in some ore veins. It is found in lilac masses in Peru and Chile and is abundant in giant 12 in. (30 cm) crystals in the gangue of the Faraday Mine, Bancroft, Ontario. Free-standing blue crystals are found with the Naica (Mexico) lead ores.

Beds once occurred in Nova Scotia, but they are now largely altered to gypsum, an expansion with hydration that caused a beautiful crumpling of the weak layers and made very graphic small-scale illustrations of the geologic process of the folding of stratified beds under compression.

W. New York localities with anhydrite in cavities in limestone (like celestite) have been described, but even if true these occurrences must be rare. Pressure or elevated temperatures, or both, seem essential to its formation.

GLAUBERITE $Na_2Ca(SO_4)_2$ **Pl. 25**

Monoclinic — prismatic $\dfrac{2}{m}$

Environment: Dry salt-like beds in desert climates.

Crystal description: The steeply inclined bipyramidal crystals are very characteristic. May also be tabular to the base.

Physical properties: White or light yellow to a mud-filled gray or buff. *Luster* glassy; *hardness* $2\frac{1}{2}$–3; *gravity* 2.7–2.8; *fracture* conchoidal; *cleavage* perfect basal. Brittle; transparent to translucent; salt taste; may phosphoresce.

Composition: Sodium calcium sulfate (22.3% NaO, 20.2% CaO, 57.5% SO_3).

Tests: Decrepitates, then fuses easily to a white enamel, coloring the flame yellow (Na). In water it turns white and partially dissolves, leaving a residue of calcium sulfate. Bitter taste.

Distinguishing characteristics: It can be recognized as a sulfate by a chemical sulfate test with calcite in a hydrochloric acid solution. It is distinguished in this way from the water-soluble halides. Can be told from thenardite by the slow solubility and residue of calcium sulfate left after its solution in a little water.

Occurrence: Glauberite commonly forms in and with salt beds upon the evaporation of salt lakes, occurring thus in East Germany (at Stassfurt), U.S.S.R., Kenya, Chile, India, Spain, and Austria. It is found in the U.S. in San Bernardino Co. at Searles Lake (California), and in Arizona at Camp Verde. Once more widespread, since casts of other minerals and sediments around glauberite crystal-shaped cavities are fairly common. Great opal masses (known as "pineapples" in Australia) are though to be opal pseudomorphs after this mineral. Perfect, sharp, empty glauberite crystal casts in sandstone have been found in New Jersey. In the trap quarries of Paterson, one of the unknown minerals that are commemorated by the well-known quartz casts may have been glauberite. Existing crystals are usually small, their normal size only a few centimeters.

POLYHALITE $K_2Ca_2Mg(SO_4)_4 \cdot 2H_2O$ **Pl. 26**
Triclinic — pinacoidal $\overline{1}$

Environment: Sedimentary beds associated with other products of an evaporated saline sea.

Crystal description: Usually occurs in massive, granular beds, or in fibrous or lamellar masses. Crystals simple, small, and rather rare.

Physical properties: If pure, colorless to white, but often pale cloudy red to brick-red. *Luster* resinous; *hardness* $3\frac{1}{2}$; *gravity* 2.8 (but water-soluble so not usually determined); *fracture* usually fibrous or splintery; *cleavage* 1 good.

Composition: Hydrous sulfate of potassium, calcium, and magnesium   (15.6% K_2O,   18.6% CaO,   6.7% MgO,   53.1% SO_3, 6.0% H_2O).

Tests: Bitter taste. Colors flame purple (K) and fuses easily. Dissolved in a small quantity of water, it frees an insoluble residue of calcium sulfate.

Distinguishing characteristics: Much like some of the other bedded salts, and often impure. Likely to be confused with sylvite but distinguishable by its incomplete solubility.

Occurrence: Likely to be found in commercial bedded-salt deposits where the several layers are being mined for rock salt (halite) and sylvite. In the U.S. it has been found in the salt beds near Carlsbad, New Mexico, and w. Texas. Also found in the salt deposits: near Hallstatt, Austria; in Galicia, Poland; and at Stassfurt, East Germany.

Interesting facts: The name at first glance is misleading but refers to the Greek for "many" (*poly*) "salts" (*hal*), in reference to the large number of salts that compose it.

GYPSUM $CaSO_4 \cdot 2H_2O$ Monoclinic — prismatic $\dfrac{2}{m}$ **Pl. 26**

Environment: Sedimentary rocks as massive beds, in free crystals in clay beds, and crystallized in cavities in limestone. Often in opaque, sand-filled crystal clusters.

Crystal description: Crystals are common and most often assume a tabular habit, making model-like, backward-slanting, monoclinic plates, with the horizontal axis the shortest. "Fishtail" twins are characteristic. The commonest crystals — which may be quite large — are found loose and free-growing in clay beds, and come out whole; this glassy form is known as selenite. Fibrous veins are known as "satin spar."

Physical properties: Colorless, white, and light tints. *Luster* glassy, pearly (on cleavage face), and silky; *hardness* 2; *gravity* 2.3; *fracture* conchoidal and fibrous; *cleavage* 2, 1 perfect micaceous. Sectile; often fluorescent in yellow, showing hourglass pattern within crystal; also phosphorescent.

Composition: Hydrous calcium sulfate (32.6% CaO, 46.5% SO_3, 20.9% H_2O).

Tests: Soluble in hot dilute hydrochloric acid; the addition of barium chloride solution makes a white precipitate. After firing, fluorescent and phosphorescent in longwave ultraviolet light.

Distinguishing characteristics: The low degree of hardness, the observation that it is easily scratched by a fingernail, is about the only test needed. The clear plates bend but lack the elasticity of mica, and are softer than brucite. Massive beds are softer than those of anhydrite or marble, and gypsum will not bubble in acid like the latter.

Occurrence: A widespread, commercially important mineral. The massive beds are quarried, or mined, for the manufacture of plaster of paris and various plaster products. Alabaster is a name for massive gypsum and "satin spar" is the fibrous variety. The most abundant deposits are the sedimentary beds, some of which have formed from the alteration of the water-free variety, anhydrite. It is such beds that are mined for economic applications in New York State, Michigan, Texas, Iowa, and California. Nova Scotia has great beds of altered anhydrite that show interesting crumpling of the layers as they swelled with the addition of water — geologic structures on a micro scale!

Good crystals are found in clay beds of Ohio and Maryland, and interesting cave rosettes of spreading fibers (gypsum flowers) come from Kentucky.

The most beautiful gypsum (selenite) crystals are foreign in origin, though the largest probably came from a cave in Utah. The large water-clear crystals from the Sicilian sulfur mines, often with inclusions of sulfur, are classics of all collections. In Naica, Chihuahua, n. Mexico, a cavern in the mine ("Cave of the Swords") contains meter-long, slender, slightly milky needles with tubular water-filled cavities and movable bubbles.

Interesting facts: The name plaster of paris comes from its early production in the Montmartre quarries of Paris. The name gypsum comes from the Greek word for the calcined (or "burned") material. "Selenite" comes from a Greek comparison of the pearly luster of the cleavage to moonlight.

CHALCANTHITE $CuSO_4 \cdot 5H_2O$ Triclinic — pinacoidal $\bar{1}$

Environment: Always a secondary mineral that forms during copper sulfide mineral oxidation and likely to persist only in arid environments because of its high solubility in water.

Crystal description: Usually forms botryoidal or stalactitic masses, and rarely in blue fibrous veins. Sharp crystals like those so easily grown artificially are so exceptional in nature as to be unbelievable when offered by dealers.

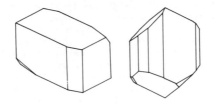

Physical properties: Sky-blue. *Luster* vitreous; *hardness* $2\frac{1}{2}$; *gravity* 2.3; *fracture* conchoidal; *cleavage* 3 poor. Translucent to transparent; sweetish metallic taste.

Composition: Hydrous copper sulfate (31.9% CuO, 32.1% SO_3, 36.1% H_2O).

Tests: None necessary as a rule; the taste and color are enough to identify it. *Poisonous*. Do not taste too freely!

Distinguishing characteristics: Not likely to be mistaken for any other water-soluble salt except the related iron sulfate (melanterite $FeSO_4 \cdot 7H_2O$) or iron copper sulfate (pisanite), which are greener. Chalcanthite is sufficiently abundant in fibrous veins at Chuquicamata and El Teniente (Sewell), Chile, to form an important ore of copper. Elsewhere it is too rare to have any value alone, though copper can be recovered from the water solutions of copper sulfate by exchanging the copper in solution for iron, which goes into solution as a sulfate. This is a valuable source of copper at Minas de Ríotinto, Spain.

Occurrence: Aside from its occurrence in actual veins in rock in Chile, it usually forms on mine timbers and on the walls of tunnels as a result of the exposure of wet sulfide ores to air as the mine is worked. Fine blue stalactites have formed in many mines, notably at: Bingham, Utah; Ducktown, Tennessee; and the Arizona copper mines. Almost without exception, the dealers' fine crystals perched on matrix are artificial, and can be regarded as fakes.

Interesting facts: "Chalcanthite" comes from Greek for "flower of copper." It is an unsatisfactory mineral for collections because it usually loses water and crumbles to a white powder in a short time. The artificial crystals, easily grown from slowly evaporating solutions, make it one of the most satisfactory salts for the amateur's experiments in crystal-growing. To survive in collections it seems to have to be very pure and free of iron.

EPSOMITE $MgSO_4 \cdot 7H_2O$
      Orthorhombic — Rhombic bisphenoidal 2 2 2
    Environment: Cave walls, as a white efflorescence deposited by salt springs.
    Crystal description: Usually not in crystals, but in white hairlike or cottony efflorescences. Also in botryoidal masses and small prismatic crystals.
    Physical properties: White. *Luster* silky, glassy to earthy; *hardness* 2–2½; *gravity* 1.7 (but water-soluble, so not readily determined); *fracture* conchoidal; *cleavage* 1 perfect and 2 less perfect. Brittle to cottony; translucent to transparent; bitter taste.
    Composition: Hydrous magnesium sulfate (16.3% MgO, 32.5% SO_3, 51.2% H_2O).
    Tests: Rapidly and completely water-soluble; has bitter taste. Melts readily to a liquid in its own water of crystallization.
    Distinguishing characteristics: Its taste and ready solubility, together with its occurrence, are usually distinctive.
    Occurrence: In the U.S. epsomite's principle occurrences are as white efflorescences on the walls of limestone caves, where they are protected from solution by rain or much dampness. It has been found in large crystals in lake-bed deposits on Kruger Mountain, Oroville, Washington. In some very dry localities, as in South Africa, it may form beds of considerable thickness, but in general it can be considered rare. It has also been found around fumaroles on Vesuvius lavas.
    The name is derived from its occurrence in solution in a medicinal mineral spring at Epsom, England.

BROCHANTITE $Cu_4(SO_4)(OH)_6$ **Pl. 27**
      Monoclinic — prismatic $\dfrac{2}{m}$
    Environment: Oxidized (weathered) zones of copper deposits, particularly in rocks low in carbonates.
    Crystal description: Small, prismatic to short-prismatic or tabular crystals; also soft masses like malachite. Commonly twinned to look orthorhombic, with terminal faces that are characteristically rounded, lacking the even surfaces and sharp definition usual in the prism and pinacoid faces. A smooth shiny face will always lie in the prism zone, making orientation easy.

Physical properties: Bright to dark green. *Luster* glassy (slightly pearly on the cleavage faces); *hardness* $3\frac{1}{2}$–4; *gravity* 4.0; *fracture* conchoidal; *cleavage* perfect side pinacoidal. Splintery or flaky fragments form on crushing; translucent to transparent.

Composition: A basic sulfate of copper (70.4% CuO, 17.7% SO_3, 11.9% H_2O).

Tests: Same as for antlerite (next).

Distinguishing characteristics: See next mineral.

Occurrence: A common mineral of deeply altered copper deposits, especially in rocks other than limestone; and consequently has been found in many of the western copper localities. Especially well crystallized specimens have come from Nevada, but it is also found in Arizona, New Mexico, Utah, and California. It was abundant in the old European localities, in Russia, Rumania, Italy, and England. It was named for a French geologist, Brochant de Villiers.

ANTLERITE $Cu_3(SO_4)(OH)_4$ **Pl. 27**

Orthorhombic — Rhombic bipyramidal $\dfrac{2}{m}\dfrac{2}{m}\dfrac{2}{m}$

Environment: Secondary (weathered) zone of copper deposits.

Crystal description: Forms small tabular to short-prismatic green crystals; also occurs in soft, fibrous, green masses resembling malachite and in painfully skin-penetrating needles.

Physical properties: Bright to dark green. *Luster* glassy; *hardness* $3\frac{1}{2}$–4; *gravity* 3.9; *fracture* uneven; *cleavage* pinacoidal, perfect side, poor front. Splintery; translucent to transparent.

Composition: Basic sulfate of copper (67.3% CuO, 22.6% SO_3, 10.1% H_2O).

Tests: Dissolves in hydrochloric acid without effervescence; chip of calcite added to solution causes white needles (of calcium sulfate) to form.

Distinguishing characteristics: Distinguished from malachite by lack of bubbling in acid and from copper phosphates and arsenates by the sulfate test. Antlerite is chemically indistinguishable from brochantite, though dome faces are flatter and more even than the base (pseudodomes) of brochantite.

Occurrence: Antlerite, like brochantite, is a mineral of the oxidized zones of copper deposits in siliceous rocks that cannot supply an abundance of the CO_2 required for the formation of the carbonate group of copper minerals. It was thought to be rare, but since its recognition as the principal secondary ore of copper at Chuquicamata, Chile, its greater abundance and more widespread distribution has been recognized. It has often been confused with brochantite, from which it is nearly indistinguishable by simple tests, and is far more common than was thought. It was named from the Antler Mine in Arizona, and is probably fairly common in copper deposits in the West.

LINARITE $PbCu(SO_4)(OH)_2$ **Pl. 27**

Monoclinic — prismatic $\dfrac{2}{m}$

Environment: Secondary (weathered) zone of ore deposits.
Crystal description: Slender prismatic blades to tabular parallel to the base. Usually not as upstanding as azurites.
Physical properties: Deep blue. *Luster* glassy to adamantine; *hardness* $2\frac{1}{2}$; *gravity* 5.3–5.4; *fracture* conchoidal; *cleavage* 1 perfect and 1 fair. Brittle; translucent to transparent in thin blades.
Composition: Basic sulfate of lead and copper (19.8% CuO, 55.7% PbO, 20.0% SO_3, 4.5% H_2O).
Tests: Decomposed and partially dissolved by 1:1 nitric acid, leaving a white insoluble residue of lead sulfate, and forming a green solution that turns blue with the addition of ammonia (Cu).
Distinguishing characteristics: It could only be confused with azurite among the common minerals, and can be distinguished from that by its lack of effervescence and the incomplete solubility in acid. Diaboleite $[Pb_2CuCl_2(OH_4)]$, a rare tetragonal associate at the Mammoth Mine, Tiger, Arizona, is a chloride and will not give the sulfate precipitate.
Occurrence: The blue masses and crystals of linarite are probably more common than is generally thought, but they are so similar to azurite in appearance that they are usually mistaken for those of the commoner mineral. Large crystals are rare; some of the best — 4 in. (10 cm) or more long — have been found at the Mammoth Mine. Elsewhere it is usually in small crystals, as at: Tintic, Utah; Eureka, Nevada; and Cerro Gordo, Inyo Co., California. Better than average 2 in. (2–3 cm) crystals come from Graham Co., Arizona. The richest U.S. locality is Bingham, New Mexico. Named for Linares, Spain, where it was first recognized; also found in Great Britain in Cornwall, Cumberland, and Scotland, and in Germany, Siberia, Chile, Argentina, and South West Africa.

ALUNITE $KAl_3(SO_4)_2(OH)_6$ **Pl. 26**

Hexagonal — Ditrigonal pyramidal 3 m

Environment: A rock-making mineral where acid, often ore-bearing, solutions have altered orthoclase feldspar-rich rocks.
Crystal description: Usually massive, crystals are rare and most often cubelike rhombohedrons. When seen they are likely to be coating the walls of a fissure in massive alunite.
Physical properties: White, light gray, or flesh-red. *Luster*

vitreous to pearly; *hardness* 3½–4; *gravity* 2.6–2.9; *fracture* flat conchoidal to uneven; *cleavage* fair basal and poor rhombohedral. Brittle; translucent to transparent, sometimes fluorescent orange in longwave ultraviolet light.

Composition: Basic hydrous sulfate of aluminum and potassium (11.4% K_2O, 36.9% Al_2O_3, 38.7% SO_3, 13.0% H_2O).

Tests: High heating in closed tube gives water that tests acid with litmus paper (a blue paper that turns pink in acid). Colors flame purple (K). Infusible, but becomes soluble in nitric acid after blowpiping.

Distinguishing characteristics: Closely resembles, in its massive form, limestone and dolomite. A test is essential for identification if alunite is suspected. Its eventual solubility, and then without effervescence, is a favorable sign.

Occurrence: A great mountain of alunite is to be found at Marysvale, Utah, and several attempts have been made to work it commercially, both by the exploitation of the potash as a fertilizer and the balance as an ore of aluminum. Similar large alunite deposits are known in Colorado, at Red Mountain, and associated with the ores at Goldfield, Nevada. Although uninteresting from the specimen standpoint, it is potentially valuable as a raw material.

JAROSITE $KFe_3(SO_4)_2(OH)_6$ Pl. 46
Hexagonal — Ditrigonal pyramidal 3 m

Environment: Secondary mineral, forming under conditions of weathering in arid climates.

Crystal description: Often in minute or microscopic crystals of hexagonal or, more commonly, triangular habit; also in fibrous crusts, granular and massive ocherous aggregates.

Physical properties: Ocher-yellow to clove-brown. *Luster* vitreous to subadamantine; *hardness* 2½–3½; *gravity* 2.9–3.3; *fracture* uneven; *cleavage* perfect basal. Brittle to sectile; translucent.

Composition: Basic hydrous sulfate of iron and potassium (9.4% K_2O, 47.8% Fe_2O_3, 32.0% SO_3, 10.8% H_2O).

Tests: On charcoal, with the blowpipe, gives black magnetic bead, colors flame purple (best seen by touching grain with drop of nitric acid and noting first flash of color). A partially fused mass gives the blackening test for sulfur obtained by crushing and moistening on silver disk.

Distinguishing characteristics: The crystallized specimens are easily recognized by the hexagonal and rhombohedral shapes. The massive material resembles limonite but can be distinguished by the blowpipe tests listed above. In routine testing, potassium and sulfur are good indication of jarosite, but it is not an easy mineral to identify without crystals.

Occurrence: Most frequently found near western ore veins in rocks that are rich in silica, supposedly formed by alteration of pyrite in the vein. Good specimens have been found in: Chaffee Co., Colorado; Maricopa Co., Arizona; and Tintic, Utah. Jarosite has been found in nodules with iron phosphates in Midvale, Virginia.

COPIAPITE $(Fe,Mg)Fe_4(So_4)_6(OH)_2 \cdot 20H_2O$ **Pl. 27**

Triclinic — pinacoidal $\overline{1}$

Environment: Oxidized iron sulfide deposits.

Crystal description: Usually occurs as loose masses of crystalline scales, also in compact granular crusts. No good crystals.

Physical properties: Ocher to sulfur-yellow. *Luster* pearly; *hardness* $2\frac{1}{2}$–3; *gravity* 2.1; *cleavage* micaceous. Translucent: metallic taste.

Composition: Basic ferric sulfate (about 25.6% Fe_2O_3, 38.5% SO_3, 30.3% H_2O, often with some MgO, CuO, and Al_2O_3).

Tests: Water-soluble; clear solution becomes and remains cloudy on boiling. Gives magnetic bead on charcoal before the blowpipe.

Distinguishing characteristics: Difficult to distinguish, without extensive tests, from several other iron sulfates that closely resemble it in appearance and occurrence. However, the taste and the water solubility distinguish them from similar-appearing minerals of unrelated species. It is also less brilliantly yellow (and nonfluorescent) than several oxides of uranium minerals.

Occurrence: Copiapite is the commonest of the ferric sulfates and is selected here as representative of a large group of similar and related species, all of which form in the same fashion. The only reliable method of distinguishing between them is with X-rays.

Copiapite is likely to be found in the U.S. wherever pyrite is oxidizing rapidly, as on coal mine refuse piles, or at a burning copper mine in Jerome, Arizona. It has also been noted at Sulphur Bank, California, and in some of the California mercury mines, like Mt. Diablo. It formed continously in some of the Missouri sinkhole iron sulfide deposits as soon as they were exposed to the air.

CALEDONITE $Cu_2Pb_5(SO_4)_3(CO_3)(OH)_6$ **Pl. 28**

Orthorhombic — Rhombic bipyramidal $\dfrac{2\ \ 2\ \ 2}{m\,m\,m}$

Environment: Secondary (weathered) zone of lead and copper ores.

Crystal description: Usually in small well-formed prismatic crystals, often with several prisms and a series of parallel truncating faces. Though small they make very attractive specimens, especially for micromounts.

Physical properties: Light blue to light blue-green. *Luster* resinous; *hardness* $2\frac{1}{2}$–3; *gravity* 5.8; *fracture* uneven; *cleavage* 1 good and 2 poor. Brittle; translucent.

Composition: Basic carbonate sulfate of lead and copper (9.9% CuO, 69.2% PbO, 14.9% SO_3, 2.7% CO_2, 3.3% H_2O).

Tests: Fuses easily to a metal bead on charcoal. The bead dissolves easily in nitric acid to give a green solution, which turns blue with ammonia (Cu). Added HCl makes a milky (Pb) solution.

Distinguishing characteristics: The mineral is quite rare. Its prismatic crystals and color (both of which are very characteristic), together with its occurrence and associates, make its recognition very easy.

Occurrence: Probably the world's finest examples of caledonite are the $\frac{1}{2}$ in. (1–1.5 cm) crystals from the Mammoth Mine at Tiger, Arizona. Also found at Cerro Gordo, Inyo Co., California, Beaver Creek, Utah, and Dona Ana Co., New Mexico, in lead-copper mines. It is not a common mineral, even in Scotland, where it was first found (whence the name), nor in Cornwall, Sardinia, Chile, or other important occurrences.

CROCOITE $PbCrO_4$ Monoclinic — prismatic $\dfrac{2}{m}$ **Pl. 28**

Environment: Oxidized lead veins, as a secondary mineral.

Crystal description: Almost always in prismatic crystals, often striated parallel to their length, commonly poorly terminated with deep-pitted depressions.

Physical properties: Brilliant orange. *Luster* adamantine; *hardness* $2\frac{1}{2}$–3; *gravity* 5.9–6.1; *fracture* uneven; *cleavage* poor prismatic. Brittle; translucent.

Composition: Lead chromate (69.1% PbO, 30.9% CrO_3).

Tests: Fuses very easily to black bead. In borax bead gives the green (chromium) color. Darkens in closed tube and flies apart (decrepitates); upon cooling, regains orange color.

Distinguishing characteristics: Distinguished from wulfenite by the prismatic crystal habit and the borax-bead and closed-tube test (plus its lower specific gravity). Realgar volatilizes completely on charcoal.

Occurrence: A very rare but very spectacular mineral that was first found in Russia. Its finest development was reached in Tasmania as crystals several inches (10–20 cm) long. It appears to form under the unusual condition of chromium-bearing solutions altering lead deposits. It has been reported from the Mammoth Mine, Tiger, Arizona, and in California at the Darwin Mine, Inyo Co., and the Eldorado Mine, Indio, Riverside Co., but never in noteworthy specimens.

It is among the most showy and colorful of mineral species. The supply of truly fine Tasmanian specimens with elongated sturdy crystals seems to have been exhausted many years ago; recent specimens are much smaller and rather fragile.

The Phosphates, Arsenates, Vanadates, and Uranates

Some of these are primary minerals (one in particular, apatite) but most are secondary, forming through alteration processes from ore minerals. This is especially true of the vanadates and the arsenates, which are mostly secondary (weathered) zone minerals. None are hard; the maximum hardness is about 6. Since many of them contain heavy elements, their gravity is relatively high. The secondary members of this group are often highly colored. Many of the uranates are brilliantly fluorescent.

There are some chemical tests for the different elements which will prove useful. Phosphorus makes a yellow precipitate in a solution of ammonium molybdate when a few drops of a nitric acid solution of the phosphate compound is added to it. The precipitate may take a few minutes to appear. Arsenates can usually be detected by the garlic smell when they are blowpiped on the charcoal, though arsenic in this form is not as easily volatilized as in the sulfides. With the common vanadates and uranates, it usually is quite unnecessary to test, since most of the former are distinctively crystallized and unmistakable; the latter are likely to be fluorescent.

TRIPHYLITE $LiFePO_4$ ⎫
LITHIOPHILITE $LiMnPO_4$ ⎬   **Pl. 26**

Orthorhombic — Rhombic bipyramidal $\dfrac{2}{m}\dfrac{2}{m}\dfrac{2}{m}$

Environment: Pegmatite dikes.

Crystal description: Crystals rare, usually embedded and simple, commonly in solid masses of large crystal units without external faces.

Physical properties: Gray-blue to gray-blue-green (triphylite), or pinkish to greenish brown (lithiophilite). *Luster* glassy; *hardness* $4\frac{1}{2}$–5; *gravity* 3.4–3.6; *fracture* uneven to numerous small conchoidal patches; *cleavage* 1 fair and 2 imperfect. Brittle; transparent to translucent.

Composition: An isomorphous series of lithium, iron, and manganese phosphate (about 9.5% Li_2O, about 45% Fe_2O_3 plus Mn_2O_3 — both are always present — and about 45% P_2O_5).

Tests: Fuse on charcoal to black bead, lithiophilite fusing more readily than triphylite. Triphylite bead magnetic. Crushed powder moistened with hydrochloric acid gives lithium flame color. Moistened with sulfuric acid gives red lithium flash and then the continued blue-green flame of phosphorus.

Distinguishing characteristics: The lithium flame coloration, with the dark color and the easy fusibility, distinguishes these from similar minerals. Their geological associations (pegmatite mineral) eliminate most other substances which might be confusing. In case of doubt, a chemical phosphorus test would be helpful.

Occurrence: Triphylite and lithiophilite are comparatively rare minerals, but have been found in a number of pegmatites, which are in consequence called phosphate pegmatites. They may form tremendous irregular masses, often with secondary alteration products around their margins. Good crystals (triphylite) have been found at Chandler's Mill, Newport, New Hampshire. Great masses of both varieties are found at the Palermo quarry, North Groton, New Hampshire. Reported from Custer, South Dakota, and Pala, San Diego Co., California, in similar masses; some now exhausted quarries and one active quarry (at Hagendorf) in Bavaria; from Rajasthan, India, and Mangualde, Portugal; and from several quarries in Rio Grande do Norte, Brazil, in great abundance.

Interesting facts: Wherever these minerals occur, but especially with the manganese-rich variety lithiophilite, one may expect to find whole series of interesting phosphates derived from the alteration of the primary phosphate. Cracks and fissures in the fresh mineral are often lined with microscopic crystals of secondary phosphates. Branchville, Connecticut, became famous as a mineral locality because of the secondary phosphates formed from the lithiophilite found there. The final stage in the alteration of lithiophilite is a black manganese oxide. This substance is likely to stain heavily such a phosphate-rich pegmatite, and serves as a good guide to pegmatites of this character. Lithia-phosphate pegmatites are among the most rewarding localities for mineral collectors because altering lithiophilite yields a wealth of colorful species.

HETEROSITE $(Fe,Mn)PO_4$ ⎱
PURPURITE $(Mn,Fe)PO_4$ ⎰   **Pl. 28**

Orthorhombic — Rhombic bipyramidal $\dfrac{2\ 2\ 2}{m\ m\ m}$

Environment: Secondary (weathered) pegmatite-phosphate minerals.

Crystal description: Do not form free-standing crystals, but usually occur in large masses of a single crystal unit, making cleavage surface reflections come from the same plane over a large area encasing and replacing a lithiophilite crystal.

Physical properties: Dark violet-brown to bright purple.

Luster pearly, almost metallic; *hardness* $4-4\frac{1}{2}$; *gravity* 3.2–3.4; *streak* purple; *fracture* uneven; *cleavage* good basal and fair side pinacoid, but crinkly and discontinuous. Brittle; almost opaque.

Composition: Iron manganese phosphate (about 53% Mn_2O_3 and Fe_2O_3, with 47.0% P_2O_5).

Tests: None necessary; these fuse easily.

Distinguishing characteristics: They are identified by their bright purple color, invariable occurrence, and associated phosphates.

Occurrence: Heterosite-purpurite is always an alteration product that forms on the surface of altered masses of triphylite-lithiophilite. It is relatively rare because its primary mineral is relatively rare, but is a very frequent associate of that mineral when it does form. Appears to be more likely to form when the manganese phosphate is present, and does not so often form from triphylite alone.

Purpurite was first described from Kings Mountain, North Carolina, but subsequently was recognized as isomorphous with heterosite and as an abundant mineral in some of the New England pegmatites, particularly in Maine and New Hampshire. Also found in the Black Hills, South Dakota, in the Pala district in California, and abroad.

Interesting facts: Most specimens of purpurite require a short immersion in weak acid to bring out the beautiful color. Dark brown specimens are cleaned on their cleavage surfaces by the acid and become beautifully pearly in luster, with a bright purple color. Such specimens are attractive, but since this is not the natural condition of the minerals, purists may frown on the practice.

BERYLLONITE $NaBePO_4$ **Pl. 26**

Monoclinic — prismatic $\dfrac{2}{m}$

Environment: Pegmatite dikes.

Crystal description: Well-formed, transparent, slightly frosted and very complex crystals an inch (2–3 cm) or more across were the first found. Subsequently found in rosettes and in larger embedded white masses with columnar cleavage.

Physical properties: Colorless or white. *Luster* glassy; *hardness* $5\frac{1}{2}$–6; *gravity* 2.8; *fracture* conchoidal; *cleavage* good basal and several less good cleavages. Brittle; transparent to translucent.

Composition: Sodium beryllium phosphate (19.7% BeO, 24.4% Na_2O, 55.9% P_2O_5).

Tests: Fuses with difficulty to a cloudy glass. Wet with sulfuric acid, powdered mineral froths, coloring the flame yellow (Na), and later shows the greenish phosphorus flame.

Distinguishing characteristics: The clear crystals might be confused with many minerals of the pegmatites, but the low fusibility, the flame colorations, and the solubility would be very significant. More easily fusible than herderite, and neither phosphorescent nor fluorescent.

Occurrence: A rare beryllium mineral found in remarkably perfect crystals at the only good locality, a decomposed pegmatite dike on Harnden Peak, Stoneham, Maine, where the loose colorless crystals were associated with quartz, feldspar, beryl, and columbite.

Large white crystals, breaking with a vertically striated surface, have been found at Newry, Maine, in a complex pegmatite in the usual associations of cleavelandite, lithia tourmaline, and the like. In Brazil it has been found with rose-quartz crystals and amblygonite at the Sapucaia pegmatite in Minas Gerais.

MONAZITE   (Ce,La,Y,Th)(PO₄)   Pl. 29

Monoclinic — prismatic $\dfrac{2}{m}$

Environment: Pegmatites, plutonic rocks, and heavy sands.

Crystal description: Usually in small, red-brown, embedded, opaque, flattened crystals whose monoclinic symmetry is very apparent. Also found in sand, in light yellow-brown, transparent, rolled grains.

Physical properties: Yellow to reddish brown. *Luster* subadamantine to resinous; *hardness* $5-5\frac{1}{2}$; *gravity* 4.9–5.3; *streak* light yellow-brown; *fracture* conchoidal to uneven; *cleavage* 1 good, several poor, with well-developed basal parting (especially in embedded crystals). Brittle; transparent to translucent.

Composition: Phosphate of cerium, and lanthanum — usually with some yttrium — a little uranium, and considerable amounts of thorium and silica (about 35% Ce_2O_3, 35% La_2O_3, and 30% P_2O_5).

Tests: On charcoal infusible, but turns gray. After fired grain is moistened with sulfuric acid and reheated, a bluish-green flash (P) can be seen around the assay.

Distinguishing characteristics: In color and occurrence resembles some zircons, but is not fluorescent and the crystal shape is very different. The oblique cleavages and parting make it break into splinters (red-brown fragments) that are rather characteristic. Difficult to identify in sand.

Occurrence: Monazite forms small primary grains that are disseminated through many gneisses and granites. Since it is more resistant to weathering than the rock-making minerals, it frequently persists, along with quartz and other resistant minerals, in the resultant sand. Deposits of heavy monazite-bearing sands are dug and separated for the recovery of several of the heavy minerals. The thorium oxide content is high enough to make the monazite valuable as an ore of that substance. Once in great demand for the manufacture of Welsbach gas mantles, but now more interesting as a source of radioactive material. Commercial deposits of monazite occur in Travancore, India, in Brazil, and along the North Carolina and Florida coasts.

Monazite forms larger crystals in pegmatites that may sometimes be several inches (10 cm) across. Divino de Ubá, Minas Gerais, Brazil, is particularly rich in the mineral, associated with euxenite, polycrase, samarskite, and columbite. Similar large crystals are found in the Norwegian pegmatites, with xenotime, fergusonite, and black biotite mica. In the U.S. it has been found in pegmatites in Maine, Connecticut (Norwich), Virginia (Amelia), Colorado (Boulder Co.), and New Mexico (Petaca district). Monazite sands are found from North Carolina to Florida, and in Idaho and California.

The Alpine crystal cavities sometimes contain small, clear, golden monazite crystals perched on clear quartz, a type that was described under the name of "turnerite." This type of monazite is widespread in France, Switzerland, and Austria.

HUREAULITE $H_2Mn_5(PO_4)_4 \cdot 4H_2O$ **Pl. 26**

Monoclinic — prismatic $\dfrac{2}{m}$

Environment: A secondary pegmatite phosphate, often within the confines of an altering lithiophilite crystal.

Crystal description: Relatively small crystals, usually subparallel aggregates and sheaves of obvious monoclinic symmetry (steeply slanting summits).

Physical properties: Predominantly pink; to grayish, yellowish, or reddish brown. *Luster* glassy; *hardness* $3\frac{1}{2}$; *gravity* 3.2; *streak* white; *fracture* uneven; *cleavage* frontal, good. Brittle; translucent to almost transparent.

Composition: Hydrous manganese (with some iron substituting for the Mn) phosphate (about 48% MnO, 38% PO_4, and 12% H_2O).

Tests: Melts quietly, with a few bubbles, drawing into a fine spherical bead that is dull black while hot and turns red-brown to golden and becomes shinier when cool. Gives water in a closed tube. Attacked by acid (only slowly soluble in HCl or oxalic acid, but luster dulls).

Distinguishing characteristics: Invariably associated with other secondary pegmatite phosphates, usually distinctively pink and often in good crystal clusters. Does not bubble in HCl like rhodochrosite and lacks the rhombohedral cleavage of that mineral. There are few other likely possibilities with this association.

Occurrence: The finest specimens of this very attractive phosphate have come from Hagendorf, Bavaria, where crystal sheaves to $1\frac{1}{2}$ in. (4 cm) have been found in phosphate-crystal-lined pockets. The largest crystal masses are clinkerlike, with crystal pockets, found at Mesquitela quarry, Mangualde, Portugal. Small brownish crystals deck the surfaces of openings in lithiophilite from several pegmatites in the Rio Grande do Norte–Paraíba region of Brazil.

The best American localities are the old ones of New England: Branchville, Connecticut, and the Palermo Mine, North Groton, New Hampshire. It was observed in San Diego Co., California, with other secondary phosphates in tourmaline pegmatites.

The name comes from a locality in France, Huréaux; hence the anglicized pronunciation should be *hoo-ray'o-lite.*

ROSELITE $Ca_2(Co,Mg)(AsO_4)_2 \cdot 2H_2O$

Monoclinic — prismatic $\frac{2}{m}$

Environment: Oxidized zone of cobalt arsenide-rich ore veins.
Crystal description: Small, ill-formed crystals and crystal-lized crusts. Largest crystals about $\frac{1}{4}$ in. (6 mm).
Physical properties: Depending on cobalt content, deep rose to pink. *Luster* glassy; *hardness* $3\frac{1}{2}$; *gravity* 3.5–3.7 (darker is heavier); *streak* pink; *fracture* uneven; *cleavage* side pinacoid and easy. Translucent to transparent.
Composition: Hydrous calcium cobalt magnesium arsenate (CoO content variable, from 8.6 to almost 16%, CaO about 23%, MgO about 4%, As_2O_5 about 50%, and water about 10%).
Tests: Fusible with difficulty, giving As fumes. Heated crystals turn blue (and remain so after cooling). Gives fine cobalt-blue bead (use thoroughly roasted assay; any remaining arsenic will spoil the platinum wire).
Distinguishing characteristics: The association with cobalt ores and the rich blue-red color are sufficient to alert collectors to the possibility of finding roselite. Very cleavable foliaceous erythrite is similar in hue but makes needles or micaceous flakes; turns blue on the surface at even lesser temperatures. Sphaero-cobaltite is very rare, has rhombohedral cleavage, and bubbles in warm HCl. Contrary to Dana, the rose hue does not return to heated crystals after cooling.
Occurrence: First found in Schneeberg, Saxony, but always in tiny crystals, and very rare. Named not for its hue but for a German mineralogist, Gustav Rose (1798–1873). The complex twinning characteristic of the small crystals made it difficult to solve the structure in the days before X-rays.

Larger and more abundant crystals have been found in the upper secondary mineral levels of the two Moroccan cobalt mines, particularly at Bou Azzer, where it is commonly associated with erythrite. Since roselite is so colorful, it is popular among collectors; almost all specimens available to them come from Morocco.

A triclinic, dimorphous mineral of the same composition, very similar in appearance and superficially indistinguishable has been called beta-roselite. Examples from Morocco seem to be deep rose overgrowths bordering an isomorphous zinc arsenate. Beta-roselite is like the darker roselite examples in hue, and is essentially free of MgO. In Schneeberg it was in granular masses, with no distinct crystals. The original describers supposed both of these arsenates to be of primary hydrothermal origin; but this is not a likelihood for the Moroccan occurrence, which is clearly an oxidized upper level of the mine. Free-standing crystals of beta-roselite have been found with roselite in Morocco.

PHOSPHOPHYLLITE $Zn_2(Fe,Mn)(PO_4)_2 \cdot 4H_2O$

Monoclinic — prismatic $\dfrac{2}{m}$

Environment: Only 3 occurrences: 2 pegmatitic, the 3rd in a tin vein; all probably late hydrothermal and primary.

Crystal description: Well-developed isolated crystals, more or less equidimensional, often paired in fishtail-type contact twins.

Physical properties: Light blue-green when clear, to gray or black (inclusions?). *Luster* glassy; *hardness* $3\frac{1}{2}$; *gravity* 3.1; *streak* white; *fracture* conchoidal; *cleavage* frontal and perfect. Transparent to translucent.

Composition: Fundamentally a hydrous phosphate of zinc, with iron and manganese (ZnO about 35%, FeO about 12%, MnO about 5%, P_2O_5 about 32%, and H_2O 16%).

Tests: Swells and exfoliates under the flame, becomes (cooled) chalky and pale yellow-brown, with continued heating finally fuses. Soluble in acids.

Distinguishing characteristics: Few minerals have this color: some apophyllites, which will only be in zeolite associations; and euclase, which is very much harder ($7\frac{1}{2}$). Environment probably the best guide. We might expect it in other vein occurrences where Zn and P_2O_5 are present, such as Zacatecas, Mexico, and Trepča, Yugoslavia.

Occurrence: First found in pockets in greisenlike mica masses, and in proximity to triphyllite in the Hagendorf (Bavaria) pegmatite. It has not been found there lately, despite an abundance of secondary phosphates, so may be primary and not one of the triphyllite-lithiophilite alteration products so well developed at that locality. Also, similarly, at the Palermo Mine, North Groton, New Hampshire.

Beautiful gemmy crystals to 4 in. (10 cm) long, mostly

twinned, have been found in the Potosí (Bolivia) tin mine. Their beauty has made them important; despite great rarity, collectors vie for them. Fortunately, unlike vivianite, another Bolivian phosphate of great charm, phosphophyllite seems not to deteriorate with time.

Pronounced *fos-fo-fill'ite* (the name refers to its composition and ready cleavage). It seems possible that further localities will be discovered in time.

VIVIANITE $Fe_3(PO_4)_2 \cdot 8H_2O$ Pl. 29
Monoclinic — prismatic $\dfrac{2}{m}$

Environment: Late or secondary mineral in ore veins and phosphate pegmatites and in sedimentary clays as a concretion.
Crystal description: Usually in small tabular crystals with a prominent cleavage parallel to the plates, and a conspicuous pearly luster on those faces. May be pulverulent and earthy, then bright blue in color. Also forms fibrous crusts.
Physical properties: Nearly colorless to light blue-green, indigo blue, and violet. *Luster* glassy to pearly; *hardness* $1\frac{1}{2}$–2; *gravity* 2.6–2.7; *streak* white, turns blue on exposure to light; *fracture* subconchoidal with striations; *cleavage* micaceous, parallel to side pinacoid. Flexible laminae; transparent to translucent; gliding plane across elongations make bent crystals customary.
Composition: Hydrous iron phosphate (43.0% FeO, 28.3% P_2O_5, 28.7% H_2O).
Tests: Fuses readily to a dull black magnetic globule. Dissolved in nitric acid it makes a yellow (P test) precipitate when added to a solution of ammonium molybdate.
Distinguishing characteristics: Not likely to be confused with other minerals; its streak, bright blue color, and soft, micaceous, tabular crystals are distinctive.
Occurrence: The best specimens of vivianite are late deposits in ore veins, as in Idaho, Utah, and Colorado. Particularly fine Bolivian specimens — the crystals are several inches (10 cm) long and light blue-green in color — have been found in cavities in the tin ore veins. Good clusters have been found in Trepča, Yugoslavia. Crusts of rounded tabular crystals were found in the Ibex Mine in Leadville, Colorado. In time these crystals have a tendency to darken and crack parallel to their cleavage direction. Crystals comparable to the Bolivian ones were found many years ago in Cornwall. Fine crystals have been found at Bingham, Utah, and Cobalt, Idaho.

Smaller and less showy crystals are often found in fossils in sedimentary rocks, as at Mullica Hill, New Jersey, where dark blue crystals line cavities formed by fossil casts in a brown sandstone. Vivianite has been found in a mammoth skull in Mexico, in a fossil tusk in Idaho, and adjacent to whale bones in Richmond, Virginia. The largest crystals ever found, yard (or meter) long "broad swords," were of similar origin, having been dug from a tropical swamp in Anloua, N'Gaoundéré, French Cameroons. Small crystals and powdery blue coatings are found as alterations of other phosphates in pegmatites. Slender crystals often coat such minerals as triphylite; in fact, much of the blue stain in slightly altered pegmatite phosphates (triphylite) may be this mineral. In highly oxidized pegmatites, it will form bright blue spots on the black manganese oxides, which were derived through the surface weathering of the pegmatite phosphates.

For the collector vivianite usually is an unwise purchase, since it tends to dry out, darken, and cleave apart in time. Primary (vein) vivianite persists better than that from secondary formations.

ERYTHRITE $(Co,Ni)_3(AsO_4)_2 \cdot 8H_2O$ **Pl. 28**

Monoclinic — prismatic $\dfrac{2}{m}$

Environment: Secondary (weathered) portions of cobalt ore deposits.
Crystal description: Usually forms pink earthy crusts and coatings, sometimes in slender prisms, and rarely in clusters of long flat needles.
Physical properties: Bluish pink to deep raspberry-red. *Luster* glassy to pearly; *hardness* $1\frac{1}{2}$–$2\frac{1}{2}$; *gravity* 2.9; *fracture* not significant; *cleavage* perfect micaceous, parallel to the side pinacoid. Laminae flexible; sectile; transparent to translucent.
Composition: Hydrous cobalt arsenate (37.5% CoO, 38.4% As_2O_5, 24.1% H_2O, with some nickel in place of the cobalt). Actually forms a continuous series with annabergite, the nickel equivalent (see next mineral), but much commoner.
Tests: Fuses into flattened gray mass with arsenical smell. Borax added to a fragment of this mass turns deep blue (Co). (Do not put on platinum wire, because of the arsenic.) Lightly heated crystal flake (on hot plate) turns blue on surface.
Distinguishing characteristics: There is almost no mineral resembling this except a rare cobalt carbonate (sphaerocobaltite, which effervesces in acid) and a rare related arsenate (roselite, p. 186). Kaemmererite, a violet-red chlorite, does not give the cobalt bead.
Occurrence: Erythrite forms as a result of the surface alteration of primary cobalt arsenides. It is known as "cobalt bloom" and is the most significant guide to cobalt ore. It is found almost everywhere that cobalt ores occur, but rarely makes attractive

specimens. Among the finest crystals are the 4 in. (10 cm) radiating blades in cavities in quartz from Schneeberg (Saxony, East Germany) that were found in the early days of mining in the area. Outstanding specimens are provided by the Bou Azzer (Morocco) skutterudite occurrence, where it is associated with equally fine examples of the rare roselite pair. Solid crusts of slender interpenetrating needles have come from Queensland, Australia, and Alamos, Mexico. Found in Cobalt, Ontario, in pinkish crusts and small crystals. Good specimens are not at all common in the U.S., although erythrite has been noted in Nevada, Idaho, Arizona, New Mexico, and California.

ANNABERGITE $(Ni,Co)_3(AsO_4)_2 \cdot 8H_2O$ **Pl. 28**

Monoclinic — prismatic $\dfrac{2}{m}$

Environment: Secondary (weathered) portion of nickel ore deposits.

Crystal description: Usually in light green earthy crusts and films; crystals slender capillary needles, always small.

Physical properties: Light apple-green to pale pink. *Luster* silky or glassy; *hardness* $2\frac{1}{2}-3$; *gravity* 3.0; never solid enough to show a fracture; *cleavage* side pinacoid, usually not visible. Earthy; translucent.

Composition: Hydrous nickel arsenate (35.5% NiO, 38.4% As_2O_5, and 24.1% H_2O, usually with some Co replacing part of the Ni). See erythrite (preceding). From its ability to impart color, Co appears to dominate the Ni, and examples that are actually higher in Ni than in Co can still be pink in hue.

Tests: Fuses, and with strong heating in reducing flame can be fused into a magnetic metallic bead. In case of doubt, the chemical test for nickel can be made: the mineral dissolved in nitric acid, neutralized with ammonia (NH_4OH), and a little dimethylglyoxime solution added. Boiling makes a bright pink solution.

Distinguishing characteristics: The green nickel color might be confused with a copper color, but the magnetic bead would prove nickel. Green minerals owing their color to chromium do not reduce to a magnetic bead under the blowpipe.

Occurrence: A rare mineral, forming near the surfaces of cobalt-nickel-silver arsenide sulfide veins, usually just a greenish film, as in Cobalt, Ontario, and Saxony, East Germany. Good small crystals are almost restricted to a Lavrion (Greece) occurrence, where it is known as cabrerite (from a Spanish occurrence in the Sierra Cabrera). Unlike erythrite, has never been found in really outstanding specimens. The best U.S. occurrence is in Humboldt Co., Nevada. Like erythrite, the green annabergite coating also has a prospector's name, "nickel bloom," and has served as a good guide to ore.

VARISCITE $Al(PO_4) \cdot 2H_2O$ }
STRENGITE $Fe(PO_4) \cdot 2H_2O$ }   **Pls. 28, 46**

Orthorhombic — Rhombic bipyramidal $\dfrac{2}{m} \dfrac{2}{m} \dfrac{2}{m}$

Environment: Really of two very different origins (parageneses). Variscite forms in secondary deposits near the surface in clay-rich rocks sometimes associated with other secondary phosphates. Strengite is generally a secondary phosphate of pegmatite associations.

Crystal description: Variscite usually massive, sometimes in thin crusts of small crystals of pyramidal habit. Strengite in crystals and botryoidal crusts.

Physical properties: Light green or emerald-green (variscite); deep pink or amethyst (strengite). *Luster* porcelaneous; *hardness* $3\frac{1}{2}$–$4\frac{1}{2}$; *gravity* 2.2–2.8; *fracture* smooth to conchoidal; *cleavage* not obtainable as a rule. Brittle; translucent in thin splinters to transparent in crystals.

Composition: Hydrous aluminum iron phosphates (variscite about 32.3% Al_2O_3, 44.9% P_2O_5, and 22.8% H_2O). Variscite forms an isomorphous series with strengite, the iron phosphate equivalent.

Tests: Infusible, but most variscite specimens turn violet and brittle on light heating. Decompose, but insoluble in dilute hydrochloric acid before heating; become soluble afterward. Will then give P test with ammonium molybdate. Strengite crystals turn ocherous and cleave up on heating.

Distinguishing characteristics: The green color, acid insolubility, and lack of copper or nickel tests eliminate any minerals of those metals. Variscite resembles turquoise but is greener and contains no copper. Strengite can be distinguished from amethyst by its softness and by blowpipe reactions; and from other substances by the P test.

Occurrence: Both minerals appear to be secondary. Like turquoise, their ingredients are derived from the breakdown of minerals in the surrounding rock. Variscite may form veins, crystallized crusts, and nodular masses; the best occurrence is the rounded nodules, up to a foot (30 cm) across, which are embedded in a soft rock at Fairfield, Utah. The cores of these nodules vary in color from dark green to pale green, though the darker pieces have a tendency in time to become paler, probably through the evaporation of moisture. The nodules of this locality are framed with rims of other phosphates, minerals derived from the alteration of the variscite with some shrinkage, so that an open space is commonly found between the differently colored rims and remaining variscite. In Lucin, Utah, variscite forms in greenish veins. Both localities have produced material used in jewelry. An interesting occurrence of thin crystallized greenish crusts of variscite has been noted in Montgomery Co.,

Arkansas. Also found in Pontevedra, Spain, and in large masses at Pannecé (Loire-Atlantique), France, and Freiberg, East Germany.

Strengite is very different in occurrence. It is found in iron mines as a late mineral, in crusts and small crystals. However, the best crystals came from altered phosphates in an old West German pegmatite at Pleystein. Radiating pink rosettes and coatings of an intermediate variscite-strengite are found in a phosphate-bearing pegmatite in Rio Grande do Norte, Brazil. Good strengite crystals have been found in altered triphylite at the Bull Moose Mine, Custer, South Dakota. Attractive microrosettes of strengite were found at Indian Mountain, Alabama (Pl. 46), associated with a number of other phosphates.

SCORODITE $Fe(AsO_4) \cdot 2H_2O$ Pl. 46

Orthorhombic — Rhombic bipyramidal $\dfrac{2\ 2\ 2}{m\ m\ m}$

Environment: Oxidized, weathered zone of ore deposits.

Crystal description: Short-prismatic to pyramidal (octahedral-appearing) crystals, which are very typical; also banded and scoriaceous gray-green masses.

Physical properties: Light green, greenish brown, blue, violet. *Luster* glassy to subadamantine; *hardness* $3\frac{1}{2}$–4; *gravity* 3.1–3.3; *fracture* uneven; *cleavage* several poor. Brittle; transparent to translucent.

Composition: Hydrous ferric arsenate (34.6% Fe_2O_3, 49.8% As_2O_5, 15.6% H_2O, although aluminum can replace most of the iron).

Tests: On charcoal it gives arsenic (garlic) fumes and melts more or less readily to a gray magnetic globule. Soluble in hydrochloric acid.

Distinguishing characteristics: Its crystals resemble zircon, but scorodite is much softer and is fusible and nonfluorescent. The massive varieties resemble a number of minerals, especially fine-grained rocks that have been impregnated and stained with iron sulfate solutions from pyrite alteration, but scorodite's fusibility, fumes, and acid solubility eliminate them.

Occurrence: Scorodite is virtually always a secondary mineral, forming in the oxidized upper portions of an ore vein that contains arsenic minerals, especially arsenopyrite. It also occurs as a thin deposit from hot springs; very rarely found in primary veins, and (like vivianite) may be late primary in genesis.

Among the best crystals are some light green ones that have come from a Brazilian occurrence, near Ouro Prêto in Minas Gerais, where they have reached about $\frac{3}{8}$ in. (1 cm) across. Small crystals have been found at several places, with other oxidized minerals: Carinthia, Austria; Cornwall, England; and Lavrion, Greece. It is common in the U.S.: at Gold Hill, Utah, and in the Tintic district; in New York at Carmel in a gray-green vein of crystalline material with arsenopyrite; and at many other localities, but nowhere in attractive specimens.

There are two outstanding specimen localities. 1 in. (2-3 cm) crystals in clusters have been found in Tsumeb, South West Africa. In the Noche Buena Mine, Zacatecas, Mexico, beautifully developed, deep blue crystals are scattered on white quartz crusts. They are strongly dichroic in blue and violet and reach about 1 in. (2.5 cm) in size. Smaller blue crystals can be numbered among the great variety of Mapimí (Mexico) species.

DESCLOIZITE $(Zn,Cu)Pb(VO_4)(OH)$ }
MOTTRAMITE $(Cu,Zn)Pb(VO_4)(OH)$ } **Pl. 29**

Orthorhombic — Rhombic bipyramidal $\dfrac{2\ \ 2\ \ 2}{m\ m\ m}$

Environment: Secondary (weathered) zone of ore deposits.

Crystal description: Usually in small to very small, transparent, yellow-brown, short spearlike blades, or in velvety black druses of microscopic crystals. Large solid crystals at one locality. Also stalactitic as mammillary crusts.

Physical properties: Cherry-red to yellow-brown, chestnut-brown, green, or black. *Luster* greasy; *hardness* $3\frac{1}{2}$; *gravity* 5.9 (mottramite)-6.2 (descloizite); *streak* yellowish orange to brownish red; *fracture* small conchoidal areas; *cleavage* none. *Brittle;* transparent to translucent.

Composition: Basic lead, zinc-copper, vanadates of variable composition (making a series, with approximately 55.4% PbO, 22.7% V_2O_5, 2.2% H_2O, and about 20% divided between Cu and Zn; the Zn member is descloizite, but when Cu is more abundant it is mottramite).

Tests: Fuse readily on charcoal, boiling at first, even after flame is removed, eventually making a ball of lead surrounded by a black slag. The powder is dissolved by hydrochloric acid and makes a yellow-green solution. A piece of pure zinc added to this solution turns it blue, then violet (V test).

Distinguishing characteristics: They are usually recognized by their color, crystal form, and associations, and do not greatly resemble any other mineral in their kind of associations.

Occurrence: The descloizite-mottramite series is commonly associated with wulfenite and vanadinite, in the usual secondary mineral suites from oxidized areas of ore deposits. It is especially widespread in both Arizona and New Mexico, and is commonly found crusting the rock matrix of specimens of wulfenite and vanadinite. Black velvety crusts of descloizite came from Sierra Co., New Mexico, and also from Bisbee and Tombstone, Arizona. The most remarkable occurrence known was in Otavi, South West Africa, where some mammoth crystals of mottramite — over an inch (3 cm) in size, dark brown in color, and resembling sphalerite — were found, forming great crystal clusters. Unfortunately, they are not as aesthetically appealing as the small brown or green "trees" from Berg Aukas, Grootfontein.

HERDERITE   CaBe(PO₄)(OH,F)   **Pl. 29**

Monoclinic — prismatic $\dfrac{2}{m}$

Environment: Pegmatite dikes.

Crystal description: Found in well-formed crystals several inches (10 cm) long at best, often very complex, with many forms. Prism-zone faces commonly rounded, not really flat. Monoclinic symmetry usually visible, but sometimes symmetrically intergrown with a second crystal (twinned) so that it looks orthorhombic (Topsham, Maine). Also in rounded nodules, radiating fibrous aggregates, and scattered grains.

Physical properties: Colorless, white, yellowish, or light bluish green. *Luster* greasy to glassy; *hardness* $5-5\frac{1}{2}$; *gravity* 2.9–3.0; *fracture* subconchoidal; *cleavage* interupted prismatic. Brittle; transparent to translucent; sometimes fluorescent deep blue in longwave ultraviolet light.

Composition: Fluophosphate of beryllium and calcium [15.5% BeO, 34.8% CaO, 44.0% P_2O_5, and 5.6% H_2O — except that some of the (OH) is always replaced by fluorine].

Tests: Thermoluminescent, glowing briefly with a blue-white phosphorescence on the charcoal just before becoming incandescent. After light heating (enough only to crack and slightly whiten the specimen) it is usually fluorescent in longwave ultraviolet light. Fuses with difficulty, becoming white and opaque. Dissolves slowly in acid, giving phosphorus test (P).

Distinguishing characteristics: The crystals are usually slightly etched and if large enough have a distinctive and recognizable rounded, greasy look. The fluorescence and thermoluminescence are usually obtainable.

Occurrence: Herderite was first described from some high-temperature tin veins in Germany, but it turned out to be very rare there and was later found to be fairly common in some of the New England pegmatites. Topsham, Maine, has produced a great many white and pale blue crystals, twinned so that they look something like barite. Probably some of the largest crystals are those from Stoneham, Maine, of a light yellow-brown color, slightly etched but well formed. Not uncommon at several other Maine localities, and nearby at the Fletcher Mine, Alexandria, New Hampshire, in crystals that equal the best from Maine. Small crystals have turned up in San Diego Co., California. Large crystals have been found at the Golconda Mine, near Governador Valadares, Minas Gerais, Brazil. Most are twinned like "fishtail" gypsum.

AMBLYGONITE $LiAl(PO_4)(F,OH)$ **Pl. 29**

Triclinic — pinacoidal $\bar{1}$

Environment: Lithia-bearing pegmatite dikes.

Crystal description: In its usual occurrence it forms medium-to-large embedded crystals with rough, irregular outlines. Now, however, being found in fine white and transparent crystals with numerous forms, several inches (to 20 cm) in length.

Physical properties: Colorless, yellow to white, light gray-green, lilac, or gray-blue. *Luster* glassy; *hardness* $5\frac{1}{2}$–6; *gravity* 3.0–3.1; *fracture* uneven to subconchoidal; *cleavage* perfect basal, and interrupted cleavages on other planes. Brittle; transparent to translucent; often fluorescent, weakly orange in long-wave ultraviolet light.

Composition: Basic lithium aluminum fluophosphate (10.1% Li_2O, 34.5% Al_2O_3, 48.0% P_2O_5, 12.8% F, but some of the F replaces O, 5.4% of O equals F).

Tests: Fuses easily to white porcelaneous sphere that fluoresces white in shortwave ultraviolet light. Acid on powder gives red (Li) flame. Dissolves in acid to give a good phosphorus test.

Distinguishing characteristics: In pegmatites it might be confused with feldspar, from which it is easily distinguished by its fusibility. A difference in luster is apparent to the trained eye.

Occurrence: Amblygonite is a mineral of complex pegmatites and may be abundant locally, occurring in large masses embedded in quartz or feldspar. Such masses are found in Ceará, Brazil, where it almost seems to substitute for the feldspar of a dike. It is found similarly in pegmatites in Sweden, Western Australia, the Black Hills of South Dakota, California (Pala), and Maine. Although a potential source of lithium, it is not now used for that purpose to any extent. The Newry (Maine) occurrence of well-formed, colorless and transparent to milky-white crystals is apparently a late stage of pegmatite formation — later than is usually the case with this mineral. In normal occurrences the amblygonite is embedded in other minerals and is only crudely formed into crystals. Brazil appears to have at least two good occurrences in Minas Gerais, near Governador Valadares. Gemmy yellow crystals as much as 4 in. (10 cm) across characterize one source; elongated, flattened twins as much as 6 in. long, 1 in. wide, and $\frac{1}{4}$ in. thick (15 x 2 x 0.5 cm) come from the other locality (Mendes Pimentel).

BRAZILIANITE $NaAl_3(PO_4)_2(OH)_4$ **Pl. 30**

Monoclinic — prismatic $\frac{2}{m}$

Environment: A primary pegmatite phosphate.

Crystal description: Well-developed crystals, sometimes very large. Single crystals on mica and divergent as aggregates of somewhat elongated (on the a-axis) points.

Physical properties: Yellow to greenish yellow, sometimes gemmy. *Luster* glassy; *hardness* $5\frac{1}{2}$; *gravity* 2.98; *streak* white; *fracture* shelly (conchoidal); *cleavage* perfect side, 1 direction. Brittle; translucent to transparent.

Composition: Basic sodium aluminum phosphate (8.6% Na_2O, 42.5% Al_2O_3, 39.0% P_2O_5, and 9.9% H_2O).

Tests: Soon turns white on heating; on charcoal it swells slightly and finally fuses on edges. Yellow hue fades while the chip is still intact and glass clear. Some white gemstones of brazilianite have been sold that owe their lack of color to mild heating, perhaps during dopping. Nonfluorescent at any time.

Distinguishing characteristics: Since brazilianite is always yellow and always crystallized, there are few minerals resembling it. Most of the gemmy minerals like chrysoberyl are harder; apatite does not have its ready side cleavage; amblygonite is usually orange fluorescent and gives a red coloration to the flame as it melts into a white bleb on the edge of the chip. The blowpipe differentiation is very simple.

Occurrence: This was a remarkable mineral to turn up in a pegmatite so late in time. Seldom do new minerals first appear in conventional deposits in 6 in. (15 cm) gemmy and well-formed crystals. The first examples were of uncertain origin; Conselheiro Pena in Minas Gerais was reported to have been their source. It has subsequently been found in several other Minas Gerais pegmatites (Córrego Feio, Galileia; Mendes Pimentel and Gramados, Conselheiro Pena) and, strangely enough, in New Hampshire in the already well-studied Palermo Mine, North Groton, and the G. E. Smith Mine at Chandler's Mill, Newport. The early Brazilian crystals were mainly equidimensional, with a readily recognizable prism zone, but the later finds, in both Brazil and New Hampshire, have shown that an elongation parallel to the front and back axis, the a-axis, is more usual.

OLIVENITE $Cu_2(AsO_4)(OH)$ **Pl. 30**

Orthorhombic — Rhombic bipyramidal $\dfrac{2\ \ 2\ \ 2}{m\,m\,m}$

Environment: Secondary (weathered) zone of ore deposits.

Crystal description: Small prismatic crystals, with few faces. Also commonly in long slender prisms, and in silky crusts of slender fibers, with color bands, sometimes very pale.

Physical properties: Pistachio-green to greenish black. *Luster* adamantine or silky; *hardness* 3; *gravity* 3.9–4.4; *fracture* conchoidal to uneven; *cleavage* 2 indistinct. Brittle; translucent to opaque.

Composition: Basic copper arsenate (56.2% CuO, 40.6% As_2O_5, 3.2% H_2O).

Tests: After slowly melting on charcoal, it suddenly boils and volatilizes with arsenical fumes. Dissolves readily in nitric acid with the typical copper blue-green, becoming intense blue when ammonia is added.

Distinguishing characteristics: Can be separated from similar-appearing sulfates and phosphates by the arsenical (garlicky) smell and unusual behavior on the charcoal. It can be proved to contain copper by the chemical color tests. Resembles several other green minerals — like epidote, which has identical coloration — but none of these is so fusible or so easily tested for copper.

Occurrence: A descriptively named but rather rare secondary mineral that forms in the upper zone of copper deposits, where it is associated with malachite, azurite, cerussite, and cuprite, and often coats limonite. Still found on mine dumps in some quantity in Cornwall, in crusts of vertical needles, but color-banded in various tints (deepest near the top) that gave it the local name "wood-copper." Good specimens of stubby crystals have been found at Tsumeb, South West Africa. In the U.S. good crystals were found in the old Arizona copper mines; particularly good examples of both crystallized and "wood-copper" olivenite, at Tintic, Utah.

LIBETHENITE $Cu_2(OH)PO_4$ **Pl. 29**

Orthorhombic — Rhombic bipyramidal $\frac{2\ 2\ 2}{m\ m\ m}$

Environment: Secondary (weathered) zone of copper ore deposits.

Crystal description: Crystals common, solid layers (druses) of usually short-prismatic crystals, diamond-shaped in cross section. Also in globular crusts.

Physical properties: Dark olive-green. *Luster* resinous; *hardness* 4; *gravity* 3.6–3.8; *fracture* subconchoidal to uneven; *cleavage* 2 good. Brittle; translucent.

Composition: A basic copper phosphate (66.4% CuO, 29.8% P_2O_5, 3.8% H_2O).

Tests: Fuses easily with boiling, eventually drawing into black, spherical bead. Gives copper and phosphorus tests in solutions.

Distinguishing characteristics: Distinguished from malachite by lack of effervescence in acid; from brochantite and olivenite by the phosphorus test; and from other green minerals by the fusibility and solubility. There are, however, a number of other related minerals with similar associations, too rare to list here, with which it might be confused. They require further tests for certain identification.

Occurrence: Libethenite, like olivenite, brochantite, and malachite — all of which are likely associations — is one of the secondary minerals formed in the alteration through weathering of sulfide ore minerals. Usually best developed where weathering is deep and concentrations high.

Originally found with many of the normally associated minerals at Libethen, Rumania (now Lubětová, Czechoslovakia), where it formed typical crystals. Those of Cornwall formed in similar associations. The best U.S. occurrence of this group of minerals has been in the Tintic region (Utah) and occasionally in Arizona and Nevada.

ADAMITE $Zn_2(AsO_4)(OH)$ Pl. 30

Orthorhombic — Rhombic bipyramidal $\dfrac{2\ 2\ 2}{m\ m\ m}$

Environment: Secondary (weathered) zone of ore deposits.
Crystal description: Drusy crusts of short-prismatic or horizontally elongated crystals.
Physical properties: Light yellow, greenish, rose, or violet. *Luster* glassy; *hardness* $3\frac{1}{2}$; *gravity* 4.3–4.4; *fracture* uneven; *cleavage* domal. Brittle; transparent to translucent; often brilliantly fluorescent yellow-green.
Composition: Basic zinc arsenate (56.7% ZnO, 40.2% As_2O_5, 3.1% H_2O).
Tests: Fuses reluctantly, with slight decrepitation. Loses fluorescence on first heating, as it whitens and becomes opaque. Slight arsenic smell. Becomes less fusible as water bubbles away. Green zinc color appears after cobalt nitrate drop on fusion is heated.
Distinguishing characteristics: The light yellow to white varieties (free of copper, which "poisons" fluorescence) can be identified by their brilliant fluorescence. Nonfluorescent green crusts can be distinguished from smithsonite by the lack of CO_2 bubbles on solution in HCl. The cobalt nitrate test shows zinc.
Occurrence: A secondary mineral found in the oxidized portion of metal ore veins at a few localities. The pink and green colorations are caused by cobalt and copper impurities, and both are found at Cap Garonne, France. Fine fluorescent specimens have long been known from the ancient mines at Lavrion, Greece, which also yield attractive copper-green specimens. Similar specimens may be collected at Gold Hill, Utah, and magnificent yellow fluorescent specimens in considerable abundance at the Ojuela Mine, Mapimí, Durango, Mexico. At all these localities, except Cap Garonne, the crystals line cavities in limonite. In Mexico, where it assumes an infinite variety of hues from white to brick-red, yellow-green, blue-green, and violet, it is associated with: hemimorphite; austinite [$CaZn(AsO_4)(OH)$]; the rare legrandite in elongated yellow straws and sprays of $Zn_2(AsO_4)(OH)\cdot H_2O$; the still rarer triclinic dimorphous $Zn_2(AsO_4)(OH)$, paradamite; and with aurichalcite, wulfenite, and mimetite.

AUGELITE $Al_2(PO_4) \cdot (OH)_3$ **Pl. 31**

Monoclinic — prismatic $\dfrac{2}{m}$

Environment: Hydrothermal deposits; a late mineral.

Crystal description: Microscopic tabular crystals in most occurrences; in one occurrence transparent and colorless, up to an inch (2.5 cm) across, and about equidimensional.

Physical properties: Colorless to white, yellowish, or rose. *Luster* glassy; *hardness* $4\frac{1}{2}$–5; *gravity* 2.7; *fracture* conchoidal; *cleavage* 2 good. Brittle; transparent to translucent.

Composition: Basic aluminum phosphate (51.0% Al_2O_3, 35.5% P_2O_5, 13.5% H_2O).

Tests: Swells and whitens, retaining angular shape under blowpipe. Cobalt nitrate drop added to mass gives good blue color on second firing. Can be dissolved in acid after sodium carbonate fusion, to give chemical phosphorus test.

Distinguishing characteristics: It would be difficult for the amateur to recognize the small crystals, since any colorless substance resembles many minerals; tests above are significant.

Occurrence: Originally described from a Swedish occurrence where it forms no crystals. Later it was recognized as a scattering of small crystals on ore minerals in tin mines at Oruro and near Potosí, Bolivia. Became interesting when found as large (over 1 in.; 2.5 cm) well-formed, transparent, gemmy crystals at White Mountain, California, associated with other phosphates in a metamorphic andalusite deposit, and in New Hampshire pegmatites at North Groton and Newport (G. E. Smith Mine, Chandler's Mill).

DUFRENITE $Fe_5(PO_4)_3(OH)_5 \cdot 2H_2O$ Monoclinic   **Pl. 31**

Environment: Weathered ore deposits; with pegmatite phosphates; and limonite formations.

Crystal description: Most commonly as dull green powdery films coating other minerals. Sometimes in rounded nodules or crusts with a fibrous radiating structure.

Physical properties: Dull olive-green to green-black. *Luster* earthy (pulverulent) to silky; *hardness* $3\frac{1}{2}$–$4\frac{1}{2}$; *gravity* 3.2–3.4; *streak* yellow-green; *fracture* none visible as a rule; *cleavage* side and front pinacoid. Brittle to earthy; translucent.

Composition: Basic hydrous iron phosphate (57.1% Fe_2O_3 and FeO, 31.1% P_2O_5, 11.8% H_2O). Related species of very similar composition have been named rockbridgeite and frondelite.

Tests: Turns brown, then fuses with a little difficulty to a dull black, slightly magnetic bead. As glowing bead cools, a new wave of light passes over it, caused by heat release with crystallization, and a dimple forms simultaneously on the surface.

Distinguishing characteristics: The green-yellow film might resemble greenockite; the best test is to make the phosphorus test of dropping a few drops of the acid solution into ammonium molybdate, producing the yellow precipitate that indicates P. The radiating spheres resemble several phosphates, but none that would become magnetic under the blowpipe.

Occurrence: Usually found as a thin, dull green film on other minerals, especially in iron mines and sometimes in pegmatites. Also (the best specimens), in thick, botryoidal, black fibrous crusts without any crystal faces. Good specimens are uncommon. Most old dufrenite specimens are actually now called frondelite or rockbridgeite; the distinction would be difficult without the tests available to specialists. Rockbridgeite forms rich masses at Midvale, Rockbridge Co., Virginia, and in Sevier Co., Arkansas. It fills geodes in a sandstone at Greenbelt, Maryland. Often found associated with primary phosphates in pegmatites, as at the old and new Palermo Mine, North Groton, New Hampshire, in radiating rosettes associated with other phosphates. Crusts of appreciable thickness coat fresh, colorless rhombohedral whitlockite (a calcium magnesium phosphate). Also found in Cornwall, England, and Wesphalia, West Germany. Fine solid crusts have been found at Hagendorf, Bavaria, with other secondary pegmatite phosphates.

PHOSPHURANYLITE $Ca(UO_2), (PO_4)_2(OH)_4 \cdot 7H_2O$

Orthorhombic — Rhombic bipyramidal $\dfrac{2}{m}\dfrac{2}{m}\dfrac{2}{m}$

Environment: Secondary mineral of uranium-bearing rocks.

Crystal description: Forms crusts of thin tabular crystals of microscopic dimensions.

Physical properties: Straw to golden yellow. *Luster* glassy; *hardness* (soft); *gravity* (undetermined); *fracture* undeterminable; *cleavage* basal. Brittle; transparent; not fluorescent.

Composition: Basic hydrous calcium uranium phosphate of uncertain composition.

Tests: Blackens, but not easily fusible. Makes fluorescent bead with sodium fluoride. Readily soluble in nitric acid, drying to leave fluorescent residue. The nitric acid solution dropped into solution of ammonium molybdate forms a yellow (P test) precipitate.

Distinguishing characteristics: This is one of a dozen similar minerals that form yellow, nonfluorescent, or weakly fluorescent crusts and are difficult to determine accurately. Absence of vanadium is shown by failure of flake to turn red in the acid. Usually associated with autunite, a highly fluorescent mineral; hence the uranium content of such crusts becomes at once apparent.

Occurrence: Considered rare but probably a very common mineral, forming nonfluorescent yellow films on seams in rocks containing radioactive minerals. Often associated with the fluorescent autunite as an inner band in a rim of alteration products around uraninite. Originally described from Spruce Pine, North Carolina. Since then it has been found in Spain, Zaïre (Belgian Congo), Bavaria (Wölsendorf), Brazil (Rio Grande do Norte), and in New Hampshire at the Ruggles Mine, Grafton, and the Palermo Mine, North Groton.

APATITE $Ca_5(Cl,F)(PO_4)_3$ **Pl. 30**

Hexagonal — Hexagonal bipyramidal $\dfrac{6}{m}$

Environment: Plutonic rocks, pegmatite dikes, ore veins, bedded sedimentary deposits.

Crystal description: Often crystallized, with considerable variation in crystal habit: long-prismatic, short-prismatic, to tabular. Also in botryoidal crusts and in great massive beds.

Physical properties: Colorless, white, brown, green, violet, blue, or yellow. *Luster* glassy; *hardness* 5; *gravity* 3.1–3.2; *fracture* conchoidal; *cleavage* inconspicuous basal and prism. Brittle; transparent to translucent; sometimes fluorescent yellow-orange (manganapatite — to 10.5% Mn replacing Ca), and thermoluminescent blue-white; usually becomes fluorescent orange (longwave ultraviolet light) after strong heating.

Composition: Calcium fluophosphate or calcium chlorophosphate, or an intermediate (about 54.5% Ca, 41.5% P_2O_5, and about 4% F and Cl). There is so large a range of composition in the various apatites that they are labeled a group by some authorities. However, the examples usually called apatite are relatively constant in appearance and associations; and the mere fact that vanadates, arsenates, or metallic phosphates have a like structure does not make them apatites. Ordinary apatite is not isomorphous with the far-afield species like pyromorphite and mimetite.

Tests: Does not fuse, but chip held in the Bunsen burner flame melts on the edges, coloring the flame reddish yellow (Ca). Crushed and moistened with sulfuric acid gives green-white flame (P). Soluble in acids; fluorescent after heating (if not already so).

Distinguishing characteristics: Crystals resemble beryl but can be distinguished by the hardness. Manganapatite resembles green tourmaline, but also is softer than that mineral, and is usually fluorescent. Herderite and beryllonite fuse.

Occurrence: Apatite is a common minor constituent of rocks, and is the source of the phosphorus required by plants. Specimens come from crystallized concentrations in pegmatites, in some ore veins, and in the form of the occasional rich masses of igneous segregations. Green manganapatite is a common mineral of the early stages of mineral formation in pegmatites; it occurs embedded in feldspar and quartz. Colorful short-prismatic and tabular apatite crystals form in cavities in cleavelandite in the late replacement phases of complex pegmatite formation. Apatite also forms good crystals in some ore veins, such as the violet crystals in the Ehrenfriedersdorf tin veins in East Germany, the gemmy yellow crystals associated with the Durango iron deposits (Mexico). The colorless, brilliant plates in the Austrian Tyrol reflect an Alpine assemblage.

Entirely different in occurrence are the indigo-blue apatites of Campo Formosa, Bahia, Brazil, and the large brown and green corroded crystals found in Ontario, embedded in flesh-colored calcite. These crystals are to 18 in. (40 cm) or more in length and may be several inches deep. Clear, gemmy, violet crystals to 1 in. (2.5 cm) across have been collected in some New England pegmatites, especially at Mt. Apatite, Maine. Granular beds of apatite that can be mined for fertilizer use are found in the Russian Kola Peninsula, and in Brazil. The apatites of Panasqueira, Portugal, are among the most attractive ones of open pockets. Bolivia yields fine colorless to violet crystals. Among the most abundant crystals are the yellow ones from Durango, Mexico, which can be 3 in. long (8 cm) and are often gemmy. Giant crystals of this type have been found near Copiapó, Chile, and in Brazil.

Interesting facts: Bone has essentially an apatite composition and structure. Apatite has an interesting crystal symmetry often revealed in the smaller, shiny crystals by faces to the right or left of the horizontal axis unpaired with a corresponding face on the other side. These are known as 3rd-order faces.

PYROMORPHITE $Pb_5(PO_4,AsO_4)_3Cl$ Pl. 30

Hexagonal — Hexagonal bipyramidal $\dfrac{6}{m}$

Environment: Secondary (weathered) zone of lead ore deposits.

Crystal description: Short hexagonal prisms up to $\frac{1}{2}$ in. (ca. 1 cm) across and twice as long. However, coarse crystals are nearly always cavernous; good terminations will be found only on slender needles.

Physical properties: Dark green, yellow-green, light gray, brown. *Luster* resinous; *hardness* $3\frac{1}{2}$–4; *gravity* 6.5–7.1; *fracture* subconchoidal to uneven; *cleavage* prismatic. Brittle; translucent.

Composition: Lead chlorophosphate (81.2% PbO, 2.5% Cl, 16.3% P_2O_5, but the P is usually replaced in part by arsenic, which grades into mimetite [next]).

Tests: Fuses easily on charcoal to a globule, which on cooling assumes an angular shape with shiny faces, like a crystal.

Distinguishing characteristics: The cavernous crystals and color are very characteristic. They can be confused only with others of the same group, and are distinguished from mimetite and vanadinite by the blowpipe test.

Occurrence: A secondary mineral forming in oxidized lead deposits, the P presumably coming from the apatite of neighboring rocks. Not common, and for this reason not an important ore of lead. Good brown crystals were found in Germany; some had been altered back to galena in pseudomorphs. Fine specimens have come from: Phoenixville, Pennsylvania, which in the 19th century was one of the world's best localities, yielding fine crusts of large green crystals; and Davidson Co., North Carolina, which produced thinner crusts of small yellow-green crystals. Not abundant in the West except in the Coeur D'Alene district of Idaho, since it does not appear to be (in spite of what one might expect) a compound best developed by desert climates. Some of the finest ever found came from El Horcajo, cen. Spain.

Interesting facts: The name means "fire form" in Greek, and refers to the unique behavior of a grain under the blowpipe. Compare with cerussite (p. 153). Green crystals are invariably characteristic of more highly altered ore levels, and limonite is generally visible in the matrix. White to brown crystals can actually grow on galena, far below an oxidation level that would result in the development of limonite.

MIMETITE $Pb_5(AsO_4,PO_4)_3Cl$ **Pl. 30**

Hexagonal — Hexagonal bipyramidal $\dfrac{6}{m}$

Environment: Secondary (weathered) zone of lead ore deposits.

Crystal description: Slender to thick needles, sometimes in yellowish mammillary crusts. Orange-yellow rounded crystals (melon-shaped) called "campylite."

Physical properties: White, yellow, yellow-orange to brown. *Luster* resinous; *hardness* $3\frac{1}{2}$; *gravity* 7.0–7.3; *fracture* uneven; *cleavage* pyramidal. Brittle; transparent to translucent.

Composition: Lead chloroarsenate (74.6% PbO, 23.2% As_2O_5, 2.4% Cl).

Tests: Fuses readily on charcoal; suddenly boils, giving off arsenical fumes (garlic odor), and reduces to a lead bead.

Distinguishing characteristics: Appearance, the associations, and occurrence show it to be a member of this group. Distinguished from pyromorphite and vanadinite by arsenic smell.

Occurrence: Like pyromorphite and vanadinite, mimetite is a secondary mineral. It is rather rare, being far less common than the other two, and only occasionally is it of importance as an ore of lead.

Best distributed in collections are the old campylite specimens. Campylite occurs in small (to $\frac{3}{8}$ in.; 1 cm) crystals at several British localities. Mimetite is rare in the U.S. Most frequent occurrence is across the border in Durango, Mexico, where it forms orange-yellow botryoidal coatings of great charm at San Pedro Corralitos. Brilliant orange blobs illuminate thin yellow wulfenites at Cerro Prieto, Sonora, Mexico, and at the Rowley and 79 Mines in Theba and Hayden, Arizona. It has been found at Eureka, Utah. The best and largest isolated crystals of former times were found in the old mine visited by Goethe at Johanngeorgenstadt, Saxony. Remarkable, gemmy, pale yellow, beautifully terminated 2 in. (4–5 cm) crystals have lately been found at Tsumeb, South West Africa, and provide what is probably the all-time great for this mineral.

VANADINITE $Pb_5(VO_4)_3Cl$ **Pl. 32**

Hexagonal — Hexagonal bipyramidal $\dfrac{6}{m}$

Environment: Secondary (weathered) zone of lead ore deposits.

Crystal description: Small 6-sided prisms, and often in larger crystals in built-up masses that are cavernous in the center. Pyramidal terminations only on slender crystals.

Physical properties: Bright red-brown-orange to yellow-brown, or brown. *Luster* resinous; *hardness* $2\frac{3}{4}$–3; *gravity* 6.7–7.1; *fracture* uneven; *cleavage* none. Brittle; transparent to translucent.

Composition: Lead chlorovanadate (78.7% PbO, 19.4% V_2O_5, 2.5% Cl; As sometimes substitutes for the V; a 1:1 ratio of V to As is known as endlichite).

Tests: Fuses to a black mass with a shiny, slightly angular surface. After continued blowing, little beads of lead eventually appear (like the yolk in a frying egg) and the slag slowly goes away.

Distinguishing characteristics: Separated from pyromorphite and mimetite by its blowpipe reactions.

Occurrence: A secondary mineral forming in desert country as a result of the alteration, by weathering, of lead ores. Associated with descloizite, wulfenite, cerussite, and other secondary ore minerals. A unique occurrence of very large crystals completely coated with descloizite was found in South West Africa. There are numerous U.S. localities in Arizona and New Mexico, among which the bright orange-red crystals from the old Yuma Mine near Tucson, Arizona, are especially well known. The orange skeletal crystals from Stein's Pass, New Mexico, are also popular. The clear, light yellow arsenical variety called endlichite is found at Hillsboro and Lake Valley, New Mexico. Flat, bright orange, hexagonal, platy crystals characterize the Mibladen (Morocco) occurrence, which seems to be about the best for this mineral.

Interesting facts: Though apparently abundant, vanadinite did not prove to be rich enough in any southwestern occurrence to be workable as an ore during World War II, when vanadium was much sought after. Since bright mahogany-red crystals have a tendency to darken and dull on prolonged exposure to light, museum displays may be disappointing.

LAZULITE $(Mg,Fe)Al_2(PO_4)_2(OH)_2$ ⎫
SCORZALITE $(Fe,Mg)Al_2(PO_4)_2(OH)_2$ ⎬   **Pl. 31**

Monoclinic — prismatic $\dfrac{2}{m}$

Environment: Pegmatite dikes, metamorphic rocks, and quartz veins in metamorphics.

Crystal description: Good crystals uncommon; when found, they are wedge-shaped and embedded as a rule. Also in small solid masses without external crystal forms.

Physical properties: Bright blue to dark blue (scorzalite). *Luster* glassy; *hardness* $5\frac{1}{2}$–6; *gravity* 3.1–3.4; *fracture* uneven; *cleavage* poor prismatic. Brittle; transparent to translucent.

Composition: Form an isomorphous series (from a basic high-magnesium phosphate [lazulite] to a high-iron phosphate [scorzalite]; about 32% Al_2O_3, 45% P_2O_5, and 5.5% H_2O, with the remainder divided between MgO and FeO).

Tests: Only slowly soluble in hot acids. In the blowpipe flame they turn white to dark brown (depending on iron content), crack open, swell up, and the pieces blow away.

Distinguishing characteristics: The light to deep blue color is rather distinctive. Blue vesuvianite fuses readily to a glass, sodalite and lazurite whiten and fuse with some difficulty to a glass, blue spinels are infusible. The copper-blue minerals are readily soluble in acid and easily fused.

Occurrence: Lazulite and scorzalite are high-temperature hydrothermal minerals of limited occurrence. Crystals have been found at very few localities. In Zermatt, Switzerland, and in w. Austria, lazulite forms good blue crystals with shiny faces in quartz veins. In Brazil it forms rich masses in veins cutting the sandstone near Diamantina. The very dark blue high-iron variety, scorzalite, from a phosphate-bearing pegmatite in e. Minas Gerais, is a recent breakdown from a series once lumped as lazulite, a mineral of variable composition. A few truly gemmy bits of the lazulite type have been found in Minas Gerais pegmatite detritus. They are strongly pleochroic: when turned, changing from yellowish to nearly colorless to sapphire-blue. The largest is about hazelnut size.

In the U.S. it forms in nodules in a vein near Death Valley, California, which cuts a light-colored schist. Scattered grains may be found in a phosphate-rich pegmatite at North Groton, New Hampshire. The best U.S. crystals are the slightly sandy ones, often slightly altered on the surface, which are found embedded in a quartzite at Graves Mountain, Georgia, associated with rutile and kyanite. There is a similar formation, with the same paragenesis, near Copiapó, Chile. In a remarkable find, 1 in. (2.5 cm) deep blue crystals were collected from a phosphate-rich vein in the Yukon Territory, Alaska. Associated minerals are wardite, brazilianite, and siderite, on quartz.

LIROCONITE $Cu_2Al(AsO_4)(OH)_4 \cdot 4H_2O$

Monoclinic — prismatic $\dfrac{2}{m}$

Environment: Secondary mineralized zone of copper arsenide deposits.

Crystal description: Usually individually crystallized, occasional crusts with crystals on edge. Isolated single crystals are pseudotetragonal bipyramids, though the faces present are actually 4 prism faces and 4 clinodomes (inclined only 1°27'). In specimens the crystals are usually attached on one side and give the impression of 4-faced low pyramids. The largest known crystal (Truro Museum, Cornwall) is about ¾ in. (almost 2 cm); most are only about ¼ in. (0.5 cm).

Physical properties: Rich sky-blue to slightly greenish blue. *Luster* glassy; *hardness* 2–2½; *gravity* 3.0; *streak* pale blue (giving it its name from the Greek for "pale powder"); *fracture* uneven; *cleavage* 2, poor, paralleling the usual faces. Brittle, translucent.

Composition: Hydrated basic copper aluminum arsenate (CuO about 37% Al_2O_3 11%, As_2O_5 [plus P_2O_5] 27%, and H_2O 25%).

Tests: In the blowpipe it turns deep blue, then blackens, fusing to a black bead. Soluble in acid.

Distinguishing characteristics: No testing needed as a rule; the color, crystals, and specimen's character usually suffice. The few similarly hued other minerals have entirely different associations. Crystals are very distinctive and localities few.

Occurrence: From a practical standpoint, this is only a Cornwall mineral, for it was found there in good specimens at three different mines and, so far, nowhere else as more than a few small crystals. Wheal Gorland, Gwennap, is most often listed as a source. Microscopic crystals have been reported from Germany, Czechoslovakia, and the U.S.S.R. No specimens have been found recently, though the Gwennap dumps might still yield a few. Collectors, who greatly admire the mineral, have to content themselves with the old-timers gleaned from private collections and museum duplicates.

The Cerro Gordo Mine, Inyo Co., California, is said to have yielded some liroconite (pronounced with emphasis on *roc*), where it was associated with caledonite and linarite.

CHILDRENITE $(Fe,Mn)Al(PO_4)(OH)_2 \cdot H_2O$
EOSPHORITE $(Mn,Fe)Al(PO_4)(OH)_2 \cdot H_2O$ **Pl. 31**

Orthorhombic — bipyramidal $\dfrac{2\ 2\ 2}{m\ m\ m}$

Environment: Late-mineral ore veins and a pegmatite phosphate (probably primary).

Crystal description: Two completely distinct types; one consisting of large, pink, well-formed (though usually corroded or altered) crystals; the other sheaves of subparallel crystals and radiating sprays of the bundles, with rough, very dark terminations. Vein crystals sharper, but usually small and dark.

Physical properties: Salmon-pink, light to dark brown, gray, and almost black. *Luster* glassy (to pearly on the front face of the brown bundles); *hardness* $4\frac{1}{2}$; *gravity* 3.06–3.25; *fracture* conchoidal; *cleavage* front and side pinacoid. Brittle; translucent to transparent.

Composition: Hydrous basic iron and manganese aluminum phosphate (an isomorphous series with MnO-FeO 31%, Al_2O_3 22%, P_2O_5 31%, and H_2O 16%). In my experience, though they form an isomorphous series, the pegmatite occurrences are wholly unlike the small crystals in the ore veins, and the large pink eosphorites bear little superficial resemblance to the much more frequent dark brown ones.

Tests: On heating, both types swell and lose weight, and are easily crushed to powder. Brown material turns black and becomes magnetic. Pink variety turns buff color and is but weakly magnetic.

Distinguishing characteristics: The brown sprays are distinctive in a pegmatite environment, though they resemble some stilbites in appearance. The pink crystals resemble nothing else in such an environment but hureaulite, which fuses easily into an orange-brown sphere.

Occurrence: This series has come due for restudy since the discovery of unique large salmon-pink (but corroded, or even altered completely to limonite) crystals in Minas Gerais, Brazil. Brown sprays — like some from Branchville, Connecticut, and several of the New Hampshire and Maine pegmatites — contain more iron. Perhaps the proper name for the browner material should be childrenite rather than the eosphorite it has always been called. The Brazilian rose-quartz crystal locality, Taquaral, has fine sprays of the brown crystals, some even on the rose quartz itself. They seem fresher, later, and perhaps more of a secondary mineral then the larger corroded pink crystals.

On simple inspection one would not suspect the two types to belong to the same species, for they seem so very different. Bolivian childrenite crystal crusts are made up of very small individual crystals and are dark gray. Cornwall childrenite occurs as sparsely scattered, small, bright brown, rather equi-dimensional crystals. With so tremendous a habit variation in this series — almost too unlike for members of one series — it seems difficult to believe that they are truly completely iso-morphous.

The brown crystals and sprays of Taquaral can be $1\frac{1}{4}$ in. (about 3 cm) long, whereas the pink crystals are as much as $2-2\frac{1}{2}$ in. (5-7.5 cm) long and $\frac{1}{2}$ in. (1 cm) across.

WARDITE $NaAl_3(PO_4)_2(OH)_4 \cdot 2H_2O$ **Pl. 31**
Tetragonal — Tetragonal pyramidal   4

Environment: Secondary alteration mineral on aluminum phosphates. Late mineral in pegmatite dikes.

Crystal description: In crusts of small, light blue-green pyram-idal crystals or white coarser crystals and crusts; also granular masses.

Physical properties: Bluish green to white. *Luster* glassy; *hardness* 5; *gravity* 2.8–2.9; *fracture* conchoidal; *cleavage* good basal. Brittle; translucent to transparent.

Composition: Hydrous basic sodium calcium aluminum phos-phate (7.6% Na_2O, 3.4% CaO, 37.5% Al_2O_3, 34.8% P_2O_5, 16.6% H_2O).

Tests: Before the blowpipe it whitens and swells. Cobalt nitrate drop gives, after refiring, the blue aluminum test. Chemical tests show phosphorus.

Distinguishing characteristics: The appearance and occur-rence at the principal American locality is characteristic, but the white, pseudo-octahedral crystals of the rare pegmatitic occurrences look like several other minerals, and would be diffi-cult for the amateur to recognize if crystals are not present.

Occurrence: Wardite in its best-known occurrence forms the innermost mineral border of the altering variscite in the nodules from Fairfield, Utah. Striated white $\frac{3}{8}$ in. (7 mm) crystals have lately been found in lazulite veins in Alaska (Yukon Territory). It was described from a French pegmatite occurrence at Mon-tebras as a secondary mineral under another name, soumansite, when it was not recognized as the same substance. Also found in a New Hampshire pegmatite at Beryl Mountain, South Ac-worth, and in a German pegmatite in $\frac{1}{4}$ in. (5 mm) unimpressive white tetragonal bipyramids. Larger crystals of like hue were found on feldspar and on the rose-quartz crystals at the Mina de Ilha, Taquaral, Minas Gerais, Brazil.

Interesting facts: Named for Professor Henry A. Ward, the founder of Ward's Natural Science Establishment.

TURQUOISE $CuAl_6(PO_4)_4(OH)_8 \cdot 4H_2O$ **Pl. 32**
Triclinic — pinacoidal $\overline{1}$

Environment: A secondary mineral, forming veins in alumina-rich rocks of desert regions.
Crystal description: Usually in fine-grained solid veins. Crystals found only in Virginia, where they formed thin crusts and small rosettes of microscopic short-prismatic crystals.
Physical properties: Sky-blue to light greenish blue. *Luster* porcelaneous; *hardness* 5–6; *gravity* 2.6–2.8; *fracture* smooth. Brittle; translucent on thin edges.
Composition: Hydrous basic aluminum phosphate plus copper (about 9.8% CuO, 37.6% Al_2O_3, 34.9% P_2O_5, 17.7% H_2O).
Tests: Decrepitates violently and will not stay on the charcoal. In closed tube it flies to pieces and turns brown. Gives chemical phosphorus and copper tests.
Distinguishing characteristics: Not likely to be confused with many other minerals. Turquoise can be distinguished from the more glassy chrysocolla by the phosphorus test, from fine-grained quartz (with Cu stain) by its solubility in acid, and from variscite by the behavior under the blowpipe.
Occurrence: Turquoise appears to be almost invariably a mineral of arid climates. It is commonly found where rocks have been deeply altered, usually forming veins in broken igneous rocks. The necessary phosphorus probably came from apatite in the fresh rock; the alumina from the feldspar and the copper from chalcopyrite grains.

New Mexico, Nevada, and Colorado are all important turquoise states. The most expensive turquoise comes from Iran and Tibet, where the matrix appears more often to be black. The American matrix is commonly brown to white. It has been found in Chuquicamata, Chile, in large veins.

The only crystallized occurrence so far known is further unique in that the turquoise is not in solid veins but forms druses of small crystals on a schist in a copper mining prospect in Virginia. The crystals are light blue to greenish blue, scattered singly and in rosettes over the surface of seams, the more spectacular crystals coating white quartz.
Interesting facts: There is an iron-stained fossil bone known as "odontolite" or "bone turquoise" which has often been confused with and used in the same ways as true turquoise. Can be distinguished by testing for copper.

WAVELLITE $Al_3(OH)_3(PO_4)_2 \cdot 5H_2O$ **Pl. 31**
Orthorhombic $\dfrac{2\ \ 2\ \ 2}{m\ m\ m}$

Environment: Late low-temperature mineral in hydrothermal veins.
Crystal description: Usually in crusts of very small crystals,

coating other minerals with the individuals poorly defined. More often in spherulitic masses with a radiating structure, sometimes filling a seam.

Physical properties: White to gray, yellow, green, brown, or black. *Luster* glassy to silky; *hardness* $3\frac{1}{2}$–4; *gravity* 2.4; *fracture* uneven to subconchoidal, splinters; *cleavage* domal and side pinacoid. Brittle; transparent to translucent.

Composition: Hydrous basic aluminum phosphate (37.1% Al, 34.5% P_2O_5, 28.4% H_2O).

Tests: The fine fibers glow whitely and exfoliate. The mass can be kept together by gently heating one end. Touched with cobalt nitrate and refired, it gives the blue aluminum test. A chemical test will show phosphorus.

Distinguishing characteristics: Except for one occurrence, not a striking mineral and could be confused with many others. The two tests given above are very useful for minerals answering this general description. A botryoidal crust may resemble chalcedony, but it is softer and soluble in acid.

Occurrence: Wavellite is a late mineral when found in hydrothermal veins with other minerals, and it usually incrusts the earlier minerals. It is also scattered throughout sedimentary beds, such as limonite and phosphate beds, in small quantities. The most attractive examples are the approximately 1 in. (2–3 cm) radiating spherules of a yellow-green color found in veins in a gray rock at Dug Hill, Avant, Garland Co., Arkansas. Small crystal faces may be seen truncating the radiating crystals that build the spheres. Considerable quantities of a pale, botryoidal, compact wavellite have been found at Llallagua, Bolivia, where it forms incrustations on the earlier vein minerals in the tin mines. Black shale surfaces are coated with greenish sunburst at Ronneburg, East Germany. Arkansas-like rosettes have been found, many coated with variscite crystals, at Pannecé (Loire-Atlantique), France.

TORBERNITE $Cu(UO_2)(PO_4)_2 \cdot 8$–$12(H_2O)$ **Pl. 32**

Tetragonal — Ditetragonal bipyramidal $\dfrac{4\ 2\ 2}{m\ m\ m}$

Environment: A secondary mineral in weathered zones of ore deposits, and seams in pegmatites.

Crystal description: Usually in thin square plates, more rarely in small bipyramids. Also micaceous flakes with indefinite outlines.

Physical properties: Emerald- to yellow-green. *Luster* pearly on base, vitreous in prism directions; *hardness* 2–$2\frac{1}{2}$; *gravity* 3.2–3.6; *fracture* not visible as a rule; *cleavage* perfect basal and good frontal pinacoid. Brittle; translucent to transparent.

Composition: Hydrous copper uranium phosphate (56.6% UO_3, 7.9% CuO, 14.1% P_2O_5, 21.4% H_2O, but part of the water is likely to evaporate spontaneously; metatorbernite has 8% H_2O). In a collection, it is assumed that all crystals are dehydrated and should probably be labeled metatorbernite for nitpicking accuracy.

Tests: Fuses easily to a black bead. Gives copper flame in acid solution, fluorescent bead with sodium fluoride.

Distinguishing characteristics: Can be confused with some rare copper phosphates and arsenates, though none have the square outline characteristic of torbernite. Resembles others of its group (like autunite), but torbernite is not fluorescent and the others are. Zeunerite, the arsenic equivalent, resembles it closely, but would give arsenic fumes on charcoal.

Occurrence: Appears to be a late mineral, and its most frequent appearance is in thin green micaceous plates coating fissures in pegmatites and small square crystals very lightly attached to the matrix. It has also been found in some ore veins, associated with other uranium minerals. Large, thin, concave crystals over 1 in. (3 cm) across were found at Gunnislake, near Calstock, Cornwall. Next in size are the large crystals from Mt. Painter, South Australia. It also occurred in Portugal at Trancoso, in the Bois Noir, France, and in Saxony and Bohemia; but it constitutes an ore of uranium only at Shaba (Katanga) in Zaïre (Belgian Congo), where it forms magnificent, giant specimens and is associated with the world's most colorful and remarkable uranium mineral suite.

U.S. occurrences are infrequent, the best are well-formed $\frac{1}{4}$ to $\frac{3}{8}$ in. (5–10 mm) plates coating a gray quartz in a quarry at Little Switzerland, North Carolina. Scattered crystals are found at many localities, but it is far rarer than autunite (next). Small pyramidal crystals have been found at the Kinkel Quarry, Bedford, New York.

AUTUNITE $Ca(UO_2)_2(PO_4)_2 \cdot 10-12H_2O$ **Pl. 32**

Tetragonal — Ditetragonal bipyramidal $\dfrac{4\ 2\ 2}{m\,m\,m}$

Environment: Secondary mineral in weathered zones of ore deposits and seams in pegmatites.

Crystal description: Square plates, also scattered thin flakes and solid micaceous crusts, with crystals standing on the edge.

Physical properties: Greenish yellow to lemon-yellow. *Luster* pearly to glassy; *hardness* $2-2\frac{1}{2}$; *gravity* 3.1; *fracture* not notable; *cleavage* perfect basal and prismatic. Brittle; translucent; one of the most brilliantly fluorescent (green) of all minerals in ultraviolet light.

Composition: Hydrous calcium uranium phosphate (58.0% UO_3, 5.7% CaO, 14.4% P_2O_5, 21.9% H_2O), but usually loses water after capture and becomes meta-autunite (see torbernite, preceding).

Tests: The brilliant fluorescence makes all other testing unnecessary.

Distinguishing characteristics: The fluorescence and the square plates distinguish it from all other minerals except rare members of the same group. The presence of Ca can be confirmed by obtaining the calcium sulfate precipitate, produced when sulfuric acid is added to the nitric acid solution.

Occurrence: Autunite is probably always a secondary mineral that forms as a result of the surface alteration of uranium ores. It may be almost invisible on a rock face, but form a fluorescent "eye" around a center of less altered nonfluorescent uranium minerals in a pegmatite. Ultraviolet light examination of rocks with altered uraninite usually shows an unexpected abundance of autunite in flakes so thin that they were not noted in the examination in ordinary light.

Very abundant in uranium-bearing pegmatites all over the world. Especially rich masses have been found at Spruce Pine, North Carolina. In Portugal at Urgeiriça and in South Australia at Mt. Painter, it has formed veins that were rich enough to be mined, those of Mt. Painter being up to 9 in. or a foot thick (20–30 cm). Rich greenish-yellow crusts are found at Saône-et-Loire, and Margnac, Haute-Vienne, France.

It tends to crumble in collections and many of the finest U.S. specimens, very rich crusts of pure mineral from the Daybreak Mine, near Spokane, Washington, have to be lacquered or otherwise treated to preserve them.

CARNOTITE $K_2(UO_2)_2(VO_4)_2 \cdot 3H_2O$
Orthorhombic (?)

Environment: Secondary mineral in sedimentary rocks.

Crystal description: No recognizable crystals; microscopic plates sometimes visible. Usually earthy disseminations or films.

Physical properties: Bright yellow. *Luster* earthy; *hardness* indeterminate (soft); *gravity* 4.1; powdery and crumbling; *cleavage* crystal plates said to have a basal cleavage, but would not be visible. Sectile; opaque like an ocher.

Composition: Hydrous potassium uranium vanadate (10.4% K_2O, 63.4% UO_3, 20.2% V_2O_5, 6.0% H_2O).

Tests: Infusible. Powder turns red-brown when dropped in boiling nitric acid, and dissolves to green solution. Cold borax bead is fluorescent green. Residue of evaporation of acid is fluorescent.

Distinguishing characteristics: The bright yellow uranium color without the normal uranium fluorescence is significant. A bead test with ultraviolet light will prove uranium.

Occurrence: The only important deposits are in sandstones in w. Colorado and e. Utah, with some in Arizona and New Mexico. Its exact origin is uncertain; presumably it has formed from pre-existing uranium and vanadium minerals. It is disseminated through a red-brown sandstone, often replacing fossil wood, then making rich masses of relatively pure carnotite. Yellow stains of carnotite have been found in a conglomerate along a railroad cut at Mauch Chunk, Pennsylvania. It has been found in n. Mexico, at Radium Hill, South Australia, and with the uranium ores at Shaba (Katanga), Zaïre (Belgian Congo). The only actual crystals seem to be those of small limestone pockets at Grants, New Mexico.

Interesting facts: For some years, before the discovery of the Belgian Congo U-ores, the U.S. carnotite deposits were the world's chief source of radium ore. These deposits were closed when the development of the Congo ores reduced the price of radium. Now that the interest has shifted to uranium they have become an important U.S. source of that precious metal.

The Tungstates (Wolframates) and Molybdates

This is a small group of ore minerals that are colorful and interesting. Wulfenite belongs to a rare tetragonal crystal class characterized by 3rd-order faces. Scheelite and powellite are both desirable minerals on account of their fluorescence, besides being members of the same crystal class as wulfenite. The wolframite group of minerals are important tungsten (wolfram) ores.

Tungsten and molybdenum can replace each other in some minerals to a limited extent. The blue color of molybdenum oxide noted in an evaporated acid solution residue is conspicuous and helps in the distinction between powellite and scheelite. The fluorescence of powellite is a guide to the identification of molybdenite, its usual parent.

WOLFRAMITE   (Fe,Mn)WO$_4$ **Pl. 33**

    Ferberite   FeWO$_4$ } Monoclinic — prismatic $\dfrac{2}{m}$
    Huebnerite MnWO$_4$ }

Environment: High-temperature and medium-temperature quartz veins, and in granitic rocks enriched by pegmatite solutions.

Crystal description: Wolframite usually occurs in fair-sized, 1–2 in. (3–6 cm) black blades commonly embedded in white vein quartz, revealing the perfect cleavage on the fracture face. More often than not the crystals are twinned on the front face, so the termination has a V-shaped notch. Ferberite usually forms crusts of small stubby black blades on rock surfaces in open cavities; also massive granular. Huebnerite tends toward brown, showing its color by the translucence on the cleavage faces from inner parallel cracks.

Physical properties: Black to red-brown. *Luster* submetallic; *hardness* 4–4½; *gravity* 7.1–7.5; *fracture* uneven; *cleavage* perfect side pinacoid. Brittle; huebnerite is translucent in thin flakes.

Composition: Tungstates of iron and manganese, the two elements form a continuous series in which the end-members are known as ferberite (with 23.7% FeO and 76.3% WO_3) and huebnerite (with 23.4% MnO and 76.6% WO_3).

Tests: Decrepitates, then fuses to a globule that assumes, on solidifying, a slightly faceted (crystalline) surface and is magnetic. The best tungsten test is to fuse the material in sodium carbonate, dissolve the mixture in strong hydrochloric acid, and add pure tin, which imparts a blue color to the solution. Best to try this test out several times with known tungsten-bearing ores, to acquire the technique. Exaggerated heat sensitivity makes specimens vulnerable to damage if too intensely illuminated, as in the mineral-show display cases.

Distinguishing characteristics: The tungsten test is the best guide and many be essential. Huebnerite can resemble goethite, which will give no W test. It often resembles columbite, tantalite and manganotantalite, and again the tungsten test is the one to apply, although tungsten sometimes can be found in these minerals; then the problem may be difficult.

Occurrence: Wolframite is a widespread mineral most often found in deep-seated quartz veins. Frequently shows embedded blades extending in from the wall, so perfect that they would serve as textbook illustrations. The perfect cleavage is very pronounced and helps to distinguish it from the interrupted surface of columbite. However, pegmatitic occurrences of wolframite are rare, though they are the customary environment of columbite-tantalite, so a distinction is largely one of academic interest. Ferberite, on the other hand, forms typical drusy crusts of small, free-growing, brilliant black crystals over rock surfaces in open low-pressure but high-temperature veins, like those of Nederland, Boulder Co., Colorado, and Llallagua, Bolivia. The finest examples come from Panasqueira, Portugal, from n. Peru, and from Tong Wha, Korea.

Good specimens have been found in quartz veins at: Fredericktown, Missouri; Ouray Co., Colorado; Lincoln Co., New Mexico; Nye Co., Nevada; and Townsville, North Carolina. Ferberite is best developed in Colorado, and similar specimens have come from Bolivia. Colorado huebnerite forms brown quartz-coated sprays. Dealers dissolve the quartz with hydrofluoric acid — a risky procedure — to obtain fragile specimens of the crystals.

Economic importance: An important ore of tungsten. Its name refers to the early name for tungsten, which in an ore mixture with tin ore reduced the recovery of that metal by "wolfing" the ore. "Wolfram" was accepted as a change in name by the chemists but is not general in popular speech.

SCHEELITE CaWO₄ **Pl. 32**

Tetragonal — Tetragonal bipyramidal $\frac{4}{m}$

Environment: Contact-metamorphic deposits, high-temperature quartz veins, and, rarely, in pegmatites.

Crystal description: Usually occurs in well-formed bipyramidal crystals, often with a suggestion of asymmetrical truncation on one side (3rd-order forms). The crystals may be small and brilliant or fairly large, even to 3 or 4 in. (15 cm). Transparent white and amber crystals suitable for cutting into gemstones have been found. Also in grains embedded in rock, without regular external form.

Physical properties: White, light brown, light green. *Luster* adamantine; *hardness* 4½–5; *gravity* 5.9–6.1; *fracture* uneven; *cleavage* 3, bipyramidal best. Translucent to transparent; most specimens are fluorescent (shortwave ultraviolet) blue to yellow (depending upon molybdenum content).

Composition: Calcium tungstate, usually with some of the tungsten replaced by molybdenum (19.5% CaO, 80.5% WO₃).

Tests: Tests are rarely necessary, since the fluorescence in ultraviolet light is the recognized method of prospecting. A gravity test and the blue tungsten test mentioned under wolframite (preceding) may be given, but the yellow precipitate and coating obtained by simply boiling a powder in hydrochloric acid are usually sufficient.

Distinguishing characteristics: The fluorescence may be confusing, especially when it becomes whitish or yellow from molybdenum substitution, but the high gravity differentiates it from fluorescent fluorite and the crystals are so common that they will often be seen.

Occurrence: Most frequently found in contact-metamorphic deposits, where granitic rocks have intruded an impure limestone and the heat and gases have caused the typical minerals of this occurrence to form. Associates will be garnet, epidote, and vesuvianite. Scheelite should always be looked for under these circumstances. It will also be found in high-temperature quartz veins, often in crystals associated with cassiterite, topaz, fluorite, wolframite, and apatite.

Good crystals have been found at many localities, particularly at Bishop and Atolia, California, and in Mohave and Cochise Cos., Arizona. Interesting crystals and replacements of wolframite after scheelite crystals have been found at Trumbull, Connecticut. Most of the commercially important Mill City (Nevada) scheelite is in grains embedded in a very compact rock. Gemmy, orange-brown crystals have been found in Sonora, Mexico, with black tourmaline.

Foreign localities of note include Málaga, Spain, Slavkov (Schlaggenwald, Bohemia), Czechoslovakia, and Tong Wha, Korea. It is abundant in n. Brazil in metamorphic formations with vesuvianite.

A seemingly secondary cool-water type has been found in n. Mexico where the scheelite is later than chrysocolla.

Interesting facts: An important ore of tungsten and, as a result of prospecting with ultraviolet light, has been discovered at many localities where it was not previously recognized. Resembles quartz when seen in the rock and probably has often not been recognized.

POWELLITE $CaMoO_4$ **Pl. 33**

Tetragonal — Tetragonal bipyramidal $\frac{4}{m}$

Environment: May form, like scheelite, in medium-temperature quartz veins, but usually is a result of the alteration of molybdenite. Rarely it is an associate of zeolites.

Crystal description: Crystals small and rare, but resemble those of scheelite in development. Commonly forms as thin yellowish films and plates intimately mixed with more or less altered molybdenite.

Physical properties: White, yellowish brown, light blue. *Luster* adamantine; *hardness* $3\frac{1}{2}-4$; *gravity* 4.2; *fracture* uneven; *cleavage* bipyramidal. Transparent to translucent; fluorescent yellow.

Composition: Calcium molybdate with some tungsten replacing the molybdenum (28.0% CaO, 72.0% MoO_3, with up to 10.0% WO_3 replacing the latter in part).

Tests: Distinguished from scheelite by its yellow fluorescence and lower gravity. Chemical tests rarely necessary, but it is decomposed by hydrochloric acid to give yellow solution; a drop of solution evaporated on streak plate leaves blue residue (molybdenum).

Distinguishing characteristics: The crystals are much like those of scheelite, which is far more common. The earthy material usually shows some residues of the molybdenite, which immediately suggests its identity.

Occurrence: Good specimens are excessively rare. The original material, in microscopic crystals from a mine in Utah, was named for Major John Wesley Powell, once a director of the U.S. Geological Survey. Magnificent crystals, the best known, were found in the Michigan copper district at the Isle Royale and South Hecla mines. Brown crystal crusts have been found at Goldfield, Nevada. Colorless, brilliant crystals occur with zeolites in basalt at the Clayton Quarry, Panama Canal Zone. Has been described in a similar paragenesis in Scotland and noted in a Pune (India) zeolite crust.

The identification of the normal alteration of molybdenite as powellite, often in pseudomorphs after flaky crystals of molybdenite, was only recognized after it was known as a crystallized mineral. It is probably a very common occurrence and should always be looked for in any altered or weathered specimen of molybdenite-bearing rock. However, at Superior, Arizona, it was noted that crystallized powellite was always very close to obvious small veins, with altering molybdenite and the green scaly copper molybdate, lindgrenite, $Cu_3(MoO_4)_2(OH)_2$.

WULFENITE PbMoO$_4$ **Pl. 32**
           Tetragonal — Tetragonal pyramidal 4
Environment: A secondary mineral forming near the surface in lead veins.
Crystal description: Almost always in crystals, usually tabular, often very thin. Basal plane well developed; occasional 3rd-order pyramid faces make base appear interestingly twisted in relation to the crystal outline. Prismatic and pyramidal habits less frequent. On the large thin plates the prism faces are often irregularly developed so that the crystals are not sharply bounded.
Physical properties: Yellow, orange, brown, gray, almost white. *Luster* adamantine; *hardness* $2\frac{3}{4}$–3; *gravity* 6.8; *fracture* subconchoidal; *cleavage* pyramidal good, 2 poor. Transparent to translucent.
Composition: Lead molybdate (60.7% PbO, 39.3% MoO$_3$).
Test: The brilliant color, high luster, and platy habit make most tests unnecessary. Fuses easily to slag that is yellow when hot, gray when cold. Shiny fragment in hot hydrochloric acid becomes frosted on the surface, turns blue when removed and rubbed with steel needle while still wet.
Distinguishing characteristics: The brilliant colors characteristic of this mineral, together with the tabular development of the crystals, make it one of the easiest minerals to recognize. There is almost nothing with which there is any danger of confusing it except stolzite, the rare tungsten equivalent (PbWO$_4$).
Occurrence: Best developed in dry climates where weathering has extended fairly deep. The American Southwest and Mexico are particularly notable for their occurrences of wulfenite. (See comment under molybdenite, p. 97, about the fugitive character of Mo solutions.) The most brilliant orange crystals ever

found were at the Red Cloud Mine, Yuma Co., Arizona, and at Chah-Kharbose, Iran. There are many occurrences in the Southwest however, far too many to list. The orange to caramel crystals of Los Lamentos, Chihuahua, Mexico, tend to be more prismatic in habit than is common. Rare and unusual e. U.S. occurrences were at a lead mine in Southampton, Massachusetts; and at Phoenixville, Pennsylvania, with the pyromorphite.

The thickest crystals of wulfenite are almost colorless (within), 2 in. (5 cm) square ones from M'fouati, Congo Republic, usually coated with quartz, which adheres tightly to the base face (it chips free from the pyramid faces). Spectacular thin yellow crystals, with orange mimetite, come from the San Francisco Mine in Sonora, Mexico. Cerro Prieto has smaller but similar crystals. Scheelite-like crystals from Broken Hill, New South Wales, will be stolzite.

The first occurrence, in Carinthia, Austria, was described by Xavier Wulfen in 1785, who made recognizable pictures of many prismatic and pyramidal crystals before the importance of the shape of crystals was widely known.

The Silicates

This group of minerals is the largest and commonest, and its members are the most difficult to identify individually. Recognition of the group as a whole is easy, since most of the silicates are completely or relatively insoluble in our acids. They are translucent — at least in their splinters, giving a pale or white streak — and average higher in hardness and lower in specific gravity than most minerals. Their resistance to acids, and in many cases to fusion, makes them more difficult to identify by the tests in vogue among amateurs than minerals of other groups. In some cases a series of negative test results are about all that can be obtained.

The sequence of this group was originally changed in anticipation of the seventh edition of *Dana's System of Mineralogy,* which has not yet been published in entirety. Since this work is the accepted standard reference work of all professionals, and the sequence will be the sequence of most museum collections, it seems desirable to follow that arrangement here. Beginners will then not have to rearrange what they have learned as they advance their knowledge and add to their libraries.

The determination of the atomic arrangements within crystals, briefly discussed in the section on crystallography, has led to the present classification of the silicates. It is based upon the recognition that all of the silicate minerals are characterized by groups of 4 oxygen atoms equidistant in space from a central silicon atom. This 4-cornered imaginary solid is called a tetrahedron, and the tetrahedrons are linked together by sharing their corners or edges in one way or another to create 6 different sorts of arrangements (or structures). The structures are responsible for some of the properties. A sheet structure, for example, is revealed by unusually good cleavage in one plane, chain structures encourage good cleavages in two planes, and so on. For this reason it is both logical and convenient to group them in this fashion, even though it results in the separation of some minerals that occur naturally together in the same environment and are chemically somewhat similar.

The silicate section is subdivided into the following types:

Silica	SiO_2	Framework structure
Disilicate	Si_2O_5	Sheet structure
Metasilicate	Si_3O_8 ⎫	
	Si_4O_{11} ⎬	Chain structures
	SiO_3 ⎭	
	Si_nO_{3n}	Ring structure
Pyrosilicate	Si_2O_7	Isolated groups of tetrahedrons
Orthosilicate	SiO_4	Isolated single tetrahedrons
Subsilicate	SiO_5	Isolated tetrahedrons with additional O

The Silica Type $Si:O = 1:2$

Mainly sodium, calcium, and potassium aluminum silicates, sometimes with water, in an open network. This arrangement gives its members a low specific gravity and is responsible for a tendency toward an equidimensional crystal habit.

Silica Group

QUARTZ SiO_2 **Pls. 33, 34**
Hexagonal — Trigonal trapezohedral 3 2
Environment: Commonest of minerals, found in every class of rocks and forming under all sorts of conditions.
Crystal description: This can be divided into two groups on the basis of its appearance: crystallized and microcrystalline. The microcrystalline group can in turn be subdivided into a parallel fibrous crystal arrangement and a heterogeneous finely granular type.
1. Crystallized quartz often occurs in large well-formed colorless crystals or crystal crusts. Violet-colored crystals are

known as amethyst; gray to black crystals are known as smoky quartz. Also forms veins or masses of this coarsely crystallized material and may be milky quartz or rose quartz.

2a. Chalcedony is a microscopically crystallized variety of the same mineral, but the individual crystals are arranged in slender fibers in parallel bands. Chalcedony surfaces tend to be botryoidal and are often smooth and translucent. The banding is very obvious in the type called agate.

2b. The chert, flint, and jasper group also have microscopically grained quartz, but these do not have the definite banding and the translucency of the chalcedony group and usually have more impurities.

Massive quartz, quartz sand, and disseminated grains of quartz in other rocks, or in pebbles of quartz or quartzite, are very common, and usually are the most important constituents of any gravel or sand beach.

Free-growing quartz crystals vary in habit from long slender prisms to crusts or "points." Prism faces are usually horizontally striated; terminal faces usually exhibit alternating development of larger and smaller faces, thus indicating the rhombohedral rather than hexagonal character of the mineral.

Because of the composition, quartz and the other SiO_2 minerals have always been considered with the oxides, but their physical properties and their crystal structures are more in accord with those of the silicate group, so it seems appropriate to transfer them to the silicates. Quartz itself has several crystal-class modifications, and although it has only a right- or a left-hand rhombohedral symmetry at normal temperatures, it is fully developed or paired rhombohedral at temperatures above 573°C. This greater symmetry form is known as beta-quartz (β-quartz), and frequently forms when quartz crystallizes from really hot solutions. However, after crystallizing — on cooling below 573°C — the structure then changes to alpha-quartz (α-quartz), and all quartz that we now find is of course α-quartz. Quartz has been used as a geological thermometer, because the crystal shape it assumes sometimes indicates whether it formed above or below 573°C.

Two chemically identical minerals to be described after quartz carry the geological thermometer higher. SiO_2 crystallizing above 870°C forms platy orthorhombic crystals, and the mineral known as tridymite. SiO_2 crystallizing above 1470°C forms in white cubic-system crystals, and this substance is known as cristobalite. Hence, from the series of differently crystallizing compounds of this fortunately common substance, we can deduce the temperature of the formation of many rocks. The 2 high-temperature SiO_2 compounds are rarer than would be expected, for in solidifying, cooling rocks stay liquid down to far lower temperatures than expected if we were to judge by the heat that is required to remelt them, once they have crystallized to a solid. Under some conditions it is thought that tridymite and cristobalite can form at temperatures slightly lower than those at which they are really stable.

Physical properties: Colorless, white, smoky, rose, violet, brown, also translucent and tinted any hue by impurities. *Luster* glassy; *hardness* 7; *gravity* 2.6; *fracture* conchoidal; *cleavage* rhombohedral, sometimes observable. Transparent to subtranslucent from impurities. Rock crystal often triboluminescent.

Composition: Silicon dioxide (46.7% Si, 53.3% O).

Tests: Hardness of 7 is important; infusible, insoluble. Powder mixed with sodium carbonate fuses to a clear glass.

Distinguishing characteristics: The luster and fracture are typical, and hardness is greater than that of most similar minerals. Crystals are easy to recognize if the hexagonal pattern or the typical points can be seen, and the striations on the prism are very helpful. Specific gravity is a useful test for this mineral. A flake held in gas flame always breaks up (as soon as it reaches 573°C).

Occurrence: Quartz can occur almost anywhere. High-temperature veins are usually coarsely crystallized, whereas low-temperature veins in sedimentary rocks may show one of the finer-grained varieties.

Good colorless crystals of "rock crystal" have been found: in Arkansas in the Hot Springs area; at Little Falls, New York, in small, brilliant, doubly terminated crystals ("Herkimer diamonds"); in Ontario near Lyndhurst. The smoky crystals of the Pikes Peak area of Colorado are often spectacular, and some fine crystals have come from the Maine and the California pegmatite areas. Foreign localities include the famous Alpine crystal-lined pocket occurrences (the higher their elevation, the smokier their crystals) and the commercially important Madagascar and Brazilian rock crystals.

Amethyst is found in Maine, Pennsylvania, North Carolina, and elsewhere in the U.S. The purple variety is rarely in tall prismatic crystals, but Mexico is the home of two fine sources, one in Guerrero (veins) with steep rhombohedron faces, and a second at Las Vigas, in the state of Vera Cruz (pockets in lava). Bahia and Rio Grande do Sul are the two important amethyst-producing states in Brazil. Rose quartz is a pegmatite mineral and crystals are scarce; they were found long ago at Newry, Maine, and at one or two Brazilian localities. The failure to find large well-formed crystals of rose quartz is a geological mystery and even now there seem to be some possibly basic differences between the common solid rose quartz of pegmatite cores and the three isolated occurrences of pink-hued, late-

formed crystals often associated with pink chalcedony. Sapucaia and Taquaral in Minas Gerais, Brazil, have produced some
beautiful specimens of pink crystals.

The best agate forms in cavities in basaltic rock, as in the
w. U.S. and in Rio Grande do Sul, Brazil, the chief source of
commercial agate. The famous Idar gem-cutting industry of
Germany owes its start to the occurrence there of agate concretions in a lava flow.

Whole books have been written on quartz and its relatives.
Consult *Quartz Family Minerals* by Dake, Fleener, and Wilson
for further locality information and descriptions of types. Vol.
3 of the 7th edition of Dana is devoted to SiO_2.

Interesting facts: An important industrial material from
many standpoints. Sand is used in glass manufacture or to
make fused silica. The clear rock crystal is of great value for
electronic equipment, as in oscillators for controlling radio fre-
quencies and in the latest models. The beautifully colored
varieties have gem value. Rose quartz often shows asterism
when cut in a sphere or hemisphere. White quartz veins are
common guides to gold in some regions. Chalcedony and agate
have decorative use but are also of value for bearings and in
mortars. Flint is a black compact variety once valued for the
sparks it gave when struck by steel, as in flintlock guns.

TRIDYMITE SiO_2 **Pl. 33**
Orthorhombic — Rhombic bipyramidal $\dfrac{2\ 2\ 2}{m\ m\ m}$
(pseudohexagonal)

Environment: Rare mineral of volcanic rocks.

Crystal description: Usually seen in thin rock slices when
they are examined under the microscope, but may sometimes
be observed in small cavities in volcanic rocks. They appear
as thin tabular crystals, often developed so that they look hexagonal, but commonly grouped into sheaves of crystals, or in
intergrowths of 3 in the commonly pseudohexagonal twinning.

Physical properties: White or colorless. *Luster* glassy; *hardness* 7; *gravity* 2.3; *fracture* conchoidal; *cleavage* prismatic.
Transparent to translucent.

Composition: Silicon dioxide; like quartz, but seems to contain
a significant percentage of sodium aluminum silicate.

Tests: Same as for quartz (p. 219), but the amateur collector
will have to recognize it by its crystal form and manner of
occurrence.

Distinguishing characteristics: The tabular crystals and the
rock associations are typical.

Occurrence: Significant as a high-temperature silicate mineral,
forming only in rocks solidifying at high temperatures. Quartz,
tridymite, and cristobalite (next) all have the same composition
but form under different conditions. Tridymite undoubtedly

sometimes forms at temperatures below its theoretically stable limit, 870°C, just as does cristobalite. Then it often changes to quartz, and many specimens are really quartz pseudomorphs after tridymite.

Crystals of tridymite are usually microscopic, the largest are under $\frac{1}{2}$ in. (1 cm) long and very thin. Good crystals have been found in gas cavities in the lavas of the San Juan Mountains of Colorado and on the flanks of Mt. Lassen in California. Reported in the crystallizing nuclei (lithophysae) of the Yellowstone Natl. Park obsidian, with quartz, feldspar, and fayalite. **Interesting facts:** The name refers to its usual habit of crystallizing in trillings, or groups of 3 individuals.

CRISTOBALITE SiO_2 **Pl. 33**
Tetragonal — trapezohedral (pseudo-isometric) 4 2 2
Environment: A high-temperature mineral of volcanic rocks.
Crystal description: Forms small white crystals, usually pseudo-octahedrons and twinned intergrowths. Crystal faces rarely smooth and crystals always microscopic. Commonly in little spherical masses.
Physical properties: White. *Luster* glassy; *hardness* 5–7; *gravity* 2.3. Translucent; often fluorescent.
Composition: Silicon dioxide; like quartz, with various impurities.
Tests: The white milky look disappears on heating to about 175°C without otherwise affecting the crystal, and on cooling it resumes its white, frosty appearance.
Distinguishing characteristics: There are, of course, many minerals with which cristobalite might be confused, but the manner of occurrence, like that of tridymite — and indeed it is often associated with that mineral — is all that is needed for identification.
Occurrence: In small cavities (as lithophysae) in volcanic rocks. One of the best occurrences is in small (under $\frac{1}{16}$ in.; 1 mm) crystals in the shrinkage cracks in lithophysae of Inyo Co. (Little Lake, Coso Hot Springs), California, obsidian, associated with small blades of fayalite (Pl. 46). Also in the lavas of San Juan Mountains of Colorado, and at the Cerro San Cristóbal (from which it got its name) near Pachuca, Mexico.

OPAL $SiO_2 \cdot nH_2O$ Amorphous **Pls. 34, 35**
Environment: In recent volcanics, deposits from hot springs, and in sediments.
Crystal description: Amorphous, therefore not in crystals except as pseudomorphs. In amygdules, veins, and seams; also botryoidal, reniform, stalactitic. Commonly pseudomorphous after wood, shells, or bone. Electron microscope photographs of precious opal reveal its structure to consist of regularly

packed tiny spheres that are responsible for the light interference creating the color play.

Physical properties: Colorless or with all light tints; also with rainbow play of color. *Luster* glassy to resinous; *hardness* 5–6; *gravity* 1.9–2.2; *fracture* conchoidal. Transparent to translucent; often highly fluorescent (yellow-green).

Composition: Silicon dioxide, like quartz, but with water to 10%.

Tests: Infusible and insoluble, but gives water in closed tube upon intense ignition; usually decrepitates in flame; may whiten. Distinguished from chalcedony by the glassy fracture surface.

Distinguishing characteristics: Broken fragment might be confused with quartz, but opal's lesser hardness is a good guide.

Occurrence: One of the varieties of opal, the variety characterized by a play of rainbow colors from what is essentially clear material, is known as precious opal and is a valuable jewelry stone. A clear orange-red variety is known as fire opal and also finds jewelry use in faceted stones. Common opal has no particular value, though it is often highly fluorescent and collected for that reason. Clear, colorless opal is known as hyalite.

There are many occurrences of opal deposited from hot water, as in the geyserite of Yellowstone Natl. Park. A light yellow altered wood occurs in Virgin Valley, Nevada. Diatomaceous earth is made from the fossil external skeletons of microscopic plants. Precious opal was found in volcanic rocks in the first known occurrence, in Czechoslovakia, and later in Idaho and California, and pre-eminently in the Querétaro district of Mexico. Of greater value, however, are the opals of the sedimentary rocks of e. Australia, which at many different places yield numerous types of precious opal. It is found in concretions and in cracks and crevices in the rocks, and often in Queensland as opalized fossils. There is an occurrence of similar white precious opal in Brazil, at Dom Pedro II, Ceará. Colorless to blue hyalite is common on seams in pegmatites in the Spruce Pine district, North Carolina.

The Feldspars

This group of minerals might, with some justification, be regarded as varieties of a single mineral species. With this premise feldspar, rather than quartz, can be considered the most abundant of all minerals. All feldspars are aluminum silicates of soda, potash, or lime (with a few rarer varieties), and all are closely related in structure and composition. Soda and lime can replace each other in one series so that the differences are quite gradational and different names are arbitrarily assigned. Importance of the group lies in the fact that feldspars are the principal constituents of igneous and plutonic rocks.

The feldspars include orthoclase, microcline, and the plagioclase group of albite, oligoclase, andesine, labradorite, bytownite, and anorthite.

ORTHOCLASE KAlSi$_3$O$_8$ **Pl. 35**

Monoclinic — prismatic $\dfrac{2}{m}$

Environment: A mineral of igneous, plutonic, and metamorphic rocks, and occasionally of high-temperature veins.

Crystal description: The best crystals are found in porphyries, and are usually best developed parallel to the base, so that the pair of prisms is rather short. Intergrowths of 2 individuals are common; the twins are named according to localities where they were first conspicuous. In sanidine the base is even more prominent, as a rule. In adularia, the prisms are dominant.

Physical properties: White, flesh, yellow, brown, colorless. *Luster* glassy; *hardness* 6; *gravity* 2.6; *fracture* conchoidal; *cleavage* 2 good, 90°, also fair prismatic. Transparent to translucent.

Composition: Potassium aluminum silicate (16.9% K$_2$O, 18.4% Al$_2$O$_3$, 64.7% SiO$_2$). Sodium can replace up to 50% of the potassium in sanidine.

Tests: Fusible only with some difficulty, insoluble in acids. Sanidine glows blue-white in gas flame but colors flame only slightly. Fuses only on thin edges. Nonfluorescent after blowpiping.

Distinguishing characteristics: A common mineral that resembles several other silicates, but it may usually be distinguishable: from spodumene by its blocky cleavage (as opposed to splintery), by its lack of twin striations on the good cleavage face (a distinction from the plagioclases), and by its 90° cleavages. The hardness and acid insolubility distinguish it from calcite, its slight fusibility from amblygonite.

Occurrence: As a constituent of aplite (a granite composed of orthoclase and quartz), orthoclase is used in the ceramic and glass industry. Transparent varieties have slight gem use. Much microcline has been called orthoclase. Although orthoclase is primarily a rock-making mineral of igneous or plutonic rocks, mineral specimens and free crystals usually come in veins and in porphyritic rocks.

The variety known as sanidine is glassy, and forms tabular crystals embedded in volcanic rocks. It sometimes reflects a bluish sheen in certain crystal directions. This phenomenon is known as adularescence, and such feldspar is moonstone. Good sanidine and moonstone have come from New Mexico. A transparent yellow variety from an unusual Madagascar pegmatite has been cut into brilliant jewelry stones.

Adularia forms colorless to white prismatic crystals (most abundant in Switzerland, where they occur in cavities in the metamorphosed rocks). The name comes from one locality, Adular. Some of these glassy crystals are large.

Common orthoclase is best formed in phenocrysts in porphyritic granitic rock, from which it sometimes weathers — as at Robinson, Colorado, and Goodsprings, Nevada — providing collectors with fresh, model-like crystals.

MICROCLINE $KAlSi_3O_8$ Triclinic — pinacoidal $\overline{1}$ **Pl. 34**
Environment: Usually found in granite pegmatites, where it takes the place of orthoclase, and in plutonic rocks.
Crystal description: Crystals common and often large, frequently twinned like orthoclase. The inclination of the 3rd axis is only a few minutes, so the forms are most easily compared with monoclinic crystals. The crystals may be several inches or feet (a meter) across, in contrast to the small crystals of orthoclase.
Physical properties: White, flesh, red-brown, green. *Luster* glassy; *hardness* 6; *gravity* 2.5–2.6; *fracture* conchoidal; *cleavage* 2 good, almost at right angles, and poor prismatic. Translucent.
Composition: Potassium aluminum silicate, the same as orthoclase (preceding).
Tests: The hardness and the cleavage are usually sufficient for identification, when considered in relation to the associated minerals.
Distinguishing characteristics: Microcline is the only bright green feldspar. If of another hue it is distinguished from orthoclase by the pegmatitic occurrence. (Pegmatite orthoclase is almost unknown.) Distinguished from the markedly triclinic plagioclases by the lack of twin striations on the prominent cleavage face.
Occurrence: Microcline is the characteristic feldspar of granite pegmatites, and may grow into tremendous crystals, several feet (a meter) on an edge. Good crystals may be obtained from open cavities or be broken free from massive quartz, which is easily chipped away. A green variety is sometimes used in jewelry under the name amazonstone. It is quarried for ceramics, ceramic glazes, and for a scouring powder.

The best green crystals have come from scattered pegmatitic pockets in schist near Crystal Peak and at Pikes Peak, Colorado, associated with smoky quartz. Good green crystals were found at Amelia, Virginia, in Brazil, India, Russia, and Madagascar. Ordinary microcline is found in almost every pegmatite.

PLAGIOCLASE SERIES   **Pls. 34, 35**

Triclinic — pinacoidal $\overline{1}$

Albite $NaAlSi_3O_8$
Oligoclase
Andesine
Labradorite   to
Bytownite
Anorthite $CaAl_2Si_2O_8$

Environment: The plagioclase feldspars are principally found in the igneous, metamorphic, and plutonic rocks.

Crystal description: Crystals, except albite, are not common. Albite is frequently a late mineral in pegmatites and forms thin blades (known as cleavelandite) and late growths in parallel position on microcline. Sometimes in small crystals in low-temperature veins. Oligoclase forms crystals in impure marbles. Anorthite may form free phenocrysts in a porphyry. Usually granular, sometimes quite coarse; multiply twinned on the base or on a side pinacoid plane, giving striated cleavage surfaces ("polysynthetically twinned").

Physical properties: White, yellow, reddish gray to black. *Luster* glassy; *hardness* 6; *gravity* 2.6–2.8; *fracture* conchoidal; *cleavage* 2 good at about 94° to each other, and 2 poor prismatic. Transparent to translucent; bluish to whitish internal flashes, marked in albite moonstone and in labradorite.

Composition: A continuous series of mixtures of sodium and calcium aluminum silicates: albite has 11.8% Na_2O, 19.5% Al_2O_3, and 68.7% SiO_2; anorthite has 20.1% CaO, 36.7% Al_2O_3, and 43.2% SiO_2.

Tests: More easily fused than the potash feldspars, but still with difficulty. The soda-rich members give a good Na flame coloration. The lime-rich members are attacked by, and form a silica gel in, hydrochloric acid. Intensely fired albite often fluoresces blue on edge where flame touched.

Distinguishing characteristics: Since these are rock-forming minerals, they should always be suspected in any rock specimen showing smooth cleavage surfaces that are too hard to scratch with a knife. Repeated twinning, showing as many fine parallel lines on good cleavage faces, are diagnostic of a member of this group when the associations and other properties are right.

The recognition of which member is present is more difficult, and the amateur can best determine them by a very careful gravity determination on pure material. In general, gravities are as follows:

albite	2.63	labradorite	2.71
oligoclase	2.65	bytownite	2.74
andesine	2.68	anorthite	2.76

Occurrence: *Albite* (Pl. 35) is a mineral of plutonic rocks, and its substitution for orthoclase in a granite-like rock classifies it as a quartz monzonite instead of a granite. The classification of the igneous and plutonic rocks is based upon the type of feldspar present. Albite is also found in pegmatites in granular replacements of microcline and in thin platy crystals. Pegmatites in Maine, Connecticut, and at Amelia, Virginia, are especially noted for the fine examples of this variety (known as cleavelandite), which is common in the U.S. but appears rare in Europe. Fine albite crystals are found in the Swiss and Austrian Alps. Moonstone is a variety with bluish reflections, found in Sri Lanka (Ceylon), Madagascar, and rarely in the U.S.

Oligoclase (Pl. 35) often has a bluish cast; clear, pale blue masses are found in North Carolina. Much of the feldspar in coarse-grained Manhattan Island rocks is oligoclase, and fair, rounded crystals weathered from a marble can be found in St. Lawrence Co., New York. Reddish-golden inclusions in Norwegian and Canadian oligoclase reflect brilliantly in one plane to produce "sunstone."

Andesine is a feldspar of fine-grained common andesite lavas (named from the Andes), rare in mineral specimens.

Labradorite (Pl. 34) makes up rock masses, often very coarsely crystalline — as in Labrador — and is used as a decorative stone for carvings and building façades, where it is valued for the beautiful bluish reflections, often resembling a Brazilian butterfly's wing. Little of the Adirondack material shows the "schiller." Clear, glassy labradorite occurs as phenocrysts in basalt flows in Oregon (Plush), Utah, and in n. Mexico. Sometimes the Oregon crystals are sunstone-like with hematite-flake coppery reflections; a few are tinted red and green and can make transparent gemstones.

Bytownite is a rare feldspar forming grains in lime-rich igneous rocks. It is gradational from labradorite, but the original Canadian source at Bytown is discredited.

Anorthite is very rare, but forms good crystals in the lava-digested limestone blocks thrown out by Vesuvius and in some lavas as glassy crystals with crusted, altered surfaces, as in Miyake-jima, Japan. Rough, greenish crystals have been described from a Franklin (New Jersey) marble quarry.

The Feldspathoids

These minerals form in a lava or magma when the available silica is insufficient to completely satisfy the alkalis present: the potash, lime, or soda. The common feldspathoids are leucite and nepheline. Since feldspars would have formed in their place, if there had been an abundance of silica, quartz (SiO_2) will not be found as a primary mineral in association with them.

LEUCITE $KAlSi_2O_6$ **Pl. 35**
Tetragonal — trapezohedral (pseudo-isometric) 4 2 2
Environment: Fresh examples are found only in recent lavas.
Crystal description: Always found in dull-surfaced embedded crystals with the trapezohedron dominant.
Physical properties: Gray to white to colorless. *Luster* glassy (altering in old examples to dull); *hardness* $5\frac{1}{2}$-6; *gravity* 2.4-2.5; *fracture* conchoidal; *cleavage* imperfect dodecahedral. Translucent to transparent.
Composition: A potassium aluminum silicate (21.5% K_2O, 23.5% Al_2O_3, 55.0% SiO_2).
Tests: Unnecessary; usually in crystals that are characteristic.
Distinguishing characteristics: The crystals resemble only those of garnet, which is fusible (and usually dark), and analcime, which is fusible and gives water in a closed glass tube.
Occurrence: The best examples of leucite are the fresh crystals embedded in Vesuvius lavas. It alters readily to pseudoleucite (a mixture of nepheline, orthoclase, and analcime) and then to clay. Very large, more or less altered, white crystals of this type are found in Austria and Brazil. Good embedded crystals are found at Magnet Cove, Arkansas, in loose boulders on the shores of Vancouver I., British Columbia, and in the Leucite Hills, Wyoming.
Interesting facts: Has been used locally in Italy as a source of potash for fertilizer and tried as a source of aluminum.

NEPHELINE $(Na,K)(Al,Si)_2O_4$ **Pl. 35**
Hexagonal — Hexagonal pyramidal 6
Environment: Low-silica plutonic and igneous rocks.
Crystal description: Flat hexagonal prisms; the volcanic crystals are very small and clear, with few modifications. Larger coarse 6-sided crystals with corroded surfaces have been found in pegmatitic nepheline syenite dikes. Usually in grains in rock.
Physical properties: Colorless, white, gray, reddish, smoky. *Luster* greasy; *hardness* $5\frac{1}{2}$-6; *gravity* 2.5-2.6; *fracture* subconchoidal; *cleavage* good prismatic. Transparent to translucent; often fluorescent orange-red in portions of crystals.
Composition: Sodium, potassium, aluminum silicate (21.8% Na_2O — very little K_2O — 35.9% Al_2O_3, 42.3% SiO_3).
Tests: Splinter rounds to a clear glass droplet with a brilliant yellow Na flame. A powder is easily soluble in hydrochloric acid, evaporating to leave a silica gel.
Distinguishing characteristics: The easy fusibility, usual associates, and peculiar luster distinguish it from almost all minerals except the even more fusible cryolite, which it resembles. It is softer than feldspar and quartz. The very similar scapolite melts to a white blebby glass. Old exposed surfaces of nepheline-bearing rock always show pits where the nepheline

has been dissolved out; feldspar veins through such outcrops stand out in relief.

Occurrence: Crystals are found in cavities in metamorphosed limestone blocks thrown out by the volcano at Vesuvius. Nepheline forms grains in coarse plutonic rocks in Karelia (now Karelskaya, U.S.S.R.) and at Bancroft, Ontario. Small glassy crystals line cavities in volcanic rocks. Large coarse crystals are found in pegmatitic segregations in the Bancroft region, where dull crystals to 6 in. (15 cm) or more across have been noted.

Interesting facts: In recent years nepheline has become an important glass and ceramic raw material. Nepheline-bearing rocks cannot contain quartz. If the silica necessary to form quartz had been present in the molten rock, feldspar would have formed in place of nepheline.

Sodalite Group

SODALITE $Na_4Al_3Si_3O_{12}Cl$ **Pl. 34**

Cubic — hexoctahedral $\frac{4}{m}\,\overline{3}\,\frac{2}{m}$

Environment: A mineral of alkaline igneous and plutonic rocks, low in silica.

Crystal description: Crystals small, in cavities of rock, commonly in dodecahedrons. Usually massive and in considerable concentrations.

Physical properties: Colorless, white, blue, violet, pink (hackmanite). *Luster* glassy; *hardness* $5\frac{1}{2}$–6; *gravity* 2.2–2.3; *fracture* conchoidal to uneven; *cleavage* poor dodecahedral. Transparent to translucent; frequently fluorescent yellow to orange, in longwave ultraviolet.

Composition: Sodium aluminum silicate with chlorine (25.6% Na_2O, 31.6% Al_2O_3, 37.2% SiO_2; 7.3% Cl replaces some of the O). Hackmanite contains sulfur in place of chlorine.

Tests: Soon loses color and eventually fuses to a white glass with yellow flame coloration. After being fired, heated specimen fluoresces brilliant orange in longwave ultraviolet, and the fused area fluoresces blue in shortwave ultraviolet.

Distinguishing characteristics: The color blue is very typical and likely to be confused only with lazulite and lazurite (see next). Blue grains in rock may not originally be fluorescent but the pink variety (hackmanite) is brilliantly fluorescent and reversibly sensitive to light, fading to white in daylight and reverting to pink on exposure to ultraviolet light.

Occurrence: Rich blue masses are found near Bancroft, Ontario, and nearby along the York River there are several massive occurrences of hackmanite. Thinner veins of blue sodalite are found in nepheline rocks on the Ice River, British Columbia. Litchfield, Maine, yields sodalite in smaller masses of moderate richness. Hackmanite, some perpetually pink, occurs in coarse rock areas at St. Hilaire, Quebec. Large sodalite formations are quarried as decorative stone in Bahia, Brazil, and in South Africa. Colorless crystals are found in the altered limestone blocks thrown out by the eruptions of Vesuvius.

LAZURITE $Na_{4-5}Al_3Si_3O_{12}S$ **Pl. 36**

Cubic — hexoctahedral $\dfrac{4}{m}\,\bar{3}\,\dfrac{2}{m}$

Environment: A mineral of metamorphosed limestones.
Crystal description: Crystals dodecahedral and to 1 in. (2.5 cm) in size, but rare. Usually granular, massive, disseminated in limestone.
Physical properties: Blue, violet-blue, or greenish blue. *Luster* glassy; *hardness* $5-5\frac{1}{2}$; *gravity* $2.4-2.5$; *fracture* uneven; *cleavage* poor dodecahedral. Translucent.
Composition: Sodium aluminum silicate, with sulfur; and some admixture of related minerals like sodalite (approximately 23.1% Na_2O, 30.7% Al_2O_3, 39.3% SiO_2, 8.4% S).
Tests: Retains color even after heating to incandescence. Fuses with difficulty.
Distinguishing characteristics: Almost invariably associated with pyrite and so distinguishable from the similar blue minerals lazulite and sodalite. On heating does not swell as lazulite does; usually deeper in color and finer-grained than sodalite. Commonly associated with calcite, which dissolves with effervescence in the hydrochloric acid. Not associated with copper minerals.
Occurrence: A rather rare mineral, found in the U.S. only in Colorado, where it occurs as small grains in a dark rock. The best occurrence is in Afghanistan, where fairly large rich masses are found. The dull crystals found here are embedded in white marble and range to 1 in. (2.5 cm) or more in diameter. Also found in disseminated grains near Lake Baikal, Siberia, and in Ovalle, Chile.
Interesting facts: Lazurite forms a decorative and jewelry stone known as lapis lazuli, the "sapphires" of the ancients. Selected crushed grains of lapis lazuli colored the "ultramarine" of the old masters. A synthetic lazurite has now replaced it as a pigment.

Scapolite (Wernerite) Series   Pl. 37

MARIALITE $Na_4Al_3(Al,Si)_3Si_6O_{24}(Cl,CO_3,SO_4)$ ⎫
MEIONITE $Ca_4Al_3(Al,Si)_3Si_6O_{24}(Cl,CO_3,SO_4)$ ⎬

Tetragonal — Ditetragonal bipyramidal $\dfrac{4}{m}\,\dfrac{2}{m}\,\dfrac{2}{m}$

Environment: Metamorphic rocks, especially metamorphosed impure limestones, and pegmatites.

Crystal description: Commonly in prismatic crystals, often large and usually milky, with dull surfaces; also in great, massive, single crystals or in aggregates of coarse crystals.

Physical properties: Colorless, white, violet, yellow, pink, gray. *Luster* glassy; *hardness* $5\frac{1}{2}$-6; *gravity* 2.5-2.7; *fracture* subconchoidal; *cleavage* poor prismatic. Transparent to translucent; often fluorescent orange to bright yellow, less often red.

Composition: Sodium and calcium aluminum silicate, with chlorine, carbonate, and sulfate; sodium and calcium mutually replace each other to any amount, making a series which have been named marialite for the NaCl rich end-member and meionite for the $CaCO_3$ end. The average composition is 7.15% Na_2O, 12.9% CaO, 26.5% Al_2O_3, 51.9% SiO_2, and about 2% Cl, etc.

Tests: Fuses to a white bubbly glass, coloring the flame yellow. After heating (without fusion), fluorescence is yellower and brighter; best in longwave ultraviolet light.

Distinguishing characteristics: The color and the frequent fluorescence are suggestive of scapolite; the fusibility, flame color, and solubility distinguish it from feldspar. Crystals are common. The cleavage surface has a typical, interrupted, irregularly striated character.

Occurrence: The largest and purest masses are found in impure limestones that have been altered by igneous intrusions, forming large and (when recognizable) dull-surfaced crystals. Good crystals of this type are found at Rossie and Pierrepont in St. Lawrence Co., New York, and in Bedford and Renfrew, Ontario. Pegmatitic crystals are found in unusual pegmatites with pyroxene and apatite in Arendal, Norway, and Madagascar. Crystals of the pegmatite type are sometimes transparent, and suitable for cutting, as in Madagascar, Minas Gerais, Brazil, and Tremorgio, Switzerland. Gemmy pink and violet scapolite has come from Burma. Weak cat's-eyes can be produced from some of the less transparent bits.

Zeolite Family

This is a large family of related minerals: related in composition, in occurrence, and, many of them, in appearance. There are several other minerals (including apophyllite, pectolite, datolite, and prehnite), described later, that are usually associated with zeolites in occurrence but differ too greatly in composition to belong to this family. The group includes about 30 members. Many of the individuals are not easily distinguished without tests too complicated for the beginner. Only the most common are included here. In their compositions sodium and calcium readily substitute for each other, and each can actually replace the other in the solid mineral. This easy substitution of elements is utilized in zeolite water softeners. Calcium in solution makes water "hard," but the calcium is removed and replaced by sodium from the synthetic zeolite linings of the water-softener containers. The water with sodium substituted for calcium is far better for washing. The reverse substitution can also take place, and the softener is renewed by occasional rinsings with a concentrated brine that drives out the calcium and replaces it in the zeolite structure with sodium. The name zeolite is a Greek reference to the ease with which these minerals boil in fusing under the blowpipe flame.

All the zeolites are very late minerals, forming best in cavities in lava flows, probably as late deposits either from water dissolved in the lava itself or from later supergene solutions working over lavas that have been preconditioned for such alteration and deposition by the water originally present in the lava. Also, sometimes, late deposits in plutonic rock crevices during the last stages of pegmatite formation and rarely in veins and alpine fissures.

The following members of the group are described here: heulandite, stilbite, chabazite, natrolite, and analcime.

HEULANDITE $(Ca,Na,K)_6Al_{10}(Al,Si)Si_{29}O_{80} \cdot 25H_2O$ **Pl. 37**

Monoclinic — prismatic $\dfrac{2}{m}$

Environment: Typical zeolite associations.
Crystal description: Always in elongated tabular crystals, to 1 in. (2.5 cm) in length but usually smaller. Shape characteristic, widest at center, like an old-fashioned coffin; hence called "coffin-shaped."
Physical properties: White, reddish, yellowish. *Luster* pearly on cleavage face and glassy otherwise; *hardness* $3\frac{1}{2}$–4; *gravity* 2.2; *streak* white; *fracture* subconchoidal to uneven; *cleavage* perfect side pinacoid. Transparent to translucent.
Composition: Hydrous sodium, calcium, potassium aluminum silicate (9.2% CaO, 16.8% Al_2O_3, 59.2% SiO_2, 14.8% H_2O).
Tests: On fusion swells and writhes, finally fusing at ends to white droplets; fused mass often has a stringy look.
Distinguishing characteristics: Crystal form very typical and usually suffices, when considered in its associations as a zeolite. Stilbite and apophyllite have a pearly luster in one direction but usually the crystal form is distinctive. Stilbite fuses in more splintery fragments; apophyllite fuses with bubbling but much less swelling.
Occurrence: Beautifully developed in the trap quarries of the Paterson (New Jersey) region near New York City. Also in fine crystals in Nova Scotia in the Partridge I. area. Good crystals were found years ago in Berufjördhur, Iceland, and it was named for an early English mineral dealer, H. Heuland, who went there to collect specimens. Common, but usually small,

in Oregon and Washington traprock localities. Good red crystals are found at Gunnedah, New South Wales.

STILBITE $(Ca,Na)_3Al_5(Al,Si)Si_{14}O_{40} \cdot 15H_2O$ **Pl. 37**

Monoclinic — prismatic $\dfrac{2}{m}$

Environment: Typical zeolite associations.

Crystal description: In tabular crystals, commonly intergrown to give an orthorhombic symmetry, and often in bundles spreading slightly at either end to give the impression of wheat sheaves. Sometimes rounded knobs with radiating structures.

Physical properties: Yellow, brown, reddish, white. *Luster* glassy, pearly on cleavage face; *hardness* $3\frac{1}{2}$–4; *gravity* 2.1–2.2; *fracture* irregular; *cleavage* 1 perfect. Transparent to translucent.

Composition: Hydrous calcium, sodium, aluminum silicate (1.4% Na_2O, 7.7% CaO, 16.3% Al_2O_3, 57.4% SiO_2, 17.2% H_2O).

Tests: On fusion swells and writhes like heulandite, but the protuberances are more wormlike.

Distinguishing characteristics: The larger and sheaflike crystals are sufficiently typical to distinguish stilbite from the other common zeolites. In fusing, the worms are more splintery than in heulandite. Apophyllite boils and melts to droplets with less swelling.

Occurrence: Excellent specimens come from the Paterson (New Jersey) district and from Nova Scotia around the Bay of Fundy. Bright orange crystals have been found at: Great Notch, New Jersey; Victoria, Australia; and Kilpatrick, Scotland (at the latter, $1\frac{1}{2}$ in. [4 cm] long). There are numerous other localities for stilbite; it may be encountered in many types of occurrences. The crystals of Iceland, Rio Grande do Sul, Brazil, and Pune, India, are notable.

CHABAZITE $(Ca,Na,K)_7Al_{12}(Al,Si)_2Si_{26}O_{80} \cdot 40H_2O$ **Pl. 36**

Hexagonal — Hexagonal scalenohedral $\overline{3}\dfrac{2}{m}$

Environment: Typical zeolite associations.

Crystal description: Rhombohedral crystals that look like slightly distorted cubes are the rule. Frequently penetration-twinned so that the corners of a smaller individual project from the faces of the larger. May be an inch (2.5 cm) or more across. Usually show crackled appearance just beneath shiny surface of the faces. White penetration twins are known as phacolite.

Physical properties: Colorless, white, pink. *Luster* glassy; *hardness* 4–5; *gravity* 2.1–2.2; *fracture* uneven; *cleavage* good rhombohedral. Transparent to translucent.

Composition: Hydrous calcium, sodium, aluminum silicate, usually with potassium, and in varying proportions (averaging about 47% SiO_2, 20% Al_2O_3, 5.5% CaO, 6% Na_2O, and 21% H_2O). **Tests:** Fuses with less swelling than many zeolites, retaining better the original shape. Often fluorescent blue after heating, particularly the area in contact with the charcoal.

Distinguishing characteristics: The melting behavior under the blowpipe identifies it at once as zeolite. With the rhombohedral (pseudocubic) outline and without a pearly cleavage surface, it can be distinguished from all the other zeolites or zeolite associates.

Occurrence: The localities are in general the same as for the other zeolites — Paterson, New Jersey, and along the Bay of Fundy in Nova Scotia being particularly good. Also Goble, Oregon, and Richmond, Victoria, Australia.

NATROLITE $Na_2Al_2Si_3O_{10} \cdot 2H_2O$ **Pl. 37**
     Orthorhombic — Rhombic pyramidal m m 2

Environment: Typical zeolite associations.

Crystal description: In prismatic, often very slender, square needle crystals commonly terminated by a low 4-faced pyramid that gives the impression of a tetragonal crystal. Also white radiating nodules or compact masses.

Physical properties: Colorless or white. *Luster* glassy; *hardness* 5-5½; *gravity* 2.2; *fracture* uneven across the prism; *cleavage* good prismatic. Transparent to translucent; often fluorescent orange.

Composition: Hydrous sodium aluminum silicate (16.3% NaO, 26.8% Al_2O_3, 47.4% SiO_2, 9.5% H_2O).

Tests: Melts rather quietly to a bubbly but colorless glass. Heated needles and glass fluoresce greenish white or blue. Partially melted crystals fluoresce brightest.

Distinguishing characteristics: Its ready fusibility distinguishes it from most acicular crystals, and the crystal form is characteristic among the zeolites. The hardness distinguishes it from prismatic gypsum; its fluorescence is a help when it forms embedded radiating masses.

Natrolite is one of 3 very similar minerals. Scolecite, a calcium equivalent [$Ca(Al_2Si_3)O_{10} \cdot 3H_2O$], forms comparable large sprays and in many zeolite occurrences of the volcanic type substitutes for natrolite. It fuses with wormlike extrusions; hence the name, which is derived from the Greek for "worm."

Mesolite is intermediate in composition, having both Ca and Na [$Na_2Ca_2(Al_6Si_9)O_{30} \cdot 8H_2O$]. The Ca-bearing pair are monoclinic in symmetry, but with no inclination of the front axis. Usually twinned on the front face, they appear to be as orthorhombic as natrolite. As a rule (1 known exception), mesolite crystals are very slender. Scolecite, on the other hand, tends to be sturdier than natrolite in the volcanic pockets.

Occurrence: Natrolite can form part of the groundmass of igneous rocks and can occur in large individual crystals in pegmatitic phases of such rock, as at St. Hilaire, Quebec, and in the Kola Peninsula, U.S.S.R. More often it forms crystal sprays in vesicles in lavas. Scolecite and mesolite occur in the same way but are slightly less frequent. Natrolite is found in New Jersey, Colorado (Table Mountain), and in Oregon traprock areas. Large crystals to 8 in. (12 cm) in length have been found, mainly as loose and sometimes doubly terminated singles in Bound Brook, New Jersey. 1–2 in. (2.5–5 cm) crystals were found in California in an asbestos quarry near Coalinga.

Many old European localities like Ustí nad Labem (Aussig), Bohemia, County Antrim, Ireland, and the Faroe Is. are famous. Very large crystals, even bigger than those of Bound Brook, have been found in the U.S.S.R.

Veins of natrolite cut other rocks, as in San Benito Co., California, where it fills the seams that are lined with neptunite and benitoite; these can be exposed by dissolving away the natrolite with hydrochloric acid.

Scolecite has turned out to be relatively abundant in many important localities, such as: Theigerhorn and Berufjördhur, Iceland; Pune, India; and Santa Catarina, Brazil. In each of these deposits it forms long sprays, those of Brazil and India being as much as 6 in. (15 cm) long.

Mesolite is usually in thinner needles, but in the building of a dam at Skookumchuck, Washington, crystals of a size comparable to the normal ones of scolecite were found in what appears to have been a unique occurrence. Mesolite is common in the Oregon-Washington traprock, but is usually hairlike in dimension.

ANALCIME (Analcite) $NaAlSi_2O_6 \cdot H_2O$ **Pl. 37**

Cubic — hexoctahedral $\dfrac{4}{m} \, \overline{3} \, \dfrac{2}{m}$

Environment: Typical zeolite associations.

Crystal description: This, with garnet and leucite, is a classic example of a tetragonal trisoctahedron (translated, this means three 4-sided faces on each octahedron face, making 24 in all), perhaps better known as a trapezohedron. Rarely in cubes with trapezohedron faces on the corners.

Physical properties: Colorless, white, greenish, or reddish. *Luster* glassy; *hardness* 5–5½; *gravity* 2.3; *fracture* subconchoidal; *cleavage* traces of cubic. Transparent to translucent.

Composition: Hydrous sodium aluminum silicate (14.1% Na_2O, 23.2% Al_2O_3, 54.5% SiO_2, 8.2% H_2O).

Tests: Clear crystals become cloudy, then clear again as they start to melt. If cooled at this point, fluoresces yellow-green, sometimes quite brightly.

Distinguishing characteristics: Its crystals are free-growing in cavities, and usually shiny, in contrast to the embedded, dull-surfaced crystals of leucite. Softer than the rare light-colored garnet, fuses more easily, and becomes fluorescent.

Occurrence: Analcime crystals will be found in the same traprock cavities in which other zeolites grow. Therefore it will be found in association with them in the New Jersey and Nova Scotia zeolite areas. Very good examples have been found in the copper mines of the Upper Peninsula of Michigan, and in the Table Mountain traprock near Golden, Colorado, the Owyhee Dam, and elsewhere in Oregon. The largest crystals have come from Fassatal, in the Austrian Tyrol. It can form in the microscopic groundmass of basalts as a rock-making mineral constituent. Very large crystals have been found at St. Hilaire, Quebec.

CORDIERITE $(Mg,Fe)_2Mg_2Al_4Si_5O_{18}$ **Pl. 37**

Orthorhombic — Rhombic bipyramidal $\dfrac{2\ 2\ 2}{m\ m\ m}$

Environment: Usually a mineral of metamorphic rocks, considered an indication of fairly intense heat and pressure.

Crystal description: Crystals rare, and embedded, often more or less altered to a mica or chlorite. Usually in grains or masses embedded in rock without crystal outline.

Physical properties: Both gray and blue in the same grain. *Luster* glassy; *hardness* $7-7\frac{1}{2}$; *gravity* 2.6–2.7; *fracture* subconchoidal; *cleavage* poor pinacoidal (side pinacoid best). Transparent to translucent; strong transformation of hue in different crystal directions, changing in a small grain from violet-blue to grayish as it is turned (hence one of its names, "dichroite").

Composition: Magnesium, aluminum silicate; plus iron, calcium, and hydroxyl (OH): 10.2% MgO, 33.6% Al_2O_3, 49.4% SiO_2, and perhaps 5.3% FeO, and 1.5% H_2O.

Tests: No blowpipe test is necessary. The color change from blue to gray, which will be seen through most flakes, is sufficiently distinctive. In case of doubt, look through chip at light reflecting from a polished table top or glass sheet and turn it to see the 2 colors.

Distinguishing characteristics: Color and dichroism (directional change in color) are very characteristic; there is no other violet-blue schist mineral with this appearance.

Occurrence: Large altered crystals have been found in Bodenmais, West Germany. Good embedded glassy masses are found at: Orijärvi, Finland; Kragerø, Norway; and Mt. Tsilaizina, Madagascar. Gemmy waterworn pebbles are found in the Sri Lanka (Ceylon) gem gravels and in India. In the U.S. it is found near Haddam, Connecticut, on the west side of the Connecticut River. Recently found in Yellowknife, Northwest Territories.

Interesting facts: Also known as iolite, from the violet color, and as dichroite because of the remarkable color change. It has been used as a jewelry stone but is lacking in brilliance, since rarely really clear and usually too dark. A very useful geological-thermometer mineral and used as a guide in determining the grade of metamorphism. It has been suggested that this mineral was used to locate the sun's position (through polarization of sky light at 90° to the sun's position) for the Norsemen's Atlantic navigation.

The Disilicate Type   Si:O = 2:5

This group of silicates is characterized by an arrangement of the SiO_4 tetrahedrons in a way that makes their closest grouping in a horizontal plane, in closely locked sheets, giving the crystals a hexagonal or pseudohexagonal symmetry. (OH) and F are commonly present. In the members of this group the structure reveals itself by the pronounced basal cleavage; mica is a classic example of the sheet-structure type. The structure also creates other considerable directional differences in properties: differences in hardness and differences in transparency are two of the more obvious ones. It will be noted that one or several of these pronounced directional characteristics are typical of the group.

PYROPHYLLITE $Al_2Si_4O_{10}(OH)_2$ Pl. 38

Monoclinic — prismatic $\dfrac{2}{m}$

Environment: A mineral of metamorphic rocks.

Crystal description: Sometimes in radiating bundles of small crystals attached to quartz crystals or embedded in rock. Most abundantly in compact, fine-grained, soapstone-like masses.

Physical properties: White, silvery, pale green, or stained black and brown. *Luster* pearly to greasy; *hardness* 1–2; *gravity* 2.8–2.9; *cleavage* perfect micaceous; flexible flakes. Translucent to opaque.

Composition: Basic aluminum silicate (28.3% Al_2O_3, 66.7% SiO_2, 5.0% H_2O).

Tests: Micaceous or radiating masses writhe and exfoliate, and glow very white when heated on charcoal, without fusing (whence the name pyrophyllite: *pyro* = fire, *phyl* means leaf). Compact material also whitens and gives blue color on moistening with drop of cobalt nitrate solution and heating (Al test).

Distinguishing characteristics: Before heating, more silvery and lighter in color than vermiculite. Heated material is very white. Talc becomes violet rather than blue from cobalt nitrate. The fine-grained micas are harder.

Occurrence: The best specimens are the coarse crystalline masses on quartz crystals from Lincoln Co., Georgia; almost identical examples come from Quartzsite, Arizona, and Copiapó, Chile. Radiating masses are found in Montgomery Co., North Carolina, in the Chesterfield district of South Carolina, and at Indian Gulch, California.

Interesting facts: The Chinese "soapstone" carvings in agalmatolite are in a fine-grained pyrophyllite. Valued as a carrier for insecticide dusts.

KAOLIN $Al_2Si_2O_5(OH)_4$ Monoclinic — prismatic $\dfrac{2}{m}$

Environment: A secondary mineral, derived from fresh aluminum silicates in soils; and in place in rock from alteration of feldspar in granite and pegmatite.

Crystal description: Crystals fine-grained and in compact masses, the individuals usually indistinguishable. The electron microscope has produced interesting pictures of kaolin plates. Kaolin forms dull earthy masses, sometimes pseudomorphic after feldspar. Many similar clay minerals are identical in appearance.

Physical properties: White, may be stained red, brown, or black. *Luster* dull; *hardness* $2-2\frac{1}{2}$ (undeterminable because it simply breaks up); *gravity* 2.6 (also not ascertained by ordinary means); *cleavage* micaceous; can be cut or shaped. Opaque.

Composition: Basic aluminum silicate ($39.5\%\ Al_2O_3$, $46.5\%\ SiO_2$, $14.0\%\ H_2O$).

Tests: Gives earthy odor when breathed upon. Gives bright blue color from heating, after being touched with cobalt nitrate.

Distinguishing characteristics: The amateur cannot distinguish the clay minerals (which the professional identifies by heat absorption, X-ray, or electron microscope methods). It is more friable than pyrophyllite.

Occurrence: Clay beds, stream-sorted and derived from the alteration of earlier rocks, are everywhere and are widely exploited in the northern states. Farther south, pegmatites have been worked for the kaolin formed from the feldspar. In Cornwall a high-quality china clay is extracted from the altered orthoclase feldspar of a granite.

Interesting facts: Widely used in ceramics, and with other clays is the important constituent of soil.

TALC $Mg_3Si_4O_{10}(OH)_2$ Monoclinic — prismatic $\dfrac{2}{m}$

Environment: Secondary mineral formed by the alteration of magnesium silicates.

Crystal description: Rarely in free crystals, usually in embedded micaceous flakes and masses, white or apple-green color; most commonly fine-grained, massive (soapstone or steatite).

Physical properties: White, greenish, gray, almost black. *Luster* greasy to pearly; *hardness* 1; *gravity* 2.7-2.8; *cleavage* micaceous; can be easily cut; greasy feel. Translucent to opaque.

Composition: Basic magnesium silicate (31.7% MgO, 63.5% SiO_2, 4.8% H_2O).

Tests: Very soft; fuses only with difficulty. Micaceous masses swell, whiten, and give violet color with cobalt nitrate solution after blowpiping.

Distinguishing characteristics: Greasier and softer than brucite, mica, or chlorite. The violet color of the cobalt nitrate test distinguishes it from pyrophyllite, which turns blue. Brucite fluoresces blue.

Occurrence: In the metamorphosed rocks of the Appalachian Mountains, talc appears mainly in the massive (soapstone) form. It has been quarried in Vermont, Connecticut, New York, Virginia, and other states along the mountain line. Good talc in light green micaceous blades is found in: Staten I., New York; St. Lawrence Co., New York; Chester Co., Pennsylvania; Disentis, Switzerland; the Austrian Tyrol; and many other places. Interbedded and mined with magnesite in Brumado, Bahia, Brazil.

Interesting facts: Ground talc makes talcum powder. The massive variety (soapstone) is used for sinks, table tops, etc. Soapstone found a use in Babylonian days when signature cylinder seals were often carved from it. The Egyptians also used it as a base for some of their blue faience figurines, which were then fired to fuse the glaze.

SERPENTINE $Mg_3Si_2O_5(OH)_4$ **Pl. 38**

Monoclinic — prismatic $\dfrac{2}{m}$

Environment: A secondary mineral, resulting from a hot-water alteration of magnesium silicates.

Crystal description: Crystals unknown, except as the parallel fibers called chrysotile asbestos. Also massive, sometimes with a botryoidal surface as if it had been amorphous when formed.

Physical properties: White, green, brown yellow, red, black. *Luster* silky, waxy to greasy; *hardness* 2-5; *gravity* 2.2-2.6; *cleavage* none to fibrous. Translucent to opaque; yellowish varieties often fluorescent cream-yellow.

Composition: Basic magnesium silicate (43.0% MgO, 44.1% SiO_2, 12.9% H_2O, plus some iron and possibly nickel).

Tests: Infusible, but tends to decrepitate very badly. Light-colored material blackens, gives water, and then lightens in closed tube. Decomposed by hydrochloric acid, the freed silica separating as gel.

Distinguishing characteristics: A very common mineral, and one that should always be suspected in a rock with a greasy feel. Usually relatively soft and dark greenish. White varieties are not common and typically are associated with other serpentines. The serpentine asbestos varieties are softer and more flexible than the amphibole asbestoses. The blackening and the water released in the closed tube also distinguish it from amphibole asbestos. Ease with which the green massive material can be scratched distinguishes it from nephrite jade; it is harder than chlorite, however.

Occurrence: Since serpentine seems frequently to form by the alteration of primary magnesium silicates taking up the water originally present in the magma, they are found wherever dark-colored magnesium silicate rocks occur. Great serpentine formations, as in the California Coast Ranges, give it rock status as well as mineralogical identity. Readily identifiable in highway cuts by the shiny, greenish, slickensided surfaces.

Serpentinization seems commonly to invade mineralized areas, altering quite unrelated minerals to serpentine. In this way we find at the famous Tilly Foster Mine (Brewster, New York) that serpentine is pseudomorphous after numerous minerals, and also forms botryoidal coatings and films ranging from white to black. Large masses of serpentine result from the alteration of the dark intrusives, as at: Hoboken, New Jersey; Staten I., New York; Eden Mills, Vermont; Thetford and Asbestos, Quebec. Veins of fibrous asbestos cut through such bodies; there are quarries or mines for chrysotile asbestos in those regions, near Coalinga, California, and in Arizona.

Varieties:

Fibrous and silky:	chrysotile
Columnar:	picrolite
Waxy:	retinalite
Platy:	antigorite
Micaceous:	marmolite
Massive and mottled:	ophiolite
Translucent light green:	williamsite

Interesting facts: Chrysotile is considered the best asbestos. Serpentine marbles make the popular verd antique. Closely related nickel-rich serpentines are important ores of the metal (garnierite) and are mined in New Caledonia. Commonly used in decorative carvings.

APOPHYLLITE $KCa_4Si_8O_{20}(F,OH) \cdot 8H_2O$ **Pl. 38**

Tetragonal — Ditetragonal bipyramidal $\dfrac{4\ 2\ 2}{m\ m\ m}$

Environment: Associated with the zeolites.

Crystal description: Practically always in crystals, frequently distinct individuals, varying from the common, short-prismatic habit with a more or less well-formed pyramidal truncation to simple, blunt, square prisms. Tabular habit rare. Often over an inch or two (3–5 cm or more) across, or in inch-long prisms. Prism faces have parallel vertical lines; base has a very pearly look.

Physical properties: Colorless, white, pale pink, pale to emerald-green. *Luster* glassy and pearly; *hardness* $4\frac{1}{2}$–5; *gravity* 2.3–2.4; *fracture* uneven; *cleavage* perfect basal. Transparent to translucent.

Composition: Basic calcium, potassium fluosilicate (5.2% K_2O, 25.0% CaO, 53.7% SiO_2, 16.1% H_2O, with the fluorine replacing some of the oxygen).

Tests: Fuses easily, bubbling and swelling to a white vesicular enamel. The depths of the mass fluoresce weak greenish white after heating.

Distinguishing characteristics: The different (pearly) luster on the basal face distinguishes apophyllite from any cubic mineral it might otherwise suggest. The typical square pyramid and prism combination with the 2 lusters is easy to recognize. In case of doubt, the basal cleavage makes the identity certain. Distinguished from stilbite and heulandite by lesser swelling, quicker melting with boiling, and the usual fluorescence after heating.

Occurrence: Found in typical, well-formed white crystals in the traprocks of Paterson, New Jersey, and the Bay of Fundy, Nova Scotia. Beautiful crystals on prehnite were found near Washington, D.C., at Fairfax, Virginia. It is also sometimes found in cavities in pegmatitic dikes, where it is one of the last minerals to form, and in ore veins. Two notable occurrences of the latter are the delicate pink prismatic crystals at Guanajuato, Mexico, and in the Harz Mountains of Germany. Excellent crystal clusters were found at French Creek and Cornwall, Pennsylvania. Unusually clear, tabular crystals occur in the Michigan Upper Peninsula copper mines, with analcime and datolite. Particularly large, fine, pale green crystals were found in a railway cut (and now in numerous quarries) at Pune, India, and Santa Catarina, Brazil. Very clear ones have come from Iceland.

CHLORITE $(Mg,Fe,Al)_6(Si,Al)_4O_{10}(OH)_8$ **Pl. 38**

Monoclinic — prismatic $\dfrac{2}{m}$

Environment: Commonly a secondary mineral like serpentine, but usually affecting localized spots of primary iron, magnesium, aluminum silicates in the rock rather than the entire mass, as is commonly the case with the serpentines.

Crystal description: Two types form distinct crystals: penninite though monoclinic is pseudorhombohedral and forms thick crystals; clinochlore usually grows in thinner crystals and is hexagonal in outline. Also fine-grained, in masses, blades, and fibers, or in little rounded knobs.

Physical properties: Green, black, also brown, rose, yellow, and even white. *Luster* glassy to pearly; *hardness* 2-2½; *gravity* 2.6-3.0; *cleavage* perfect micaceous, with folia flexible but not elastic. Transparent to opaque.

Composition: Chlorite actually is a group name, but it is not practical for the amateur to distinguish certainly the varieties. At best, one can usually assign names only on the basis of appearance, when other tests cannot be given. The chlorites are basic iron, magnesium, aluminum silicates with about 36.1% MgO, 18.4% Al_2O_3, 32.5% SiO_2, and 13.0% H_2O. The pink varieties contain chromium in place of the aluminum, and the reddish-brown varieties contain manganese.

Tests: Whitens, but fuses only with great difficulty; gives water in the closed tube.

Distinguishing characteristics: Usually the chlorites can easily be distinguished from the micas by their color and the lack of elasticity in the cleavage flakes, and from talc by their greater hardness.

Occurrence: Most commonly as a spot of green alteration in rock; also in chlorite-rich to almost pure chlorite schists. Occasionally crystallized in triangular wedges (penninite) in cavities, as in the Alpine crevices or in rocks altered by hot-water solutions. Also in good crystals in Lancaster Co., Pennsylvania. The best (to 2 in.; 5 cm) crystals of clinochlore plates are found with magnetite and chondrodite on the surfaces of a serpentinized rock, at the old Tilly Foster Mine, Brewster, New York. Also with talc in Chester Co., Pennsylvania, and in fissures in San Benito Co. (California) serpentine formations.

The red chromiferous variety (kaemmererite) is well developed in small crystals at Texas, Lancaster Co., Pennsylvania, and in some of the chromite mines in California and Turkey.

MARGARITE $CaAl_4Si_2O_{10}(OH)_2$ **Pl. 38**

Monoclinic — prismatic $\dfrac{2}{m}$

Environment: Commonly associated with corundum in emery deposits.

Crystal description: Rarely in very thin distinct crystals, which resemble those of mica. Usually in foliated micaceous aggregates, often with fairly coarse individual cleavage surfaces.

Physical properties: Light violet, pink, white, gray. *Luster* pearly on cleavage face; *hardness* 3½ (cleavage face), 5 (prism face); *gravity* 3.0–3.1; *cleavage* perfect micaceous. Translucent to transparent; brittle.

Composition: Basic calcium, aluminum silicate (14.0% CaO, 51.3% Al_2O_3, 30.2% SiO_2, 4.5% H_2O).

Tests: Fuses with some difficulty, swelling and turning white on edges of the plates. Cobalt nitrate gives this edge a blue color after strong heating.

Distinguishing characteristics: Resembles muscovite mica but is harder, less fusible, and the flakes are more brittle. The corundum or emery association is a guide.

Occurrence: Margarite is probably usually derived from the alteration of corundum, and it may take the form of casts of the original corundum crystal. Commonly there is a residual core of fresh unaltered corundum, as in Madison Co., North Carolina, and Unionville, Pennsylvania. Good specimens of pinkish bladed masses are found in the emery deposit at Chester, Massachusetts, associated with diaspore, emery, and chlorite. The best American specimens are these veins of light lilac plates standing on edge. Also found in a similar association in the emergy deposits of Asia Minor and Greece.

PREHNITE $Ca_2Al_2Si_3O_{10}(OH)_2$ **Pl. 36**
    Orthorhombic — Rhombic pyramidal m m 2

Environment: A mineral of hot-water rock alteration origin, and the frequent associate of zeolites.

Crystal description: Isolated well-formed crystals of this mineral are very rare in much more than microscopic dimensions. Usually intergrown in botryoidal masses, with ridged surfaces marked by the edges of curving crystals. Sometimes in dull, cloudy, elongated, almost square crystals with a blunt top. Slender, pointed colorless crystal clusters, wholly unlike the usual prehnite, have been found associated with remarkably large, flat pectolite blades at Asbestos, Quebec.

Physical properties: White, light green and yellow-green to green. *Luster* glassy; *hardness* 6–6½; *gravity* 2.8–2.9; *fracture* uneven; *cleavage* basal (commonly concave, because of curved crystal-growth habit). Translucent to almost transparent.

Composition: Hydrous calcium aluminum silicate (27.1% CaO, 24.8% Al_2O_3, 43.7% SiO_2, 4.4% H_2O, often with some iron in place of part of the Al; from which the varying color).

Tests: Fuses, with swelling and bubbling, to a dirty yellowish or greenish glass. After this fusion, dissolves in hydrochloric acid to form a gelatinous mass.

Distinguishing characteristics: Crusts resemble hemimorphite and some smithsonite (though lower in luster and lighter in gravity than either). Fuses more readily than hemimorphite and does not dissolve in hydrochloric acid with bubbles like smithsonite. Its zeolite associates are often characteristic.

Occurrence: Prehnite is a common mineral found in many localities with zeolites: Paterson, New Jersey; Farmington, Connecticut (yellow-green); and Westfield, Massachusetts (bright green). The colorless, sharp, $\frac{1}{2}$ in. (1 cm) prehnite crystals from the Jeffrey Quarry, Asbestos, Quebec, are unique. Good specimens were found with the axinite in the Dauphiné province of France, sometimes in almost perfect spheres.

Mica Group

This is a group of minerals similar in structure and physical properties and related in chemical composition. They do not, however, form a complete series, with the metals substituting for each other in any percentage. All have the perfect basal cleavage, and the slight inclination of the base to the prism is so near to 90° that the crystals look hexagonal or orthorhombic, as the case may be. They develop an interesting 6-rayed star around the point of impact of a sharp point, a "percussion figure," the strongest ray of which is parallel to the side pinacoid faces. The micas included here are muscovite, biotite, phlogopite, and lepidolite.

MUSCOVITE $KAl_3Si_3O_{10}(OH)_2$ **Pl. 38**

Monoclinic — prismatic $\frac{2}{m}$

Environment: One of the common rock-forming minerals, an important constituent of granite and the main constituent of some schists, but best developed in pegmatite dikes.

Crystal description: Crystals are common in occurrences of mineralogical interest, though still rare of course in relation to the abundance of rock-forming muscovite in general. Usually tabular parallel to the cleavage, often hexagonal in outline. Also fine-grained, sometimes so granular and compact as not to resemble a mica at all.

Physical properties: White, light yellow, colorless, amber, bright rose, green. *Luster* glassy to pearly; *hardness* 2–2½; *gravity* 2.8–3.0; *cleavage* perfect basal, plates flexible. Translucent to transparent (thick crystals often transparent through the much wider sides, and pearly and opaque through the cleavage faces, even though far thinner in this direction).

Composition: Basic potassium, aluminum silicate, often with more or less impurity of many other elements (11.8% K_2O, 38.5% Al_2O_3, 45.2% SiO_2, 4.5% H_2O).

Tests: Variable fusibility, sometimes almost infusible, rounding and whitening a little on the edges of the flakes; sometimes actually melting and bubbling slightly. Insoluble in acid.

Distinguishing characteristics: The thin, flexible, and elastic cleavage flakes distinguish it from most other minerals except other micas. Greater flexibility distinguishes it from margarite. Sharpness of the prism faces and elasticity of the basal plates distinguish even green crystals from the chlorites. Selenite gypsum has been mistaken for muscovite, but it cannot be split into the thin, flexible, elastic sheets obtainable from muscovite. Pink muscovite resembles lepidolite but is far less fusible and does not color the flame red. The fine-grained, compact type is difficult or impossible to recognize without microscopic tests. Phlogopite is darker and is decomposed by sulfuric acid. Biotite is very dark to black.

Occurrences: Muscovite is found wherever igneous and metamorphic rocks are found. The best crystals are in pegmatites and may be free-growing or embedded. The largest crystals are always embedded, and are mined in pegmatite areas in New England, North Carolina, the Black Hills of South Dakota, and in Colorado. Beautiful zoned green crystals have been found near Salt Lake City, Utah, and small, bright green, free crystals were found in Lincoln Co., North Carolina. Rose muscovite has been found in Massachusetts (Goshen), Virginia (Amelia), and in abundance in New Mexico (Dixon).

Other minerals are often trapped between the plates of the muscovite and grow in characteristic patterns of flattened crystals. The flat garnets of Spruce Pine, North Carolina, are particularly fine in this respect.

Interesting facts: It was once valued as window-making material, derived from Russia — whence the name muscovite — and is still used in iron-stove windows. More important today as an insulator for electrical equipment; large clear sheets are of great commercial value. Scrap mica has many uses, from lubricant to Christmas-tree "snow." A fluorine-bearing muscovite is synthesized in medium-sized crystal plates, but it is used in a crushed ceramic aggregate form, not in sheets like natural micas.

BIOTITE $K(Mg,Fe)_3AlSi_3O_{10}(OH)_2$ **Pl. 39**
                    Monoclinic — domatic m

Environment: Like muscovite, one of the rock-making minerals of igneous and metamorphic rocks, but rarer than muscovite.

Crystal description: Good crystals common in pegmatites and in metamorphosed limestones; usually tabular, sometimes somewhat barrel-shaped. Most often in embedded grains, sometimes intergrown with muscovite.

Physical properties: Dark brown to black, rarely (at Vesuvius) light yellow. *Luster* glassy; *hardness* $2\frac{1}{2}$–3; *gravity* 2.8–3.4; *cleavage* perfect basal; yielding thin flexible and elastic sheets. Opaque to translucent.

Composition: Basic potassium, magnesium, iron, aluminum

silicate (averaging about 8.5% K_2O, 21.0% MgO, 13.0% FeO plus Fe_2O_3, 16.0% Al_2O_3, 38.0% SiO_2, and 3.5% H_2O).

Tests: Fuses easily on thin edges to a dull, black magnetic glass.

Distinguishing characteristics: Distinguished from the other micas by the dark color; in its rare (Vesuvian) light phases, by its sulfuric acid reaction (forming milky solution on boiling in strong acid).

Occurrence: A common mineral of pegmatites, often taking the place of muscovite in pegmatites rich in rare-earth minerals; hence, a useful sign of that type of pegmatite. The associated feldspar is often a brick-red color. Good crystals are found in New England and elsewhere. Commonly found in the same occurrences as muscovite. Small, complex, light-colored crystals occur in cavities in the Vesuvius limestone blocks. Often in dark volcanic rocks as larger crystals (porphyry phenocrysts).

PHLOGOPITE $K(Mg,Fe)_3(AlSi_3)O_{10}(F,OH)_2$ **Pl. 39**

Monoclinic — prismatic $\dfrac{2}{m}$

Environment: Usually a mineral of metamorphosed limestones and dolomites; sometimes in serpentines and igneous rocks.

Crystal description: Good crystals common, embedded in crystalline dolomite. Often prismatic (elongated, for a mica); sometimes very large.

Physical properties: Light to dark brown. *Luster* often pearly or metallic on cleavage face; *hardness* $2\frac{1}{2}$–3; *gravity* 2.7; *cleavage* perfect basal, yielding thin, flexible, and elastic plates. Translucent, especially marked through the prism faces; commonly asteriated (shows 6- or 12-rayed star around distant or small light source when viewed through a cleavage sheet). May be triboluminescent and glow at the line of separation when sheets are pulled from a "book."

Composition: Basic potassium, magnesium, aluminum silicate (about 8% K_2O, 28% MgO, 16% Al_2O_3, 42% SiO_2, and 6% H_2O, F, and Fe).

Tests: Reacts much like muscovite but sometimes can be found to make a cloudy solution if boiled in strong sulfuric acid.

Distinguishing characteristics: Best told from muscovite by association with crystalline marbles and its golden-brown color (lighter than biotite). Usually less transparent than muscovite, with innumerable microscopic inclusions very apparent. The asterism is a useful guide, also change of color (a darkening) as the sheet is viewed on a slant instead of directly through it. Sometimes twinned sheets of phlogopite show a distinct color break across their face as this color change is observed.

Occurrence: Can occur in large sheets, and Canadian and Madagascar phlogopite is in good demand for electrical purposes. For some uses (spark plugs) phlogopite mica is preferred to muscovite. Large sheets are obtained in the Burgess area, Ontario. Well-formed several-inch (decimeter-sized) crystals of phlogopite have been found in abundance at Franklin, New Jersey, and in St. Lawrence Co., New York.

LEPIDOLITE $K_2Li_3Al_4Si_7O_{21}(OH,F)_3$ **Pl. 39**
                    Monoclinic — domatic m

Environment: A mica mineral of lithium-bearing pegmatites.
Crystal description: Commonly occurs in medium- to fine-grained aggregates; well-developed crystals of sharp hexagonal outline rare. Sometimes borders ordinary muscovite mica, but the cleavage flakes are not quite continuous. 1–2 in. (2.5–5 cm) crystals, tapering down to a slender point and more prismatic than tabular, occur at some localities, often in curving concave clusters embedded in feldspar.
Physical properties: Lilac, gray-green, pale yellow. *Luster* pearly and vitreous; *hardness* $2\frac{1}{2}$ and 4; *gravity* 2.8–3.3; *cleavage* perfect basal (micaceous), making elastic plates. Translucent to transparent.
Composition: Basic fluosilicate of lithium, potassium, and aluminum (about 5% Li_2O, 12% K_2O, 26% Al_2O_3, 51% SiO_2, 1.5% H_2O, and 4.5% F).
Tests: Fuses easily to a bubbly fluorescent glass (blue and pinkish fluorescence). Colors the flame red.
Distinguishing characteristics: Since lepidolite colors can be confusing, a melting and flame test is desirable if there is any reason (such as the presence of colored tourmalines or of other lithium minerals) for suspecting a mica to be lepidolite, rather than the more common muscovite. The fluorescence and flame tests will also distinguish it from the more intensely colored chromium chlorites, dumortierite, and similar hydrous silicates.
Occurrence: An important ore of lithium but relatively rare, since it is only found in pegmatites that show a long series of replacements by successive elements; always an associate of lithium minerals. Only found in regions where dikes of this type are exposed, as in New England, particularly in Maine, and at Portland, Connecticut, and San Diego Co., California.

Well-formed crystals up to an inch (2.5 cm) or more across are found at Auburn, Maine. Fine-grained aggregates are common in many Maine localities, and are associated with microlite at Dixon, New Mexico. The coarsest crystals form bladed aggregates at Ohio City, Colorado. Foreign localities include: Minas Gerais, Brazil; Madagascar; Varütrask, Sweden; South West Africa; Western Australia (where there are sheets as much as 6 in. (15 cm) across in the Londonderry pegmatite); U.S.S.R.; and Germany. The Alto Ligonha pegmatite in Mozambique has some notable lepidolite knobs to 12 in. high and 6 in. across (30 × 15 cm).

The Metasilicate Types

Chain Structures

Si:O = 3:8   (triple chains)
Si:O = 4:11   (double chains)
Si:O = 1:3   (single chains)

The structural crystallographer pictures the SiO_4 tetrahedrons in this subtype of the metasilicates as linked together in single or multiple chains. The important additional elements in their compositions are Mg, Fe″, Ca, Mn, Al, and Fe‴. The crystals are all distinctly prismatic and may even be fibrous. Pronounced prismatic cleavages and strong directional differences in properties like color and hardness are normal to these structures.

The Amphiboles

This large group of minerals has been subdivided into several series; optical mineralogists can distinguish the individuals by their appearance under the microscope. The average collector has neither the training nor the experience for these identifications and it is not practical for him to attempt to distinguish them. The different amphiboles show some consistency in color, which is about the only practical guide for the purposes of this book.

A second problem for the collector is differentiating all the members of the amphibole group from those of a very comparable pyroxene series. That series (described on p. 253) is similar in occurrence. It too is a rock-making group of calcium, iron, magnesium, aluminum silicates in which there are also isomorphous series and overlapping relationships. The pyroxene series can be distinguished from the amphibole series by the angles at which the prismatic cleavage planes meet. The prisms of the amphibole series lie at 56° and 124° to each other, giving a wedge-shaped cross section to the cleavage flake. The prisms of the pyroxene series are at 87° and 93° to each other, so that cleavage splinters of this group have a square or rectangular cross section.

There is also a tendency for the amphiboles to form longer and more slender crystals than the pyroxenes. Any massive specimen made up of elongated crystals should be suspected of being an amphibole. Tremolite and actinolite are particularly conspicuous in this respect.

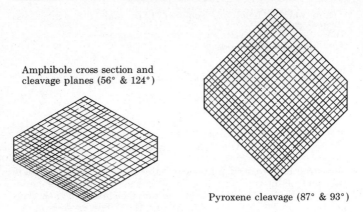

Amphibole cross section and cleavage planes (56° & 124°)

Pyroxene cleavage (87° & 93°)

The amphiboles discussed here are the following:

Anthophyllite $(Mg,Fe)_7Si_8O_{22}(OH)_2$ Orthorhombic
Tremolite-Actinolite $Ca_2(Mg,Fe)_5Si_8O_{22}(OH)_2$ Monoclinic
Hornblende $CaNa(Mg,Fe)_4(Al,Fe,Ti)_3Si_6O_{22}(O,OH)_2$ Monoclinic

ANTHOPHYLLITE $(Mg,Fe)_7Si_8O_{22}(OH)_2$

Orthorhombic — Rhombic bipyramidal $\dfrac{2\ \ 2\ \ 2}{m\ m\ m}$

Environmant: A rare mineral of metamorphic rocks, commonly associated with ore minerals.

Crystal description: Crystals rare, usually in compact masses with a fibrous structure.

Physical properties: Generally brown, sometimes with grayish or greenish tints. *Luster* glassy; *hardness* $5\frac{1}{2}$–6 (but usually splinters and appears softer); *gravity* 2.9–3.4; *cleavage* prismatic. Translucent. Sometimes with blue schiller reflections.

Composition: Basic magnesium iron silicate (27.8% MgO, 16.6% FeO, 55.6% SiO_2, plus water).

Tests: Fuses with some difficulty to a black magnetic glass. Insoluble in acid.

Distinguishing characteristics: It is not easily recognized, but is a good guess for a fibrous brown silicate mineral with the proper cleavage and hardness.

Occurrence: Anthophyllite is thought to be a secondary mineral forming from olivine under conditions of moisture and pressure. More moisture and, possibly, less pressure would have produced serpentine; therefore the two will not be associated.

Best developed in the U.S. in the metamorphic rocks of Franklin Co., North Carolina, and in feathery masses in Delaware Co., Pennsylvania. Fairly common in the Greenland schists. The closely related cummingtonite forms brown fibrous masses at Cummington, Massachusetts. Beautiful blue schiller reflections characterize an unusual anthophyllite amphibolite from near Butte, Montana.

TREMOLITE $\quad$ $Ca_2Mg_5Si_8O_{22}(OH)_2$ $\Big\}$
ACTINOLITE $\quad$ $Ca_2(Mg,Fe)_5Si_8O_{22}(OH)_2$ $\Big\}$ $\qquad$ **Pl. 39**

Monoclinic — prismatic $\dfrac{2}{m}$

Environment: Minerals resulting from the metamorphism of impure limestones or dolomites. Also in green schists and gneisses (actinolite) possibly derived from pyroxenes. Nephrite seems to develop in serpentine in nodes of higher intensity alteration during regional metamorphism.

Crystal description: The crystals of the amphiboles tend toward a more elongated prismatic habit than those of the pyroxenes. They may be stubby but quite large and well formed when growing in calcite. Also in masses of needles, from coarse blades to very fine needles.

Physical properties: White, light green, violet (hexagonite), and dark green. *Luster* glassy; *hardness* 5-6; *gravity* 3.0-3.3; *fracture* subconchoidal to uneven; *cleavage* perfect prismatic. Transparent to translucent; sometimes fluorescent.

Composition: Basic calcium magnesium (iron) silicate; when free of iron it is light in color, or white, and is called tremolite. 2% or more iron replacing the magnesium makes it green and changes the name to actinolite. There is no simple way of identifying the intermediate examples (CaO,MgO, and FeO total about 42%; and SiO_2, about 57%).

Tests: Thin splinters of tremolite and actinolite fuse to a black or white glass, the more iron-rich varieties fusing more easily. Insoluble in acid.

Distinguishing characteristics: This series of minerals is most likely to be confused with some of the related series, the pyroxenes. The well-crystallized varieties can be recognized by their prismatic habit and the characteristic cleavage angles. Wollastonite is commonly fluorescent (lost after heating), and is decomposed by hydrochloric acid. Scapolite melts more easily and is (or on heating becomes) fluorescent in longwave ultraviolet light. Tourmaline has no cleavage. Epidote melts more readily to black magnetic slag.

Occurrence: Tremolite and actinolite are minerals that have formed, usually secondarily, under conditions of moderately high temperature and pressure, in the presence of some water. They will therefore be found in metamorphosed limestones, in gneisses and schists with serpentines, and in granites. Locally they may form considerable formations of rock, when they tend to be in compact masses of rather slender crystals. The best crystals are found separately embedded in coarsely crystalline marbles, from which they are easily freed by acid or careful handwork.

Good greenish or white tremolite crystals are found in the calcite of Canaan, Connecticut. Fibrous white masses come from Ossining, New York. Coarse green or gray crystals are abundant at many localities in St. Lawrence Co., New York. An attractive lilac variety known as hexagonite occurs at Fowler, St. Lawrence Co., New York. Chrome-tremolite, an emerald-green variety, has been found in Ontario, Finland, and Tanzania.

Actinolite usually forms solid masses of slender intergrowing crystals and is quite common. Chester, Vermont, is a typical locality, but there are hundreds of others. Actinolite sometimes penetrates quartz crystals in green hairs.

Interesting facts: There are many related amphibole species. Nephrite jade is close to actinolite, but is more compact and massive. It is one of the two jade minerals. Amianthus is the ancient name for an amphibole asbestos. It melts more easily than serpentine asbestos. Mountain leather is a natural mat of light-colored interlocking amphibole asbestos fibers.

HORNBLENDE   Pl. 39

$$CaNa(Mg,Fe)_4(Al,Fe,Ti)_3Si_6O_{22}(O,OH)_2$$

Monoclinic — prismatic $\dfrac{2}{m}$

Environment: Like tremolite and actinolite, a mineral of metamorphic and igneous rocks, often replacing pyroxene (uralite).

Crystal description: Commonly crystallized, short- to longprismatic. Often several inches (1 dm) in length. Also solid crystalline aggregates.

Physical properties: Green (edenite), bluish green (pargasite), to black. *Luster* glassy; *hardness* 5–6; *gravity* 3.0–3.4; *fracture* subconchoidal to uneven; *cleavage* prismatic. Transparent to translucent on splinter edges.

Composition: The hornblendes constitute a whole series of aluminous amphiboles (some authorities include nonaluminous tremolite and actinolite) with numerous end-members, difficult even for the professional to name. The collector can usually only make a good guess on identity. (Basic calcium, sodium, magnesium, iron, aluminum silicates; with about 15% Al_2O_3, and 40% SiO_2.)

Tests: Fusible with some difficulty to a black glass. Gives water in a closed tube.

Distinguishing characteristics: Identified as an amphibole by its cleavage angles of 56° and 124° in contrast to the pyroxenes, and the individuals are recognized by their color; any black amphibole is probably hornblende. Tourmaline lacks the cleavage.

Occurrence: Hornblende is a common rock constituent and sometimes forms solid masses known as amphibolite. Hornblende schists are made up of thin, parallel, elongated crystals. Amphibole commonly forms from the pyroxenes in the late stages of the cooling of igneous rock, and fibrous uralitic amphiboles are commonly seen under the microscope.

Large but stubby hornblende crystals are found at Franklin, New Jersey, embedded in calcite. Similar large crystals are found in St. Lawrence Co., New York, and Renfrew Co., Ontario, where in carbonatite pegmatites they attain giant dimensions.

The Pyroxenes

This group parallels the amphibole series, and is a water-free equivalent of that group. They are similar in composition and have the same relationships as the hydrous series. The compositions are far simpler, however, and as a group they are well understood since their relationships have been the subject of an exhaustive investigation. Pyroxenes crystallize in both the orthorhombic and monoclinic systems but, in contrast to the amphiboles, tend toward stubbiness in prism development and the prism cleavages are at almost right angles (see illus., p. 250), making the distinction from the amphiboles easy. The cleavage angle is most easily observed on a small splinter, broken across its length and viewed through a hand lens from above. It is then quite apparent whether the cross section is wedge-shaped or rectangular.

The following pyroxenes are described here:

Enstatite-Hypersthene	$(Mg,Fe)SiO_3$	Orthorhombic
Diopside	$CaMgSi_2O_6$	Monoclinic
Hedenbergite	$Ca(Fe,Mg)Si_2O_6$	Monoclinic
Augite	$(Ca,Na)(Mg,Fe,Al)(Si,Al)_2O_6$	Monoclinic
Acmite-Aegirine	$NaFeSi_2O_6$	Monoclinic
Jadeite	$Na(Al,Fe)Si_2O_6$	Monoclinic
Spodumene	$LiAlSi_2O_6$	Monoclinic
Rhodonite	$(Mn,Fe,Mg)SiO_3$	Triclinic

ENSTATITE $MgSiO_3$
HYPERSTHENE $(Mg,Fe)SiO_3$ }   **Pl. 39**

Orthorhombic — Rhombic bipyramidal $\frac{2}{m} \frac{2}{m} \frac{2}{m}$

Environment: Minerals of igneous rocks and common constituents of meteorites.

Crystal description: Usually in coarsely crystalline aggregates, sometimes in free individuals. Crystals well formed at only a few localities, and then with few faces.

Physical properties: Grayish, greenish, yellowish, bronze-brown to almost black. *Luster* glassy to silky, or submetallic (bronzite); *hardness* 5½–6; *gravity* 3.2–3.9; *fracture* uneven; *cleavage* perfect prismatic. Transparent to translucent in splinters.

Composition: Magnesium and magnesium iron silicates [about 40% (MgO,FeO) and 60% SiO_2].

Tests: Practically infusible, except on the thinnest edges, but increasingly fusible with more iron. Hypersthene is decomposed by hot hydrochloric acid.

Distinguishing characteristics: They are most likely to be confused with the amphiboles, from which they may easily be distinguished by the 87° and 93° cleavage angles of the prism faces. Difficult to tell from other members of the pyroxene family, like augite, with tests suitable for the amateur.

Occurrence: Enstatite and hypersthene crystals will be found embedded in fine-grained igneous rocks, porphyries. Enstatite is the commoner variety and at several localities forms granular aggregates with the individuals about ½ in. (1 cm) across. Such green-black masses have been common at the Tilly Foster Mine in Brewster, New York. Similar masses are found: in Boulder Co., Colorado; in Lancaster Co., Pennsylvania; and at Bare Hills, Maryland. Weathering often changes the surfaces of such masses to the bronze color characteristic of the bronzite variety of this mineral. Hypersthene is rarer and is found in the dark plutonic rocks of the Adirondack Mountains region of New York, especially well developed in North Creek garnet occurrences. Emerald-green chrome enstatite is found in some volcanic rock regions and cut as a gemstone. 4-rayed black stars are cut in India. Brownish hypersthene is a gemstone in India and Tanzania.

Interesting facts: The iron end-member of this series is not known in nature. At high temperature (1140°C to below 955°C, depending upon the iron content) enstatite and hypersthene are transformed to a monoclinic crystal form, and are known as clinoenstatite and clinohypersthene. Though these phases are not common in plutonic rocks, they are well known in meteorites.

DIOPSIDE $CaMgSi_2O_6$ }
HEDENBERGITE $Ca(Fe,Mg)Si_2O_6$ }   **Pl. 36**

Monoclinic — prismatic $\dfrac{2}{m}$

Environment: Minerals of contact metamorphism and of regional metamorphism of dolomitic limestones. Less often in some rare types of pegmatites.

Crystal description: Crystals are common and are often large; usually they are not free-growing but are embedded in a crystalline marble from which they are easily freed. Such crystals commonly have poor end faces, though the prisms are well developed and lustrous. Also in granular aggregates.

Physical properties: White, light green, dark green, brown. *Luster* glassy; *hardness* 5–6; *gravity* 3.3–3.5; *fracture* conchoidal; *cleavage* perfect prismatic, occasional basal partings due to twinning. Translucent to transparent; light-colored varieties in dolomitic marble may fluoresce blue.

Composition: Calcium magnesium silicate (25.9% CaO, 18.5% MgO, 55.6% SiO_2). Iron may replace some or all of the magnesium, darkening the crystal and forming the variety hedenbergite, a less common calcium iron silicate.

The diopside series is the pyroxene equivalent of the tremolite-actinolite series in the amphiboles. It is a common and important group.

Tests: Splinters fuse with a little difficulty to a darker glass; insoluble in hydrochloric acid.

Distinguishing characteristics: The common light green color, cleavage angles of 87° and 93°, and the associations are usually a sufficient guide.

Occurrences: The best American diopside occurrences are in De Kalb, St. Lawrence Co., New York, where large, light green, transparent to translucent, short-prismatic crystals 2 or 3 in. (5–8 cm) long were found. There are numerous localities in the West, including several California counties, particularly Riverside Co. at Crestmore. Almost white, fluorescent crystals are found in and near New York in a dolomite marble, and are known as malacolite. Large, light smoky-brown crystals with prominent basal partings were found in a pegmatite at Laurel, Quebec, associated with idocrase.

European localities have produced better-formed crystals; some simple ones, rich enough in iron and dark enough to be considered hedenbergite are found at Nordmark, Sweden. It is one of the silicates that occur in the Broken Hill (New South Wales) galena, with garnets, pyroxmangite, and rhodonite. Fine light-colored diopside crystals have been found in the Italian, Swiss, and Austrian Alps. Many of these are much lighter, almost white, at one end and green at the other. Some, from the Tyrol, lie on a chlorite schist; those from Ala, Italy, grow in cavities with perfect brown essonite garnet crystals. Large, green, and transparent diopside crystals have been found in Madagascar and n. Korea near the 38th parallel. Emerald-green chrome-diopside of gem quality has been found in Outokumpu, Finland, and in the U.S.S.R.

Interesting facts: Sometimes cut as a collector's gemstone, either as a clear faceted gem or in a rounded shape (cabochon) to show a streak of light (a "cat's-eye diopside").

AUGITE $(Ca,Na)(Mg,Fe,Al)(Si,Al)_2O_6$ **Pl. 40**

Monoclinic — prismatic $\dfrac{2}{m}$

Environment: The most widespread of the pyroxenes and an essential component of many of the darker plutonic rocks. A constituent grain of basalt and traprock, and commonly in larger porphyritic crystals in fine-grained rocks.

Crystal description: The best crystals are found in the porphyries, but usually are not over an inch (2 cm) in size. They are commonly very perfect, however. Granular, massive augite is frequent in other rocks — including pyroxenites, which are almost wholly augite.

Physical properties: Black. *Luster* glassy; *hardness* 5–6; *gravity* 3.2–3.4; *fracture* uneven; *cleavage* perfect prismatic at 87°. Translucent only on the thinnest splinter edges.

Composition: Actually a whole series of minerals with different names, in which aluminum substitutes for both magnesium and silicon. The Al_2O_3 ranges from 3% to 9%. Magnesium and iron are present in varying percentages, as are calcium and sodium.

Tests: Fusible with some difficulty; insoluble in HCl.

Distinguishing characteristics: Free crystals are very typical and easily recognized. Massive material is distinguished from amphibole by its 87° and 93° cleavage angles, and from tourmaline by its prismatic cleavage. Acmite-aegirine crystals are more elongated, diopside-hedenbergite lighter in color.

Occurrence: Common as a rock constituent in the U.S., but well-formed free crystals from volcanic rocks are not common. At Vesuvius, $\frac{3}{4}$–1 in. (1–2 cm) crystals are frequently abundant, especially in recent, greatly corroded lavas that occupy, when there is one, the crater floor. Similar crystals are found in the ancient lavas of the German Eifel and Bohemia. Loose, perfect crystals of like size are exploded, sharp and free of all lava attachment, in the recurrent paroxysms of Stromboli.

Large crystals are found in St. Lawrence Co., New York, and in similar deposits in Renfrew Co., Ontario. A black pyroxene is one of the once abundant minerals from Franklin, New Jersey. Sharp crystals occur in the sulfide ores of Ducktown, Tennessee.

ACMITE (Aegirine) $NaFeSi_2O_6$ **Pl. 40**

Monoclinic — prismatic $\dfrac{2}{m}$

Environment: Minerals of rocks poor in silica and characterized by the presence of the low-silica equivalents of feldspar — the feldspathoids, like nepheline and leucite.

Crystal description: Visually recognizable only when crystallized; the pyroxene cleavage angles then become important.

Usually in prismatic, embedded crystals, several inches (10 cm) long, terminated by steep pyramids. Also in fibrous masses.

Physical properties: Black, brown, or green on thin edges. *Luster* glassy; *hardness* 6–6½; *gravity* 3.4–3.5; *fracture* uneven; *cleavage* easy prismatic. Brittle; translucent on thin edges.

Composition: Sodium iron silicate (13.4% Na_2O, 34.6% Fe_2O_3, 52.0% SiO_2). Acmite has exactly this composition and probably would not be separately recognizable; in any case aegirine is the acceptable identification for the mineral when it is found, since exact theoretical compositions are not the custom in nature. Only steep-tipped crystals can be called acmite.

Tests: Fuses easily to shiny, black magnetic bead, giving a yellow sodium flame.

Distinguishing characteristics: These are common minerals of their particular group of rocks; therefore, the crystal habit and associates are the usual guides to the identity. They are more fusible than most of the black silicates they resemble.

Occurrence: Aegirine is common in high-soda, low-silica rocks: the nepheline syenites with very black biotite and their fine-grained equivalents. This group of rocks, however, is not common. The best U.S. occurrence is at Magnet Cove, Arkansas, and slender crystals several inches (10 cm or more) long are abundant at this locality. Small crystals are found in a dark-colored dike of this material at Beemerville, New Jersey. Similar crystals are found in low-silica rocks in the Bear Paw and Highwood Mountains in Montana and near Colorado Springs. Abundant at St. Hilaire, Quebec, with many rare nepheline syenite minerals. The same type of rock is found: in Greenland; at Langesundfjord, Norway; and near Poços de Caldas, Brazil.

JADEITE $Na(Al,Fe)Si_2O_6$ Monoclinic — prismatic $\dfrac{2}{m}$

Environment: Little known in place, usually in waterworn boulders; freed by weathering from masses formed in serpentine by alteration of a soda-rich rock.

Crystal description: Free crystals known only from California. Usually in felted masses of elongated blades, which give thin slices their great strength. The Mexican individual crystals are coarser than most, to ¼ in. (5 mm) across, and sometimes show a silky luster from parallel cleavage cracks.

Physical properties: Emerald- to light green, white, red-brown, yellow-brown, violet, lilac, malachite-green. *Luster* glassy to silky; *hardness* 6½–7; *gravity* 3.3–3.5; *fracture* difficult, splintery; *cleavage* prismatic. Translucent to opaque.

Composition: Sodium aluminum silicate (15.4% Na_2O, 25.2% Al_2O_3, 59.4% SiO_2; some varieties, particularly the Mexican, quite high in CaO).

Tests: Fuses easily to a bubbly white glass, with a yellow sodium flame coloration.

Distinguishing characteristics: Distinguished from nephrite by its easy fusion and the flame coloration. Distinguished in worked objects by the gravity, which also separates it from serpentine and idocrase. Hardness tests also distinguish jade from soft-mineral carvings without the necessity for gravity tests.

Occurrence: Until recent years jadeite has been a mystery mineral. We now know of several California occurrences of white or grayish jadeite. Boulders are found in Clear Creek, between New Idria and Hernandez, San Benito Co. A few examples of free-standing crystals are reported. All Mexican jadeite is in carved objects (not to be confused with the modern imitations of dyed calcite-onyx) and its source (or sources) is not known. "Chinese" jadeite is found as boulders in streambeds in Burma and traded to the carving centers. It has been found in place at one locality in Japan and is now mined in Guatemala.

Interesting facts: A valuable material for gem purposes (almost transparent emerald-green is very valuable); the larger, less colorful masses are widely used for carvings in China. Color is often spotty and patterns may be used by the artists to emphasize the figure.

SPODUMENE   Pl. 40

$$LiAlSi_2O_6 \quad \text{Monoclinic — prismatic} \quad \frac{2}{m}$$

Environment: Almost exclusively a pegmatite mineral.

Crystal description: Usually in elongated, embedded crystals, commonly well developed, with striated prism and pinacoid faces and steep terminations. Very large (40 ft.; 10 m) crystals have been described in South Dakota. Networks of intergrowing crystals may not show any terminations.

Physical properties: Opaque varieties buff, white, lavender, greenish; transparent varieties colorless, lilac, yellow, or green. *Luster* glassy; *hardness* $6\frac{1}{2}$–7; *gravity* 3.1–3.2; *fracture* uneven, rather tough across prism directions, developing splinters; *cleavage* perfect prismatic 87° and 93°; good partings parallel to front pinacoid. Transparent to translucent; thermoluminescent, often fluorescent and phosphorescent orange.

Composition: Lithium aluminum silicate (8.0% Li_2O, 27.4% Al_2O_3, 64.6% SiO_2).

Tests: Fuses to a clear glass after developing small zeolite-like protuberances, and colors the flame bright red (lithium). On initial heating will show marked thermoluminescence. Fused material fluoresces blue in shortwave ultraviolet. Original material fluoresces orange, best in longwave ultraviolet or in X-rays.

Distinguishing characteristics: The pegmatitic occurrence, commonly associated with other lithia minerals, like lepidolite mica and colored tourmalines, is usually sufficient. The tough splintery fracture distinguishes it from feldspar. Distinctive in many ways, including its luminescent qualities.

Occurrence: Found only where there are lithia-rich pegmatites, and it is usually, though not always, associated with lepidolite, colored tourmalines, cesium beryl, amblygonite, and/or herderite.

The transparent colored varieties have some value as gems; the ordinary material is an important ore of lithium. Lithia pegmatites are found in New England — notably in Maine, Connecticut, and Massachusetts. The usual lithium mineral associates are lacking at Kings Mountain, North Carolina; and the Hiddenite (Alexander Co., North Carolina) locality is unusual because the small green gem (hiddenite) crystals occur in a gneiss in veins that must have been deposited largely from solutions, rather than from a rock melt.

Good crystals are found at Dixon, New Mexico (see Pl. 6, bottom), and in the Black Hills of South Dakota, especially at the Etta Mine, where the mammoth crystals mentioned earlier were mined. Gemmy lilac crystals (kunzite) are found in several San Diego Co. pegmatites in the vicinity of Pala, California. Elsewhere in the world spodumene is found in: Minas Gerais, Paraíba, and Rio Grande do Norte, Brazil; Madagascar; South West Africa; and Varütrask, Sweden. Kunzite in abundance has also come from Urupuca, Minas Gerais, Brazil; Kabul, Afghanistan (a "first" for good terminations); and Madagascar.

Interesting facts: Spodumene alters easily to greenish mica pseudomorphs ("pinite") or clay pseudomorphs after the crystals, and even the gemmy material is frequently penetrated deeply by long curving slender tubes that start at the bottom of etch pits on the crystal surface. Clear spodumene is invariably etched so that the original luster of the faces has been removed.

The Pyroxenoids

RHODONITE   (Mn,Mg,Fe)SiO$_3$ **Pl. 36**
Triclinic — pinacoidal $\overline{1}$

Environment: A mineral of metamorphic rocks, related to manganese occurrences, often with ore veins.

Crystal description: Usually massive, sometimes fine-grained. Good crystals of short-prismatic habit are well developed at Franklin, New Jersey, embedded in calcite. Smaller prismatic and flattened crystals of deeper color in open cavities are also at this deposit.

Physical properties: Pink to grayish, blackening rapidly on weathering. *Luster* glassy; *hardness* $5\frac{1}{2}$–6; *gravity* 3.4–3.7; *fracture* splintery, very tough in massive form; *cleavage* prismatic at about 88° and 92°. Crystals brittle; transparent to translucent.

Composition: Manganese silicate (54.1% MnO, 45.9% SiO$_2$, with Ca replacing Mn).

Tests: Fuses to a brown glass. Gives manganese test in borax bead.

Distinguishing characteristics: The pink material is likely to be mistaken only for rhodochrosite (but it is much harder than the manganese carbonate) and for feldspar, which gives no manganese test or easy fusion. The gemmy red crystals are practically indistinguishable from the similar, closely related iron-bearing pyroxmangite [triclinic (Mn,Fe)SiO$_3$].

Occurrence: The world's leading specimen locality for large crystal masses is Franklin, New Jersey, from which have come the crystal groups that adorn the museums of the world; the crystals had been worked by hand out of the enclosing calcite. Brighter, wedgelike, smaller crystals in later veins are also found there. Massive rhodonite is found at Plainfield, Massachusetts, and at numerous western and foreign localities — California, Brazil (Itabira, Minas Gerais), Siberia, Australia (Tamworth, New South Wales), Tanzania, to name a few.

Good and sometimes transparent red crystals are found with microcline encased in sulfide ores at Broken Hill, New South Wales. Rich, compact masses suitable for carving are found in the Ural Mountains. Small late Franklin-type crystals are found at Pajsberg and Langban, Sweden.

A closely related and very similar manganese iron silicate is called pyroxmangite; it can grow in gemmy triclinic crystals and occurs with rhodonite at Broken Hill and in the manganese ores of Japan. It is more obviously triclinic in its angles and twins are common, thus making sight identification of this rarer species sometimes possible. Usually X-ray tests are required.

WOLLASTONITE CaSiO$_3$ Triclinic — pedial 1   **Pl. 40**

Environment: A mineral of contact-metamorphic deposits in limestones.

Crystal description: Usually in fibrous masses of elongated crystals flattened parallel to the base and to the front pinacoid, giving the impression of slender prismatic needles. Also crystals, coarsely granular, compact, and massive.

Physical properties: White to colorless, pink or gray. *Luster* glassy to silky; *hardness* $4\frac{1}{2}$–5; *gravity* 2.8–2.9; *fracture* splintery; *cleavage* perfect pinacoidal (pseudoprismatic) on base and front pinacoid at 84° and 96° to each other. Translucent; often fluorescent in yellow and orange.

Composition: Calcium silicate (48.3% CaO, 51.7% SiO$_2$).

Tests: Fuses to a white globule. Dissolves in hydrochloric acid, with a separation of shreds of silica.

Distinguishing characteristics: Distinguished from tremolite by greater fusibility and the cleavage angles, which are near those of the pyroxenes and far from the 56° and 124° of the amphiboles. Distinguished from diopside and prismatic topaz (pycnite) by its fusibility and solubility in acid. The fluorescence is commonly an aid to quick identification.

Occurrence: Common where limestones have been strongly metamorphosed, as in Llano Co., Texas, and Riverside Co. (at Crestmore) and San Diego Co., California. Good examples of distinct crystals come from Natural Bridge, St. Lawrence Co., New York. Richly fluorescent specimens were found at Franklin, New Jersey.

As might be expected, crystals are found in the altered limestone blocks thrown out by the eruptions of Monte Somma on Vesuvius. Good fibrous masses come from Perheniemi, Finland, and crystals from Banat, Rumania, and in the marble of Tremorgio, Switzerland. Used in ceramics.

PECTOLITE $NaCa_2Si_3O_8(OH)$ **Pl. 40**
Triclinic — pinacoidal $\overline{1}$

Environment: Usually an associate of the zeolites in traprocks; sometimes a secondary mineral or vein in coarser rocks.

Crystal description: Mammillary masses with fibrous structures line or fill cavities in traprocks. Rarely, ends of coarser blades may protrude and have a face or two of the side pinacoids visible. Also in solid veins with groups of needles radiating from successive centers along each wall.

Physical properties: White to gray, often stained yellowish or reddish. *Luster* silky; *hardness* 5 (but easily separated into fibers and appears softer); *gravity* 2.7–2.8; *fracture* splintery; *cleavage* crumbles into fibers from its perfect basal and front pinacoid (pseudoprismatic). Translucent; usually fluorescent orange in longwave ultraviolet.

Composition: Hydrous calcium sodium silicate (33.8% CaO, 9.3% NaO, 54.2% SiO_2, 2.7% H_2O).

Tests: Fuses easily to a white glass, coloring flame yellow. Fused mass fluoresces weakly white in shortwave ultraviolet, loses longwave ultraviolet fluorescence.

Distinguishing characteristics: Usually the zeolite associates are characteristic enough. If tests are necessary it can be distinguished from the amphiboles by greater fusibility and from wollastonite by the water that escapes in the closed tube. Distinguished from fibrous zeolites by lack of a blue color (aluminum) in the cobalt nitrate test.

Occurrence: Very abundant in fine domes and in rounded

fibrous crusts and radiating bundles at Paterson, New Jersey, and the nearby zeolite occurrences. Groundmass fluorescent pectolite is found in the Magnet Cove (Arkansas) nepheline syenite. Massive white pectolite is found in Tehama Co., California, and pink masses on Isle Royale in Lake Superior. The easily separated slender needles of pectolite readily penetrate the skin and are then difficult to remove because they are so brittle. Avoid handling as much as possible. The first occurrence of distinct and well-formed crystals was the Jeffrey Quarry, Asbestos, Quebec. The up to $1\frac{1}{2}$ in. (3 cm) long bluish-white blades with good slanting "terminations" (they are probably elongated on the b-axis), partly crusted here and there with white tacharanite $[(Ca,Mg,Al)(Si,Al)O_3 \cdot H_2O]$, are really unusual and entirely unlike any pectolite previously found.

BABINGTONITE $Ca(Fe'',Mn)Fe'''Si_5O_{14}(OH)$ **Pl. 40**
Triclinic — pinacoidal $\overline{1}$

Environment: A late, hot-water, secondary mineral, commonly associated with the zeolites.

Crystal description: Crystals usually small and often very brilliant. Roughly equidimensional, with faces striated. Always in crystals.

Physical properties: Black. *Luster* glassy; *hardness* $5\frac{1}{2}$–6; *gravity* 3.4; *fracture* conchoidal; *cleavage* 2 pinacoidal (1 good) at 87° and 93°. Translucent on thin splinters.

Composition: Basic calcium iron silicate (about 19% CaO, 29% FeO plus Fe_2O_3, 51.5% SiO_2, and 0.5% H_2O, often with some manganese).

Tests: Fuses easily to a black magnetic globule. Insoluble in hydrochloric acid.

Distinguishing characteristics: In appearance it might be rather difficult to distinguish from some of the black pyroxenes, but is less prismatic than the amphiboles usually are. The easy melting and the magnetism are helpful; most of all, one can rely on the mineral associates.

Occurrence: An uncommon mineral of seams and silicate veins; found best at several localities in Massachusetts. Once, at Woburn, Massachusetts, in crevices in a diorite, with calcite and thin-bladed crystals of prehnite. Small ones uncovered by dissolving away the calcite are very brilliant and unmistakable. Larger crystals at Westfield, Massachusetts, are contemporaneous with green prehnite. Thin-bladed and often partially altered (to a bronze amphibole) crystals at Paterson and Great Notch, New Jersey.

Good crystals coat feldspar in pegmatites in granite at Baveno, Italy, and Arendal, Norway. Similarly in Devonshire, England.

NEPTUNITE $(Na,K)_2(Fe,Mn)TiSi_4O_{12}$ **Pl. 41**

Monoclinic — prismatic $\dfrac{2}{m}$

Environment: Nepheline syenite cavities and in serpentine veins with natrolite and benitoite.

Crystal description: Always in crystals, the best from California over an in. (3 cm) long, distinctly prismatic in habit, and about $\frac{3}{8}-\frac{1}{4}$ in. (4-6 mm) across.

Physical properties: Black with reddish reflections. *Luster* glassy; *hardness* 5-6; *gravity* 3.2; *fracture* splintery (conchoidal across splinters); *cleavage* perfect prismatic. Translucent red-brown on thin edges.

Composition: A soda and potash, iron manganese titanosilicate (17.8% TiO_2,   9.8% Na_2O,   5.1% K_2O,   11.6% FeO,   3.8% MnO, 51.9% SiO_2).

Tests: Fuses readily to a black nonmagnetic shiny glass sphere that crushes to a brown powder.

Distinguishing characteristics: The perfect cleavages at about 80° and 100° distinguish it from the amphiboles, and it is more fusible than most similar pyroxenes. The red-brown translucency and streak are very characteristic. In California its benitoite association is constant.

Occurrence: A rare mineral but of special interest to the collector because of the unique occurrence in San Benito Co., California, where it has formed on the walls of natrolite veins with well-crystallized benitoite in a green serpentine. It is usually freed from its white natrolite coating by a hydrochloric acid bath. Smaller and duller crystals were found in Narsarssuak, Greenland, in pockets in a nepheline syenite along the coast. Similar crystals have been found in the Kola Peninsula, U.S.S.R.

CHRYSOCOLLA $Cu_2H_2Si_2O_5(OH)_4$ Orthorhombic (?) **Pl. 41**

Environment: In the oxidized zone of copper deposits, mainly in arid climates.

Crystal description: Microcrystalline, usually in solid vein-filling or botryoidal masses, often opal-like in appearance. Slender needles have been described as crystals but were only found at one locality (Mackay, Idaho).

Physical properties: Sky-blue to greenish blue and green, often streaked with black. *Luster* glassy, dull, or earthy; *hardness* 2-4; *gravity* 2.0-2.4; *fracture* conchoidal. Sectile to brittle.

Composition: Basic copper silicate (45.2% CuO, 34.3% SiO_2, 20.5% H_2O).

Tests: Tongue usually clings to specimen. Blackens and gives water in closed tube. Practically infusible, but decomposed by hydrochloric acid with a separation of silica.

Distinguishing characteristics: Only likely to be confused with turquoise, which decrepitates violently and is much harder (6, and cannot be scratched by a knife), and with chrysocolla-impregnated chalcedony (quartz), which has, of course, a hardness of 7.

Occurrence: Chrysocolla occurs very widely in the Southwest in copper deposits. Blue chrysocolla-impregnated quartz, covered by small crystals of white quartz, from the Globe Mine, Gila Co., Arizona, are frequent in collections. Fine massive specimens were found, in the early stages, in most of the w. U.S. copper mines. Also found today in Africa and Chile. Russia and England (Cornwall and Cumberland) once produced good specimens.

Interesting facts: It is an ore of copper when associated with other secondary copper minerals. In the West, used like turquoise for jewelry; but pure chrysocolla, being free of quartz, is rather fragile and likely to crack as it loses water in artificially dry home environments.

The Metasilicate Types

Ring Structures   Si:O = n:3n

The silica tetrahedrons in this type of structure form a closed ring. There are two ring types: one of 3 tetrahedrons forming a trigonal pattern; the other of 6 forming a hexagonal pattern. As would be expected, the minerals of this structure type occur in trigonal or hexagonal crystals.

BENITOITE $BaTiSi_3O_9$ **Pl. 36**

Hexagonal — Ditrigonal bipyramidal $\overline{6}$ m 2

Environment: San Benito Co., California, the principal occurrence, in a natrolite dike cutting a green schist in serpentine, with neptunite.

Crystal description: Good tabular triangular crystals, to $1\frac{1}{2}$ in. (4 cm) across, usually unevenly colored blue and white. The triangular base is likely to be duller in luster and whiter than the pyramids and prisms.

Physical properties: Blue to white (rarely, pink). *Luster* glassy; *hardness* 6–6½; *gravity* 3.6; *fracture* conchoidal; *cleavage* poor pyramidal. Transparent to translucent; fluorescent blue in shortwave ultraviolet light.

Composition: Barium titanium silicate (36.3% BaO, 20.2% TiO_2, 43.5% SiO_2).

Tests: Crystals are so distinctive that no tests are necessary.

Distinguishing characteristics: Since there is but one significant occurrence, with constant associates and appearance, it has been unnecessary to test specimens; for it resembles no other mineral.

Occurrence: Mainly known from a limited deposit of compact granular natrolite veins cutting a gray-green fibrous schist interlayered with serpentine. Collectors should eventually turn up other occurrences of this attractive mineral. Small pinkish "roses" of benitoite have been found near the California occurrence, and embedded grains of benitoite have been noted in rock thin-sections in Belgium. In 6-sided blue crystals at Ōmi Machi, Nishi-kubiki Gun, Niigata Prefecture, Japan.

Interesting facts: Until this mineral was found in 1907, the mineral world has no naturally-occurring representative of this crystal class. Even now it is the only mineral of the class. It is a valuable gemstone when transparent, free of flaws, and of good color.

EUDIALYTE $Na_4(Ca,Ce,Fe)_2ZrSi_6O_{17}(OH,Cl)_2$ **Pl. 41**

Hexagonal — Hexagonal scalenohedral $\overline{3}\,\dfrac{2}{m}$

Environment: A mineral of the coarse or pegmatitic phases of nepheline syenite.

Crystal description: Usually embedded in rock, with the grains occasionally showing a few free crystal faces, but always surrounded by other minerals and distorted in development. Large crystals to 2 in. (5 cm) have been found in pegmatitic zones in Greenland.

Physical properties: Brick-red; pink, brown. *Luster* dull; *hardness* 5–6; *gravity* 2.9–3.0; *fracture* uneven; *cleavage* poor basal. Translucent.

Composition: A complex silicate of calcium, sodium, zirconium, cerium, iron, and manganese, with hydroxyl and chlorine (about 50% SiO_2, 14% ZrO_2, and 2% to 3% Ce_2O_3).

Tests: Fuses fairly easily to a shiny green glass.

Distinguishing characteristics: The nepheline syenite associations of feldspar and nepheline, usually with aegirine, are sufficiently characteristic in most cases. The fusibility of the eudialyte would distinguish the brown varieties from zircon, and the red varieties are unlike most of the more common minerals.

Occurrence: Eudialyte is one of the rarer minerals but one that is attractive and popular with collectors. In the U.S. it is found in good crystals in the coarse phases of the Magnet Cove (Arkansas) nepheline syenite, where it has a good pink-red color. In Greenland it sometimes forms rich red bands in the rock, so abundant are the disseminated grains. Also found on the Kola Peninsula, U.S.S.R., in Norway, and in Madagascar.

TOURMALINE GROUP Pl. 41
Hexagonal — Ditrigonal pyramidal 3 m

Schorl   black $NaFe_3B_3Al_3(Al_3Si_6O_{27})(OH)_4$

Dravite $\begin{cases}\text{garnet-red} \\ \text{brown}\end{cases}$ $NaMg_3B_3Al_3(Al_3Si_6O_{27})(OH)_4$

Uvite   white $CaMg_3B_3Al_3(Al_3Si_6O_{27})(O,OH)_4$

Elbaite $\begin{cases}\text{red} \\ \text{green} \\ \text{blue, etc.}\end{cases}$ $Na(Al,Fe,Li,Mg)_3B_3Al_3(Al_3Si_6O_{27})(O,OH,F)_4$

Environment: A high-temperature and pressure mineral, forming in igneous and metamorphic rocks, and best developed in pegmatites, less often in high-temperature veins.

Crystal description: Commonly in prismatic crystals, sometimes very large and up to a yard (1 m) long. Usually triangular or nearly triangular in cross section. Tabular crystals are rare enough to be notable. In the colored crystals the colors often change from one end to the other or from the center outward. Also in veins of fine needles or in black masses.

Physical properties: Black, white, blue, green, red, pink, brown, colorless. *Luster* glassy; *hardness* 7–7½; *gravity* 3.0–3.3; *fracture* easy across the crystal, uneven to conchoidal; *cleavage* poor prismatic and rhombohedral. Opaque to transparent; strongly charged electrically on heating and cooling; magnesia varieties (forming in dolomite) fluorescent yellow in shortwave ultraviolet light.

Composition: A complex series of compounds with varying quantities and ratios of sodium, calcium, magnesium, lithium, aluminum, and iron but with a constant structure and content of boron, aluminum, silica, and the volatiles (B_2O_3 averages about 10%; Li_2O in colored varieties is only 1.0 to 1.5%).

Tests: Fusibility depends upon the composition; the brown magnesium varieties are most easily fused and lithia varieties are infusible. Some form a crust of brownish powder. Will attract dust, ashes, or bits of paper if warmed and cooled.

Distinguishing characteristics: The bulging triangular cross section of the crystal is usually all that is required. The poor cleavage separates it from the pyroxenes and amphiboles.

Occurrence: Tourmaline is found in the U.S. wherever coarse granitic rocks and their related pegmatite dikes come to the surface. New England — particularly the vicinity of West Paris, Maine — and San Diego Co., California, are famous for their colored tourmalines. Black tourmalines are found in pegmatites in many states, and tourmaline-bearing schists are also found in Maine and California. The brown magnesium dravite tourmalines of St. Lawrence Co., New York, are formed in a metamorphosed limestone. Similar small brown crystals have been found in the Inwood dolomite along the Harlem River in New

York City, and giant ones at Yinniethara, Western Australia. It has been noted that dravite morphologically seems to be alike at both ends. The prism faces are sharp, there is no rounding, and the Australian crystals could be taken for slightly elongated dodecahedrons. A colorless "dravite" from Gouverneur, New York, suggests a possibility of providing the (till now) only synthetic uvite variety. An odd schorl found in Mexico, with iron replacing Na, has been called buergerite.

Since tourmaline is valued as a gem mineral, foreign localities have been sought out, and the state of Minas Gerais, Brazil, is the chief present source of gem material. Many localities in Madagascar have yielded large crystals with interesting color-zoning in triangular patterns following the growth stages of the terminations. South West Africa yields fine green crystals; the island of Elba, off the Italian coast, is famous for its pink crystals, often tipped with black; and the Urals produced some fine deep reds. Chainpur, Nepal, produces light-hued elbaites of gemstone quality, with Kabul, Afghanistan, a recent contributor.

Interesting facts: The colored tourmaline varieties make valuable gems, and these as well as the more glassy black varieties are used for electrical apparatus that depends upon their pressure-electric (piezoelectricity) characteristic. The gem varieties have been given special names: the red known as rubellite, the blue as indicolite. Tourmaline to the gem trade means the green variety.

BERYL $Be_3Al_2Si_6O_{18}$ **Pl. 41**

Hexagonal — Dihexagonal bipyramidal $\dfrac{6\ 2\ 2}{m\ m\ m}$

Environment: Almost exclusively a pegmatite mineral, rarely in high-temperature veins and pockets where it has been formed from beryllium-bearing gases or very hot solutions.

Crystal description: One of the most beautifully crystallized minerals, usually in prismatic hexagons, sometimes several feet long and weighing many pounds. Rarely in tabular crystals; the pink cesium beryls more likely to have this flat habit. Also massive and embedded as grains or columnar masses.

Physical properties: White, blue, yellow, green, pink. *Luster* glassy; *hardness* 8; *gravity* 2.6–2.8; *fracture* conchoidal; *cleavage* poor basal. Transparent to translucent; sometimes weakly fluorescent yellow (emerald may be pink to deep red also, especially the synthetics).

Composition: Beryllium aluminum silicate (14.0% BeO, 19.0% Al_2O_3, 67.0% SiO_2; sodium, lithium, and cesium may replace parts of the beryllium, thus reducing the BeO content and lowering its value as an ore).

Tests: Glows white, does not decrepitate too violently to remain intact in the flame, and fuses with great difficulty to a white glass. Insoluble in the common acids.

Distinguishing characteristics: The pegmatitic occurrence and 6-sided outline are very characteristic. Only likely to be confused with apatite (which is much softer and is fluorescent and soluble in acid), with white, massive topaz (wholly infusible), and with quartz (decrepitates violently).

Occurrence: Ordinary beryl is the chief ore of beryllium. Transparent varieties have gem value and are aquamarine (blue and blue-green), emerald (green), golden beryl (yellow-brown), and morganite (pink). Since as a rule it is a mineral of the ancient, deeply buried rocks, it will be found where pegmatites have been exposed at the surface by weathering. New England has many localities; the beryls usually appear as well-formed crystals in quartz and feldspar and ordinarily are broken free without much difficulty. North Carolina is also a source of common beryl, and the emerald variety occurs at several localities in the state. Tabular beryl crystals have been found in some abundance in New Mexico at Dixon. Large crystals are found in the Black Hills of South Dakota. Short-prismatic pink beryls occur with the blue beryl, kunzite, and colored tourmaline in San Diego Co., California. An unusual occurrence for beryl is that of deep pink crystals in the Wha Wha Mountains, Utah. In one area they are more or less embedded in gray-white rhyolite, $1-1\frac{1}{2}$ in. (2-3 cm) long and deep rose in hue. Smaller, flatter, and paler raspberry-pink crystals have been found in gas cavities in the Thomas Range (Utah) rhyolite, best known for its topaz and bixbyite.

Emeralds are found in veins in a black limestone at Muso, and in a pegmatite-like vein at Chivor, Colombia. Biotite schists bordering a pegmatite are the source of the emeralds in the Takowaja River, U.S.S.R., accompanied there by chrysoberyl and phenakite. Large crystals of aquamarine and fine morganites come from Madagascar. Brazil is the chief source of aquamarine, and crystals weighing several hundred pounds (100-150 kg) have been recovered from streambeds, principally in Minas Gerais, Brazil. In a tin mine of South Africa, clusters of slender needles are important gangue minerals in an unusual vein deposit.

The Pyrosilicate Type   Si:O $=$ Si$_2$O$_7$

Silicates of this type contain groups of two SiO$_4$ tetrahedrons, sharing one of the oxygens. Aluminum is usually not present. They have no special characteristics that make them distinctive.

The crystals are often tabular, and, because of the frequent presence of heavy elements, may be high in specific gravity.

HEMIMORPHITE $Zn_4Si_2O_7(OH)_2 \cdot 2(H_2O)$ **Pl. 42**
Orthorhombic — Rhombic pyramidal m m 2
Environment: The oxidized zone of zinc deposits.
Crystal description: Commonly crystallized in flattened prismatic plates up to an inch (2–3 cm) in length, attached at the base so that the different development of the lower end (indicative of its rare symmetry) is not apparent. Also in mammillary rounded groups with crystallized surfaces (Franklin, New Jersey) and in smoother botryoidal knobs, granular, massive, and earthy.
Physical properties: White, sometimes slightly stained with iron or copper (brown and blue or green). *Luster* glassy; *hardness* $4\frac{1}{2}$–5; *gravity* 3.4–3.5; *fracture* uneven to poor conchoidal; *cleavage* prismatic. Transparent to translucent. Strongly susceptible to electrical charges with changing temperature; often fluorescent pale orange in longwave ultraviolet light.
Composition: Basic hydrated zinc silicate (67.5% ZnO, 25.0% SiO_2, 7.5% H_2O).
Tests: Decrepitates, and readily becomes frosted; the coating yellow when hot, turning white when cold. Then fluoresces bright orange in longwave ultraviolet, white in shortwave ultraviolet.
Distinguishing characteristics: Distinguished from smithsonite by its lack of bubbling in acid; recognized as a zinc mineral by its colored coating from blowpiping. Heavier than prehnite and the similar zeolites.
Occurrence: The best U.S. specimens were found in the Stone Mine, Leadville, Colorado, and at Elkhorn, Montana. Solid masses of botryoidal, white, wormlike crystalline surfaces were obtained in the early days at Franklin, New Jersey. Excellent examples have come from Mapimí, Durango, Mexico, with crystals an inch (2.5 cm) and more in length standing up on a cavernous matrix of limonite and hematite. Crusts of upstanding, flat, and well-terminated crystals $\frac{1}{2}$–1 in. (1–2 cm) long and $\frac{1}{8}$–$\frac{1}{4}$ in. (1–3 mm) thick have been found at Santa Eulalia, Chihuahua, Mexico — many piercing white rhombohedral calcite. They are very unlike most hemimorphites. The sw. Missouri crystals are small and there is much earthy hemimorphite mixed with earthy smithsonite ("drybone ore").
Interesting facts: The old name, calamine, is widely used but has been changed by international agreement to hemimorphite, which describes the interesting crystal class to which it belongs, and at the same time will eliminate international confusion resulting from the European use of "calamine" for the carbonate and "smithsonite" for the silicate.

BERTRANDITE Be$_4$Si$_2$O$_7$(OH)$_2$ **Pl. 46**
Orthorhombic — Rhombic pyramidal m m 2

Environment: A secondary mineral forming in hot-water-altered pegmatites from an attack on beryl.

Crystal description: Recognizable only when in distinct crystals, always small, commonly tabular parallel to the base. The pearly luster of the base is quite characteristic, and is probably due to a lamellar parallel growth of individual crystals. Often twinned into "heart-shaped" twins, which are then not tabular in habit but are very typical.

Physical properties: Colorless, flesh color. *Luster* pearly on base, glassy otherwise; *hardness* 6; *gravity* 2.6; *fracture* flaky; *cleavage* perfect basal, good prismatic. Transparent to translucent; strongly affected electrically by temperature changes.

Composition: Basic beryllium silicate (42.1% BeO, 50.3% SiO$_2$, 7.6% H$_2$O).

Tests: Whitens but will hardly fuse on charcoal, insoluble in acid. Turns blue with cobalt nitrate test.

Distinguishing characteristics: Found almost exclusively in beryl pegmatites, thus eliminating most other minerals. It is less fusible than the feldspars, but is difficult to distinguish from late feldspar growths in pockets. Usually these will be attached to earlier feldspars and aligned with them so that a group of prominences will reflect light simultaneously, while the randomly oriented bertrandites reflect as individuals. Twinned crystals are more easily recognized. The zeolites (stilbite) will fuse easily.

Occurrence: Bertrandite is usually considered rare, but actually is far more common than realized. It is likely to be encountered in any beryl pegmatite that clearly has a history of secondary mineral formation, such as etching of the beryl, the formation of albite — especially the cleavelandite variety — or sulfide and calcite deposition in late cavities. The best crystals came from Mt. Antero, Colorado, and are to ½ in. (1 cm) long. Excellent small crystals are found in pockets in the cleavelandite feldspar at Portland, Connecticut. Small crystals were found coating beryl of Bedford, Westchester Co., New York. It is associated with apatite at Stoneham, Maine.

Pseudomorphs of masses of bertrandite plates after beryl are found in a pegmatite in Jefferson Co., Colorado, and similarly in the state of Rio Grande do Norte in Brazil. Small primary crystals have been found on cassiterite-mica seams in Portugal and on beryl at Raade, Norway. Most European examples are inconspicuous, occupying cavities where beryl once grew.

Interesting facts: Though hemimorphic, like hemimorphite, the symmetry is less apparent in this mineral because the crystals are so commonly flattened parallel to the basal pinacoid. Hence, the slight difference in truncations on upper and lower edges is not especially noticeable.

DANBURITE $CaB_2Si_2O_8$ **Pl. 42**

Orthorhombic — Rhombic bipyramidal $\frac{2}{m}\frac{2}{m}\frac{2}{m}$

Environment: Typically in high-temperature deposits, either in veins or contact-metamorphosed rocks. Also in pegmatites. May be more common than supposed.

Crystal description: Usually prismatic crystals, often resembling topaz. May be very small and slender, or as much as 12 in. (30 cm) long and 1 in. (2.5 cm) across. Sometimes corroded so that they shatter easily. Grow free in pockets or embedded in rock.

Physical properties: Colorless, white, pale pink, gray, brownish, straw-yellow. *Luster* glassy; *hardness* 7; *gravity* 3.0; *fracture* uneven to conchoidal; *cleavage* poor basal. Transparent to translucent.

Composition: Calcium borosilicate (22.8% CaO, 28.4% B_2O_3, 48.8% SiO_2).

Tests: Fuses with little difficulty to a milky glass that fluoresces bright blue in shortwave ultraviolet.

Distinguishing characteristics: The crystal form of danburite is similar to that of barite and topaz; its hardness distinguishes it from the barite group and the fusibility distinguishes it from the topaz group.

Occurrence: Formerly the most spectacular danburite crystals were regarded as those from the Toruku and Obira Mines in Miyazaki and Ôita Prefectures, Kyushu I., Japan, which are clear at the summit and may grade down to milky. They are as much as 4 in. (10 cm) long and were implanted on axinite. The original occurrence at Danbury, Connecticut, was of corroded brownish crystals with dolomite in white feldspar, but appears to have been lost. A somewhat similar occurrence is at Russell, St. Lawrence Co., New York. At De Kalb, New York, it occurs in corroded embedded grains in a white pegmatite quartz.

Slender, colorless prismatic crystals by the thousands lined a fissure at Skopi, Switzerland, associated with chlorite. Danburite occurs in Burma in the dolomitic marble with the rubies, often in large straw-yellow, gemmy masses. In Bolivia doubly terminated crystals have been found embedded in a dolomite with gypsum, colored white to gray from inclusions of foreign matter. Once in abundance in crystal clusters, from Charcas, San Luis Potosí, Mexico. Large milky crystals to 4 in. (10 cm) and half as broad have been found in a pegmatite in Baja California. Giant crystals, white and milky but well formed, have been found at Vostochnaya, Siberia. Some are as much as 10 or 12 in. (25–30 cm) long.

Microscopic crystals have been observed in salt-dome insoluble residues in the Gulf states.

Interesting facts: Sometimes it is cut as a colorless or straw-colored gem for collectors.

The Orthosilicate Type   Si:O = 1:4

The silicates of this type have the highest ratio of O to Si, which means that the tetrahedrons are independent, not interlocking. Chemically they differ greatly and there is no notable tendency for any elements to be present or lacking. The packing is close, with the heavier elements dominant over silica, so the members are fairly high in specific gravity, and hard. The crystals are rather equant in their development, with little tendency toward prismatic or platy habits.

Olivine Series

OLIVINE $(Mg,Fe)_2SiO_4$ **Pl. 42, 46**

Orthorhombic — Rhombic bipyramidal $\dfrac{2\ \ 2\ \ 2}{m\ m\ m}$

Environment: A common rock-forming mineral of the darker rocks, never found with free quartz. Common in meteorites.

Crystal description: Usually in embedded grains, rarely in free-growing crystals; commonly any free crystals that are found will be altered to serpentine. Solid granular masses of olivine are known (dunite).

Physical properties: Green, light gray, brown. *Luster* glassy; *hardness* $6\frac{1}{2}$–7; *gravity* 3.3–3.4; *fracture* conchoidal; *cleavage* 1 fair and 1 poor. Transparent to translucent.

Composition: Olivine is really a series of minerals of varying compositions, ranging from the pure magnesium silicate (forsterite) through chrysolite, the magnesium iron silicate, to fayalite, the iron silicate (SiO_2 will average about 36.1% for a 1:1 Mg:Fe ratio).

Tests: Infusible but slowly soluble in hydrochloric acid. High-iron varieties fuse to dark magnetic globule; but even if unfused, powder may still become slightly magnetic, if high enough in iron.

Distinguishing characteristics: It is usually identified by its color and occurrence. No similar mineral of this hardness and color is likely to be encountered in the same environment. Apatite is usually fluorescent and softer; green tourmaline comes in granite pegmatites where olivine could not form; garnet is easily fusible. A green glass produced by assayers is often confused with olivine, but it is unstable and an efflorescence forms on the surface.

Occurrence: Solid, granular masses are found in basalt bombs in Arizona, near volcanic cinder cones, and in the Hawaiian lavas. A bed of slightly finer granular material is found near Webster, Jackson Co., North Carolina. Isolated crystals will be found in many porphyries of the Southwest, and fair-sized rounded grains may be found on anthills, with garnets, near Holbrook, Arizona. Common in the Italian volcanic bombs and in the old German volcanoes of the Eifel district. Large crystals formed near Møre and Snarum, Norway, but most were then altered to serpentine. A vein of shattered and serpentinized chrysolite which cements a number of fresh unaltered crystals cuts serpentine on St. John's I. in the Red Sea. It is the chief source of jewelry peridots, but large corroded crystals have also been found in Burma. The crystals may be $2\frac{1}{2}$–3 in. (7–8 cm) long and about the same across and through. See also basalt and peridotite (pp. 15, 18).

Interesting facts: Dunite has been considered for refractory use and as a source of magnesium. The gem peridot is the chrysolite variety of olivine.

PHENAKITE Be_2SiO_4 **Pl. 42**

Hexagonal — rhombohedral $\overline{3}$

Environment: A mineral of pegmatites and high-temperature veins.

Crystal description: Almost always in free, well-developed crystals, which range from rhombohedral scales to short, or even long, prisms. Usually small, commonly only a fraction of an inch (0.5 cm) across, and often penetration-twinned.

Physical properties: Colorless and white. *Luster* glassy; *hardness* $7\frac{1}{2}$–8; *gravity* 3.0; *fracture* condhoidal; *cleavage* poor prismatic. Transparent to translucent.

Composition: Beryllium silicate (45.6% BeO, 54.4% SiO_2).

Tests: Infusible and insoluble in acids. Usually does not decrepitate.

Distinguishing characteristics: Crystals provide the best clues; the rhombohedral scales can only be confused with one of the carbonates, which will be acid-soluble, and soft. The prismatic crystals often resemble those of quartz, but quartz is striated horizontally on the prisms, whereas phenakite is striated vertically. Topaz has a basal, and better, cleavage. Quartz decrepitates, beryl will whiten and fuse on thinnest edges.

Occurrence: The best U.S. specimens are from Mt. Antero, Colorado, in pegmatitic pockets in short-prismatic, commonly penetration-twinned crystals, associated with beryl, fluorite, and quartz. Also near Colorado Springs at several localities in the Cheyenne Mountains district in rhombohedral-habit crystals, often perched on microcline feldspar, with smoky quartz. Similar crystals are found on Baldface Mountain in New Hampshire on the Maine border, and not far away, at Lord's Hill, Maine, prismatic crystals to $3/4$ in. (1.5 cm) long grow on smoky quartz.

The most attractive specimens are flat crystals up to 2 in. (5 cm) across, with short-prism zones, often grouped in great clusters at São Miguel de Piraçicaba, Minas Gerais, Brazil. The largest crystals are prisms embedded in cleavelandite feldspar or white quartz at Kragero, Norway. They attain 6 or 8 in. (15–20 cm) in length and are an inch or more (2–3 cm) thick. The original occurrence was of 2–3 in. (5–8 cm) crystals in mica, with the emeralds of Sverdlovsk (Ekaterinburg) in the U.S.S.R. **Interesting facts:** Named from a Greek word for "to deceive," because it was long confused with quartz. A specimen was pictured in a British mineralogical work in 1811 and described as white tourmaline twenty years before it was recognized as a new mineral.

WILLEMITE Zn_2SiO_4 **Pl. 42**
Hexagonal — rhombohedral $\overline{3}$

Environment: Secondary, in oxidized portions of zinc veins, and in one metamorphosed oxidized zinc deposit.
Crystal description: Usually small and simple, short-prismatic or rhombohedral. The freak Franklin (New Jersey) occurrence has produced very large embedded crystals (troostite) in white calcite and, in cavities, well-formed small and highly fluorescent ones, sometimes with steep terminations on slender prisms. Also massive, fibrous, radiating.
Physical properties: White or colorless, commonly stained reddish brown by iron (Belgian occurrence), or pale blue by copper (w. U.S. occurrences); also reddish, green, yellow-green, yellow, orange, black. *Luster* resinous to glassy; *hardness* $5\frac{1}{2}$; *gravity* 3.9–4.2; *fracture* uneven to conchoidal; *cleavage* basal. Transparent to translucent; often strongly fluorescent and sometimes phosphorescent and triboluminescent (gives flash of light when struck with metal point).
Composition: Zinc silicate (73.0% ZnO, 27.0% SiO_2, with manganese replacing up to 12% of the Zn at Franklin, New Jersey, where it may be in large, dull, reddish or grayish crystals and be the variety known as troostite.
Tests: Ordinary willemite is nearly infusible, but the Franklin variety fuses with difficulty. A chip dipped in sodium carbonate fuses to a dark brown enamel, a small tip of which is colored green after reheating with a drop of cobalt nitrate placed on it. Soluble in hydrochloric acid.
Distinguishing characteristics: A mineral recognized as a zinc mineral by the cobalt nitrate test can be distinguished from hemimorphite by the failure to give off moisture in the closed

tube. It would be distinguished from smithsonite by a greater hardness and by slow, quiet solution in hydrochloric acid (smithsonite bubbles). Recognized in Franklin specimens usually by its brilliant green fluorescence and by its associates of zincite and franklinite. Often fluorescent also in the other occurrences.

Occurrence: The pre-eminent willemite occurrence is at Franklin, New Jersey, where, with franklinite and zincite in a green, black, and red mixture, it is a principal zinc ore. At this locality it has had several stages of formation and is also present in free crystals lining cavity walls and in large coarse crystals embedded in crystalline limestone. It has been suggested that the Franklin deposit, with its unique mineralogy, is the result of the metamorphism of an oxidized zinc-sulfide ore body, once composed of the conventional hemimorphite and smithsonite. Willemite is generally recognized as an important secondary zinc ore in African occurrences, where at Tsumeb it forms blue and green crystal crusts, and at Grootfontein, in South West Africa, where it forms almost gemmy light brown crystal clusters.

The American Southwest is now known to have a number of willemite occurrences; some of the best white and pale bluish crusts came from the Mammoth Mine at Tiger, Arizona. Small, colorless, platy crystals are embedded in a greenish serpentine rock at Balmat, New York. The pale blue gemmy crystals found in nepheline syenites in Greenland and at St. Hilaire, Quebec, seem to be primary in origin.

The original occurrence was at Altenberg, Moresnet, Belgium, in small reddish-brown crystals. It was named for William I of Belgium in 1830, even though the substance was described before that from Franklin, without having been given a mineral name at the time.

DIOPTASE H_2CuSiO_4 **Pl. 43**
Hexagonal — rhombohedral $\overline{3}$

Environment: Oxidized zones of copper ores, particularly in arid climates.

Crystal description: Usually crystallized, with the crystals generally quite small; short-prismatic to rhombohedral habit; long-prismatic habit rare.

Physical properties: Emerald-green. *Luster* glassy; *hardness* 5; *gravity* 3.3–3.4; *fracture* uneven to conchoidal; *cleavage* perfect rhombohedral. Transparent to translucent.

Composition: Hydrous silicate of copper (50.4% CuO, 38.2% SiO_2, 11.4% H_2O).

Tests: Crystals dull in hydrochloric acid; decrepitate, blacken, and give water in closed tube; turn brown on charcoal, without fusing.

Distinguishing characteristics: It is harder than most similar green minerals — the copper sulfates, carbonates, and the phosphates. Rhombohedral termination is invariable and typical. Brochantite reacts on charcoal, is softer, and crushes easily to a green powder. Malachite disolves in hydrochloric acid with effervescence. The bluish cast of dioptase's green is very distinctive; experienced collectors can spot this typical shade at some distance. Once found, it becomes unmistakable.

Occurrence: There is no outstanding U.S. occurrence. Rich crusts of very slender, short, upright green needles associated with willemite and wulfenite were found at Tiger, Arizona, in the Mammoth Mine. Other Arizona localities include the Christmas Mine and Salome, always as crusts of tiny crystals. Because of the similarity to brochantite and malachite, it is probably more common than generally realized at many of the western copper mines. Copiapó, Chile, has two mines where the thin U.S.-type crystals have been found. Mexico has small crystals too, but Western Hemisphere examples take second place to those of the Eastern Hemisphere.

Tsumeb, South West Africa, is remarkable as the source of the largest dioptase crystals, which may be as much as 1 in. (2.5 cm) long. More slender prismatic crystals to 2 in. (5 cm) long have been found at Mindouli in the Congo Republic. The original locality was in the Kirghiz Steppe, Ural Mountains, in seams in a limestone, on brownish quartz. Dioptase has always been one of the most popular and desirable minerals to the general collector. Good specimens are usually expensive.

Humite Group   Pl. 43

This is a group of closely related minerals that chemically can be considered a mixture of forsterite (Mg_2SiO_4) with brucite [$Mg(OH)_2$], the layer of brucite alternating or lying between 2, 3, or 4 layers of forsterite. The members of the group and their formulas are:

NORBERGITE	$Mg_2SiO_4 \cdot Mg(OH,F)_2$	or $Mg_3(SiO_4)(F,OH)_2$
CHONDRODITE	$2Mg_2SiO_4 \cdot Mg(OH,F)_2$	or $Mg_5(SiO_4)_2(F,OH)_2$
HUMITE	$3Mg_2SiO_4 \cdot Mg(OH,F)_2$	or $Mg_7(SiO_4)_3(F,OH)_2$
CLINOHUMITE	$4Mg_2SiO_4 \cdot Mg(OH,F)_2$	or $Mg_9(SiO_4)_4(F,OH)_2$

Humite and norbergite: orthorhombic $\dfrac{2\ 2\ 2}{m\ m\ m}$

Clinohumite and chondrodite: monoclinic $\dfrac{2}{m}$

The relative length of the vertical axis varies, depending on the composition; the two other axes remain constant. Consequently, the general appearance, as well as the blowpipe properties, are about the same in all, and the amateur collector cannot distinguish the members of the group. Chondrodite, found in metamorphic iron deposits, is the most frequent and the most spectacular member of the group. With the others, it is also found in contact and regionally metamorphosed dolomitic marbles. Iron is usually present, replacing some of the magnesium. Formulas are often written thus: humite $(Mg,Fe)_7Si_3O_{12}(F,OH)_2$.

Crystal description: Commonly in embedded, shapeless or nearly shapeless grains in crystalline limestones. Well-formed crystals with good, shiny faces (but rather complex and difficult to orient) are found in a few places: Tilly Foster Mine, Brewster, New York, and Kafveltorp, Sweden. The Italian crystals are smaller.

Physical properties: Red-brown to yellow. *Luster* glassy; *hardness* 6-6½; *gravity* 3.1-3.2; *fracture* subconchoidal; *cleavage* basal, not always easy to observe. Transparent to translucent; sometimes yellow fluorescence.

Composition: Basic magnesium fluosilicates (see above; about 57% MgO, several percent of FeO, and 35% SiO_2).

Tests: Infusible, but give water in closed tube.

Distinguishing characteristics: None of the similar minerals give water in the closed tube. Likely to be confused with garnet (which, however, is fusible), with brown tourmaline (usually fusible), and with staurolite (which is heavier and unlikely to be found in the same environment).

Occurrence: The world's finest locality for chondrodite is the famous Tilly Foster Mine, at Brewster, New York, where free-growing crystals up to 2 in. (5 cm) across were found in a serpentine, associated with magnetite and equally remarkable clinochlore crystals. The finest are deep red-brown, shiny, and transparent, but many are more or less altered to serpentine. Smaller yellower brown and less well-formed crystals are found in metal sulfides at Kafveltorp, Sweden. Yellow-brown grains of chondrodite are common in the crystalline limestones of n. New Jersey, associated with dark gray spinel octahedrons.

All members of the humite group have been reported in paler crystals in the altered limestone blocks thrown out on the flanks of Vesuvius (Monte Somma).

The Garnets Pl. 43

On the basis of chemical analyses, the members of this common group have been divided into two series that mix with each other to a limited extent, but within each group they appear to grade into each other without sharp lines of demarcation. The amateur can only approximate identities from color, gravity, and associations. One series has been christened the "pyralspite" series, from the names pyrope, almandine, and spessartine; the other series, the "ugrandite," from uvarovite, grossular, and andradite.

PYROPE	$Mg_3Al_2Si_3O_{12}$	
ALMANDINE	$Fe_3Al_2Si_3O_{12}$	
SPESSARTINE	$Mn_3Al_2Si_3O_{12}$	Cubic — hexoctahedral
UVAROVITE	$Ca_3Cr_2Si_3O_{12}$	$\dfrac{4}{m}\dfrac{2}{3}\dfrac{2}{m}$
GROSSULAR	$Ca_3Al_2Si_3O_{12}$	
ANDRADITE	$Ca_3Fe_2Si_3O_{12}$	

In detail they are as follows:

Name	Color	Principal occurrence	Specific gravity
Pyrope	Deep yellow-red	In igneous rocks	3.5
Almandine	Deep violet-red	Metamorphic rocks	4.3
Spessartine	Brown, with a reddish or pinkish tone	Rhyolite pockets, pegmatites, and in metamorphic rocks with Mn	4.2
Uvarovite	Emerald-green	Chromium deposits	3.8
Grossular	Various usually pale tints, not reds	Metamorphosed limestones	3.5
Andradite	Pale tints to brown and black, not reds	Igneous and metamorphics; on seams, and in crusts but not in mica schists	3.8

Crystal description: Crystals are very common, especially in some varieties, depending in part on the type of their usual occurrence. Pyropes in volcanic rocks ordinarily are not in well-formed crystals. Almandine, growing in mica schists, usually shows faces of the dodecahedron or the trapezohedron; as does spessartine, which forms in open cavities. Uvarovite commonly coats seams in chromite and so is free to form good dodecahedral crystals. Grossular forms on seams and shows smooth trapezohedral and dodecahedral faces, crystallizes in pockets in pegmatite (essonite or "cinnamon stone," light brown in color), or is embedded in limestone, where it is usually in good dodecahedrons. Andradite commonly coats seams and forms small lustrous crystals, unless embedded in asbestos (demantoid, in Val Malenco, Italy, and in the Urals), when it may be rounded. Occasionally in sandy aggregates of fine grains, or in massive white, pink, or green veins (grossular, particularly: "South African jade").
Physical properties: Red, brown, black, green, yellow, white. *Luster* glassy; *hardness* 6–7½; *gravity* 3.5–4.3; *fracture* con-

choidal to uneven; *cleavage* none; but occasional partings. Transparent to translucent. Almandine weakly magnetic.

Composition: A series of aluminum silicates with magnesium, iron, and manganese; and a 2nd series of calcium silicates with chromium, aluminum, and iron in which the SiO_2 amounts to about 35%.

Tests: Theoretically, distinguished by their variation in color, fusibility, and behavior:

Pyrope	Fuses with slight difficulty to black nonmagnetic globule
Almandine	Fuses to black magnetic globule
Spessartine	Fuses with boiling to gray or black nonmagnetic globule
Uvarovite	Almost infusible, but always bright green
Grossular	Fuses easily to light-colored nonmagnetic globule that colors blue when a cobalt nitrate drop is added and it is remelted
Andradite	Darkens, and then fuses to black magnetic globule

However, enough iron is present in many garnets to make the globule magnetic anyway.

Distinguishing characteristics: The garnet varieties are so generally crystallized and so typical in their occurrence that the group is very easily recognized. Red grains seen embedded in metamorphic and igneous rocks are most likely to be garnets. Apatite is softer and does not melt. Altered pyrite gives a limonite streak; zircons often fluoresce and will not fuse. Short tourmalines can look like dodecahedrons, but tourmaline will not fuse like garnet.

Occurrence: Garnet is one of the commonest of all minerals, and ordinary localities are far too numerous to list. Special localities might be worth mentioning. Pyrope is found in transparent grains in Arizona and New Mexico, in Bohemia, and in the South African diamond pipes. Large almandine crystals are found in the Adirondacks at North Creek, New York, where it is mined for garnet paper. Almandine is the most widely used of the jewelry stones and comes, for this use, from Madagascar and India. Spessartine is less common; it is usually pegmatitic or associated with metamorphic manganese deposits. At Nathrop, Colorado, and in the Thomas Range, Utah, it occurs in brown-black crystals in gas cavities in a light-colored lava flow (rhyolite).

Uvarovite occurs mainly as green crusts often associated with other minerals of chromium, usually on seams and in fissures in that mineral. The largest crystals, to 1 in. (2 cm), have been found at a Finnish copper mine — an untypical occurrence.

Grossular has been found in light-colored crystals most often in contact-metamorphic deposits, as in Morelos and Lake Jaco,

Mexico, where it forms light pink and white crystals associated with vesuvianite. Massive white grossular has been found with jade in Burma and has been carved by the Chinese. Green grossular garnet occurs in Africa in a solid vein, and some has been carved and sold as "South African jade." A Tanzanian emerald-green chrome grossular rivals demantoid as a gemstone, but lacks its fire (tsavorite). Andradite is probably the rarest of the garnets, and may form on metamorphic rock crevices as crusts of lustrous crystals; yellow-green topazolite and emerald-green demantoid are varieties. Black melanite andradite is found in San Benito Co., California.

Interesting facts: Some varieties are important gemstones; pyrope is used in garnet paper, a variety of sandpaper esteemed for its better cutting qualities.

VESUVIANITE (Idocrase) $Ca_{10}Mg_2Al_4(SiO_4)_5(Si_2O_7)_2(OH)_4$

Tetragonal — Ditetragonal bipyramidal $\frac{4\ 2\ 2}{m\ m\ m}$ **Pl. 43**

Environment: Contact-metamorphic deposits in impure limestones, associated with garnet, diopside, and wollastonite; rare in pegmatite.

Crystal description: Almost always in crystals, either free-growing and tending toward a prismatic habit with shiny faces, or embedded in crystalline calcite and tending toward a stubby or bipyramidal habit. Also massive.

Physical properties: Green, brown, yellow, blue ("cyprine"), violet. *Luster* glassy; *hardness* $6\frac{1}{2}$; *gravity* 3.4–3.5; *fracture* conchoidal to uneven; *cleavage* poor prismatic. Transparent to translucent.

Composition: Basic calcium, iron, magnesium silicate (about 36% CaO, often 5% FeO, plus Fe_2O_3, about 3% MgO, and 16.5% Al_2O_3, 36.5% SiO_2, 3.0% H_2O). Some BeO has been reported in a brown idocrase from Franklin, New Jersey, and a little F is often recorded.

Tests: Fuses easily, with large bubbles, to a shiny, brownish, glassy nonmagnetic sphere.

Distinguishing characteristics: Recognized by its square cross section and very typical crystals. Zircon is infusible and usually fluorescent. The massive material (californite) resembles jade, but jadeite jade fuses even more easily and colors the flame yellow, and nephrite jade is much harder to fuse, eventually making a black glass. Epidote and garnet are magnetic after fusion; tourmaline fuses with great difficulty or not at all.

Occurrence: The finest U.S. vesuvianite crystals have come from an asbestos quarry at Eden Mills, Vermont, embedded in quartz, where they form green, brilliant, prismatic crystals terminated by a pyramid. At the Jeffrey Mine, Asbestos, Quebec, vesuvianite forms loose agregates of pale green crystals — rarely tipped with violet. Large, brown, corroded but shiny crystals with rounded edges and consisting of a base and prisms are found near Olmstedville, New York, where they have been freed from crystalline calcite by weathering. Large, green, corroded, short-prismatic, and bipyramidal crystals have been uncovered in the fields at Magnet Cove, Arkansas.

Limestone quarries at Crestmore, California, were famous for their green-brown bipyramidal crystals in blue calcite. Small emerald-green prismatic crystals of gem quality have been found at Georgetown, California. The massive green vesuvianite known as californite has been found in Butte and Fresno Cos., and along Indian Creek in Siskiyou Co. in California. In Mexico it is associated with the grossular crystals.

Vesuvianite is also common abroad and was first recognized as a distinct mineral in Italy, where it was found on the slopes of Vesuvius (Monte Somma) in metamorphosed limestone blocks expelled from the crater; thus the name vesuvianite. At Pitkäranta (U.S.S.R., but formerly Finland) the light brown vesuvianite crystals are long and thin, like a bundle of nails. Steep, gemmy pyramidal crystals are found in Pakistan. Cuttable yellow-brown crystals come from Quebec and Tanzania.

Epidote Group

This is a rather complex group with several members, most of which are rare and do not grade into more common varieties in a continuous series. There may be considerable substitution of iron and manganese for aluminum. The varieties discussed here are relatively common and sufficiently distinctive in all their properties to be easily recognizable from the descriptions and tests. Crystals are mainly monoclinic.

ZOISITE $Ca_2Al_3(SiO_4)_3(OH)$ **Pl. 44**

Orthorhombic — Rhombic bipyramidal $\dfrac{2}{m}\dfrac{2}{m}\dfrac{2}{m}$

Environment: Metamorphic rocks; also in quartz veins, pegmatites, and some ore deposits.

Crystal description: Usually in crystals, sometimes several in. (10 cm) long, but generally poorly terminated. Best developed when embedded in quartz or sulfides, from which it breaks easily. Also in interlocking masses of needles.

Physical properties: Gray, brown, pink (thulite), blue, violet (tanzanite). *Luster* glassy; *hardness* 6; *gravity* 3.3–3.4; *fracture* subconchoidal to uneven; *cleavage* perfect side pinacoid. Translucent. Thulite may fluoresce yellow-orange in longwave ultraviolet.

Composition: Basic calcium aluminum silicate (24.6% CaO, 33.7% Al_2O_3, 39.7% SiO_2, 2.0% H_2O). Some Fe may replace the

Ca, and when enough is present — over 5% Fe_2O_3 — it tends to grade into clinozoisite and epidote.

Tests: Grows "worms," swells, and fuses in a dark bubbly mass that does not easily melt down to a sphere. Light-colored varieties color blue with 2nd melting after touch with drop of cobalt nitrate solution.

Distinguishing characteristics: Distinguished from the amphiboles by the single plane of cleavage (and a pearly luster on the cleavage face). Tourmaline has no cleavage. Zoisite much lighter color than other members of group. Pink tourmaline is not fluorescent like some thulite. Strong directional coloring (pleochroic), especially tanzanite.

Occurrence: Not uncommon in metamorphic rock areas in the U.S., as in New England, and most easily recognized as gray prismatic crystals in quartz veins. The fluorescent pink variety, thulite, is found in Mitchell Co., North Carolina, in a pegmatite with albite feldspar. Good brown crystals are found embedded in the sulfide ores at Ducktown, Tennessee. In California it occurs in green schists near Sulphur Bank. Thulite derives its name from the ancient one for Norway (Thule), where it occurs associated with blue cryprine at Telemark in attractive specimens. The transparent gemmy variety from Tanzania has been a late, completely unforeseen gemmological wonder that, as tanzanite, has been assiduously promoted into popularity.

EPIDOTE $Ca_2(Al,Fe)_3(SiO_4)_3(OH)$ **Pl. 44**

Monoclinic — prismatic $\dfrac{2}{m}$

Environment: Metamorphic rocks, contact-metamorphosed limestones, altered igneous rocks, pegmatites, and traprocks with zeolites. Common on shrinkage seams in granite, formed from the last gases or solutions to escape.

Crystal description: Commonly crystallized, usually in long, slender, grooved prisms, which are actually stretched out along a horizontal direction and give the impression that the side faces are slanting, if we follow our normal inclination to set the crystals upright. Also in very thin crusts, of small crystals, paler in color, and in greenish films of massive or fine-grained "pistacite" (from the color).

Physical properties: Pistachio-green, green, blackish green, brown, light yellow brown. *Luster* glassy (pearly on cleavage); *hardness* 6–7; *gravity* 3.4–3.5; *fracture* uneven; *cleavage* perfect basal, but base is usually parallel to the length of the crystal. Transparent to translucent; strongly 2 different colors as a translucent prism is rotated, usually showing green and dark brown.

Composition: Basic calcium iron silicate (averaging about

23.5% CaO, 11.5% Fe_2O_3, 25.0% Al_2O_3, 38.0% SiO_2, and just under 2% H_2O).

Tests: Fuses with bubbling to a dull black scoriaceous glass, usually magnetic. Since it is insoluble in dilute hydrochloric acid, can be exposed in calcite veins by an acid soaking of the specimen.

Distinguishing characteristics: The color and the general appearance of epidote are so characteristic that tests are rarely necessary. Actinolite, the green amphibole, has 2 cleavages and does not show the pronounced color change as the prism is rotated. Tourmaline shows no color change this way and has no cleavage.

Occurrence: This mineral is so common that there is little value in mentioning any localities. Prince of Wales I. (Alaska) crystals are remarkable for their size (to 3 in.; 7–8 cm), and their short-prismatic, almost tablet shape. Slender prisms are found in the Mitchell Co. area (North Carolina) on pegmatite feldspar. Epidote and garnet are abundant at several localities in California, where they sometimes can form alternating layers, the shape of the garnet crystal determining the outline. The world's leading locality is Untersulzbachtal, in the Austrian Tyrol, where magnificent, dark, lustrous crystals up to a foot (30 cm) long and an inch (3 cm) or more across were found in a pocket in a chlorite-actinolite schist with colorless apatite crystals. Small sprays of crystals, and large singles and crusts have been found in Baja California and on Guadalupe I. in the Gulf. Larger sprays, up to 3 in. (7–8 cm) long, have been found in Minas Gerais, Brazil, in pegmatites.

ALLANITE (Orthite)   Pl. 44
$(Ca,Ce,La,Na)_2(Al,Fe,Be,Mn,Mg)_3(SiO_4)_3(OH)$

Monoclinic — prismatic $\dfrac{2}{m}$

Environment: Pegmatites, and as a minor mineral in igneous rocks.

Crystal description: Usually in elongated, dull-surfaced crystal grains, embedded in feldspar but so shattered that it is difficult to remove them intact. Large crystals are often thin, dull-surfaced plates.

Physical properties: Black to dark brown. *Luster* pitchy or resinous; *hardness* $5\frac{1}{2}$–6; *gravity* 2.7–4.2; *fracture* subconchoidal to uneven; *cleavage* several poor, not conspicuous. Translucent only on thin edges of splinters; radioactive and showing staining of feldspar dark red around grain, with radiating cracks leading away from it.

Composition: An extremely variable silicate containing rareearth minerals, including thorium, cerium, disprosium, lanthanum, yttrium, and erbium, which may total — as oxides — as much as 20% of the weight.

Tests: Fuses quickly with bubbling to a dull, black magnetic glass. Weakly affects photographic film by its radioactivity. Attacked by acid.

Distinguishing characteristics: It is easily recognized as a radioactive mineral by its effect on the bordering rocks. The magnetism after fusion distinguishes it from uraninite. Similar-looking radioactive minerals, which will have halos of alteration around them in the rock, react very differently under the blowpipe. Magnetite is magnetic without fusion.

Occurrence: Fairly common as small black radioactive grains in coarse granite pegmatite. Also in concentrations in some magnetite and apatite veins, as in Essex and Orange Cos., New York. Fine crystals from Madawaska, Ontario. Small crystals are common in New York City rocks; many specimens were found in the excavations for the Brooklyn-Battery tunnel. Larger crystals have come from: Llano Co., Texas; Chester Co., Pennsylvania; and Warwick, New York. Very large crystals have been found in Oaxaca, Mexico, and in San Diego Co., California. Also common in Europe; particularly good crystals have been found at Arendal, Norway (orthite).

ZIRCON $ZrSiO_4$ Pl. 44

Tetragonal — Ditetragonal bipyramidal $\dfrac{4\ 2\ 2}{m\,m\,m}$

Environment: Common minor accessory of granitic rocks, occasionally in metamorphosed limestones, also in veins in fine-grained nepheline-rich rocks and in pegmatites. Frequently found as a residual heavy mineral in sands and gravels.

Crystal description: Always in crystals, which may be an inch (2 cm) or more across, and in Canada and Australia even larger ones have been found. Usually short-prismatic, sometimes bipyramidal.

Physical properties: Brown, colorless, gray, green, reddish, bluish, violet. *Luster* adamantine; *hardness* $6\frac{1}{2}$-$7\frac{1}{2}$; *gravity* 4.0-4.7; *fracture* conchoidal; *cleavage* 2, usually poor. Transparent to translucent; commonly fluorescent yellow-orange.

Composition: Zirconium silicate (67.2% ZrO_2 with up to 4.0% of hafnium oxide and, often, rare earths, which make it weakly radioactive, 32.8% SiO_2).

Tests: Infusible, but colored varieties may whiten and some varieties glow intensely for a moment (thermoluminescent), although only one time. Fluorescent frequently enough for this to be a good test.

Distinguishing characteristics: The tetragonal shape is very typical, the only common similarly shaped mineral is idocrase, which is much lighter in weight and is readily fusible.

Occurrence: Well-formed sharp crystals are found loose in Henderson Co., North Carolina. Bluish-skinned brown crystals are found in marble at Sparta in n. New Jersey, and very long slender crystals similarly at Natural Bridge, New York. Brown crystals occur in magnetite at an iron mine in Pricetown, Pennsylvania. Small grains are common in heavy sands in North Carolina and south to Florida. Often these are sharp, colorless, perfect crystals.

Very large crystals are found in Renfrew, Ontario. Smaller good crystals come from Tory Hill, Wilberforce, Ontario. Isolated crystals and crusts are common on Cheyenne Mountain, near Colorado Springs, Colorado, with a neighboring occurrence of violet-brown bipyramids in white quartz.

In Brazil it is found in the Poços de Caldas district of Minas Gerais as isolated large crystals in the coarse nepheline syenite. Similar crystals have come from Madagascar and cen. Australia.

Interesting facts: The presence of radioactive elements is indicated by the frequency of radioactive halos around the grains embedded in mica. Often the mineral has broken down and does not have the internal structure required by the crystal shape. Heating makes it revert to the original structure (when it glows) and raises the specific gravity to the upper level. It may also change the color, and the blue zircons of the jewelry commerce are heated brown stones. These often tend to revert to brown, a process hastened by sunlight.

Related species: Cyrtolite is a radioactive zircon easy to recognize by the identical crystal shape, but it has dull convex pyramid faces. On analysis it is found to contain uranium and yttrium. It is abundant in some pegmatites, particularly in Norway, and masses from Bedford, Westchester Co., New York, have actually been used for the recovery of rare earths. Cyrtolite in pegmatites tends to group more than the isolated zircon crystals of the coarse granitic rocks do, and to form a row of crystals, all with rounded faces. It is usually red-brown in color.

DATOLITE $Ca_2B_2(SiO_4)_2(OH)$ **Pl. 44**

Monoclinic — prismatic $\dfrac{2}{m}$

Environment: An associate of the zeolites, in cavities in traprock. Rarely in ore veins.

Crystal description: Usually in crystals, which may be 2 in. (5 cm) across. Often well formed, more or less equidimensional, but all faces not equally lustrous; some usually dull. Also (in Michigan) in white porcelaneous opaque masses of microscopically granular material, commonly stained reddish by iron.

Physical properties: Colorless, light yellow-green, white, stained reddish (fine-grained material). *Luster* glassy and por-

celaneous; *hardness* 5–5½; *gravity* 2.8–3.0; *fracture* conchoidal to uneven; *cleavage* none. Transparent to translucent.
Composition: Basic calcium, boron silicate (35.0% CaO, 21.8% B_2O_3, 37.6% SiO_2, 5.6% H_2O).
Tests: Fuses very easily with bubbling to form a viscous, clear glass ball that fluoresces blue in shortwave ultraviolet.
Distinguishing characteristics: In appearance datolite resembles a zeolite, but the green boron flame, with the easy fusibility and but moderate swelling, is a certain test.
Occurrence: Fine examples are found in the traprocks of the ne. U.S. coast, with the biggest and best examples coming from the Lane Quarry at Westfield, Massachusetts, where it is associated with prehnite, babingtonite, and epidote. The best of the Paterson (New Jersey) specimens, from a similar occurrence, are almost as good.

The cluster of small crystals and the gas-cavity fillings of fine-grained material in the Lake Superior copper mines are also good. The fine-grained porcelaneous Michigan datolite appears not to be found elsewhere. Good crystals are found in Andreasberg in the German Harz, in the Italian and Austrian Alps, and in Tasmania. Remarkably large greenish crystals, closely intergrown and ill defined, have lately come from the Charcas (Mexico) danburite locality. Clear, pseudo-orthorhombic crystals to 1 in. (2 cm) have been found in the Faraday Mine, Bancroft, Ontario.

EUCLASE BeAlSiO$_4$(OH)   **Pl. 42**

Monoclinic — prismatic $\dfrac{2}{m}$

Environment: Almost exclusively a pegmatite mineral, though it has been reported from a Tyrolean locality in crystals to ½ in. (1 cm) and with topaz and emerald in veins.
Crystal description: Probably always in more or less well formed crystals generally very late in a depositional sequence. Usually prismatic and very obviously monoclinic, with well-developed downward-slanting front faces. Rarely flattened enough on the sides to give them a blocky outline.
Physical properties: Colorless, light blue, sapphire-blue, green-blue, pale yellow, pale amethyst, light green. *Luster* glassy; *hardness* 7½; *gravity* 3.09–3.11; *fracture* shelly (conchoidal); *cleavage* perfect side; front and back dome poor. Transparent; often gemmy.
Composition: Basic aluminum silicate (with about 17.2% BeO, 35.2% Al_2O_3, 41.4% SiO_2, 6.2% H_2O).
Tests: Testing seldom necessary, the environment and the crystal shape being so typical. One does not look for barite or celestite in a pegmatite pocket (usual site for euclase). In topaz veins, as in Brazil, it would be very obvious from its color.

Nonfluorescent, holds together with heat, but edges of splinter whiten and finally fuse with little points of white incandescence. **Distinguishing characteristics:** In its associations might be confused with topaz, but the cleavage is parallel to the prism instead of across it, as in topaz. The easy cleavage, which gives it its name, is very distinctive. The color is likely to be irregularly distributed in the crystal.

Occurrence: One of the rare but popular minerals for collectors. It has been cut as an unusual gem, and the green and blue examples command a high price. It is associated in Brazil with the topaz seams in the Ouro Prêto region of Minas Gerais, and has recently been found in São Sebastião de Maranhão in Minas Gerais and in another pegmatite, Alto Santino, in Rio Grande do Norte. In Russia crystals were found with pink topaz in the Sanarka River in gold placers; surprisingly, considering their cleavability, the lovely blue-green crystals were intact and a little waterworn. The largest crystal found is a light blue milky one from Kenya, now in the British Museum (Natural History) and about 6 in. (15 cm) tall. Large colorless cleavages have been found in Brazil and would indicate still bigger crystals. Some fine, blue, side pinacoid-flattened, 1 in. or more (3 cm) crystals have been found with emeralds in Colombia.

TOPAZ $Al_2SiO_4(F,OH)_2$ **Pl. 44**

Orthorhombic — Rhombic bipyramidal $\dfrac{2}{m}\dfrac{2}{m}\dfrac{2}{m}$

Environment: Pegmatites, seams in granitic rock, high-temperature veins and replacements, gas cavities in rhyolite.

Crystal description: Commonly crystallized, often in free-growing transparent crystals, sometimes very large. The base may be conspicuous or may be entirely missing; it is usually present. Also in columnar growth (pycnite); in pseudomorphs after feldspar crystals; granular.

Physical properties: Colorless, white, pale blue, light yellow, yellow-brown, pinkish brown, and pink. *Luster* glassy; *hardness* 8; *gravity* 3.5–3.6; *fracture* conchoidal; *cleavage* perfect basal. Transparent to translucent.

Composition: Aluminum fluohydroxysilicate (56.5% Al_2O_3, 33.3% SiO_2, and about 10% F and OH).

Tests: Infusible, and insoluble in acid. The powder turns blue (alumina) when moistened with cobalt nitrate and heated.

Distinguishing characteristics: Great hardness and its good cleavage are excellent indications, along with its crystal form and typical occurrence and pegmatitic associations. Beryl fuses on thin edges; quartz decrepitates more.

Occurrence: A valuable jewelry stone, especially in the brown and pink tints. Not to be confused with the brown quartz generally sold under the name topaz.

Large topaz crystals are not common in the U.S.; the biggest are probably some crudely shaped white ones found in the pegmatite at Amelia, Virginia, associated with microcline. Clear crystals, several inches (10 cm) across and somewhat etched, came from Devils Head, Colorado. Smaller crystals have come from several Colorado localities near Colorado Springs and on Pikes Peak. Large but deeply etched blue crystals were found at Topsham, Maine, and many 1–2 in. (2–5 cm) crystals were found in small miarolitic cavities in granite with smoky quartz, feldspar, and phenakite at Baldface Mountain, New Hampshire. Less etched blue crystals were found in Mason Co., Texas. Also important in San Diego Co., California, associated with beryl and tourmaline.

The rhyolite flows of the Thomas Range, Utah, and, less conspicuously, of Nathrop, Colorado, contain many gas cavities in which there are 1 in. (3 cm) light brown crystals, which fade to colorless on exposure to light. Larger crystals in the rhyolite are filled with quartz and look opaque; they are always simpler in their terminations. It is associated in Utah with rose beryl and in Colorado with garnet. In San Luis Potosí, Mexico, topaz appears to be alone in the rhyolite seams.

Brazilian topaz is outstanding and comes in pegmatitic colorless and blue crystals, and in a series of quartz veins in rich brown gemmy crystals. Pink crystals of this type have been found in nearby manganese mines. Russian topaz resembles some of the brown Brazilian crystals; and there are occurrences in Afghanistan and in the Ural Mountains, Sanarka River, U.S.S.R., of natural pink crystals of this same growth habit. The finest blue topaz crystals were found years ago in pegmatites in the Ural Mountains. The Saxon crown jewel topazes came from the Schneckenstein in the Erzgebirge near the Czechoslovakian border.

Interesting facts: The brown Brazilian topaz turns pink on heating, and most pink jewelry topaz has been heated. Topaz is a very attractive mineral that forms beautiful crystals and is among the popular gemstones with collectors.

AXINITE $H(Ca,Mn,Fe)_3Al_2B(SiO_4)_4$ **Pl. 45**

Triclinic — pinacoidal $\overline{1}$

Environment: Veins in granitic rock and in contact-metamorphic deposits near granite intrusions.

Crystal description: Always in flattened crystals or crystalline bladed aggregates with many parallel lines on the crystal surfaces. Crystals are extremely characteristic; they often reach 2 in. (5 cm) or more in size, and are the best examples of the triclinic system.

Physical properties: Violet-brown, gray, yellow-orange (Franklin, New Jersey). *Luster* glassy; *hardness* $6\frac{1}{2}$–7; *gravity*

3.3–3.4; *fracture* conchoidal; *cleavage* 1 good and several poor. Transparent to translucent.

Composition: Hydrous calcium, manganese, and iron aluminum borosilicate (about 21% CaO, 3.5% MnO, 9% FeO plus Fe_2O_3, 17.5% Al_2O_3, 5% B_2O_3, 42.5% SiO_2, and 1.5% H_2O; but subject to considerable minor variation).

Tests: Fuses easily all over the grain to a frothy glass, remaining frothy on cooling. Insoluble in hydrochloric acid.

Distinguishing characteristics: The color and crystal form are very distinctive and not likely to be mistaken for any other mineral. Titanite is usually not striated and fuses much less easily, without remaining as a froth upon cooling.

Occurrences: Large crystals have been found in a contact-metamorphic deposit with epidote at Luning, Nevada. Good crystals have been found in Nevada and in Riverside Co., California. The Franklin (New Jersey) occurrence of a red, fluorescent manganese-rich variety is most unusual for color; the light orange-yellow crystals are small but very attractive. Other U.S. occurrences are not rare, but except for some isolated sites in California none is outstanding in quality. N. Baja California has been a good source, in scheelite pits. The Le Bourg-d'Oisans occurrence, in s. France, with epidote, prehnite, and quartz is one of the world's best. Axinite veins are very abundant in the granite and the altered slates of Cornwall. The less flattened crystals from Obira, Japan, are browner and build up into aggregates of parallel crystals, rather than single individuals. Bahia, Brazil, has yielded the largest known complete crystal, 9 in. (22 cm) from point to point.

The Subsilicate Type Si:O = 1:5

This type has independent SiO_4 tetrahedrons, like the orthosilicates, but its minerals contain additional O, which is not in the silica tetrahedrons. In this way we can get a ratio of Si:O in their formulas that is as low as 2:27, and the silicates merge into the titanates, borates, and rare-earth minerals. They might be considered a subtype of the orthosilicate group, since they have the isolated SiO_4 tetrahedrons. They have no diagnostically distinctive characteristics.

ANDALUSITE Al_2SiO_5 **Pl. 45**

Orthorhombic — Rhombic bipyramidal $\dfrac{2\ 2\ 2}{m\,m\,m}$

Environment: Metamorphic rocks and in contact-metamorphic zones near granite intrusions.

Crystal description: Usually in coarse, dull-surfaced crystals with blunt terminations, commonly slightly altered on the surface so that the original luster is lost. The variety chiastolite is embedded in dark schist in cigarlike crystals which in cross section show a pattern of light and dark areas, caused as the growing crystal thrust carbon particles into definite areas. The pattern changes in successive slices through the length of the crystal. Small, gemmy, waterworn andalusite crystals have been found in Brazil and Sri Lanka (Ceylon).

Physical properties: Gray, pink, brown, white (gemmy varieties, greenish and reddish brown). *Luster* glassy; *hardness* $7\frac{1}{2}$; *gravity* 3.1–3.2; *fracture* conchoidal; *cleavage* fair to good prismatic. Transparent to translucent.

Composition: Aluminum silicate (63.2% Al_2O_3, 36.8% SiO_2).

Tests: Infusible and insoluble, but powder is slightly colored blue by strong firing after it is moistened with cobalt nitrate (Al test).

Distinguishing characteristics: The variety chiastolite is easily recognized. The altered appearance and dull surface with the square cross section (dominant prisms are virtually at right angles to each other) are very distinctive. The cobalt nitrate coloration test is much easier to obtain with kyanite and sillimanite than with andalusite.

Occurrence: Like the next two aluminum silicates, andalusite can be used in spark plugs and other porcelains requiring high heat resistance. The clear material makes an interesting gem because of its 2-color effect. Chiastolite is found in Fresno, Kern, and Mariposa Cos., California, and near Lancaster, Massachusetts. Clear pinkish andalusite grains are found in the mica schist of Mt. Washington, New Hampshire. Great gray to white masses were mined at White Mountain, Laws, Inyo Co., California. Good opaque crystals have come from Standish, Maine, and Delaware Co., Pennsylvania. The green Brazilian variety has been called viridine and is said to be manganiferous.

Gemmy andalusite comes from Minas Gerais in Brazil and from Sri Lanka (Ceylon). It is distinctive because of the 2 colors it shows in the sides and ends of the cut stone — green on the sides, red-brown on the ends.

SILLIMANITE Al_2SiO_5 **Pl. 45**

Orthorhombic — Rhombic bipyramidal $\frac{2\ 2\ 2}{m\ m\ m}$

Environment: Mica schists and gneisses, and in contact-metamorphic deposits.

Crystal description: Usually in finely fibrous masses, embedded in rock. Distinct prismatic crystals, clear and transparent, with good pinacoidal cleavage in a rare gemmy variety.

Physical properties: Usually white, sometimes brownish or greenish (clear variety light blue). *Luster* satiny (glassy when clear); *hardness* 6–7 (but splinters and is difficult to determine; gemmy examples are $7\frac{1}{2}$); *gravity* 3.2–3.3; *fracture* splinters, but conchoidal across elongation; *cleavage* perfect pinacoid, usually fibrous. Translucent to transparent.

Composition: Aluminum silicate (63.2% Al_2O_3, 36.8% SiO_2).

Tests: Infusible and insoluble, but the crushed mineral, or a little group of fibers, turns blue when heated with cobalt nitrate solution.

Distinguishing characteristics: Infusibility distinguishes it from fibrous anthophyllite, which it may resemble (anthophyllite fuses to a black magnetic bead). Hardness and brittleness of the fibers distinguish them from those of asbestos.

Occurrence: Relatively rare, in fibrous parallel masses in schist, and often altered to mica; therefore lacking in normal hardness. Interesting because its Burma and Sri Lanka occurrences (where it is found in waterworn, clear, blue, gemmy pebbles) are so unlike the fibrous embedded masses of New England at Worcester, Massachusetts, and Norwich and Willimantic, Connecticut. Also in New York and Pennsylvania. Sometimes, as in Brazil, it is compact enough to form waterworn pebbles that may be cut to resemble a cat's-eye. Pebbles of compact fibers water-wear into very smooth and shiny surfaces, even more lustrous than waterworn jade masses. Another name, fibrolite, comes from its appearance; the accepted name sillimanite was given in honor of Yale's first professor of mineralogy, Benjamin Silliman. New Mexican Indians produced many stone tools from sillimanite masses.

KYANITE Al_2SiO_5 Triclinic — pinacoidal $\overline{1}$ **Pl. 45**

Environment: Schists and gneisses formed from clay-rich rocks.

Crystal description: Always in embedded bladed crystals, sometimes in solid aggregates, sometimes isolated in a mica schist. May be up to a foot (30 cm) or more long; usually shorter.

Physical properties: Bluish, greenish, to colorless, usually colored in splotches. *Luster* glassy; *hardness* 5 along the prism, 7 across; *gravity* 3.6–3.7; *fracture* splintery across crystals; *cleavage* perfect pinacoidal. Transparent to translucent.

Composition: Aluminum silicate (63.2% Al_2O_3, 36.8% SiO_2).

Tests: Infusible and insoluble. Best tested by the unique hardness test in which the knife can scratch parallel to the crystal length and not across.

Distinguishing characteristics: Very distinctive in appearance; in case of doubt the hardness test should settle it.

Occurrence: Kyanite is an important refractory for porcelains, high-temperature bricks, and spark plugs. It is common in the New England schists and gneisses, and is found in some of the building excavations of New York City. Rich minable masses occur in Virginia and North Carolina. Typical crystals occur at Graves Mountain, Georgia, associated with rutile and lazulite.

The Swiss Pizzo Forno occurrence in a white schist with brown staurolite is a classic locality. In recent years mining operations in Kenya, East Africa, have produced some of the largest, clearest crystals. Clear waterworn pebbles have been found in São Paulo, Brazil. Also spelled "cyanite" and known in some countries as disthene (France).

STAUROLITE $FeAl_4Si_2O_{10}(OH)_2$ Pl. 45

Monoclinic — prismatic $\frac{2}{m}$ (pseudo-orthorhombic)

Environment: Regionally metamorphosed schists and gneisses.
Crystal description: Always crystallized, commonly with two individuals intergrown at right angles (twinned) so as to produce a cross; they may also intergrow at other angles. To 2 in. (5 cm) in length.
Physical properties: Dark brown. *Luster* glassy; *hardness* 7–7½; *gravity* 3.6–3.7; *fracture* subconchoidal; *cleavage* fair pinacoidal. Translucent to almost transparent.
Composition: Iron aluminum silicate, can be regarded chemically as a mixture of kyanite with iron hydroxide (15.8% FeO, 55.9% Al_2O_3, 26.3% SiO_2, 2.0% H_2O).
Tests: Infusible and insoluble, but after firing, grain crushes easily to a brown, weakly magnetic powder.
Distinguishing characteristics: Since staurolite is always in schist in typical brown crystals, with some individuals commonly twinned, it presents no special problem. Andalusite is unaffected by the blowpiping; tourmaline of this color would fuse.
Occurrence: Large and well-formed crystals are found in Fannin and Cherokee Cos., Georgia, and near Taos, New Mexico. Smaller ones are commercially exploited in Fairfax Co., Virginia, as good luck charms. However, many of the twins one sees appear to have been carved from a soft brown clay and are not the real mineral, though some may be pseudomorphs.

Untwinned, lustrous crystals of more than usual transparency are associated with the blue kyanite of Pizzo Forno, Switzerland, and make attractive specimens, with their matrix of fine-grained white mica. Still larger ones, also untwinned or twinned, are found in Bahia and in Minas Gerais, Brazil.

TITANITE (Sphene) $CaTiSiO_5$ Pl. 45

Monoclinic — prismatic $\frac{2}{m}$

Environment: Best developed in metamorphic rocks, in

marbles, schists, and gneisses; also common in small crystals in the lighter-colored coarse igneous rocks and in some pegmatites in an epidote and albite association in dioritic and gabbroic rocks.

Crystal description: Usually crystallized, in brown "envelope-shaped" crystals in granitic igneous rocks, but forming larger and more complex crystals when growing free in cavities in gneisses and schists. Commonly twinned so that the crystal edge shows a sharp re-entrant angle. Crystals may be several in. (10 cm) across. Also massive and granular.

Physical properties: Brown, yellow, green, gray. *Luster* adamantine; *hardness* 5–5½; *gravity* 3.4–3.5; *fracture* conchoidal; *cleavage* fair prismatic, with several others, and commonly also a parting. Transparent to translucent.

Composition: Calcium titanium silicate (28.6% CaO, 40.8% TiO_2, 30.6% SiO_2).

Tests: Fuses, with bubbling only on hottest places, to a dark mass. Brown specimens turn lighter and are frosted on the surface if heated without fusion. Practically insoluble in hydrochloric acid.

Distinguishing characteristics: The high luster, color, and typical wedge-shaped crystal cross section are very characteristic. Brown type distinguished from staurolite by the melting under blowpipe; the greenish-yellow type from sphalerite by greater hardness. Axinite fuses readily, with abundant froth.

Occurrence: The gemmy varieties have been cut for collectors; gem titanite has great brilliance and fire. In the U.S.S.R. it is mined as a source of titanium, but is too rare elsewhere.

The best North American specimens are the large dark brown crystals from Renfrew, Ontario, where it occurs in a coarse marble. Good, clear, yellow-brown crystals were once found in the Tilly Foster Mine at Brewster, New York, and in Bridgewater, Pennsylvania. Gemmy brown crystals were found in a pegmatite near Butte, Montana. Large wedge-shaped chocolate-colored embedded crystals occurred in the pegmatites at the babingtonite locality near Woburn, Massachusetts, and smaller crystals like the Canadian ones are common in St. Lawrence Co., New York.

The most beautiful and the clearest titanite crystals have come from the Alps and the Tyrol, associated with transparent or white albite feldspar crystals and often more or less coated with chlorite. The largest crystals (from n. Baja California) are some etched, flat, brown-yellow ones, more significant for their 6 in. (15 cm) size than for their beauty. A pegmatite at Capelinha in Minas Gerais, Brazil, has become an abundant source of twinned greenish-yellow, gemmy crystals.

DUMORTIERITE $Al_8BSi_3O_{19}(OH)$

Orthorhombic — Rhombic bipyramidal $\frac{2\ 2\ 2}{m\ m\ m}$

Environment: Scattered in pegmatites, in quartz concentrations in metamorphic rocks, and in gneisses and schists.

Crystal description: Rarely in small embedded distinct crystals; usually in very finely fibrous compact masses.

Physical properties: Violet, pink-violet, or blue. *Luster* glassy to pearly; *hardness* 7; *gravity* 3.3–3.4 (but usually impure); *fracture* conchoidal; *cleavage* poor pinacoidal. Translucent.

Composition: Basic aluminum borosilicate (64.6% Al_2O_3, 5.5% B_2O_3, 28.5% SiO_2, 1.4% H_2O).

Tests: On the charcoal, under the blowpipe, it whitens; with cooling, the color partially or entirely returns. Sometimes fluorescent blue after firing, sometimes naturally purple fluorescent.

Distinguishing characteristics: Bright color and fibrous appearance distinctive, and distinguish it from nonfibrous-looking lazulite and lazurite (which usually have fluorescent associates). The great hardness distinguishes the purple variety from similar-appearing rare species, or lepidolite.

Occurrence: In the U.S. dumortierite most common in the West, and has been mined in Oreana, Nevada, for spark plug ceramics. The blue is found in Los Angeles Co., California, with a gray quartz, and has been carved as an imitation lapis lazuli in China. Scattered needles through quartz are found in many localities and are recognized by their color. New York City building excavations produce fair dumortierite needles. Alpine, San Diego Co., California, dumortierite has a purple fluorescence. Blue "knots" in white quartz occur near Karibib, S.W. Africa.

URANOPHANE $CaU_2Si_2O_{11} \cdot 7H_2O$

Orthorhombic — Rhombic bipyramidal (?) $\frac{2\ 2\ 2}{m\ m\ m}$

Environment: Secondary mineral associated with uraninite or pitchblende.

Crystal description: Usually in minute tufts of light yellow crystals on open fracture surfaces. Uranotile is probably about the same, but is thought to be triclinic and to occur in thicker crystals.

Physical properties: Yellow, orange-yellow. *Luster* glassy to pearly; *hardness* 2–3 (undeterminable as a rule); *gravity* 3.8–3.9; *fracture* undeterminable; *cleavage* probably pinacoidal. Translucent; weakly fluorescent yellow-green.

Composition: Hydrated calcium uranium silicate (about 6.5% CaO, 67% UO_3, 13.9% SiO_2, 12.6% H_2O).

Tests: Soluble, quietly, in warm hydrochloric, without effervescence and with a separation of silica gel. Drop of nitric acid solution, poured on streak plate and allowed to dry, is very fluorescent.

Distinguishing characteristics: Likely to be confused with other U compounds, some of which may be carbonates that dissolve with bubbling in cold acid. Distinguished from yellow iron compounds by its fluorescence and by the fluorescence of the evaporated drop.

Occurrence: Not too rare a mineral as an alteration product of pitchblende, and often found in cavities in pegmatites from which uraninite may have been leached. Uranotile needles of this type occur at Bedford, Westchester Co., New York, and the more slender uranophane is found: in Mitchell Co., North Carolina; at Stone Mountain, Georgia; Avondale, Pennsylvania; Marysvale, Utah; and Grants, New Mexico. The most notable foreign occurrence is the Zaïre (Belgian Congo) uranium mines, where velvety uranophane coats other uranium alteration minerals. Also found in Schneeberg (Saxony, East Germany), and elsewhere in the Jáchymov uranium district (Czechoslovakia).

Glossary

Acicular. Needlelike; refers to the growth of a mineral in long and slender crystals.

Adamantine. The word used to describe a very high luster, like the luster of a diamond. It is a submetallic luster on a translucent material.

Adularescence. A bluish reflection coming from a definite plane in a mineral. Comes from the feldspar variety *adularia,* and is best known in the gemstone "moonstone."

Amygdule. A rounded mass of mineral formed in a gas cavity in a volcanic rock, a rock that solidified before all the gas bubbled out.

Botryoidal. Descriptive of a mineral surface that is rounded like the surface of a compact mass of grapes.

Boule. The name given to the form of synthetic ruby or sapphire grown from molten drops in a furnace. The word is French for "ball" and persists from the round pea-sized shapes of the first synthetic rubies and sapphires.

Country rock. The underlying basic geological formation of an area.

Decrepitation. The explosive shattering of mineral grains on heating, commonly observed during blowpipe testing or in the open- and closed-tube tests.

Detrital. Descriptive of a form of occurrence for minerals, in gravels that came from a mineral deposit. Hard or heavy minerals, like diamonds and gold, are often found in detrital deposits (see **Placer**).

Dichroism. Literally, "two colors." It refers to mineral crystals whose color is disparate in different crystal directions. Tourmaline is the commonest example: in one direction it may be green and in the other brown to almost black (see **Pleochroism**).

Dike. An intrusive, cross-cutting, thin sheet of igneous rock.

Double refraction. The property possessed by minerals crystallizing in anything but the cubic system of bending (refracting) light differently in different crystal directions. Very pronounced in some minerals, like calcite, and related to *dichroism* and *pleochroism,* which will be seen, of course, only in the colored minerals.

Druse. A crystal-coated surface of rock, commonly used interchangeably (but erroneously) with *vug.*

297

Ductile. Able to be drawn into a wire; a characteristic of some of the metals.

Fluorescence. A luminescence originating in substances while being irradiated by rays of invisible light, like ultraviolet light or X-rays, but stopping with the cessation of the stimulus.

Foliated. Made up of thin leaves, like a mica schist.

Gangue. The minerals of no value associated in veins with ore minerals.

Geniculated. Said of "kneelike" intergrowths of crystals; especially common in rutile and cassiterite.

Geode. A rounded concretionary rock mass, often hollow and lined with crystals.

Gliding plane. A crystal direction along which the atoms within a crystal can slip a definite distance without destroying the coherence of the crystal. Best noted in stibnite and vivianite.

Habit. The general shape of a crystal, sometimes long and thin, other times short and flat. Often an indication of the temperature and pressure conditions under which a crystal formed.

Hackly. The fracture characteristic of metals in rock, like gold and copper. Drawn to points as the rock breaks, the metal grains catch the skin as the finger is scraped across a hackly surface.

Hemimorphic. "Half formed"; descriptive of crystals in which the faces that grow on one end are different in angle and position from the faces to be found on the other end.

Hydrothermal. A self-explanatory word, "hydro" meaning water and "thermal" meaning heat. Hydrothermal solutions, from which so many minerals are deposited, are solutions of hot water escaping from subterranean sources, possibly of molten rock. Hydrothermal solutions may have the temperatures of superheated steam or be as cool as bath water.

Isomorphous. "Iso" means equal and "morph" means form — minerals in which two or more elements can replace each other to any extent without notably changing the appearance of the crystal. See dufrenite or lazulite (pp. 199, 205).

Lithophysae. Rounded nodular areas in obsidian which represent centers where crystallization of the molten rock began before it cooled into glass. Usually contracted and cracked, creating crystal-coated surfaces.

Litmus paper. Colored paper (pale blue) used in chemistry to show whether a solution is acid (turns pink) or alkaline.

Magma. The name given to molten rock under the surface of the earth. Magma becomes lava if it escapes on the surface at a volcano.

Magmatic. Describes changes in the rocks or minerals that form as a result of magma movements. *Magmatic segregations* are mineral deposits created directly as a result of the separation of one part of a mass of molten rock in one spot. Some iron deposits are thought to have formed in this way, by a separation and concentration of magnetite crystals from a mass of magma.

Malleable. Can be flattened out by pounding, a characteristic of the native metals and of the metals freed from ores in blow-pipe testing.

Mammillary. Descriptive of some mineral surfaces, rounded like botryoidal and reniform but larger.

Metamorphism. Changes in the rocks brought about, in the general usage of the word, by heat and pressure acting in the rocks below the immediate surface. *Contact metamorphism* is the result of heat and hydrothermal solutions accompanying and preceding intrusions of magma, with pressure playing no important part.

Native. Uncombined with other elements, native metals are those found as minerals, like gold, silver, and copper.

Ore. A mineral occurring in sufficient quantity and containing enough metal to permit its recovery and extraction at a profit. The term is also applied to rock containing such a mineral or metal, as "gold ore" and "copper ore."

Orientation. Applied to crystals, this means visualizing the disposition of the principal directions (top and bottom, front and back, side to side) within the crystal. It is essential to the recognition of the crystal system to which a crystal belongs, and soon becomes automatic.

Outcrop. A place where bed rock is exposed on the surface without any soil capping to conceal it.

Paleontology. A division of geology that concerns itself with prehistoric life and the fossilized remains of that life found in the rocks.

Paragenesis: The sequence in time in which a mineral crystallizes with respect to the other minerals. Important for what it tells us of the requirements for each mineral's formation in pressure, temperature, and geological environment.

Paramorph. A paramorph is chemically identical with the original crystal, but the atoms have been rearranged so that they no longer conform to the original outline (see **Pseudomorph**). The change of brookite to rutile or of aragonite to calcite is this type of paramorph.

Parting. A smooth fracture in minerals that looks like a cleavage but takes place only in certain planes in the crystal, not between any set of atoms, like cleavage. The planes along which parting takes place seem to be planes along which a row of atoms lie in a twinned position, and for this reason the bonding along that particular plane is weaker. Parting that looks like cleavage is particularly common in corundum.

Pegmatite. A very coarse plutonic rock, generally granitic in composition. Usually forming dikes that cut granite or the gneisses and schists that border granite masses. They represent the last liquid portion of the crystallizing magma. They are coarse because the liquid residue at the time of their crystallization contained a high percentage of water and other volatile elements that did not go into the makeup of the common minerals of granite, and which were for that reason concentrated in the residue. They are interesting mineralogically because minerals of the rarer elements are found with the coarse quartz, feldspar, and mica that principally compose them.

Percussion figure. The 6-rayed starlike cracks that radiate outward in a sheet of mica from the point of impact of a sharp, hard-driven needle.

Petrography. A division of geology that concerns itself with the mineral makeup of rocks. It is usually carried on with the assistance of the "petrographic microscope" and thin, transparent slices of rock, known as "thin sections," ground to $\frac{3}{1000}$ in. (0.07 mm) thickness.

Petrology. A division of geology concerning itself with the origin of rocks, trying to understand and explain some of the unusual mineral combinations that have been found as rock masses of considerable volume.

Phosphorescence. A luminescence emanating from substances that have been irradiated with ultraviolet light or X-rays, but persisting after the source of the stimulation has been removed (see **Fluorescence**).

Piezoelectric. Describes a substance that becomes electrically charged by pressure; it can only occur in certain crystals belonging to classes of low symmetry. Always associated with *pyroelectricity*.

Placer. A deposit of heavy minerals in streambeds, in which the valuable substances have been concentrated as the lighter-weight minerals have been carried away by the stream.

Pleochroism. Like dichroism except that it is applied to minerals with 3 instead of 2 different colors.

Plumose. Describes a feathery mineral growth, composed of a compact mass of slender branching crystals. A common appearance of some of the sulfosalt minerals.

Polarized light. Light that has been forced to vibrate in a single plane rather than in all planes. Limited polarization takes place when light is reflected from polished nonmetallic surfaces. Light escaping from a Nicol prism (made from calcite) or coming through a green tourmaline or a sheet of Polaroid is almost completely polarized.

Polysynthetic twinning. A term that has been applied to multiple intergrowths of a mineral in twinned positions, giving the effect of many narrow striations on a cleavage or fracture surface. It is best observed in the triclinic feldspars and aids in their recognition, since it is almost invariably present.

Primary. Refers to a mineral deposit that formed directly from hot-water solutions or from molten rocks.

Pseudomorph. A substance with the crystal form of some other mineral, forming as the result of the alteration of the original mineral without losing the original shape. Pseudomorphs may form by a breakdown and rearrangement of the same atoms (a paramorph), by a slight change in composition, by a coating over another crystal, or by a complete replacement by an entirely different mineral.

Pyroelectric. Describes a substance that becomes electrically charged by temperature changes (see **Piezoelectric**).

Re-entrant angle. An angular depression, bounded by crystal faces, that characterizes twinned crystal intergrowths.

Refraction. The bending of light as it passes from air into transparent substances. Each mineral has a very definite ability to bend light differently in different crystal directions as a rule (making "double refraction"), and the determination of the "indices of refraction" is a method of mineral identification. A petrographic microscope and considerable training are required to make this a useful tool for mineral recognition.

Reniform. A descriptive term for rounded mineral surfaces, meaning kidney-like. It is coarser than botryoidal and finer than mammillary.

Schiller. A German term, from the name of a turbid German wine, for the almost metallic, sometimes bronzy, reflections that come from certain planes in some minerals. They are due to minute platy particles within the crystals, forced into a parallel arrangement by the atomic pattern of the host.

Secondary enrichment. A mineral deposit that has been altered, and enriched in valuable metals like copper, as a result of the weathering of the surface portion of the vein. The dissolved metals seep downward and reach the fresh unweathered section of the vein, where they react chemically with the lower-grade minerals to form new compounds richer in copper.

Sectile. Can be cut by a knife, with a shaving curling away, like horn silver and some of the softer metals.

Slickenside. A smooth, often striated, gliding or fault-rock surface. Very common in serpentinous rock outcroppings.

Sphenoidal. An incomplete type of crystal growth, in which upper and lower pyramid faces develop alternately. A simple sphenoidal crystal will look like a wedge with 4 flat faces. See chalcopyrite (p. 84).

Sublimate. A deposit that has grown from a vapor rather than from a solution. Sublimates are often seen in blowpipe testing, and some minerals around volcanoes form this way.

Thermoluminescence. A luminescence resulting from the mild heating of a substance, released and visible well below the point of incandescence. Best observed in fluorite.

Triboluminescence. A luminescent phenomenon taking the appearance of tiny sparks observed in the dark in some minerals (sphalerite, corundum) when a hard point is dragged across the surface of the mineral.

Trillings. An intergrowth of 3 separate orthorhombic crystals, crossing at a center and giving the effect of a 6-sided (hexagonal) crystal.

Twin. Two (or more) crystals intergrown with a definite relationship between the crystal structures, so that one or more of the faces of one are parallel to unlike faces on the other. Twinning is sometimes difficult to recognize, and amateurs are likely to confuse true twinning with parallel growths, in which like faces are parallel (instead of unlike faces), or with random intergrowths, in which no consistent angular relationship is to be seen.

Valence. The relative combining capacity of an atom in relation to hydrogen, which has a valence of 1. Some elements, like iron, sometimes have more than one valence, so that you can get either FeO, or Fe_2O_3.

Vein. A more or less upright sheet deposit of minerals, cutting other rocks and formed from solutions rather than from a molten magma like a dike.

Volatilize. To change into a gaseous state, sometimes without melting (as with ammonium chloride).

Vug. Open cavity in rocks, often lined with druses of crystals.

Vulcanism. The phenomena associated with volcanoes: fumaroles, hot springs, and lava flows.

Weathering. In the broadest sense, any of the destructive effects of the atmosphere and the exposure of rocks to the temperature extremes of the surface. In a mineral sense we usually mean the chemical effects of water, carbon dioxide, and oxygen attacking and destroying the minerals that are near the surface of the earth. Minerals that formed deep in the earth, at high temperatures and pressures, become unstable under surface conditions and alter to form new compounds.

X-ray pattern. The arrangement of spots or lines revealed in a photographic negative that has been exposed behind a crystal or the powder of crystals at the time a slender beam of X-rays is directed at it. Such photographs are used for the determination of the crystal structures of minerals, and by comparison with known minerals, for identification.

Annotated Bibliography

Dana, Edward Salisbury. *Minerals and How to Study Them,* 3rd edition, revised by Cornelius S. Hurlbut, Jr. New York, Wiley, 1971.

An elementary version of the *Manual of Mineralogy,* and although excellent not to be preferred to it except for juniors.

———. *A Textbook of Mineralogy,* 5th edition, revised and enlarged by William E. Ford. New York, Wiley, 1954.

This one-volume work lists all the minerals and gives some descriptive data on each. For the average collector, this will suffice. The seldom-used introductory material on testing and crystallography is noteworthy, but of college level. The best all-around advanced textbook.

Dana, James Dwight. *Manual of Mineralogy,* 18th edition, revised by Cornelius Hurlbut, Jr. New York, Wiley, 1971.

An excellent textbook of mineralogy, giving considerable space to the properties of minerals and their identification, together with descriptions of the more common and important varieties.

———, and Edward Salisbury Dana. *The System of Mineralogy,* 7th edition, rewritten and enlarged by Charles Palache, Harry Berman, and Clifford Frondel. New York, Wiley, 1944-. Vol. 1, 1944; Vol. 2, 1951; Vol. 3, 1962; Vol. 4, in preparation.

This is the standard international reference work on minerals, a revision and an expansion of the original work begun by James Dwight Dana in 1837 and brought up to date in 1892 by his son Edward Salisbury Dana. It is usually referred to as *Dana's System of Mineralogy.* No serious mineralogist should be without these works.

Dake, Henry C., Frank L. Fleener, and Ben Hur Wilson. *Quartz Family Minerals.* New York, Whittlesey House, 1938. Out of print.

Useful summary of information aimed at the amateur lapidary, especially with reference to agate varieties. Now badly dated, of course, but still a useful reference. Numerous inaccuracies, but reference to Vol. 3 of *Dana's System of Mineralogy* (quartz volume) will give the correct scientific relationships.

Hey, Max H. *An Index of Mineral Species and Varieties, Arranged Chemically,* 2nd edition. London, British Museum (Natural History), 1962. (Second Appendix, 1974.)

A complete listing of minerals described up to the date of publication and a handy reference book. Provides a numbering series that might be useful in cataloguing a collection. It would not take the place of the Dana books; it is only supplemental.

Holmes, Arthur. *Principles of Physical Geology,* rev. edition. New York, Ronald Press, 1965.

An introductory college text on general geology, but more stimulating than most textbooks, and very readable.

Read, Herbert H. *Geology: An Introduction to Earth-History.* London and New York, Oxford, 1949.

A small popular book from this press's "Home University Library of Modern Knowledge" by a leading British geologist, and good, though many of the references are to British scenic features.

Roberts, Willard L., George R. Rapp, Jr., and Julius Weber. *Encyclopedia of Minerals.* New York, Van Nostrand Reinhold Company, 1974.

A complete, beautifully illustrated compendium of all the most recent data on almost all known species. Although costly, because of the numerous superb color photographs (the work of Julius Weber), it is indispensable for the advanced collector and a very convenient one-volume reference work for professionals.

Short, M. N. *Microscopic Determination of the Ore Minerals.* Washington, D.C., U.S. Geological Survey Bulletin 825, U.S. Govt. Printing Office, 1931.

Intended for the student of polished-ore specimens, as seen under the microscope, but the latter half of the book has an excellent set of tests, some of which need not be microscopic in dimension, for the identification of the metals in those minerals.

Sinkankas, John. *Mineralogy for Amateurs.* Princeton, Van Nostrand, 1964.

———. *Prospecting for Gemstones and Minerals.* New York, Van Nostrand Reinhold, 1970.

———. *Gemstone and Mineral Data Book.* New York, Winchester Press, 1972.

———. *Gemstones of North America.* Princeton, Van Nostrand, 1959.

All of the Sinkankas books are authoritative and readable, and can be highly recommended for serious amateurs. There are large amounts of original data not available elsewhere, as well as useful compilations that make scattered facts readily accessible.

Smith, Orsino C. *Identification and Qualitative Chemical Analysis of Minerals,* 2nd edition. Princeton, Van Nostrand, 1953.

A series of tables listing all minerals to 1946 by hardness and specific gravity, and suggesting chemical confirmatory tests. Good section on qualitative analysis precedes tables, with all the data required to begin this type of testing. Highly recommended as a reference and a guide, but only to supplement other books.

Vanders, Iris, and Paul F. Kerr. *Mineral Recognition.* New York, Wiley, 1967.

A useful, fairly complete, well-illustrated book with data clearly presented but descriptions regrettably terse.

Winchell, Alexander N., and Newton Horace Winchell. *Elements of Optical Mineralogy.* New York, Wiley, 1951. Three volumes: Part I, *Principles and Methods;* Part II, *Description of Minerals;* Part III, *Determinative Tables.*

The standard reference work on optical mineralogy and the identification of non-opaque minerals under the microscope. This is a college-level text and will be found useful only by the advanced amateur with petrographic microscope equipment. The first volume is the best source of information on the discussion of principles.

In addition to the books listed above, there are a number of periodicals for the amateur and professional mineralogist. They contain articles on localities, care of the collection, lapidary techniques, equipment, and personal experiences. The advertising pages inform potential customers of sources of specimens and collecting and testing supplies.

The technical journal for serious mineralogists is *The American Mineralogist,* 1707 L Street, N.W., Washington, D.C. 20036.

For serious collectors, the indispensable journal is *The Mineralogical Record,* P. O. Box 783, Bowie, Md. 20715.

The amateur journals are numerous and specialize in different aspects of the hobby. They include:

The Earth Science Digest, Box 1815, Colorado Springs, Colo. 80901

Gems and Minerals, P. O. Box 687, Mentone, Calif. 92359

The Lapidary Journal, P. O. Box 80937, San Diego, Calif. 92138

Rocks and Gems, 16001 Ventura Blvd., Encino, Calif. 91316

Rocks and Minerals, P. O. Box 29, Peekskill, N.Y. 10566.

Good foreign magazines are:

Der Aufschluss (monthly), Kastelweg 6, 69 Heidelberg, West Germany

Schweizer Strahler (quarterly), P. O. Box 650, 6002 Lucerne, Switzerland

Gems, 84 High Street, Broadstairs, Kent, England.

Index

This index covers rock and mineral descriptions and selected important subjects. Rock and mineral names are capitalized, and those that refer to main text entries are in **boldface** type, as are all plate numbers. The abbreviation "(sp.)" follows mineral species that are briefly described in the main-entry texts of other minerals. Other rock and mineral names include varieties, synonyms, and alternate names; popular, foreign, and vernacular names are in quotation marks.

307

IGNEOUS AND
PLUTONIC INTRUSIONS
    Quartz
    Feldspar
    Mica
    Dark minerals

CONTACT-METAMORPHIC ORES
    Sulfides
    Scheelite
    Garnet
    Vesuvianite
    Epidote

PEGMATITE DIKES AND
MIAROLITIC CAVITIES
    Granite minerals
    Topaz
    Beryl
    Tourmaline
    Garnet
    Apatite

WEATHERED VEINS
    Malachite
    Azurite
    Copper
    Anglesite
    Cerussite
    Wulfenite
    Smithsonite

ORE VEINS
    Sulfides
    Gold, Tellurides

FUMAROLES
    Sal Ammoniac
    Sulfur
    Sulfates, Hematite

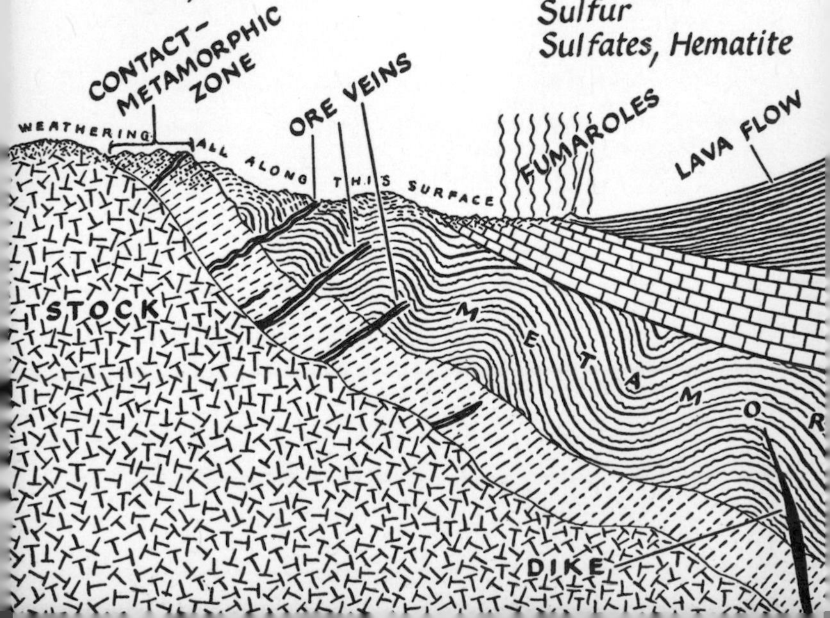

CONTACT-
METAMORPHIC
ZONE

ORE VEINS

FUMAROLES

LAVA FLOW

WEATHERING

ALL ALONG THIS SURFACE

STOCK

METAMOR

DIKE

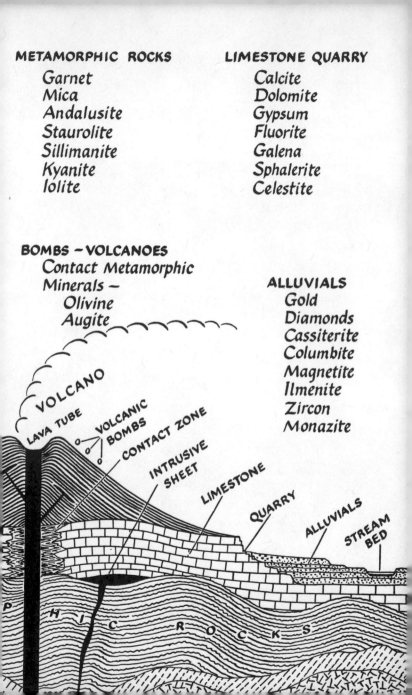

METAMORPHIC ROCKS

  Garnet
  Mica
  Andalusite
  Staurolite
  Sillimanite
  Kyanite
  Iolite

LIMESTONE QUARRY

  Calcite
  Dolomite
  Gypsum
  Fluorite
  Galena
  Sphalerite
  Celestite

BOMBS – VOLCANOES

  Contact Metamorphic
  Minerals –
    Olivine
    Augite

ALLUVIALS

  Gold
  Diamonds
  Cassiterite
  Columbite
  Magnetite
  Ilmenite
  Zircon
  Monazite

VOLCANO

LAVA TUBE

VOLCANIC BOMBS

CONTACT ZONE

INTRUSIVE SHEET

LIMESTONE

QUARRY

ALLUVIALS

STREAM BED

P H I C   R O C K S